The Splendour of

Mathurā

Art and Museum

Perspectives in Indian Art & Archaeology, no. 1

The Splendour of
Mathurā
Art and Museum

Dr. R.C. Sharma
Director General & V.C.
National Museum/Institute, New Delhi

D.K. Printworld (P) Ltd.
NEW DELHI-110015

Cataloging in Publication Data — DK

Sharma, R.C. (Ramesh Chandra), 1936-

The Splendour of Mathurā art and Museum.
(Perspectives in Indian art & archaeology ; no. 1).
Includes bibliographical references (p.).
Includes index.

1. Sculpture, Mathurā. 2. Art -- India -- Mathurā. 3. Museums -- India -- Mathurā. 4. Mathurā, India -- Antiquities. I. Title. II. Series: Perspectives in Indian art & archaeology ; no. 1.

ISBN 81-246-0015-5

First Published in India in 1994

Published in India by :
K. Rai Mittal
Managing Director
D.K. Printworld (P) Ltd.
Regd. office : H-12, Bali Nagar
NEW DELHI - 110015
Phone : (011) 541-3463; *Fax :* (011) 559-8898

Typeset at : Easy Computer Systems, New Delhi-110015; Ph. 546 1078

Printed at : D.K. Fine Art Press (P) Ltd., Delhi-110052

Dedicated

to

all esteemed German Indologists and particularly to
Professors H. Härtel, G.V. Mitterwallner and M. Yaldiz
whose contribution in research and propagation of
Mathurā's archaeological and artistic wealth
has been magnificent.

Preface

MATHURĀ'S place in the cultural and artistic history of the country has been unique and it has always been a fascinating experience to explore and study the glory and to write about its art treasures. The request of Mrs. Pushpa Thakurel, the present Director of Mathurā Museum to update my earlier writings in the light of new researches and reshuffling of exhibits in galleries was quite alluring. Whenever I could carve some time out of the tight schedule in Delhi, I rushed to Mathurā and confined myself to the Museum galleries sometimes till midnight to analyse the fresh arrivals and to interpret the old ones wherever it was necessary.

The Splendour of Mathurā Art and Museum presents a comprehensive survey of a renowned seat of sculptural art and its grand repository. No study in Indian plastic art and iconography is complete without consulting cupboards of the Mathurā Museum. It was at Mathurā that the divinities of Brahmanism, Buddhism and Jainism were given earliest form and plethora multiplied in due course. Besides, a number of folk deities also emerged here. The followers of different creeds and sects erected a good number of temples, *stūpas, caityas,* monasteries, assembly halls, portrait gallery and several places of public utility such as wells, water tanks, gardens, refectories, etc. The remains of such establishments as exposed during the course of excavations furnish ample evidence of a flourishing and prosperous urban life at Mathurā.

The contribution of Mathurā has been manifold. Scholars, saints, philosophers have been visiting the region from time to time to disseminate their message and to propagate the fundamentals of their religion. Sculptors, artists and masons have been at their command and the businessmen were there to support. All these factors made Mathurā a metropolis of the Northern India in ancient time. Indigenous by birth, the Mathurā School of Art flourished on the banks of the Yamunā and reached pinnacle under the Kuṣāṇa patronage, further improved in quality in the Gupta period and did leave its imprints in the Medieval period.

Since the two schools of art, viz., Mathurā and Gāndhāra evolved and flourished almost simultaneously and under the patronage of the Kuṣāṇa kings there was a good deal of interaction between the two. While Mathurā used the light red or spotted red sand stone, the stone in the Gāndhāra region was of schist or state variety. It is also likely that some artists from the western frontiers visited Mathurā and a few settled here and continued to practise the art renderings. It is, therefore, natural that the alien trends are clearly discernible at Mathurā. At the same time several motifs travelled from Mathurā to the western region. The origin of the Buddha image has been a debatable subject and arguments can be advanced in favour of Gāndhāra and Mathurā both. Mathurā inspired some contemporary and subsequent art styles like Sārnāth and Amarāvatī in the field of the Buddhist art and icons.

Inscriptional records from Mathurā are of great significance for reconstruction of early political and cultural life. Same is the case of numismatic finds which shed valuable light from the pre-Mauryan period to the British rule.

After the devastation of the city by the Hunas in the end of the 6th century the ateliers of art stopped functioning for some time but the creativity revived and we have some beautiful sculptures belonging to medieval period. A good number of artists had migrated to the safer places and they continued the family tradition of sculpting. The process resulted in the evolution of regional sub-styles in the sculptural art.

Beside stone sculptures, Mathurā has also been famous for early terracottas the continuity of which is seen from about 6th century B.C. to the 6th century A.D. The discovery of a few bronze figures from the excavations at Sonkh hints to the use of metal for the artistic innovations in the 1st-2nd century A.D.

All these and allied issues have been discussed in the present book. It mainly follows the chronological sequence although the pantheon classification has also been considered as far as possible. New discoveries and fresh arrivals to the Museum upto 1993 have been taken into consideration. Inscriptions have been transliterated and translated as well. Characteristics of Mathurā art through ages have been given while describing the artifacts of a period. History of Museum and archaeological campaigns will be of much use to the researchers. Similarly, the cultural and historical background of the region has been adequately discussed. A good number of colour and black and white photographs do help in appreciating the beauty of Mathurā art. While the District and City maps locate the important archaeological sites and other places, the gallery plan projects the situation of period-wise arrangement. Provenance of objects has been given if recorded in the Museum's accession registers. List of illustrations furnishes all relevant details including measurements. Index to the exhibits will help in quickly finding the location and description of the displayed items. The select bibliography is added for future academic pursuits. While the visitors will find the book a very remunerative companion during the Museum round, the scholars will equally be benefitted through the prolific research material it reveals.

The book is the result of the keen initiative of Mrs. Pushpa Thakurel, Director of the Mathurā Museum who has helped and assisted in many ways. Without her wonderful cooperation and constant reminders this would not have come out.

In Delhi, my worthy colleague Dr. Shashi Asthana, Assistant Director, herself a meritorious scholar offered her ungrudging help in screening the script, selecting the illustrations, preparing the press copy, going through the proofs and offering useful suggestions. The Select Bibliography has also been compiled by her.

Sri K. Rai Mittal, Managing Director, D.K. Printworld and his son Sri Susheel Mittal for their special regard and affinity to Vraj region have taken extra pains in bringing out the book attractive and useful for visitors and scholars from India and abroad.

My former and present colleagues in Mathurā, Vrindāban and Delhi also came forward to lend their cooperation and mention should be made of Sri K.D. Misra, Sri Shatrughna Sharma, Sri V.K. Tulreja, Sri Rajat Shukla, Sri R.K. Dattagupta, Sri N. Shah. and Smt. Santosh Sharma, P.S., who has also prepared the Index to the Exhibits and General Index. Sri Kushal Pal has rendered his services in designing, finalising the coloured illustrations and preparing maps & gallery plan.

I have availed full advantage of the documents of the Mathurā Museum and the works of my worthy predecessors and successors. The staff of the Museum has been very generous and cooperative during my visits for this work. I express my sincere gratitude to all whose names have been mentioned and also to them who remained behind the curtain. Thanking my wife Santosh and other family members for allowing me utmost time to concentrate on the book will be thanking my ownself hence I reserve my sentiments.

I feel delighted in dedicating the book to the esteemed German Indologists whose great contribution and deep involvement in spreading the glory of Mathurā's cultural heritage has been highly inspiring. After Sonkh excavations, the Palace of Gods (Classical Art of India) Exhibition organised in Berlin in 1992 has further cemented the academic ties between the two nations. In this regard, I should specially record the name of Prof. R. Härtel, Prof. G.V. Mitterwallner and Prof. M. Yaldiz and her colleagues with whom I have often shared my views on different Indological aspects and their association has been much rewarding to me.

Vijayadaśamī, Saṃvat २०५०
October 24, 1993
New Delhi

R.C. SHARMA
Director General & V.C.
National Museum/Institute

Contents

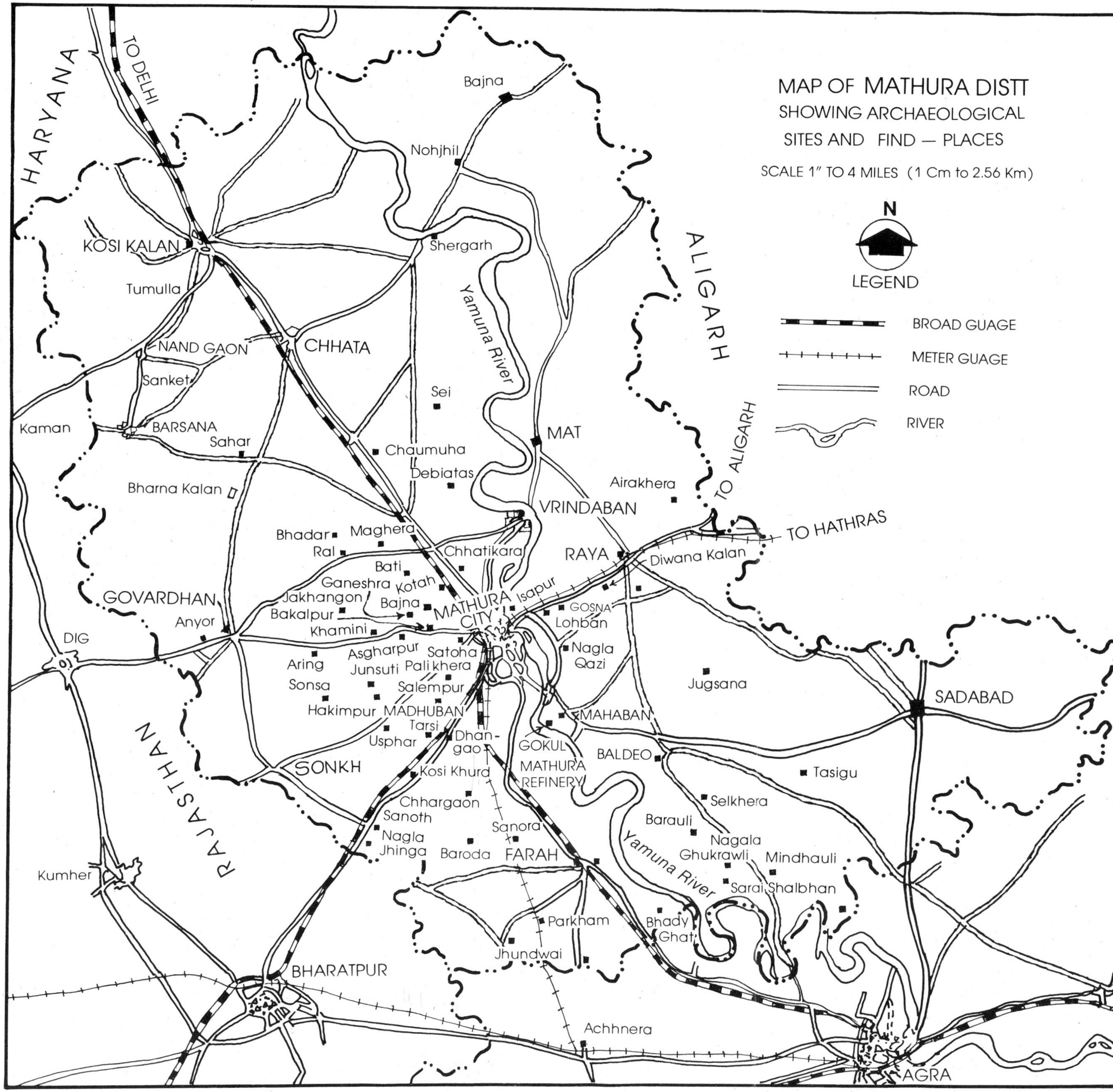
MAP OF MATHURA DISTT
SHOWING ARCHAEOLOGICAL
SITES AND FIND — PLACES
SCALE 1" TO 4 MILES (1 Cm to 2.56 Km)
N
LEGEND
BROAD GUAGE
METER GUAGE
ROAD
RIVER
HARYANA
TO DELHI
ALIGARH
TO ALIGARH
TO HATHRAS
RAJASTHAN
Bajna
Nohjhil
KOSI KALAN
Shergarh
Tumulla
Yamuna River
NAND GAON
CHHATA
Sanket
Sei
Kaman
BARSANA
Sahar
MAT
Chaumuha
Debiatas
Bharna Kalan
Airakhera
VRINDABAN
Bhadar
Maghera
Ral
Chhatikara
RAYA
Diwana Kalan
Bati
Ganeshra
Kotah
Isapur
GOVARDHAN
Jakhangon
Bajna
MATHURA CITY
GOSNA
Bakalpur
Lohban
Anyor
Khamini
DIG
Asgharpur
Satoha
Nagla Qazi
Aring
Junsuti
Pali khera
Jugsana
Sonsa
Salempur
SADABAD
Hakimpur
MADHUBAN
MAHABAN
Tarsi
Usphar
Dhangao
GOKUL
BALDEO
SONKH
Kosi Khurd
MATHURA REFINERY
Tasigu
Chhargaon
Selkhera
Sanoth
Barauli
Nagla Jhinga
Sanora
Nagala Ghukrawli
Baroda
FARAH
Mindhauli
Kumher
Yamuna River
Sarai Shalbhan
Parkham
Bhady Ghat
Jhundwai
BHARATPUR
Achhnera
AGRA

IMPORTANT SITES OF MATHURA CITY

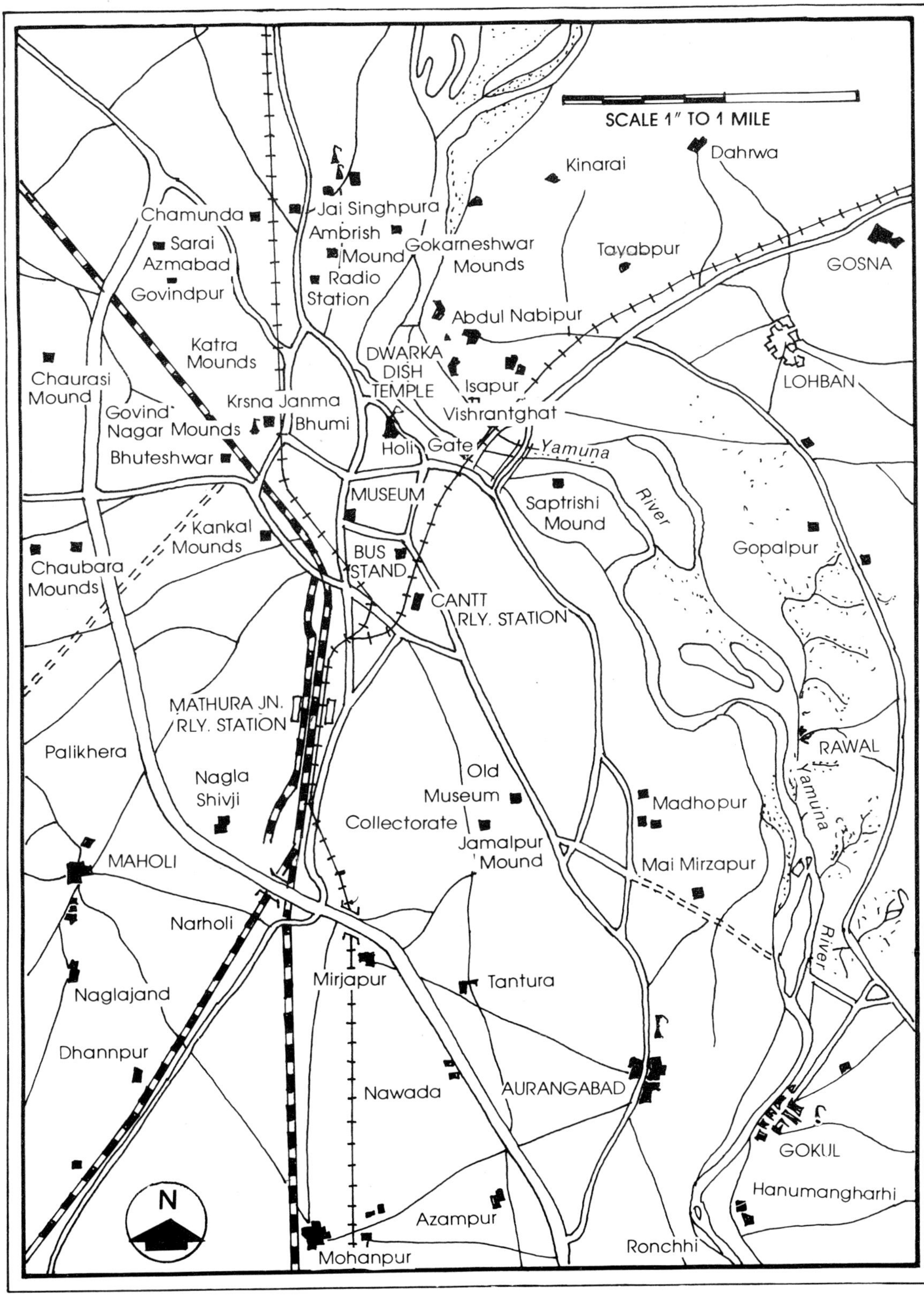

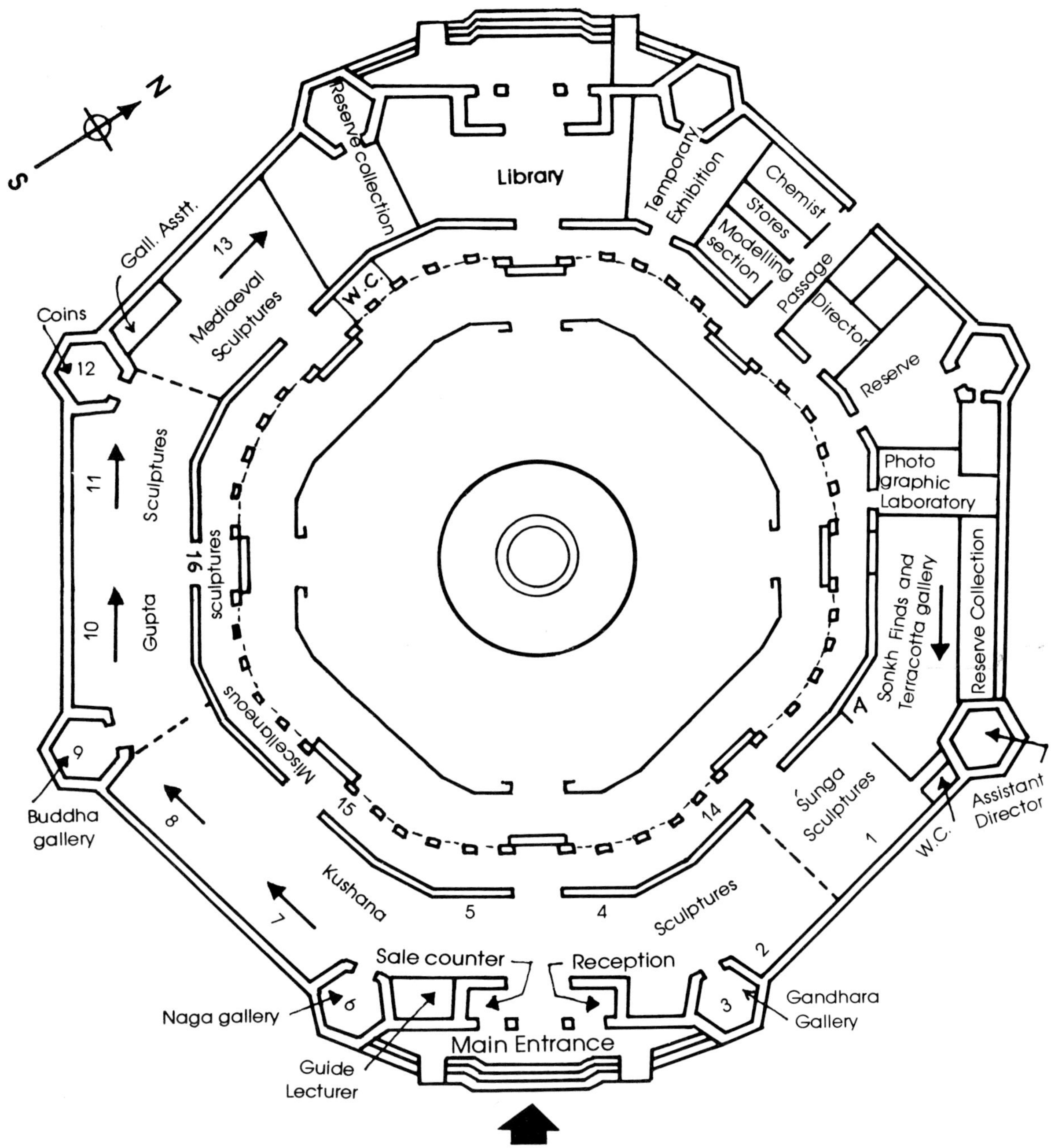

A Beginning of the tour

--- Period demarcating line

3 Figures indicate Gal. Nos.

MUSEUM GALLERY PLAN

List of Illustrations

(The code shown in the parenthesis at the end of each entry indicates the corresponding accession no. of the object in the Museum)

Colour

XI. Vema Kadphises on lion throne, Kuṣāṇa period, 1st century A.D., Māṭ, Mathurā District, red sand stone, ht. 235 cm. (12.215)

XII. Kaniṣka, Kuṣāṇa period, late 1st century A.D. Māṭ, Mathurā District, buff sand stone (behind red), ht 162.5 cm. (12.213)

XIII. Sūrya clad in Northern style, Kuṣāṇa, late 1st century A.D., Kaṅkālī, Mathurā city, buff sand stone, ht. 48 cm. (12.269)

XIV. Kārttikeya with spear and mentioned as Kārttikeya in epigraph, Kuṣāṇa period, *c.* 2nd century A.D., Kaṅkālī, Mathurā city, spotted red sand stone, ht. 48 cm. (42.2949)

XV. Yakṣa with cup and fruit, late Kuṣāṇa, 3rd century A.D., Kaṅkālī, Mathurā city, spotted red sand stone, ht. 68.5 cm. (46.3232)

XVI. Multiple *caturvyūha* form of Viṣṇu/Kṛṣṇa, Kuṣāṇa period, *c.* 2nd century A.D., Museum well, buff sand stone, ht. 46 cm. (14.392-95)

XVII. Balarāma or Nāga bust with serpent hood, Kuṣāṇa period, *c.* 2nd century A.D., Kacahrighāṭ well, Mathurā city, buff sand stone, ht. 35.5 cm. (14.406)

XVIII. Slab showing Vasudeva carrying child Kṛṣṇa in basket across Yamunā, Kuṣāṇa period, *c.* 1st century A.D., Kaṭrā, Mathurā city, spotted red sand stone, ht. 46 cm. (17.1344)

XIX. Railpost with a lady seated on a wicker seat and looking into the mirror, Kuṣāṇa period, 2nd century A.D., Govindnagar, Mathurā city, spotted red sand stone, ht. 108 cm. (76.39)

XX. Railpost with a lady in act of putting on her garment after bath, Kuṣāṇa period, *c.* 2nd century A.D., Bhūteśvar, Mathurā city, red sand stone, ht. 142 cm. (J. 4)

XXI. Railpost with a lady holding grapes and pot, Kuṣāṇa period, *c.* 2nd century A.D., Bhūteśvar, red sand stone, ht. 132 cm. (11.151)

XXII. Railpost with the scene of birth of Ṛṣyaśṛṅga, pre Kuṣāṇa period, late 1st century B.C., Govindnagar, Mathurā city, spotted red sand stone, ht. 139 cm. (76.40)

XXIII. Railpost showing Rṣyaśṛṅga in ecstasy, Kuṣāṇa period, *c.* 2nd century A.D., Caubārā mound, Mathurā, spotted red sand stone, ht. 80 cm. (J.7)

XXIV. Railpost with a lady wearing a skirt and squeezing her hair after bath while a swan takes the fallen drops in guise of pearls, Kuṣāṇa period, *c.* 2nd century A.D., Narhaulī, Mathurā district, spotted red sand stone, ht. 61 cm. (18.1509)

XXV. Upper compartment of a big railpost showing an eye ward of veterinary

Black and White

Primal

A. Mr. F. S. Growse.

B. Old building.

C. Present building.

D. Smt. Indira Gandhi, the Prime Minister of India, for the Inagural of Centenary Celebration.

Objects

1. Showcase imparting a glimpse of Sonkh mound and pottery from the site.
2. Terracotta, medallion representing a lion crushing other creatures, Kuṣāṇa period, *c.* 2nd century A.D., Sonkh, Mathurā district, dia. 9 cm. (SO I-301)
3. Kubera and Hārītī, Kuṣāṇa period, 2nd century A.D., Sonkh, Mathurā district, bronze, ht. 10.5 cm. (SO I-173)
4. Kārttikeya with spear, Kuṣāṇa period, 2nd century A.D., Sonkh, Mathurā district, bronze, ht. 9.3 cm. (SO I-178)
5. A foreigner at meals, Maurya-Śuṅga period, 3rd-2nd century B.C., provenance not known, grey terracotta, ht. 11.5 cm. (71.12)
6. Mother goddess or a lady with elaborate hairdo and ornaments, Śuṅga period, 2nd century B.C., Mathurā city, grey terracotta, ht. 30 cm. (66.2)
7. Kārttikeya on peacock, Gupta period, *c.* 5th century A.D., river bed, Mathurā, grey terracotta, ht. 34.3 cm. (38.2794)
8. Yakṣa, late Mauryan period, 3rd-2nd century B.C., inscribed, Parkham, Mathurā district, buff sand stone, ht. 262 cm. (C. 1)
9. Yakṣa inscribed as Agni (fire god), Śuṅga period, *c.* 2nd century B.C., Bharnā Kalān, Mathurā district, buff sand stone, ht. 195 cm. (87.146)
10. *Bodhi* or *caitya* tree symbolising the Enlighenment of the Buddha, Śuṅga period, *c.*1st century B.C., Mahādevghāṭ, Mathurā city, buff sand stone, ht. 40.5 cm. (18.1516)
11. *Naṭī* (female dancer) on the railpost, Śuṅga period, *c.* 2nd-1st century B.C., provenance not known, spotted red sand stone, ht. 195.5 cm. (J. 2)
12. Railpost with fine lotus medallions and narrating the '*jātaka* of the worst evil', Śuṅga period, *c.* 1st century B.C., Ṣūrajghāṭ near Saptarṣī mound, Mathurā city, red sand stone, ht. 113 cm. (15.586)
13. Flywhisk or torch bearer, Śuṅga period, *c.* 1st century B.C., Jamālpur (?),

32. Kubera enjoying drink, Kuṣāṇa period, *c.* 1st-2nd century A.D., Pālikherā, Mathurā district, red sand stone, ht. 153.5 cm. (C. 2)

33. Seated Buddha (head missing), inscribed, Kuṣāṇa period, early 2nd century A.D., near Govardhan by-pass, Mathurā, spotted red sand stone, ht. 62 cm. (78.34)

34. Siddhārtha in meditation, Kuṣāṇa period, *c.* 2nd century A.D., Maholī, Mathurā district, spotted red stone., ht. 40.5 cm. (46.3231)

35. Yakṣa carrying bowl, early Kuṣāṇa period, 1st-2nd century A.D., Govindnagar, Mathurā city, spotted red sand stone, ht. 63 cm. (71.31)

36. Buddha wearing thick pleated garment, late Kuṣāṇa period, late 2nd century A.D., Govindnagar, Mathurā city, spotted red sand stone, ht. 115 cm. (76.17)

37. Lakṣmī holding lotus in *abhaya* pose, Kuṣāṇa period, *c.* 2nd century A.D., Janmasthāna, Mathurā city, spotted red sand stone, ht. 24 cm. (80.2)

38. Dorjamb carved with harem (*Saundarananda*) scenes, Kuṣāṇa period, *c.* 2nd century A.D., Guḍgāon, Haryana, spotted red sand stone, ht. 145 cm. (12.186)

39. Stele carved with four deities (Arddhanārīśvara, Viṣṇu, Gajalakṣmī and Kubera), Kuṣāṇa period, *c.* 2nd century A.D., provenance not known, spotted red sand stone, ht. 19, L. 25.5 cm. (34.2520)

40. Square parasol which functioned as roof of a shrine, carved with auspicious motifs, late Kuṣāṇa period, 2nd-3rd century A.D., Maholī kī paur, Mathurā city, buff and red sand stone, 111 x 105 cm. (76.12)

41. Head with conical cap inscribed '*Nāyasa*', Kuṣāṇa period, *c.* 2nd century A.D., Māṭ, Mathurā district, spotted red sand stone, ht. 38 cm. (16.1252)

42. Part of a large umbrella carved with auspicious motifs, early Kuṣāṇa period, 1st century A.D., Govindnagar, Mathurā city, spotted red sand stone, dia. 208 cm. (72.5)

43. Umbrella with auspicious motifs, Kuṣāṇa period, 1st-2nd century A.D., Govindnagar, Mathurā city, spotted red sand stone, dia. 97 cm. (75.32)

44. Standing Buddha, Kuṣāṇa period, early 2nd century A.D., provenance not known, spotted red sand stone, ht. 81 cm. (A. 4)

45. Lady playing on flute under the cluster of flowers, Kuṣāṇa period, *c.* 2nd century A.D., provenance not known, spotted red sand stone, ht. 22.5 cm. (F. 17); and

    Flying celestial, Kuṣāṇa period, *c.* 2nd century A.D., Katṛā, Mathurā city, red sand stone, ht. 21.5 cm. (58.4479)

46. Stele bearing Kubera with Lakṣmī and Hārītī and worshippers, Kuṣāṇa period, *c.* 2nd century A.D., Manoharpur mound, Mathurā city, spotted red sand stone, L. 16.5 cm. (C. 30)

47. Bracket showing mother and child under a tree, Kuṣāṇa period, *c.* 2nd century A.D., provenance not known, spotted red sand stone, ht. 31.5 cm. (F. 16)

48. Bracket figure (*śālabhañjikā*) from the doorway of the *Nāga* shrine, Kuṣāṇa period, *c.* 100 A.D., Sonkh, Mathurā district, spotted red sand stone, 77.5 cm. (SO IV-27)

49. Lintel of the gateway of the *Nāga* shrine showing probably a court scene, Kuṣāṇa period, *c.* 100 A.D., Sonkh, Mathurā district, red sand stone, L. 121 cm. (SO IV-36)

50. Fragment of beam showing a fish-tailed elephant with stalked lotus in his trunk, Kuṣāṇa period, 100 A.D., Sonkh, Mathurā district, red sand stone, L. 67 cm. (SO IV-36)

51. Upper half of the famous Buddha image installed/carved by Yaśadinna, Gupta period, *c.* 5th century A.D., Jamālpur mound, Collectorate Mathurā, red sand stone, ht. of the full figure 220 cm., (A. 5)

52. Lower half of Buddha image with inscribed pedestal dated year 93 = A.D. 171, Mathurā city, red sand stone with buff patched. ht. 46 cm. (76.1)

53. Inscribed pedestal of Amitābha Buddha of the year 26 = A.D. 106, Govindnagar, Mathurā city, spotted red sand stone, L. 51 cm. (77.30)

54. Inscribed pedestal of a Buddha image installed in the reign of Budha Gupta dated 161 (A.D. 480), Govindnagar, Mathurā city, red sand stone, L. 44.5 cm. (82.240)

55-56. Standing Buddha image carved by Yaśadinna in the year 115 (A.D. 434), Govindnagar, Mathurā city, red sand stone, ht. 147 cm. (76.25)

57. Architectural component representing the Buddha in preaching pose and *caitya* window (*kīrttimukha*) motif above, Gupta period, *c.* 5th century A.D., provenance not known, spotted red sand stone. ht. 57 cm. (87.25)

58. Bust of Viṣṇu in cosmic form, Gupta period, *c.* 5th century A.D., Bhaṅkhri, Aligarh district, red sand stone, ht. 46 cm. (42-43.2989)

59. Part of a doorframe representing Gaṅgā on crocodile, late Gupta period, *c.* 6th century A.D., provenance not known, buff sand stone, ht. 107.5 cm. (OA 8/7)

60. *Śivaliṅga* with human face on both sides and third eye, Kuṣāṇo-Gupta phase, *c.* 3rd century A.D., Arīng, Mathurā district, red sand stone, ht. 61 cm. (14-15.462)

61. Upper half of Śiva with matted hair, rosary and erect phallus, Gupta period, *c.* 5th century A.D., provenance not known, red sand stone, ht. 38 cm. (71.23)

62. Head of Arddhanārīśvara (combined form of Śiva and Pārvatī), Gupta period, *c.* 5th century A.D., Mathurā city, red sand stone, ht. 26.5 cm. (13.362)

63. Gaṇeśa, probably the earliest representation of the elephant headed deity, early Gupta period, *c.* early 4th century A.D., spotted red sand stone, ht. 20.5 cm. (15.758)

64. Arddhanārīśvara bust, a unique specimen of Gupta period art, *c.* 5th century A.D., Gosna well, Mathurā district, red sand stone, ht. 32 cm. (15.772)

65. Cakreśvarī—*Yakṣī* of Ṛṣabhanātha, Medieval period, *c.* 10th century A.D., Kaṅkālī mound, Mathurā City, buff sand stone, ht. 74. 5 cm. (D. 6)

66. Quadruple Jaina image, post Gupta, *c.* 6th-7th century A.D., provenance not known, spotted red sand stone, ht. 86 cm. (B. 65)

67. Circular plaque representing Sūrya (sun god) with his retinue on both sides, Medieval period, *c.* 9th centuary A.D., Cūrīawālī ṭhek, Mathurā city, buff sand stone, dia. 51 cm. (68.1)

68. Sūrya inside a pillared ariche, drawn in the chariot of seven horses, Medieval period, *c.* 10th century A.D., Madaur, Sādābād, Mathurā district, buff sand stone, ht. 102 cm. (88.18)

69. Sūrya with ten incarnations of Viṣṇu, Medieval period, *c.* 10th century A.D., Madaur, Sādābād, Mathurā district, buff sand stone, ht. 74 cm. (88.19)

70. Viṣṇu in dwarfish form (Vāmana), Medieval period, *c.* 10th century A.D., Batnaur, Mawānā, Meerut, buff sand stone, ht. 26 cm. (78.1)

71. Four armed meditating Viṣṇu, Medieval, *c.* 10th century A.D., Gataśrama temple, Mathurā city, buff sand stone, ht. 86.5 cm. (D. 37)

72. Lakṣmī-Nārāyaṇa on Garuḍa, Medieval period, *c.* 10th-11th century A.D., provenance not known, buff sand stone, ht. 55.5 cm. (85.185)

73. Double Viṣṇu stele, Medieval period, *c.* 10th century A.D., Gokul barrage, Mathurā District, buff sand stone, ht. 58.5 cm. (93.31)

74. Viṣṇu with club, disc, conch and protection pose with other deities and attendants, Medieval period, *c.* 10th-11th century A.D., Rataul, Meerut

district, buff sand stone, ht. 67 cm. (88.10)

75. Varāha (boar incarnation of Viṣṇu) lifting earth, Medieval period, *c.* 10th century A.D., Mānasīgaṅgā, Govardhan, buff sand stone, ht. 75 cm. (87.6)

76. Durgā or Ambikā, Medieval period, *c.* 10th century A.D., Rataul, Meerut district, buff sand stone, ht. 55 cm. (88.16)

77. Marriage of Śiva and Pārvatī (*kalyāṇasundara*), Medieval period, *c.* 10th century A.D., Mānasīgaṅgā, Govardhan, buff sand stone, 79 cm. (87.8)

78. Rāhu (a planet) in offering pose (*tarpaṇa mudrā*), Medieval period, *c.* 10th century A.D., Satohā, Mathurā district, buff sand stone, ht. 48 x L. 67.5 cm. (39.2836)

79. Lower part of temple doorjamb representing Gaṅgā and attendant, Medieval period, provenance not known, buff sand stone, ht. 91.5 cm. (R. 56)

80. Umā-Maheśvara or Śiva-Pārvatī stele, Medieval, *c.* 11th century A.D., Hāzipur, Hāthras, dark basalt stone, ht. 112 cm. (85.167)

81. Architectural fragmenting three damsels between the pilasters, Medieval period, *c.* 10th century A.D., Mahāban, Mathurā district, spotted red sand stone, ht. 114 cm. (73.28)

82. Fragmentary frieze with three mother goddesses (*mātṛkās*) Kaumārī, Vaiṣṇavī and Vārāhī, Medieval period, *c.* 10th century A.D., Kagaroll, Agra district, buff sand stone, ht. 66 x L. 91.5 cm. (40. 2874/1)

Table of Transliteration

अ a	आ ā	इ i	ई ī	उ u	ऊ ū	ए e
ऐ ai	ओ o	औ au	अं ṁ	अ: ḥ	ऋ ṛ	लृ lṛ

क ka	ख kha	ग ga	घ gha	ङ ṅa
च ca	छ cha	ज ja	झ jha	ञ ña
ट ṭa	ठ ṭha	ड ḍa	ढ ḍha	ण ṇa
त ta	थ tha	द da	ध dha	न na
प pa	फ pha	ब ba	भ bha	म ma
य ya	र ra	ल la	व va	
श śa	ष ṣa	स sa	ह ha	
क्ष kṣa	त्र tra	ज्ञ jña		

Abbreviations

AI	*Ancient India.*
ASR	*Archaeological Survey of India-Reports.*
BAM	*Buddhist Art of Mathurā.*
BMA	*Bulletin of Museums & Archaeology in U.P.*
CAMM	*Catalogue of the Archaeological Museums at Mathurā.*
CHI	*Corpus Inscriptionum Indicarum.*
col. ill.	Coloured illustration.
EI	*Epigraphia Indica.*
fig.	Figure in black and white.
IA	*Indian Antiquary.*
IMC	Indian Museum, Calcutta.
JAOS	*Journal of American Oriental Society.*
JASB	*Journal of the Asiatic Society of Bengal.*
JBOR	*Journal of the Bihar Orissa Research Society.*
JBRS	*Journal of the Bihar Research Society.*
JIM	*Journal of the Indian Museums.*
JNSI	*Journal of the Numismatic Society of India.*
JRAS	*Journal of the Royal Asiatic Society of Great Britain & Ireland.*
JRAS, NS	*Journal of the Royal Asiatic Society, New Series.*

JUPHS	*Journal of the United Provinces Historical Society.*
MDM	*Mathurā: a District Memoir.*
MI	*Mathurā Inscriptions.*
MM	Mathurā Museum.
MMA	*Mathurā Museum and Art.*
MS	*Mathurā Sculptures.*
NM	National Museum
SML	State Museum, Lucknow.

Important Dates[1]

Palaeoliths, *c.* 50000 B.C.[2]

Copper implements, pre 1000 B.C.[3]

Painted Grey Ware *c.* 800 B.C. to 400 B.C.[4]

Buddha, 623 B.C. to 527 B.C.[5]

Mahāvīra, 559 B.C. to 527 B.C.

Maurya period, 325 B.C. to 184 B.C.

Śuṅga period, 184 B.C. to 72 B.C.

Kṣaharāta Satraps of Mathurā *c.* 100 B.C. to 57 B.C.

(a) Satrapas Hagan and Hagamaṣa.
(b) Mahākṣatrapa Rājula.
(c) Mahākṣatrapa Śoḍāṣa, *c.* 81 B.C.
(d) Kṣaharāta Ghaṭaka.

Revival of the Śuṅgas at Mathurā, 57 B.C. to *c.* 20 B.C. Kings Gomitra, Viṣṇumitra, etc.

Kuṣāṇas, *c.* A.D. 1 to A.D. 176.

(a) King Kuṣāṇa or Kadaphises I, *c.* 1 to *c.* A.D. 40.
(b) Wema Kadaphises II, *c.* A.D. 40 to A.D. 77.
(c) Kaniṣka A.D. 78 to A.D. 101.
(d) Vāsiṣka, A.D. 102 to A.D. 106.
(e) Huviṣka, A.D. 106 to A.D. 138.
(f) Vāsudeva, A.D. 138 to A.D. 176. Then followed the disruption of the Śāhānuśāhi empire after the death of Emperor Vāsudeva.

Guptas, A.D. 320 to *c.* A.D. 600.

Early medieval period, A.D. 600 to *c.* A.D. 900.

Late medieval period, A.D. 900 to A.D. 1200.

References

1. Mainly on the basis of the '*Hand book of the sculptures in the Curzon Museum of Archaeology*', 1939, by V.S. Agrawala.
2. Collected by Dr. R.B. Joshi and the present author in January, 1975 from Govardhana.
3. Cunningham, A., *A.S.I.R.*, Vol. III, 1873, p. 13 and A.K. Shrivastava, *Bulletin of Museum and Archaeology in U.P.*, No. 11-12, June-December, 1973, p. 41.
4. *Indian Archaeology : 1954-55, A Review*, pp. 15-16.
5. Some scholars favour 563-483 B.C.

1

Cultural Background

The city and its Religious Importance

SITUATED on the right bank of the Yamunā at a distance of 145 km. south-east of Delhi and 58 km. north-west of Agra, Mathurā occupies a foremost place in the cultural history of India. The synonymity of different names such as Madhurā, Madhupurī, Madhuṣikā, Madhupghanā, Madhuban and Mathulā or Mathurā suggests that its nomenclature is due to the tradition that the town was founded by the mighty demon Madhu. Corroborating this legend the *Rāmāyaṇa* mentions that after Madhu's death the region was governed by his son Lavaṇa who was equally powerful. Drunken in prowess the demon challenged Rāma who sent his youngest brother Śatrughna to subdue the enemy. After a fierce battle the demon was killed and the region was conquered. The real credit of founding the city thus goes to the victorious Śatrughna.[1] According to some legends lot of honey was collected in its forests hence its name Madhubvana (forest of honey). Ptolemy mentions it as Modourā.[2] Subsequently, its association with Lord Kṛṣṇa ensured for it the greatest significance and everlasting glory. As his birth place the Hindus have always regarded it a great centre of pilgrimage. *Sarveṣām daivatīrthānām Māthuram paramam mahat.* As capital of the Śūrasena dynasty the town was the hub of the contemporary political activities during the Mahābhāratan Age.

As the traditions go, the Buddha also visited the city at least once, but he did not receive a warm welcome. According to the *Madhuriya Suttanata* Avantiputra had the religious discourse with Mahākātyāyana, the disciple of the Buddha in the garden of Gunda. It was in Avantiputra's time that Buddhism gained a strong foothold in this region. Bhadrākapilānī, the wife of another disciple, Mahākāśyapa, also belonged to Mathurā.[3] The *Divyāvadāna* refers to the Buddha's prophecy that the place will emerge into a big city.[4] Aśoka bestowed special favour on the place as his spiritual[5] preceptor Upagupta hailed from Mathurā. Aśoka was converted into Buddhism by Moggaliputta Tissa. [6] Upagupta was adviser of Aśoka for dissemination of the *Dharma* and creation of *stūpas* at various places. Hiuen-Tsang, a Chinese traveller during the reign of Harṣa (7th century A.D.) mentions that Aśoka built some *stūpas* here. Besides, many scholars hold that Mathurā is responsible for the origin of the Buddha image.[7]

For the Jaina community too the place has been very sacred. While all the 24 *Tīrthaṅkaras* were worshipped, Ṛṣabhanātha (first), Supārśvanātha (seventh), Neminātha (twenty second), Pāraśvanātha (twenty third) and Mahāvīra (twenty fourth and last) commanded special respect. Neminātha is regarded as a cousin of Kṛṣṇa, who was taught the fundamentals of Jainism by the former. The early epigraphic records suggest that the Jaina community was very prosperous and had a strong hold at Mathurā.[8] The city thus equally attracted all the three sects which flourished here simultaneously till the 7th century A.D. when Brāhmanism began to dominate.

Political History

The political history of Mathurā can be traced back from about the 5th century B.C., when it was the capital of the Śūrasena country, one of the big sixteen states (*ṣoḍaṣamahājanapada*). Pāṇini, a contemporary grammarian, mentions the place and the famous Andhaka-Vṛṣṇi clans.[9] The *Arthaśāstra* refers to the Vṛṣṇis as a republican corporation while Kṛṣṇa (Vāsudeva) is called *saṅgha-mukhya* of the combined guilds of Andhakas and Vṛṣṇis.[10] Megasthenes, the Greek ambassador to the court of Candragupta Maurya, gives an account of the place as the seat of the Śūrasenas where Kṛṣṇa worship was in vogue. But in the Mauryan period it had lost its independence and had come under the administrative control of the Magadha Empire.

The city had a prosperous time under the Śuṅga kings, who ruled here after the fall of the Mauryan kingdom. Patañjali, a commentator on the *Aṣṭādhyāyī*, mentions that the conditions were good, the people were happy and good looking and probably better off than the residents of Sāṅkāśya and Pāṭaliputra.[11]

Literary evidence[12] corroborated by numismatic finds hints that during the reign of the Śuṅgas the Greek rulers of Bactria had invaded Northern India and had reached Sāketa and Pāṭaliputra. Mathurā was also a centre of attraction. But they did not stay here for long owing to their 'internal dissensions'. Subsequently, in the 1st century B.C. Mathurā came under the Kṣatrapas headed by Rājuvala and Śoḍāṣa. Then followed a period of disruption, although from the coins of Gomitra, Sūryamitra, Viṣṇumitra and others, it appears that a Hindu renaissance was on the way.

Coins, issued under the name of Puruṣadatta, Uttamadatta, Rāmadatta, Kāmadatta, Śeṣadatta and Bhavadatta found in the Mathurā region, point to some Datta dynasty having its hold over Mathurā after the end of Kṣatrapa rule.[13]

Fortune smiled in the later part of the 1st century A.D. when it became an important headquarter of the Kuṣāṇa rule in Kaniṣka's reign. The importance of the place increased further during the reign of his successors Vāsiṣka, Huviṣka and Vāsudeva, and for about a century it became a metropolis in different aspects of life. It was probably in this period that the whole region began to be called Mathurā instead of Śūrasena. A century of Kuṣāṇa rule was truly a golden age for Mathurā when cultural prosperity reached its zenith. A period of disruption again followed after the death of

Vāsudeva in 176 A.D. The Nāgas also ruled for some time. After the rise of the Gupta power in the early 4th century A.D. Mathurā fell again in the hands of the Magadha Empire, losing its great political importance.

In the beginning of the 6th century A.D. the Huns invaded the country and destroyed many cities including Mathurā. From the 6th to the 10th century A.D. Mathurā was administrered from Kanauj (Thāneśvara) under the Vardhana and Pratihāra dynasties. It was a peaceful and rather uneventful phase of Mathurā's history which ended when it was fiercely attacked in 1017, by Mahmūd Ghaznavi, who destroyed many temples and looted their wealth. According to the Sultan's Secretary Al-Utbi 'Islām or death was the alternative that Mahmūd placed before the people'.[14]

The Gahadavālas came to power in Kanauj at the end of the 11th century and Mathurā was a part of their kingdom. In 1194 A.D. Kutubuddīn defeated Jaicandra and Hindu rule came to an end. After the fall of Kanauj, Mathurā also came under the direct rule of Muslims. The most difficult time which Mathurā faced was in the reign of Sikandar Lodī (1488-1517 A.D.). Not only were the temples and images plundered, destroyed and mutilated but he also ordered their massacre, when the citizens refused conversion. Although born of a Hindu mother the king had a highly prejudiced and bigoted attitude towards his Hindu subjects.[15]

Akbar's reign, when the policy of non-interference and tolerance towards all religions (*sulahakula*) was followed, was a time of revival for Mathurā culture and many a temples were built. Jahāṅgīr and Śāhajahān remained indifferent towards other religions. Auraṅgzeb, however, followed a different policy and caused the greatest harm to the culture of Mathurā. Important temples were either demolished or replaced by mosques, beautiful statues were broken and many saints and devotees left the place with images of deities and took shelter in different Hindu states. Towards the end of his reign the Jāṭs weakened the Mughal power and ruled over Mathurā till A.D. 1770 when they were defeated by the Marāṭhās. The city also faced two attacks in A.D. 1739 and A.D. 1757 by Nādirśāh and Ahmad Śāh Abdāli which almost ruined it. The Marāṭhās who were in power for about 33 years, tried to re-build some religious places. In A.D. 1803 they were defeated by the British who ruled uptil 1947. The city never fully recovered from this chain of calamities although it has continued to enjoy a high reputation as a great religious centre to the present day.

Archaeological Significance

Mathurā's glorious past is amply corroborated by innumerable archaeological finds. Many a dated sculpture throws valuable light on the history of our country. Building activity had started from a very early period. Aśoka is said to have built some *stūpas.* Even if we do not believe this tradition, the *stūpa* fragments of the Śuṅga period are there to give it weight.[16] That sculptures were carved in an earlier age is shown by the colossal Parkham Yakṣa of the late third century B.C. Terracottas and coins are still earlier specimens belonging to the pre-Mauryan age. While the pottery goes back to the 1st millenium B.C. the copper implements are still anterior by a few centuries. The earliest remains of the human activity are, however, noticed in the shape of the pre-historic old stone age tools which might belong to pre 50000 B.C.

Several shrines and monasteries were built during the Kuṣāṇa and Gupta periods. Vodva(?) *stūpa* was perhaps the earliest monument and is mentioned as *devanirmita* i.e., built by gods, in an inscription of early 2nd century A.D.[17] This suggests that by this time its historicity had been forgotten. The Morā well inscription datable to the 1st century B.C. describes the installation of sculptures of five Vṛṣṇi heroes in a stone shrine *śaila devagṛha*.[18]

Fa-hien in the late 4th century A.D. says that twenty monasteries existed on both the banks of the river Yamunā and housed about three thousand monks. The building activity continued to flourish for centuries after. Hiuen-Tsang writes that the *stūpas* at Mathurā contained the holy relics of Sāriputra, Upāli, Rāhula, Ānanda and Mañjuśrī. He also saw twenty monasteries but the number of the monks was reduced to two thousand. Forty five names of Buddhist monasteries and establishments are mentioned in the epigraphic records and accounts of the Chinese travellers. They are 1. Huviṣka Vihāra. 2. Svarṇakāra Vihāra, 3. Śrī Vihāra, 4. Cetiya Vihāra, 5. Cutaka Vihāra, 6. Āpānaka Vihāra, 7. Mihira Vihāra, 8. Guha Vihāra, 9. Krauṣtikīya Vihāra, 10. Roṣika Vihāra, 11. Kakāṭikā Vihāra, 12. Pravarika Vihāra, 13. Yaśā Vihāra 14. Khaṇḍa Vihāra 15. Amohassī Vihāra, 16. Śrī Kunda Vihāra, 17. Dharma-hastisa Vihāra, 18. Mahāsāṅghika Vihāra, 19. Puṣyadatta Vihāra, 20. Ladyaska Vihāra, 21. Uttara Hāruṣa Vihāra, 22. Naṭabhaṭa Vihāra, 23. Upagupta Vihāra, 24. Madhura- vanaka Vihāra, 25. Guṇḍa Vihāra, 26. Saṅghamitra Sada Vihāra, 27. Kundokhara Vihāra 28. Vīradatta Vihāra, 29. Saka Vihāra, 30. Stūpa, 31. Jīvikadatta Vihāra 32. Cetiya Kaṭiya Svakaya 33. Dharmaguptaka parigraha 34. Sanghārāma 35. Sarvāstivatrana parigrah 36. Muia Vihāra 37. Svaka Vihāra 38. Sāriputra Stūpa 39. Mudgalāyana Stūpa 40. Pūrnamaitrāyaṇiputra Stūpa 41. Upāli Stūpa 42. Ānanda Stūpa 43. Rāhula Stūpa 44. Mañjuśrī Stūpa 45. Vihāra (name missing).[19] These monasteries were not the simple dwellings of monks but served as great cultural and educational centres under the supervision of eminent scholars.

These shrines, monasteries and *stūpas* were destroyed not so much by the action of time as by human agency. Religious rivalry was greatly responsible for bringing catastrophe upon this magnificent city of art or culture. While some art treasures have been dug up and displayed in a good number of museums and art galleries in the world, there still remains much antiquarian wealth buried in different mounds and awaits the archaeologist's spade.

History of Campaigns and Acquisitions

For about the last one and a half century the archaeological importance of the city has been continuously increasing. Eminent archaeologists and Indologists have been campaigning hard to reveal antiquarian wealth of this region. The first sculpture representing a bachhanalian scene was found by Colonel L.R. Stacy in 1836 and was handed over to the Asiatic Society of Bengal, now with the Indian Museum Calcutta.[20] Stacy presented another sculpture to the Society and it shows a lady standing on a dwarf and patting a bird in a cage. The reverse of the piece depicts the subjugation of Nalgiri elephant by prince Siddhārtha.[21]

The first Director General of Archaeological Survey of India Sir Alexander Cunningham was attracted by the rich sites of Mathurā and he paid his first visit in 1853, discovering some rail posts near the Kaṭrā mound, one of which represented a lady under the tree.[22] Cunningham also obtained a stone inscription recording the geneology of the Gupta rulers upto Samudra Gupta.[23] Two pillar capitals were revealed from the Kaṭrā site but their whereabouts are not known.[24]

He revisited Mathurā in 1862 and found some acrchitectural fragments of the Buddhist railing and gateway. The important lintel of Śuṅga period showing the refectory of a monastery (Mathurā Museum M. 1) was the result of these explorations.[25] The most significant acquisition of this year was the standing Buddha image (B. 10 of the Lucknow Museum) with beautiful halo and *ubhayānsika sanghāṭī* and recording its installation in the Gupta era 230 (549-50 A.D.) by a Buddhist nun Jayabhaṭṭā in the Yaśavihāra. This discovery proves that an important Buddhist monastery was existing at the Kaṭrā site in the 6th cent. A.D. Later a Viṣṇu temple was built on this site and it has been mentioned by many foreign travellers.[26]

In 1860 the Jail or Jamālpur mound (Jail according to Cunningham and Jamālpur according to Growse) was levelled up for constructing the buildings of the present Collectorate. Numerous architectural fragments and sculptures, revealed during the course of digging the foundation etc., were sent to different places and are now seen in Calcutta, Lucknow and Mathurā museums.[27] The epigraphs obtained from this site inform us the existence of a monastery of Huviṣka and a temple of Dadhikarṇa Nāga in the Kuṣāṇa period.[28] The outstanding Buddha image (A. 5; *col. ill. XXVII*) now adorning the galleries of the Mathurā Museum was the result of the Collectorate site clearance. The pedestal of the Buddha image (A. 48) dated in the Gupta era 135 corresponding to 454-55 A.D., was dug out in 1877-78.[29]

The lion capital with a Kharoṣṭhī inscription, now in the British Museum, London, was found by Bhagwan Lal Indraji in 1869. This records the building of a Buddhist monastery Guha Vihāra by queen Kambojikā, wife of the Kṣatrap king Rājavula at the present site of Saptarṣī.[30] The standing lady in the Gāndhāra style (F. 42; *Fig. 29*) identified as Kambojikā was another important acquisition of the year 1869. Out of these one pillar showing a lady after bath (J. 4) and another busy in cosmetics (J. 5) can be seen in the Mathurā Museum. Two rail posts are in the Indian Museum, Calcutta while the remaining one was sent to the Lucknow Museum. Cunningham also excavated about a dozen of mounds at Caubārā, revealing therein one golden casket and another steatite casket (the second in the Calcutta Museum). From another site of Caubārā range a Persepolitan pillar with four mythical beings was unearthed and deposited in the Calcutta Museum (M. 14).[31] In 1869 a road planned through Caubārā mounds revealed a Buddhist relic chamber containing a small golden casket which was said to be in the possession of F.S. Growse.[32]

After Cunningham, F.S. Growse also excavated some mounds of Caubārā and found a colossal Buddha head showing Egyptian features (A. 27 of Mathurā Museum). Besides, he also got an inscribed pedestal of the Buddha image recording the 33rd year in the reign of Huviṣka (Lucknow Museum No. B.2). Another significant acquisition from Caubārā is the famous rail post representing Ṛṣyaśṛṅga in ecstasy (J. 7 of Mathurā Museum). Another image of Pārśvanātha or Supārśvanātha surmounted by the snake canopy (Mathurā Museum B. 26) was obtained between Kaṅkālī and Caubārā. This figure of Kubera or Yakṣa (C. 3 of Mathurā Museum) was found between Mathurā-Maholī and Pālīkherā and the second Bachhanalian scene came from Pālīkherā (C. 2 in Mathurā Museum). Growse also dug out a number of basement stones suggesting the possibility of an early shrine at the same site.[33] Some of the antiquities were being ruthlessly reused and he rescued them. One stone inscription of the 50th year in reign of Huviṣka was set in a P.W.D. culvert (Mathurā Museum No. B. 29) and another inscription was studded in the gate of the *Tahsīl* (Mathurā Museum No. P. 22) A *nāga* figure was collected from Kukargāon (Mathurā Museum No. C. 15).[34] Although the Museum was established in 1874 yet it failed to receive any patronage from General Cunningham, the Director General of Archaeology, who continued to send the finds to Calcutta and other museums. During his last visit to Mathurā in 1882 he found the famous sculpture of subjugation of Nemaean lion by Herakles.[35] A Jaina sculpture giving 57 year (B. 15) saw its way to the Museum from Śitalā Ghāṭī. Cunningham also reports the discovery of a pillar with Mauryan *Brāhmī* characters reading *Amogharakhitā ye dānam* from Arjunapurā locality but the whereabouts of this important piece are unfortunately not known.[36] An inscribed Jaina image dated in the 62nd year was found in Rānī kī Maṇḍī but it was sent to Calcutta Museum (M. 12).[37]

Dr. Fuhrer's area excavation at the Kaṅkālī mound from 1888 to 1891 was a great archaeological mission, revealing numerous Jaina sculptures which were removed en bloc to the Lucknow Museum. This large collection ranges in date from 2nd century B.C. to the 12th century A.D. and testifies the existence of at least two Jaina *stūpas* at the site of Kaṅkālī.[38] Some of the inscribed pedestals are valuable documents to study the contemporary society and particularly the organization of the Jaina church. Dr. Fuhrer again undertook his project in 1896 and concentrated this time at the site of Kaṭrā and found some *stūpa* fragments. But he had to close his work as the walls of the old *stūpa* were continuing towards the present *Idgāh*.[39]

After a lull of about 14 years Rāi Bahādur Pt. Radha Krishna started the collection of antiquities for the Museum at mass scale in 1909. Three years later he excavated the Iṭokarī mound at Māṭ and unearthed the famous royal portrait figures of Vema Kadphises, Kaniṣka and Caṣṭana.[40] Radha Krishna further enriched the Museum collection by adding about 600 sculptures as the result of cleaning the wells in Mathurā and its vicinity. Interesting finds including some terracotta panels of the Gupta period were recovered from the river bed in 1938. M. Venkatramayya and Vallabh Saran of Northern Zone of the Archaeological Survey of India excavated some parts of the Kaṭrā mound in 1953. The details of this work are not fully known but the finds include pottery of different types, terracottas, beads and some seals. The Painted Grey Ware was also reported from the surface.[41]

Beside the regular excavations, the Museum continued to be enriched by several important accidental finds. The Delhi-Agra highway digging yielded some valuable architectural fragments, particularly the doorjambs and coping of a big gateway of a *stūpa* or a Buddhist monastery of the Kuṣāṇa period (57. 4446 to 4448). An important eight year campaign at large scale was piloted from 1966 to 1974 by the German Archaeological Mission under the direction of Prof. Harbert Härtel. Their choice fell on the lofty mound of Sonkh about 20 km. (as the crow flies) to south-east from the District head-quarter.[42] Some of the remarkable discoveries of this Mission are: the oldest Brāhmanical and *nāga* shrines belonging to Pre-Kuṣāṇa and Kuṣāṇa period, the earliest bronzes of this region, almost complete cross section of Mathurā or Braj culture from about the 1st millenium B.C. to the Medieval period and some of the outstanding sculptures from the early *nāga* shrine belonging to about 100 A.D. Excavators are inclined to suggest 78 A.D. as the starting point of the Kuṣāṇa era.[43] The objects are in the custody of the Mathurā Museum. The detailed report on the excavation has been brought out by Prof. Härtel which will shed fresh light on scientific dating of antiquities.[44]

Some hoards of copper and silver coins of different kings have also been found. A significant hoard consisting of sixteen copper age implements was discovered in the Sādābād sub-division and sent to Lucknow Museum in 1970.[45] Some of the specimens have, however, been presented to the Mathurā Museum. This hoard is of great importance as we are informed of only a solitary piece found during the last century by Cunningham. An anthropomorphic figure is in the private possession of Gokul and it was displayed on a special exhibition held at the National Museum, New Delhi in April 1992.

The Museum has further acquired some rare antiquities through purchase, present and police help.

The last expedition was conducted under the direction of Sri B.K. Thapar and Sri M.C. Joshi of the Archaeological Survey of India in 1974-75. The team aimed at the study of the plan of the old Mathurā city and particularly the behaviour of the rampart. They also took up some trenches near Mahāvidyā, Camuṇḍā, Hāthī Ṭīlā, Ambariśa and Kaṅkālī Ṭīlā. The last site revealed a brick tank of the Kuṣāṇa period. It also exposed an inscription of the 5th regnal year of Kaniṣka.[46] Some grey terracottas of the Mauryan and the Śuṅga period representing beautiful mother goddesses etc. were discovered from Hāthī Ṭīlā behind the K.R. Training College.[47]

In January 1975 Dr. R.B. Joshi of Poona reported the discovery of some palaeoliths (Old Stone Age tools) from the Govardhan hillock. Subsequently, some more tools were collected by the Archaeological Survey party and also by the present author. This event dates back the remains of human civilization in this region to an era anterior to 50000 B.C. Eminent Russian archaeologist and pre historian Prof. Alexer P. Obladnikov, Director of the Institute of History, Philology and Philosophy of Siberian Deptt. who examined these tools on 2.11.79 confirmed them as paleoliths.

The site of Govindnagar near Kṛṣṇa Janmasthān proved to be the mine of Buddhist sculptures. As a result of levelling of mound by the colonisers a large number of sculptural remains was unearthed and this antiquarian wealth was salvaged and acquired for the Mathurā Museum. Some of these are outstanding specimens of Mathurā Art and a few are dated.[48]

Mathurā School of Art

The crudely modelled stone tools were made merely for safety or hunting purpose and do not betray any artistic workmanship. The copper implements belonging to a comparatively very late period i.e. 1000 B.C. have been given a proper shape but are devoid of any decorative expression. The anthropomorphic figure the purpose of which is uncertain is of course a fine specimen. The earliest ceramics of this region known as Painted Grey Ware are marked with black lines which are indicative of the beginning of the art form. Small terracotta figurines probably representing mother goddesses and datable to the pre-Mauryan period in many respects resemble the similar figurines found in the Indus Valley. The tradition of mother goddesses continued with some occasional changes for several centuries.

Use of stone commenced probably from the Mauryan period as is evident from the earliest statue of the Parkham Yakṣa which on stylistic and inscriptional grounds should be placed in the late 3rd century B.C. It represents purely an indigenous style of art which was prevalent throughout the country. In the second century B.C. the Mathurā artists followed the artistic trends of Central India, particularly of Bharhut. The pontiffs were not yet shown in human form, instead represented through various symbols which dominated the composition.

For a short period in the 1st century B.C. the Kṣatrapas came on the scene. The inscribed lion capital now in the British Museum London and the Amohini tablet in the State Museum, Lucknow are the two famous sculptures commemorating the reign of Mahākṣatrapa Rājula and Śoḍāṣa. A doorjamb of the time of Śoḍāṣa records the installation of Mahāsthāna at the Kaṭrā site (?). It was probably for the worship of Vāsudeva.

Subsequently, the Mathurā artists developed their own style and with the impetus and encouragement given under the patronage of art-loving Kuṣāṇa rulers, Mathurā became an independent school of art influencing a vast area. Its products were in heavy demand in distant parts. Kauśāmbī and Sārnāth Bodhisattvas recording the 2nd and 3rd regnal year of Kaniṣka respectively, were imported from here. At Bodhagayā also an early Buddha image in Mathurā style was discovered.[49] The Kuṣāṇa period is rightly called the golden age for the Mathurā School of Art for it was then that several masterpieces were produced.

Maintaining its standard in the Gupta period the Mathurā school flourished but not with the same zeal and spirit. While quantitatively the manufacturing process slowed down, the quality improved and the real charm of the physical beauty was combined with spirituality. This new concept considerably refined the expression of the artist. During this period too Mathurā continued to export Buddhist and Jaina statues to different parts. The popularity of the Mathurā School in early times can well be judged from Gen. Cunningham's remark, "Everywhere in the North-West I find that the old Buddhist statues are made of Sīkrī sandstone from which it would appear that Mathurā must have been the great manufactory for the supply of Buddhist sculptures in Northern India.[50]

The Mathurā School of Art has made a great contribution in evolving the pantheon of different sects. Any serious student working on early iconography must consult the Mathurā statuary. The Brāhmanical pantheon is represented in the Kuṣāṇa period by the introduction of the following figures: Brahmā, Viṣṇu, Śiva, Sūrya, Indra, Kārttikeya, Agni, Balarāma, Kāmdeva, Durgā, Sarasvatī, Lakṣmī, Mātṛkās (Divine Mothers) and Ekānanśā. Some of these deities have figured in different forms.

Viṣṇu

His incons are found with two arms, four arms and eight arms holding different attributes viz. *śaṅkha* (conch) *cakra* (disc) and *gadā* (mace) but not the lotus which is a later addition. Among his incarnations Kṛṣṇa and Balarāma are seen either flanking Ekānanśā or Jina Nemināthа. The later is seen independently also. Varāha has been identified (?) on one sculpture (65.15). Viṣṇu is also seen in *caturvyūha* form (different figures issuing from the main body No. 13.392-395). Hayagrīva from Mathurā has seen its way to the Bhārat Kalā Bhavan, Banāras Hindū University, Varānasi.

Śiva

He is seen in *liṅga* form, human form, sometimes with Pāravatī and *arddhanārīśvara* (male and female aspects combined).

Durgā

She was carved with four arms or six arms with or without lion, holding different weapons and sometimes killing the demon Mahiṣa, (Mahiṣāsuramardinī). The earliest icon in terracotta belongs to 1st century B.C. and hails from Sonkh.

In the Gupta period a few other deities were added to the list, such as Kṛṣṇa (as independent deity), Gaṇeśa, Gaṅgā, Yamunā, Daṇḍa, Piṅgala Hari-hara *āyudhapuruṣas* (personified weapons), and the representation of heroic deeds of some important deities. The figures of *yakṣas* and *nāgas* were also quite common.

The Jaina *Tīrthaṅkaras* made their first appearance at Mathurā in the *āyāgapaṭṭas* (tablets of worship) and gradually their images were carved independently. Statues of Ādinātha, Pārśvanātha, Neminātha and Mahāvīra as Vardhamāna were the earliest to be made. Other associated figures are of Sarasvatī, Naigameśa and Āryāvatī. In the medieval period different cognizances were given to different *Tīrthaṅkaras* for their proper identification. An unmistakable characteristic which has continued through the ages is the mark of *śrīvatsa* (jewel) on the chest of the Jina.

A delicate and controversial problem associated with the Mathurā School is the origin of the Buddha image. Gāndhāra has also been favoured by some scholars, but Mathurā seems to have a superior claim. The issue has been discussed in detail by the present writer in his book *Buddhist Art of Mathurā*, ch. 7. Beside the Buddha images, the Buddhist pantheon includes Bodhisattvas, events in the Buddha's life, *jātaka* stories, Indra, Pañcaśikha Gandharva, Kubera and Hārītī, *lokapālas* and the chief disciples of the Buddha.

Although the Mathurā sculptor portrayed religious subjects, it is difficult to say whether he himself followed a particular creed. There are several illustrations which are of secular or domestic nature. Panels depicting palace scenes, ladies under trees, some musicians and dancers, the Bachhanalian groups and so on are subjects where the sculptor has tried to infuse his own imagination and has not been governed by sectarian canons. Such themes representing the free choice of the engraver are more full of life. The art motifs such as vine creeper, lotus, mythical beings and many auspicious symbols have also been tastefully represented.

Glimpses of foreign elements are occasionally found in the art of Mathurā. This was quite natural, as Mathurā was the Eastern centre of Kuṣāṇas who were foreigners. Śakas and Kṣatrapas also came from outside the country. As a cosmopolitan city, Mathurā was a meeting place of several cultural currents. Motifs freely travelled from East to West and vice versa. Exchange was a natural phenomenon. Winged lions, centaurs mythical animals, battlements, palmettes and a host of other art forms are supposed to be foreign in origin. It may, however, be pointed out that these motifs have been repeatedly mentioned in ancient literature and are respectively known as *sapakṣasihma, kinnara, vyālas, īhāmṛgas, kapiśirṣaka tālaparṇa*, etc.

In the medieval period despite repeated foreign invasions, the sculptural art of Mathurā did not entirely disappear but it lost its original quality as the place disintegrated as school of art. The red sandstone was replaced by a buff coloured sandstone and the execution in general weakened considerably. The number of arms of deities increased to show their prowess. Emphasis was laid on ornaments, vehicles and attendant figures. Al-utbi has mentioned in his *Tārīkh-e-yāminī* that there existed a great and magnificent temple which was destroyed by Mahmūd Ghaznavi (A.D. 1017).[51] His statement that the king also recovered five big idols of gold studded with jewels proves that metal statuettes of high quality were also manufactured at Mathurā. This is corroborated by the discovery of two bronze figures from Sonkh belonging to the Kuṣāṇa period. Later in A.D. 1150 Prince Vijayachandra of the Gahadavāla dynasty built a big temple on the site of Kaṭrā. In the Mughal period and particularly in Akbar's time, Mathurā introduced a new pattern of architecture combining essential characteristics of different religious buildings. This phase of eclecticism can be noticed in the temple of Govindadeva at Vrindāban. Owing to prevailing circumstances Mathurā made no significant artistic or architectural achievement in the post-Mughal period.

Sculptural art while losing its original quality, did survive to a very late date. The remarks of F.S. Growse need mention in this regard: "The temples that line both sides of the high street in the city, the monument to Seth Maṇi Rām in the Jamunā Bāgh and the porch of the Museum (old building) itself are fine specimens of the style, and are conclusive proofs that in Mathurā at all events architecture is, to this day no mere galvanized revival, of the past, but is still a living and progressive art".[52]

To sum up, the highlights for which the Mathurā School of Art is distinguished are: The grey terracotta figurines with traces of black slip and subsequently red plaques; use of red sandstone with yellowish spots; replacement of symbols by the anthropomorphic form; origin and development of Buddha and Jina images, continuation of early art traditions of Central India (particularly of Bharhut) assimilation of foreign elements; fusion of primitive *yakṣa* cult with the pantheon of other sects; development of new art forms; introduction of portrait figures; delineation of female figures with special care and charm and an overall faithful depiction of different modes of life.

References

1. *Rāmāyaṇa, Uttarakāṇḍa*, canto 61-69.
2. *Mathurā District Gazetteer*, 1968, p. 1.
3. Bajpeyi, K.D., *Mathurā* (Hindi), 1955, ch. IV.
4. *Divyāvadāna*, Pansupradānavadānam, Darbhanga, 1958, pp. 216-18.
5. *Ibid.*, pp. 218-21.
6. *2500 Years of Buddhism*, p. 45.
7. Sharma, R.C., 'Pre-Kaniṣka Buddhist Iconography at Mathurā', In *B.M.A.*, No. 5-6, pp. 15-27.
8. Jain, J.P. *The Jaina Sources of the History of Ancient India*, ch. VI.
9. *Aṣṭādhyāyī*, IV. I/14; IV. 2.82 and VI. 2.34; Also see Dr. V.S. Agrawala's book, *India As known to Pāṇini*.
10. *The Age of Imperial Unity*, p. 12.

11. मृदङ्ग शङ्ख पणवः पृथङ् नदन्ति संसदि प्रासादे धनपति रामकेशवानाम्।

    Mahābhāṣya, 2.2.34.

    सांकाश्यकेभ्यश्च पाटलिपुत्रकेभ्यश्च माथुरा अभिरूपतरा इति।

    Mahābhāṣya, 5.3.57.
12. *Yuga Purāṇa* section of *Gārgī Saṁhitā.*
13. Bajpeyi, *op. cit.*, p. 18.
14. *The Struggle for Empire*, 1957, p. 499.
15. *The Delhi Sultanate*, 1960, p. 146-47 and 626.
16. Śuṅga period sculptures as described in the present book.
17. Smith, V.A., *Jain Stūpa* etc., 1901, p. 12, Pl. VI Lucknow Museum exhibit No. 20.
18. Agrawala, V.S., *Mathurā Museum Catalogue, J.U.P.H.S.*, 1951, p. 130-32, exhibit No. 21.
19. Sharma R.C., *Buddhist Art of Mathurā*, 1984, pp. 52-58.
20. *J.A.S.B.* Vol. *V*, 1836, p. 567.
21. Cunningham, A., *A.S.I:R.* Vol. II 1871, p. 21, Pl. 7 and *Anderson's Catalogue* p. 185.
22. Cunningham, A., *A.S.I.R.* Vol. 1871, p. 237, Mathurā Museum exhibit No. J. 40.
23. Fleet, J.H., *Gupta Inscriptions, Text and Translation*, Part, 1963, p. 26-27, No. 4, Mathurā Museum No. Q. 5.
24. *A.S.I.R.*, Vol. I, 1871 p. 237; Vol. III, 1873, p. 15, Pl. XV-4 and 12 a.
25. *Ibid.*, Mathurā Museum, No. M. 1.
26. Tavernier *Voyage*, Paris 1678 Vol. 2 p. 71; Bernier *Voyage*, Amsterdam 1699, Vol. 2, p. 76; Manucci, *Storia do Mogol* Vol. I, p. 298.
27. Vogel's *Mathurā Museum Catalogue* 1910, 0.10.
28. Reference No. 1, p. 3.
29. *A.S.I.R.*, Vol. III, 1873, p. 36 pl. 36 and *Corpus Inscriptionum Indicarum*, Vol. III, 1888, p. 262-63 No. 63, pl. 39 a.
30. *Corpus Inscriptionum Indicarum, Vol.* II Part I, 1929 p. 30-49.
31. *A.S.I.R.*, Vol. III, 1873, p. pl. 3.
32. Anderson, J., *Indian Museum Catalogue*, 1883, p. 169 footnote 2.
33. Vogel's *Mathurā Museum Catalogue*, p. 15.
34. Archaeological explorations made by Growse are detailed in chapter V of his book *Mathura Memoir.*
35. *Anderson's Catalogue*, Part I, p. 190 M. 17.
36. Vogel's *Mathurā Museum Catalogue*, p. 16. The other Mauryan Inscription is in Lucknow Museum, In *A.S.R.*, 1906-7, p. 139.
37. *J.A.S.B.* (*N.S.*), Vol V No. 7, 1909, p. 239 No. 3.
38. *Jain Stūpa*, etc., 1900 *A.S.I.R.* Vol. XX.
39. *Annual Progress Report of the Archaeological Survey*, June 30, 1906, p. 1-2.
40. For details see present author's paper in the *Bulletin of Museums and Archaeology in U.P.*, No. 11-12, June-Dec., 1973, p. 21-29.

41. *Indian Archaeology-A Review*, 1954-55, pp. 15-16.
42. Salient features of Sonkh excavations have been discussed in the following issues of the *Bulletin of Museums and Archaeology in U.P.*, No. 1 March 1968 p. 3-8; No. 2 Dec. 1968, p. 3-5; No. 3, June 1960, p. 1-5; No. 5-7, June-Dec. 1970, p. 1-4; and No. 11-12, June-Dec. 1973, p. 1-6.
43. Excavations at Sonkh, *German Scholars on India*, Vol. II, 1993.
44. *Excavations at Sonkh*, 1993.
45. Dr. A.K. Srivastava's report in the *Bulletin of Museums and Archaeology in U.P.*, No. 11-12, June - December 1973, p. 37-41.
46. *Indian Archaeology, 1975-76: A Review*, pp. 53-54.
47. Joshi, M.C. and Margabandhu, C.M., 'Some Terracottas from Excavations at Mathurā - A Study', *JISOA*, No. VIII, pp. 16-17.
48. Sharma, R.C., *Buddhist Art of Mathurā*, 1984, ch. 5.
49. Vogel's *Mathurā Museum Catalogue*, p. 29.
50. *Ibid.*, p. 28.
51. Tavernier, *Voyages*, *op. cit.*, p. 23.
52. Growse, F.S., *Mathurā Memoirs*, 2nd ed. p. 162.

2

The Museum at Mathurā

THE antiquarian remains continued to be exposed but none bothered to preserve them locally and their fate remained at the mercy of the excavator or an officer interested in them. Consequently, a large number of items were sent out. When Mr. F.S. Growse became Collector he gave a serious thought to check the out-flow of antiquities from the District. He himself was an archaeologist and a good writer. He explored some sites and contributed several papers on his finds in the contemporary leading research journals. He felt the necessity of housing the available objects at one place and for this purpose he favoured an unused guest house near the Collectorate building. This was the modest beginning of the Museum in 1874.

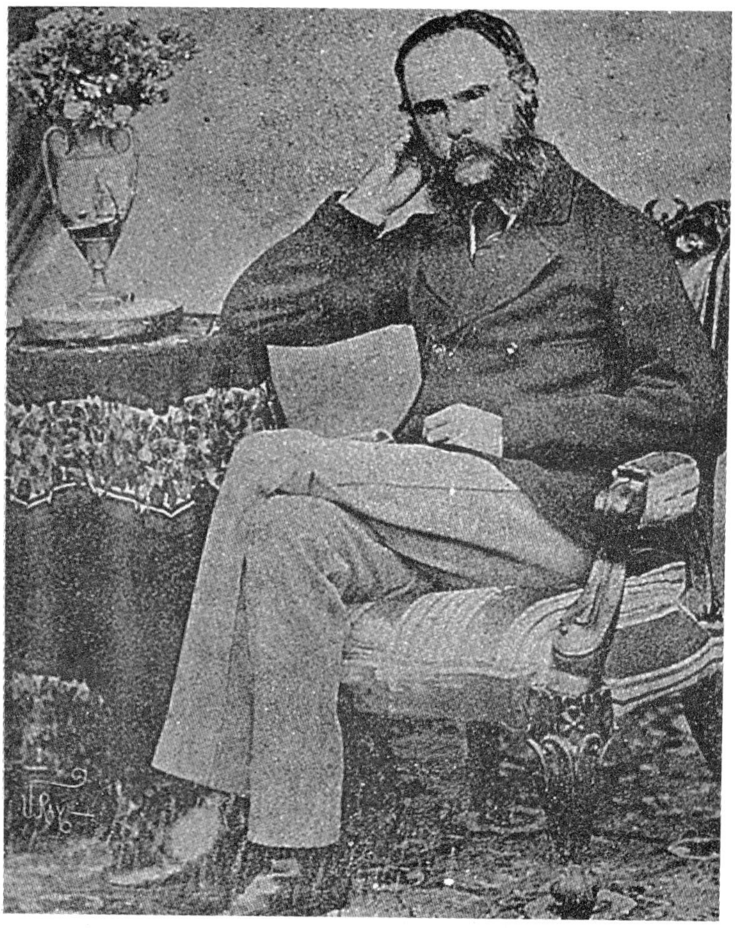

A. Mr. F.S. Growse, Founder of Museum

Old Building

The first building meant to house the Museum is a richly carved stone mansion and deserves a note of appreciation. Growse himself gives an interesting record in his '*Memoirs*'. "It was commenced by Mr. Thornhill, the Magistrate and Collector of the District, who raised the money for the purpose by public subscription, intending to make of it a rest-house for the reception of native gentlemen of rank, whenever they had occasion to visit the headquarters. Though close to the Courts, which would be a convenience, it is too far from the bazar to suit native tastes and even if it had been completed according to the original design, it is not probable that it would ever have been occupied."[1] The building originally cost Rs. 30,000 but when it was commissioned for Museum certain alterations and additions including the intricately carved front porch were introduced. It however, remained a beautiful specimen of contemporary stone carving and had less functional purposes. The observations of Growse are noteworthy in this context. "Though the cost of the building has been so very considerable, nearly Rs. 44,000, it is only a small dimension; but the whole wall surface in the central court is a mass of geometric and flowered decorations of the most artistic character. The bands of natural foliage, a feature introduced by Mr. Thornhill's own fancy, are very boldly cut and in themselves decidedly handsome but they are not altogether in accord with the conventional designs of native style by which they are surrounded."[2]

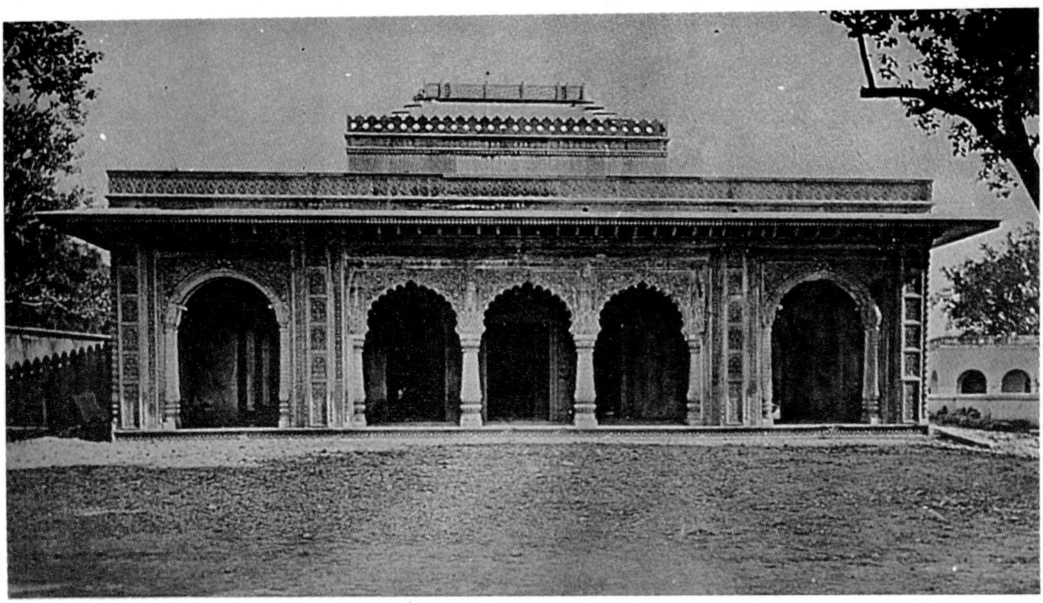

B. Old building

Early Days

Due to shortage of space the scope of the Museum was limited to the archaeological exhibits only. On transfer of Mr. Growse to Bulandshahr, Mr. Vigram, the Collector of the District, managed to collect a sum of about six thousand rupees for further completion of the building. The Museum, however, remained as a sculpture shed and till 1880 it was not open to public. Growse when visited Mathurā in that year expressed much anxiety on its future progress. He writes in his *'Memoirs'* dated June 29, 1880, "The Museum has again been taken in hand and in the course of year or so will, I trust be ready for use. Noticing in one of my recent visits to Mathurā that the collection of antiquities which I had left behind me was utterly uncared for, and that some of the valuable inscriptions had disappeared, though it is possible General Cunningham may have taken them."[3] When Cunningham paid his last visit to Mathurā in March 1882 the Museum was in function. It therefore, seems quite probable that the visitors were allowed in the Museum in 1881. The sculpture discovered by Cunningham during his visit was, however, presented to the Calcutta Museum as the local museum was ignored. The antiquity represented Herakles strangling the Nemean lion.

The Institution, however, remained mere a store house for want of staff. The Collectorate's old records reveal that the Municipal Board, Mathurā started taking some interest from 1889 and a *Farrash* was appointed for Rs. 3 per month for cleaning the rooms and dusting the objects. The formal control and responsibility for its management was taken up by the Board in 1900 but only a few persons realised the value of the objects. An interesting note was observed by Dr. Vogel in an official letter which indicates an indifferent view even at the Collectorate level. To a query regarding the ownership of the remains the reply is, "the relics were collected by Mr. Growse and Dr. Fuhrer by digging a *ṭīlā* in the city. They belong to Government, I think, and no one would buy them as they are mostly broken."[4]

Development

Even after the establishment of the Museum the new finds continued to be sent out to different places and museums. The bulk of objects excavated by Dr. Fuhrer from the site of the famous Kaṅkālī mound in the years 1888-91 was shifted *en bloc* to the Lucknow Museum which has since become another centre for the study of Mathurā art and particularly of the Kuṣāṇa period. The Mathurā Museum had its good fortune when Dr. J.Ph. Vogel, the then Superintendent of Northern Circle of the Archaeological Survey of India and a great champion of Mathurā School of Art,[5] started taking interest in its affairs from 1905. It owes to his good offices that several outstanding pieces were brought back to Mathurā. In order to apprise the scholarly world and the visitors in general with the significance of Museum collection, Dr. Vogel undertook the great task of preparing a comprehensive catalogue which came out in 1910.

Association of late Rāi Bahādur Pt. Radha Krishna with the Museum proved to be very auspicious. He first took over as Honorary Assistant Curator in 1903 and subsequently was appointed in the capacity of Honorary Curator in 1912. In 1928 his meritorious services elevated him to the position of Life Member and Vice-Chairman of the Museum Management Committee. He explored several sites in the District and acquired numerous sculptures. In 1912 he exposed the Ṭokrī or Iṭokrī mound near the village of Māṭ, 16 km. north of Mathurā, as the crow flies, and enriched the Museum with the finds of inscribed royal statues of the Kuṣāṇa rulers Vema Kadphises, Kaniṣka and Caṣṭana, the Śaka chief. This discovery was of utmost importance in the history of Museum's acquisition.[6] His next task was to clear up the wells at Mathurā and some distant places. The expedition resulted in obtaining about 600 pieces. In 1912 the administrative control of the Museum was transferred to the Provincial Government.

Present Building

With rapid growth of collection, building became inadequate and no room was left to receive and display the fresh arrivals. The progress of the Museum came to standstill and Government were moved for a new building. The proposal was generously accepted and the construction started in the Dampier Park now known as Bhagat Singh

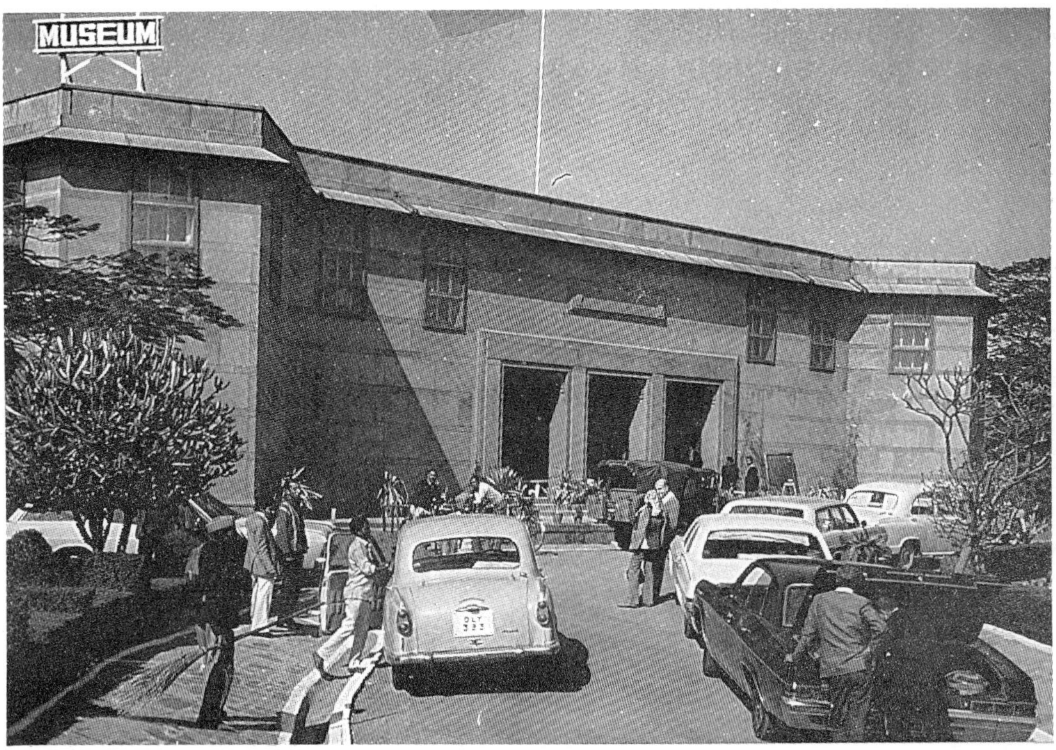

C. Present building

Park in 1926 in accordance with the design and plans prepared by Mr. A.L. Mortimer, the then Consulting Architect to U.P. Government.[7] It took about two and a half years to complete about five-eighths of present building at a cost of Rs. 1,23,000. The Government granted an additional sum of Rs. 10,000 to meet the expenses of shifting of objects from the old building and their proper arrangement in the new galleries. Rāi Bahādur Ram Prasad Chanda, late Superintendent, Archaeological Section, Indian Museum, Calcutta offered his valuable services for this purpose. The opening ceremony of the new building was performed by Sir William Malcolm Hailey, Governor of U.P. on January 25, 1933.[8] Rāi Bahādur Pt. Radha Krishna had since expired and the Government paying rich tributes for his outstanding services unveiled his portrait.

Further increase in collection and activities caused paucity of space and under the Second Five Year Plan the Government sanctioned a special sum of Rs. 2,70,000. Out of this Rs. 1,09,000 were spent on urgent repairs and relaying of roofs which had developed serious cracks and were endangering the valuable exhibits and also the visitors. The remaining part of grant was utilised to complete the three-eighth part to make it a complete octagonal rotunda according to the original plan. The work was finished by the end of 1962. The complete building of red sand stone imparts a majestic look and the beautifully laid out gardens both in and outside have further enhanced its grandeur. Although the scarcity of water makes it difficult to maintain. When the Museum was shifted from the Collectorate compound to the Dampier Park the old building was taken over by the Revenue Department. But the proper arrangement and scientific presentation of exhibits required more space and no room was left for housing the undisplayed objects. Efforts were therefore, made to acquire the old building and it again came under the charge of the Museum in 1960. Since then it serves the reserve collection.

Mathurā and its neighbourhood is a rich mine of early art objects. Almost every year a good number of sculptures, terracottas and other specimens see their way to Museum. Besides, a museum of good standing needs space for the allied sections including different labs and workshops. Some new galleries are also to come up. The Institution is again facing the problem of space, and it is hoped that the solution will be sought in the near future when the new building is put up on the adjacent ground. The Government of U.P. vide notification no. 5483/IV-9(10)-73, dated November 24, 1973 changed its nomenclature as Government Museum, Mathura in order to widen the scope and enhance its status. The posts of Curator and Assistant Curator were also redesignated as Director and Assistant Director, vide U.P. Government notification no. 6998/IV-9(10)-73, dated May 17/23, 1974.

The Museum also has a large number of objects in the reserve collection which can be seen by the research scholars on prior intimation. Proper arrangement and classification of these items has not yet been completed mainly due to shortage of space. Beside the stone sculputres and terracottas, the reserve collection includes some gold, silver and copper coins, clay seals, bricks, pottery pieces, paintings and bronzes.

Administration

The early days of this Institution have been very hard. It is surprising to note that nobody was deputed to look after it for a long period and the collection remained uncared for. After a lapse of fifteen years it could get the services of a *Farrash* for Rupees 3 per month just for dusting and sweeping. For another twenty years no officer was appointed and it was just before the visit of the Liutenant Governor in 1908 that Lt. Col. W. Vost., I.M.S., and Pandit Radha Krishna agreed to act as Curator and Assistant Curator respectively in the honorary capacity. While the old records are wanting, it appears that the Provincial Government constituted a Management Committee in 1922 with the District Collector as ex-officio Chairman. It was represented by the gentlemen of good standing, professors and officers interested in Indian art and archaeology. The Curator was made ex-officio Secretary of the Committee. From 1950 the District Collector was replaced by the non-official Chairman. In 1957 the Government of U.P. set up an independent Directorate of Cultural Affairs and Scientific Research (previously known as Directorate of Indology). Since then the Museum is controlled by the Director, Department of C.A. and S.R. (now only Cultural Affairs), U.P., Lucknow at Government level. The institutional head has been the Curator (now Director). The following chart records the names of the Curators/Officers Incharge and the tenure of their services:

Name	Period		Remarks
Lt. Col. W. Vost	1908 - 1912		Honarary
Pt. Radha Krishna	1912 - 1928		Honarary
D.B. Diskalkar	Feb. 1, 1929	- March 17, 1930	
V.S. Agrawala	June 22, 1931	- Feb. 20, 1934	
J.P. Chaturvedi	Feb. 21, 1934	- May 21, 1935	Officiating
V.S. Agrawala	May 22, 1935	- April 15, 1939	
M.M. Nagar	April 5, 1939	- April 4, 1946	
K.D. Bajpai	April 16, 1946	- May 7, 1951	
J.P. Chaturvedi	May 8, 1951	- June 30, 1953	Officiating
K.D. Bajpai	July 1, 1953	- Sept. 16, 1958	
V.N. Srivastava	Sept. 17, 1958	- June 2, 1959	Officiating
V.P. Mathur	June 3, 1959	- April 2, 1963	O.S.D./A.O.
N.P. Joshi	April 3, 1963	- Sept. 15, 1967	
V.N. Srivastava	Sept. 16, 1967	- Jan. 23, 1969	Officiating
R.C. Sharma	Jan. 24, 1969	- April 30, 1980	
A.K. Srivastava	May 1, 1980	- April 30, 1986	
Jitendra Kumar	June 1, 1986	- April 23, 1990	
Smt. Pushpa Thakural	April 24, 1990 -		

Reorganisation

During the Second, Third and Fourth Five-Year Plans the Museum received special grants for reorganising the galleries and setting up and development of different allied sections. Several posts were also created to implement the plan schemes effectively. The reorganisation scheme resulted not only in the growth of the Institution but also provided additional facilities to the visitors and the research scholars. At present the Museum, besides the galleries consists of a good reference library, photographic and chemical laboratories, modelling and carpenter's workshops, general office and a sale counter. The technical staff includes Assistant Director, Guide Lecturer, Librarian, Modeller-Cum-Artist, Chemist, Photographer and Gallery Assistant. The administrative work is run with the help of Head clerk, Stenographer and Office Assistants who look after different type of works. The post of Administrative Officer also exists to assist the Director in general administration and handling of budget. The other employees are Cabinet-cum-Pedestal Maker, Workshop-cum-Laboratory Assistant, Marksman, Gallery Attendants, Guards, Gardners and cleaning staff.

Centenary Celebration

The Museum completed hundred years of its glorious existence in 1974. The Government of Uttar Pradesh planned a grand celebration to mark this great event.[9] The late Prime Minister of India, Smt. Indira Gandhi, inaugurating the centenary programmes on January 10, 1974 paid rich tributes to the Institution for playing an important role in the service of the community. The occasion was also graced by the presence of the Governor of U.P. and several Union and State Ministers. The other important feature was a four-day seminar on the 'Kuṣāṇa Art of Mathurā' which was attended by several distinguished scholars from India and abroad. A temporary exhibition specially set up to synchronise the centenary celebration displayed several photographs exposing the development of the Museum in the last century including important landmarks and notable acquisitions. The other section presented significant sculptures of the Kuṣāṇa period from the reserve collection. The visitors then viewed the compartments of folk and decorative arts of the Braj region.

Several publications including souvenirs, brochures, posters, handbills and leaflets were brought out to honour the Institution. There were the Radio broadcasts, special talks, features, news items, *Samācāra Darśana* and commentaries. Some programmes were telecast by Dūra Darśana (T.V.).

Another grand function was held on October 9, 1974 when Sri K. Brahmananda Reddy, the then Union Minister for Communications released two special postage stamps on the Museum exhibits to commemorate the Mathurā-Museum Centenary. The then Chief Minister of Uttar Pradesh, Sri H.N. Bahuguna, who presided over the function, inaugurated the All India Museums Conference which discussed the problems of site and small museums.

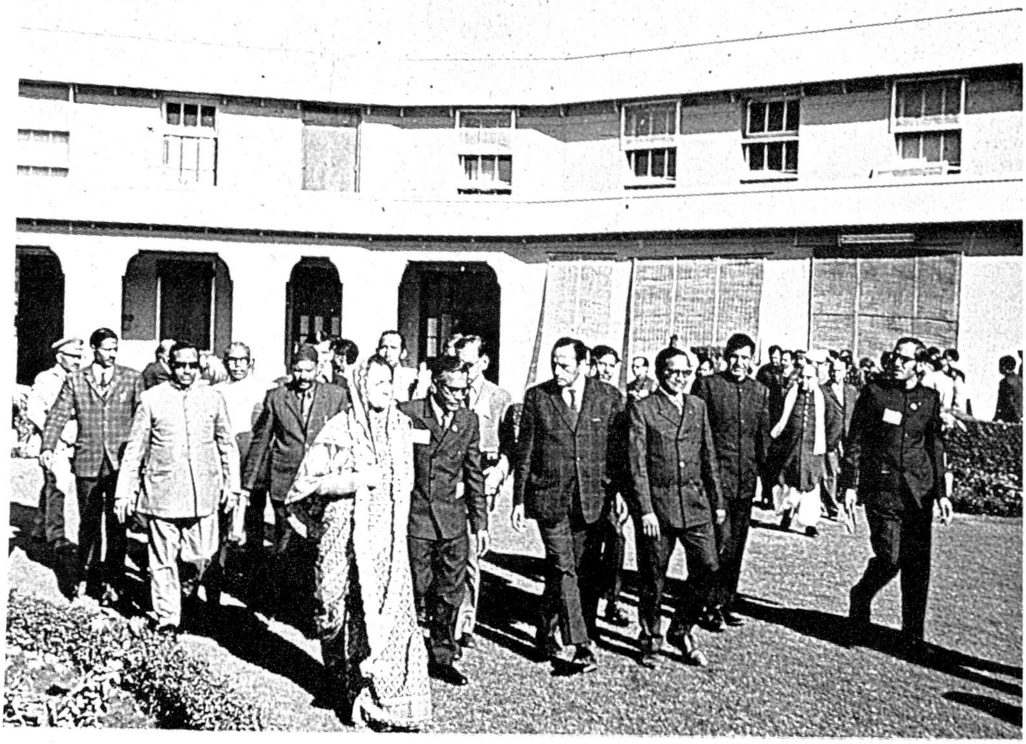

D. Smt. Indira Gandhi, the Prime Minister of India, Inaugurated the Centenary Celebration

The other salient features of the Museum Centenary were acquisition of Sonkh antiquities from the German Archaeological Mission, nomenclature of the road around the Bhagat Singh Park as 'Museum Road' by the Municipal Board, Mathurā, closer contacts with tourists, clubs, general public, educational institutions and scholars, appointment of the Museum Director as Research Examiner by universities etc.

Activities

The Museum has been constantly flourishing as an important centre for the study of early Indian art, and specialises in the pursuit of research on different aspects of the Mathurā School of Art. Its rich collection attracts art historians from distant quarters. To make their visit more useful a good reference library and a photographic laboratory are also available. The Museum, however, serves not only the scholars, it equally welcomes the general public and efforts are made to make them art conscious. Services of Guide Lecturer and Gallery Assistant are available to explain the exhibits while parties and groups of students are specially conducted. Besides its normal functions of acquisition, preservation, display and interpretation of the exhibits, the Museum has also been playing its humble role in educational and cultural awakening of this region through organising different programmes, film shows on art and archaeology, temporary exhibitions and talks of eminent scholars. Director, technical members of the staff and other scholars associated with this grand repository of art treasures have brought out several books, published research papers, popular articles and broadcast radio talks etc., interpreting the products of Mathurā art. To popularise the Museum and to develop a feeling of appreciation for our rich art traditions, plastercasts of handy and important exhibits are prepared. Besides photographs, a series of photo folders with tidy description and useful literature on art, archaeology and the museums are also available on the sale counter. A chemical laboratory and general workshop form an important part for cleaning, preservation and display of the antiquities.

Timings :

1st July to 15th April	10.30 a.m. to 4.30 p.m.
16th April to 30th June	7.30 a.m. to 12.30 p.m.

Holidays :
Mondays, Sundays following second Saturdays and every gazetted holiday.

Arrangement of Objects

The arrangement follows a chronological sequence. Display has been made as educative as possible through gallery charts and object labels. The visitor after entering the gallery is requested to turn right and walk a few steps till he sees an elaborately ornamented terracotta figure of a lady of the Śuṅga period (66.2; *fig. 6*) greeting him at the entrance of a small gallery, presenting the earliest remains of human civilization in this region followed by the finds from Sonkh and terracottas from different sites. Here he should turn to his left to commence the visit.

Museum Holdings on 1-4-93

Sculptures	4925
Terracottas	2767
Bronzes	338
Pottery-bricks	260
Paintings	379
Ornaments	32
Sonkh objects	above 12000
Others	1215

Coins	
Gold	179
Silver	4143
Copper etc.	12147

References

1. Growse, F.S., *Mathurā Memoir,* 2nd Ed., p. 153.
2. Sharma, R.C., 'Hundred years of Mathurā Museum', In *JIM,* 1973, p. 2.
3. Growse, *op. cit.,* p. III.
4. Vogel, J. Ph., *Catalogue of Archaeological Museum at Mathurā,* 1910, p. 4.
5. Beside above catalogue his other important writings on Mathurā are : 'The Mathurā School of Sculpture', In *ASR,* 1906-7; 'Explorations at Mathurā', In *ASR,* 1911-12; 'La Sculpture de Mathurā' *Ars Asiatic,* Tome 2, 1930.
6. Agrawala, V.S., Mathurā Museum Catalogue, In *JUPSH,* 1950, p. 72-79.
7. Sharma, *op. cit.,* 4.
8. *Ibid.*
9. Sharma, R.C., 'Mathurā Museum in Community Service, Museums and Museology', In *New Horizons,* 1980, pp. 164-66.

3

Prehistoric and Terracotta Finds

UNTIL about a quarter century back, the region of Mathurā was known as great religious and cultural seat beside being a centre of magnificent sculptural products upto the late Gupta period. New discoveries and explorations have, however, placed it on the pre-historic map of India as well. The notable finds are palaeoliths, copper age implements and early ceramics. Archaic terracottas representing the mother goddesses also fall in this category.

Palaeoliths

The discovery of the palaeoliths or the old stone age tools (hand axes 75.37 and 75.38) collected by the author and R.B. Joshi of Pune from the Govardhan ridge in January 1975 was a significant event as it proved that the pre-historic (palaeolithic) man had settled for some time earlier than 50000 B.C. The first small showcase presents two earliest reminiscences of human settlement in this region (75.36 and 75.37). To safeguard himself from wild animals and also for hunting, the prehistoric man gave various forms to the undressed rough stones after chipping. These were fitted with wooden or bone handles and served as weapons and also as implements for cutting and boring. Such chipped stone tools were generally made of hard rock-'quartzite', hence another nomenclature of 'Palaeolithic man' is 'Quartzite man'.

But for these tools no other remains of this age have been traced and it is not possible to give a true assessment of the life of the users. A critical analysis of these implements, however, helps us to conclude that metal was not in vogue and the people were totally ignorant of agriculture. They depended on forest vegetables and fruits besides the flesh of animals. They lived the life of nomads and did not have fixed homes except a few temporary huts made of trees and leaves. They were constantly afraid of wild animals like tigers, lions, elephants and the rhinoceros. It has been conjectured that the Palaeolithic man was distinguished by his short stature, dark skin, wooly hair and flat nose. Resembling the inhabitants of the Andaman Islands, he probably belonged to the Negrito race.

While the Palaeolithic age appears to have been succeeded by the Neolithic (new stone) age it is not possible to establish a direct relationship between these two groups.[1]

Cultivation, domestication of animals, use of fire, making of pottery first by hand and subsequently by wheel, use of cotton and woollen cloth, boating etc. were known to the Neolithic people. To some extent they had developed an aesthetic sense as indicated by some paintings in the caves mainly representing hunting and dancing scenes. The pottery was also sometimes decorated with designs. No neolithic specimen has, however, been traced in Mathurā region till now.

Copper Celts

With the discovery of metal man stepped up from stone age to Chalcolithic era. Copper preceded the other metals in Northern India. Although similar implements were in use of Indus Valley people (*c.* 2500 B.C. to 1500 B.C.) the earliest specimens from other parts of the Indian sub-continent have roughly been assigned to the middle of the 2nd millenium B.C. The exhibits on show are flat celts (75.33 and 75.34) discovered from Sādābād in Mathurā District. These form part of the 16 pieces received by the State Museum, Lucknow in 1970.[2] Scholars have advanced divergent views with regard to the people who used such copper implements.[3]

Sonkh Remains

As already discussed in the 1st chapter the site of Sonkh was excavated in eight seasons from 1966 to 1974 by the German Archaeological Mission under the direction of Prof. H. Härtel.[4] The small objects have been arranged in the first three showcases (*fig. 1*) while some rare sculptures can be seen in gallery no. 8.

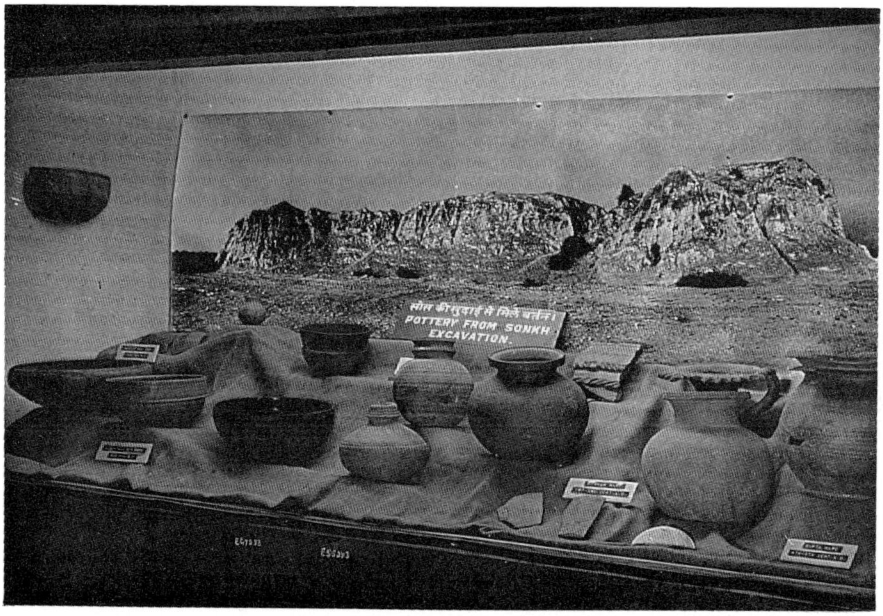

fig. 1. Sonkh ceramics showcase

Early Ceramics

Pottery plays an important role in the present day archaeology as it sufficiently helps in assigning the periods. The showcase to left represents some important types of ceramics which were used by the inhabitants of Braj region in early times. The main varieties on the show may briefly be mentioned as follows:

Painted Grey Ware

This pottery[5] which is tentatively to be dated from *c.* 800 B.C. represents the earliest ceramics of Mathurā. It is usually grey in colour with black pigments. It is also found in dull red colour with dark designs. The complete bowl is a remarkable specimen.

The Sonkh excavation has revealed a unique variety of lustrous polished pottery with lithic look, like brownish marble. The small vase also belongs to the Painted Grey Ware level.

Black and Red Ware

It is another variety which is found along with the Painted Grey Ware at Sonkh. The inner side is totally black while the exterior represents black in the upper and red in lower part[6] as a result of the firing process.

Northern Black Polished Ware

The third main variety is the Northern Black Polished group which belongs from *c.* 4th century B.C. to 2nd century B.C.[7] The steel blue or golden lustre is the main characteristic of pottery of this period. Beside the small fragments of this type, the associate ware is represented by two small jars.

Kuṣāṇa Ware

The pottery of the Kuṣāṇa period (*c.* 1st to 3rd century A.D.) excavated from Sonkh represents numerous good varieties.[8] It is usually red in colour and devoid of polish. Several decorative and auspicious motifs are stamped; sherd with creeper design is remarkable (SO I-42). Beside the fragmentary pieces, two are complete pots including one with spout.

Gupta Period

Very scanty material of this period (4th to 6th century A.D.) has been unearthed so far hence no clear picture of the Gupta period pottery has yet emerged. The next small showcase consists of two specimens viz. a double rimmed jar (SO II-839) with red slip and black pigments and an incense burner[9] with handle (SO II-1101).

The second showcase on the other side displays twenty terracottas from Sonkh[10] ranging in dates from late Mauryan to early Gupta periods (*c.* 200 B.C. to the 4th century A.D.) The remarkable pieces are: a model of a house, a jester, a *mithuna* plaque in which

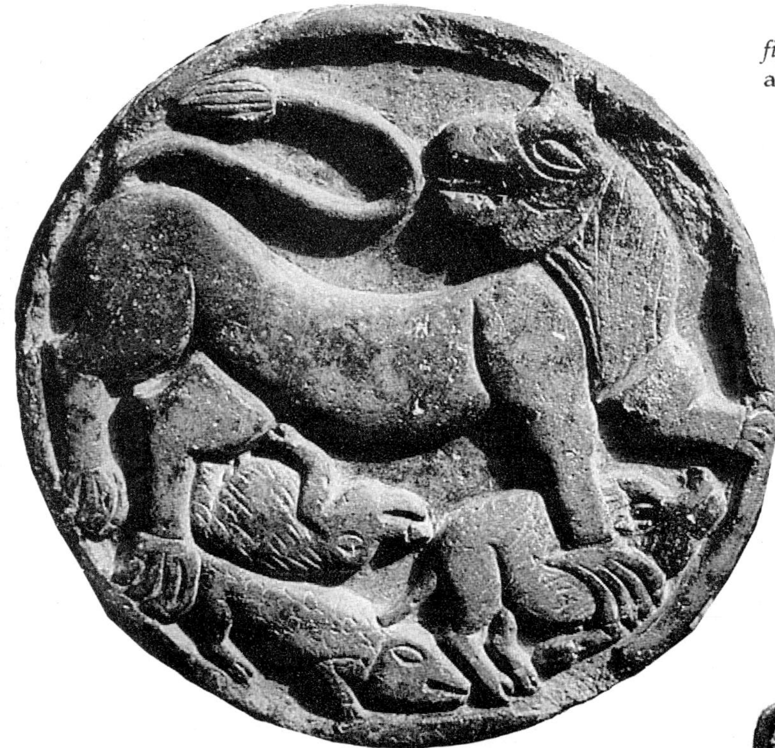

fig. 2. Lion trouncing animals, Kuṣāṇa

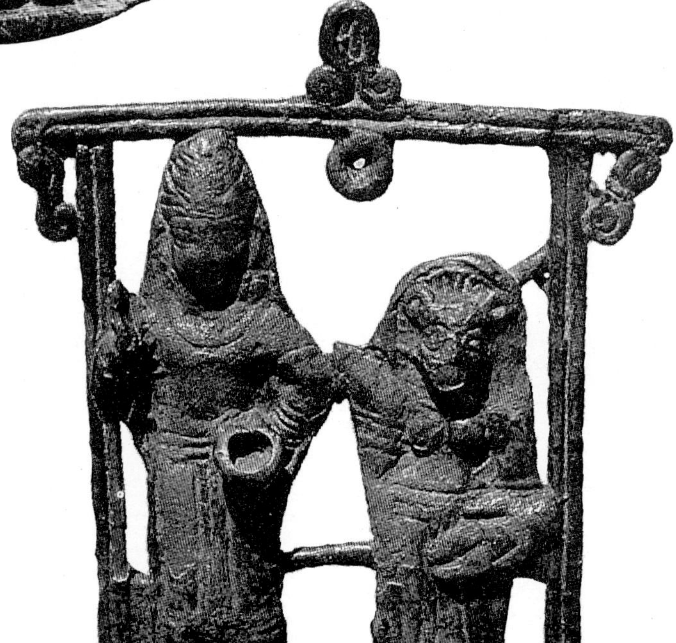

fig. 3. Kubera - Hārītī (bronze), Kuṣāṇa

the lady has been shown with a beard, mother and a child, a round hollowed object with an acrobatic scene, goddess Mahiṣāsur-mardinī, and a circular solid object representing a lion vigorously trouncing the other animals (SO I-301; *fig.* 2).

The third little corner showcase (No. 15b) consists of nine small objects but of great significance. Discovery of some bronze figures from the Kuṣāṇa layers was of high magnitude. One is almost a square plaque[11] depicting a divine couple, the male holds a bowl while his lion or cat faced spouse (*Śaṣṭhī/Carcikā/Devasenā*) carries a child to her left side (SO I-173; *fig.* 3).

The other vertical plaque represents young Kārttikeya (god of war) with a long spear (SO I-178; *fig.* 4). The third object is a trident of pre-Kuṣāṇa age. These are the earliest bronze figures of this region. The other exhibits are two bone hair pins (SO I-279 and 174) a casket and a round terracotta seal (SO I-97) reading "*Nandikarasa*" in the Śuṅga *Brāhmī* characters, a silver punch marked coin (SO I-100), small soap stone casket (SO I-252), terracotta stamp with swan (SO II-290), earliest Mahiṣāsuramardinī (SO I-245) belonging to 1st century B.C.

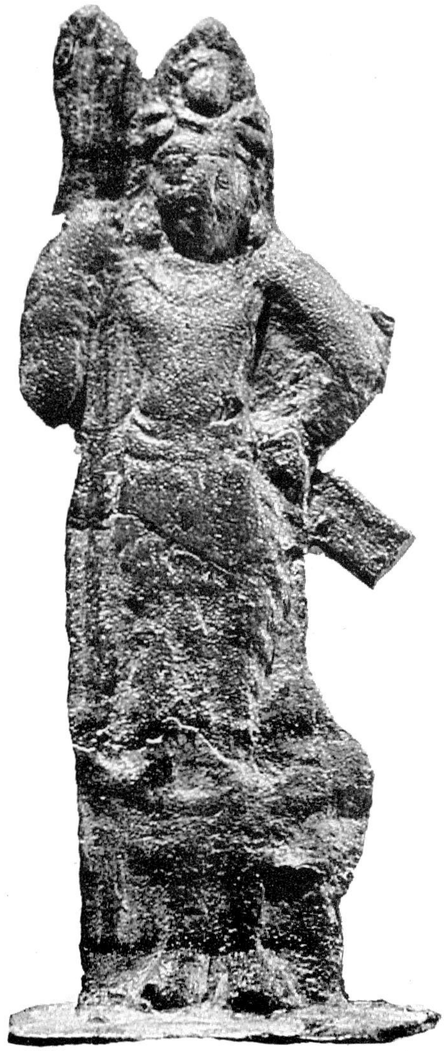

fig. 4. Kārttikeya (bronze), Kuṣāṇa

Terracotta Art

Terracotta (baked clay figure) was a medium of art expression by and for the humbler class of people to whom costly material such as stone and metal was not easily available.[12] As evidenced from the Indus Valley remains this art was practised in India from a very early period. It served both religious and secular purposes.

Archaic

The earliest figures found at Mathurā can be dated back to the pre-Mauryan period (pre 4th century B.C.). The common features of these early figures are as follows.[13]

These are completely hand modelled, the face has bird or animal characteristics, the eyes are incised and the nose has been shaped by pinching. Ornaments and some limbs are separately fixed, the body bears circular punch marks, and except where covered by ornaments the body is nude. The figures are invariably female and possibly represent the cult of mother goddess which was prevalent in different countries under different names. The early figures from Mathurā are grey in colour with black slip.[14] Showcases 1 and 2 present some of them (S. No. 3; *col. ill. I*).

Mauryan

The next two showcases (3 and 4) show the terracotta art of the Mauryan period (*c.* 4th and 3rd century B.C.). While many early features continued, some changes are noteworthy. The face is now pressed out of a mould and is no longer shown like a bird or animal. It is oval in shape with large eyes. Emphasis is laid on heavy ornaments which are still separately attached to the body. The breasts and navel are more prominent. The hair arrangement is elaborate, showing several floral motifs. Animal figures, like those of human beings, are grey with black slip, bear circular punch marks and applique decoration.[15] Twenty seven representative pieces of Mauryan terracotta art are on view in show cases 3 and 4 (42.2923; *col. ill. II*).

Śuṅga

The terracotta figurines of the Śuṅga period (2nd and 1st century B.C.) represent the revolution in this art when it shifted from hand modelling to complete moulds. The new device was responsible for the wide popularity of clay toys produced in large number.There are sixty five representative specimens of this period from different sites in six showcases (No. 5 to 10) beside a few pieces from Sonkh. The early monotonous tradition of mother goddesses was broken by a variety of subjects. The introduction of amorous couples (*mithunas*) was a landmark in art. Male figures wear double knotted or one sided turbans. Ladies have been shown in different actions; busy in toilet or arranging the coiffure, holding a fan, playing with parrots, dancing or performing music, holding a child and so on.[16] Technically, the terracotta art of this period has the following peculiarities :

Hand modelling has been replaced by moulds, no limb or ornament is made separately, the representation of nude goddesses is discontinued but the sex details have been shown despite clothing. The turban or headdress is made larger, preference is given to red colour, and a general improvement is conveyed through grace and movement.[17] The Sonkh showcase presents an interesting plaque with a couple of whom the female also has a beard (SO I-297; *col. ill. III*).

Showcase No. 5: Different styles of female coiffure are shown and some of them bear auspicious marks. Since India had already developed contacts with other countries, foreign ethnic features also appear. The figure of a Persian youth (35.2556) wearing coat, scarf, trousers and turban is a rare item. Another unique specimen is a bearded old man (foreigner) at meals sitting on a stool and holding a dish with his left hand (71.12; *fig. 5*).

Showcase No. 6: The introduction of complete mould was the most significant characteristic of the Śuṅga period and it is represented by exhibiting various original moulds. A replica of each mould has been added to give an accurate idea of the figure the mould was intended to produce. Beside the male and female figures, a monkey, a peacock and a parrot are also shown.

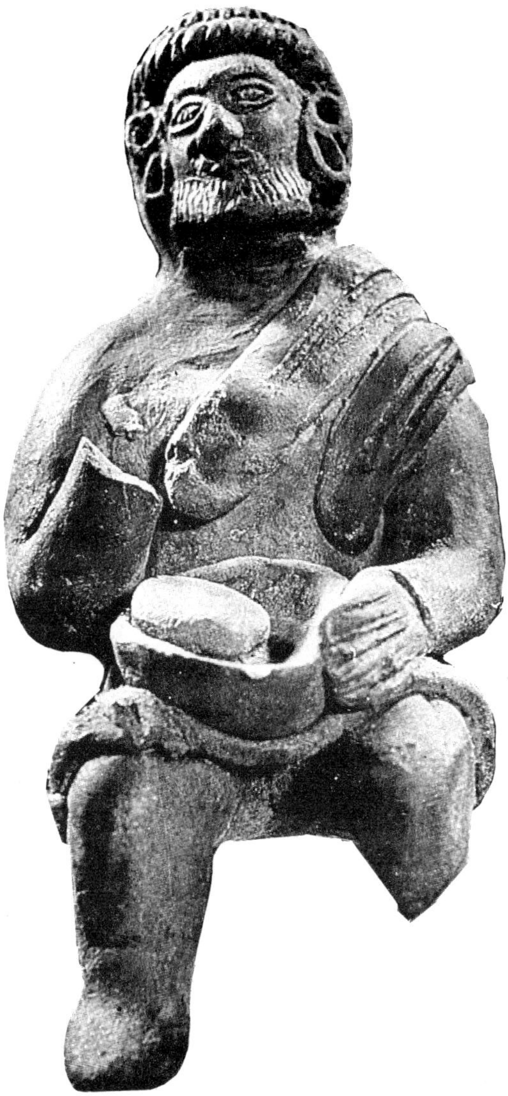

fig. 5. Foreigner at meals (T.C.), Maurya

Showcase No. 7: This case is noteworthy for some early representation of divinities. The central plaque (43.3041) is one of the earliest depictions of the goddess Gaja Lakṣmī (Lakṣmī being bathed by two elephants). It was a favourite theme of the Śuṅga period. The uppermost piece on the central shelf (39.2849) shows the winged bust of Kāmadeva (cupid) holding a bow. The spring season in which he usually attacks is probably suggested by different flowers in the background. Another headless figure (34.2552) of this deity is seen on the left shelf. He stands with a cluster of arrows, crouching a male figure under his feet and holding in left hand a wreathed bow illustrating his epithet *Puṣpadhanvā* or *Kusumāyudha* (one who holds a bow of flowers). It is late Śuṅga or early Kuṣāṇa in features. Below is seen Śrīdevī (No. 58.4696, goddess of prosperity) pressing her breast with left hand. The exhibit to our right (32.2243) is goddess Vasudhārā (associated with fertility and abundance). As her important characteristic she holds a pair of fish in her right hand. The upper object on the right plank is an interesting representation of a pot-bellied *yakṣa* supporting another figure on his shoulder (55.3880).

How the Śuṅga artist saw female beauty is explained in the next two showcases.

Showcase No. 8: This showcase presents a glimpse of taste and fashion prevalent among the women of the Śuṅga period.

The central piece (59.4748) is an embodiment of beauty. The slim and delicate treatment of body, sharp features, fine coiffure and ornaments are remarkable. Above is displayed a lady in toilet (48.3410) looking into a mirror held in her right hand while with the left she arranges her hairdo. A large cushioned seat points to the use of sophisticated furniture at this early stage. Similarly, the black figure of a lady (44.3115) playing with a bird and another (49.3498) on the right panel imparting finishing touch to her hair (*jūḍā*) is a rare piece too. Below, a parrot is seen on the waist of a lady.

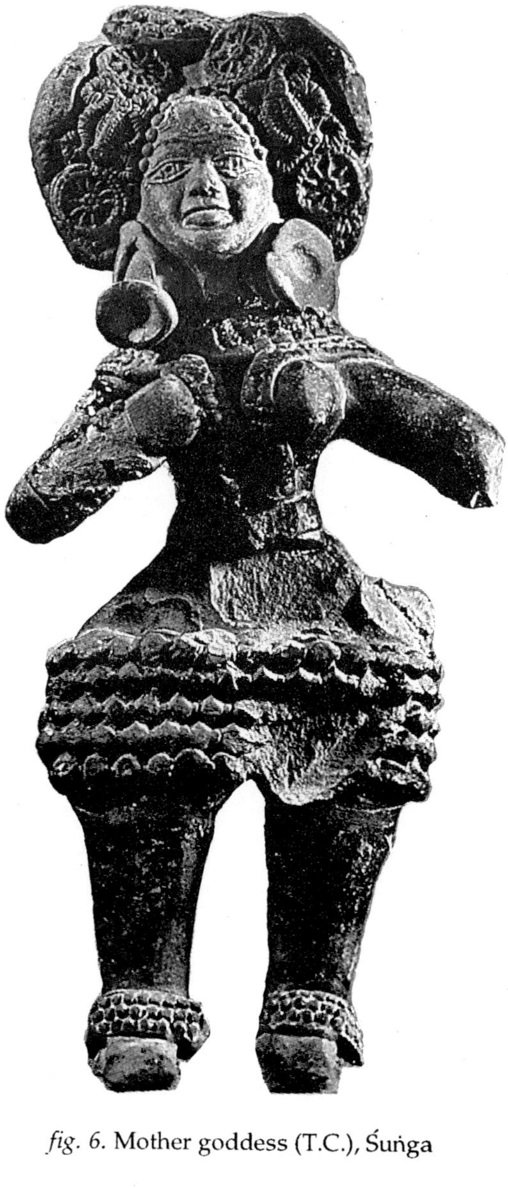

fig. 6. Mother goddess (T.C.), Śuṅga

Showcase No. 9: It consists of some finely executed plaques of amorous couples. These may probably suggest the inception of eroticism in Indian art. To the left (61.5227) the lover is seen offering wine to his beloved, while the piece on the right panel (34.2474) depicts a man putting his arm each round the necks of two ladies. The position of their heels indicates that they are in dancing attitude.

Showcase No. 10: The foreground has specimens of toy carts which was a favourite theme of the Śuṅga period. Its popularity is also known from the fact that Śūdraka in the 1st century B.C. captioned his drama as *Mṛchakaṭikam,* meaning 'Clay Cart.' The central round plaque (34.2411) bears a hunting scene with a horse rider chasing a boar. The *yakṣa* playing on a drum (32.2215) and a man with a harp (32.2258), hint at the use of musical instruments in that period.

A rare specimen of the Śuṅga period is a standing lady (66.2; *fig. 6*) already described at the entrance of the gallery.

Kuṣāṇa

In the Kuṣāṇa period (1st to 3rd century A.D.) the attention of the kings and the artists was focussed on stone carving and consequently the terracotta art suffered. While moulds continued, hand modelling revived. The body was sometimes made hollow with a double mould process.[18] The figures are crude, disproportionate and rough, yet the expression in certain cases is bold. The pantheon increased as a result of assimilation of some alien deities.[19]

Showcase No. 11: The new divinities shown are: bust of Balarāma (52.3636) with his right hand raised in protection and head surmounted by the snake hoods (as he is an incarnation of the cosmic serpent Śeṣa): a figure of a Bodhisattva (61.5258) seated cross-legged in *abhaya* (protection) pose; Durgā (36.2715) killing the buffalo demon Mahiṣa and a Nāgi (34.2434) with a stalked lotus and serpent hoods. Plaque showing Kubera and Hārītī seated in European fashion (19.1585) hints to the assimilation of foreign elements.

A peculiar head (48.3417 from Mallapurā; *col. ill. IV*) on the left half side panel wearing a large turban and heavy ear-rings looks a female but traces of moustache make it quite humorous. Kubera (31.2095) with high turban and large belly is an example of the double mould process. On the right, a lady (15.506) carrying a flywhisk resembles the contemporary figures on railing pillars. The mysterious smile on the Scythian's face (47.3361) has been beautifully expressed. Depiction of twisted moustaches, the beard and other foreign ethnic features have been successfully illustrated in this piece. As can be understood from a fragmentary piece (18.1481), use of tiles had also commenced in this period. These bear traces of glazed coating and depict different motifs. The dwarf is a rare example of glazed figurines of Kuṣāṇa period. The showcase also contains two inscribed objects, one is the potter's dabber with *Brāhmī* legend 'Kachipasa' (of Kachipa) (28.1725). The other piece is a small humped bull bearing letters '*Śivasa*' (of Śiva) on one side and a trident on the other.

Gupta

This art was revived with great zeal and enthusiasm in the Gupta period. The prosperous society of the age fell in love with decorative arts and clay figures played an important role. These were in great demand for the exterior walls of temples, and for drawing-rooms in houses. Plaques of sporting male and female figures provided a suitable and pleasing background in homes and specially in bed-rooms. Thus beside religious figures, secular and domestic scenes were also abundantly portrayed.

The terracottas of this period are of fine workmanship. The body is slim with lovely curves and contours. The youthful look is suggestive of movement, grace and elegance. The hair is arranged in various fashions. Almost all the essential characteristics of stone sculptures are infused in clay.[20] The wall panel displays some beautiful specimens. Their local provenance hints that a brick temple was built at Mathurā in the Gupta

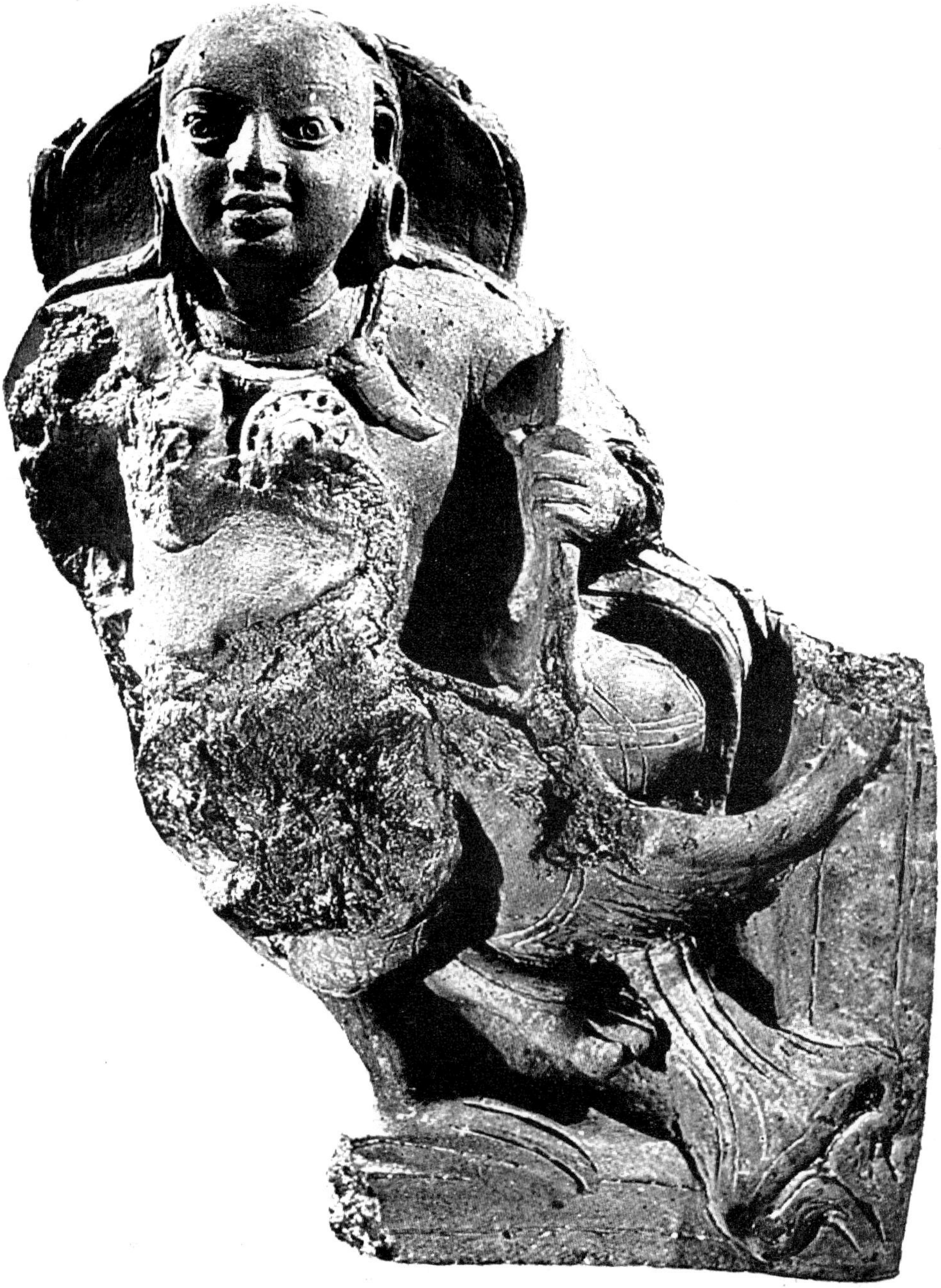

fig. 7. Kārttikeya on peacock (T.C.), Gupta

period. Kārttikeya majestically seated (38.2794; *fig. 7*) on his vehicle peacock (now mutilated) with smiling face is undoubtedly one of the masterpieces. The central exhibit (Ṭ. 6) is probably a river holding a full vase on her left hand. Unfortunately, owing to the absence of her vehicle she cannot be exactly identified. Another panel (61.5217) represents some interesting domestic quarrel in which a woman is kneeling in grief while another lady is in a furious and commanding attitude. The figure peeping through a window (65.13) was a favourite theme of the Gupta artist. This has been repeatedly shown in Bhītargāon temple (Kānpur District). An independently displayed figure is a corpulent male probably Kubera (T. I).

Showcase No. 12: Here are some other good specimens. The panel in centre (No. 38.2795 from Mallapurā; *col. ill. V*) shows a lady pulling the scarf of a man who seems busy in a ritual performance (*prāṇāyāma*). Probably he is a *vidūṣaka* (jester) whose duty was to amuse the royal family by his funny speech, overeating and other humorous actions as frequently seen in Sanskrit plays. On the left side a bearded man, probably an ascetic, (38-39.2792) is detaching his head with a dagger. Whether it is an act of highest sacrifice or of utter disappointment, is open to guess. Viṣṇu's cosmic form (34.2419) with multiplication of heads and arms and the cult of the elephant headed god Gaṇeśa (54.3867) had also evolved. Torso of a mermaid (*matsyakanyā* 55.3884) is representative of composite figures made during that period while the depiction of amorous couple (55.3914) is forceful.

Sixteen Gupta and post-Gupta terracotta objects can be seen in the front showcase (No. 13). The glamour of this art began to vanish after the 6th century A.D.

References

1. *An Advanced History of India*, Part I, 1949, pp. 9-11.
2. Srivastava, A.K., 'Treasure Trove Finds from Mathurā District', In *Bulletin of Museum and Archaeology in U.P.*, June-Dec. 1973, p. 41.
3. Gupta, S.P., Copper Hoards—the Problems of Homogeneity, Stages of Development, Origin, Authorship of Dating, In *JBRS*, Vol. IX, pp. 147-66.
4. Härtel, H., *Excavations at Sonkh*, 1993 (Berlin).
5. *Ibid.*, pp. 19, 357.
6. *Ibid.*
7. *Ibid.*, p. 357.
8. *Ibid.* , p. 360.
9. *Ibid.*, p. 361.
10. *Ibid.*, ch. Part I, ch. IV (A).
11. *Ibid.*, p. 281.
12. *The Age of Imperial Unity*, 1951, p. 531.
13. Coomaraswamy, A.K., *IPEK*, 1928, p. 68.

14. Sharma, R.C., 'Archaic Terracotta Divinities—A Case Study of Mathurā', In *Indian Museum Bulletin*, 1988, pp. 34-37.

15. Agrawala, V.S., 'Mathurā Terracottas', In *Journal of the United Provinces Historical Society*, 1933, Part II, pp. 6-38.

16. Kala, S.C., *Terracottas of North India*, 1993, pp. 2-3.

17. Sharma, R.C., 'The Terracotta Art of Mathurā', In *Independence Silver Jubilee No. of U.P. State Lalit Kala Academy*, 1972, p. 148.

18. *Ibid.*, p. 149.

19. Saraswati, S.K., *A Survey of Indian Sculpture*, 1975, p. 119.

20. Agrawala, V.S., *Studies in Indian Art*, 1965, p. 199.

4

Mauryan and Śuṅgan Sculptures

While Mathurā ushered into a celebrated school of art from the Kuṣāṇa period and continued to ascend in quantity and later in quality for about five centuries it did have a conducive background and firm foundation in the preceding centuries. The assessment is vouschsafed by the grey terracotta figurines and *yakṣa* statues installed as guardian deities at different places. Inscriptional reference to the teacher and pupil in carving out a *yakṣa* image is another positive evidence in this regard.

Mauryan

As one steps into the sculpture gallery, his eye is first caught by a dominating colossal monolithic statue of *Yakṣa* (C. I; *fig. 8*) which is the earliest known image of Mathurā art. The attention is invited to the fact that an unbroken chain of sculptures in India derives from the Mauryan period when the art flourished in two distinct varieties, viz. court art and folk art. The former is known for its lustrous polish and conventionalised treatment as evidenced by several monolithic pillars and their surmounting animals. It is supposed to have many a foreign elements. The folk art, on the other hand, is purely indigenous in character and devoid of alienism. Its chief representatives are the free standing colossal *yakṣa* statues found at several places at Parkham, Baroda, Patna, Pavāya, Bharnākalān, etc.[1]

The term *yakṣa* has been differently explained in Indian literature. It seems to have derived from the root *yaj*, to worship. In the *Vedic* texts it generally occurs to mean wonderful or terrible. *Brāhmaṇas* have so often been called a *yakṣa* in the *Vedic* literature. 'By concentrated energy I became the primal *yakṣa*'.[2] The gods have realised that *yakṣa* is *Brahman*.[3] This supremacy, however, loses its importance in the later period. Both benevolent and malevolent aspects have been associated with the *yakṣas* who are believed to be possessed of magical or supernatural powers. Their female counterparts *yakṣiṇis* are more famous for witchcrafts. In the *Atharvaveda* the subjects of Kubera i.e. *yakṣas* and *rākṣasas* are called as *puṇyajanas* but the disease *yakṣamā* (a mysterious fever) also seems to be connected with the word *yakṣa*. The *Mahābhārata* points out that the people of the *rājasika* class (passionate nature) worship the *yakṣas* and *rākṣasas*.[4] It is also held that the *rākṣasas* had two-fold division; one the guardians of treasures who

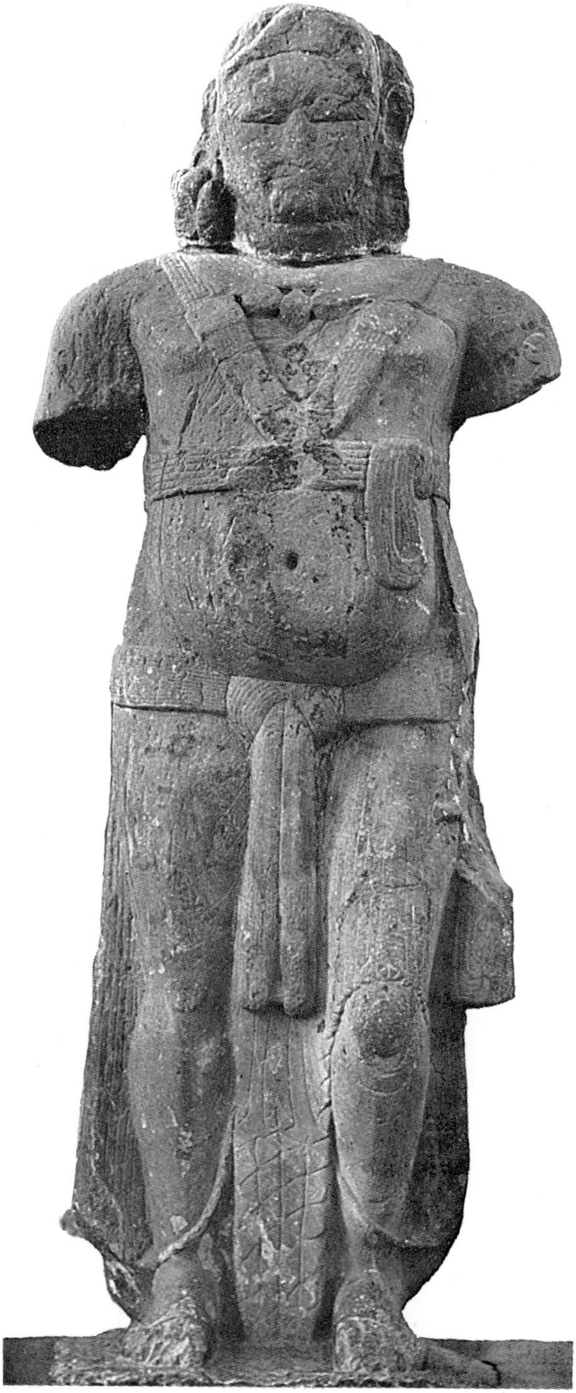

fig. 8 . Yakṣa from Parkham, late Maurya

were known as *yakṣas* while the other class being notorious by nature and disturbing the sacrifices was called *rākṣasas*. Generally, the *yakṣas* are supposed to be friendly with men while the *rākṣasas* are of evil nature. There are, however, many citations of the wicked *yakṣas* where they also behaved like *rākṣasas*. These semi-divine beings have found place in Hinduism, Buddhism and Jainism alike.[5]

The sculpture under discussion was acquired by Gen. Cunningham from the village Parkham (23 km. south of Mathurā), hence known as the Parkham Yakṣa. Heaviness, corpulence, extreme frontality, a girdle fastened round the waist and the two fillets hanging from the knot of the girdle between the thighs are some of the common features to be noticed in early *yakṣa* figures. The torque, necklace with four knots behind, flat waist and chest-bands are conspicuous. The inscription on the pedestal in early *Brāhmī* letters records that the statue was made by Gomitaka, a pupil of Kuṇika.[6] It is read as :

> Proper right side : *Nibhada-puga rāna*
> Front side : *atha . . . pi*
> Proper left side : *Kuṇikānte-vāsinā Gomitakena katā*

In the guild of *Nibhada* (in the reign of) the king . . . made by Gomitaka, the pupil of Kuṇika.[7]

The importance of the *yakṣa*

figures lies in the fact that they served as prototype for the evolution of early Indian iconography of different sects.

Just behind is seen a headless female figure (*yakṣī* 72.5) seated on the remarkably carved wicker seat. The sculpture which is badly damaged was worshipped as Manasādevī in village Naglā Jhīṅgā. The epigraph on the pedestal between her feet was read as :

1. '*Sā putehi kārito*
2. *Yakhilā ava Kuṇikāte*
3. (*vāsina Nāke*) *ne katā*

'(This image of) Yakṣī Lāyāva has been caused to be made by the sons of Sā, and made by Nāka, pupil of Kuṇika'.[8]

On the basis of the epigraph the *yakṣī* figure should be contemporary of the Parkham Yakṣa. Fortunately, the name Kuṇika is also identical. This master craftsman had two disciples i.e., Gomitaka sculptor of *yakṣa* from Parkham and Nāka who carved out Yakṣi Lāyāva. Thus there was long tradition of plastic art at Mathurā, which goes back at least to the Mauryan period.[9] In front of *yakṣī* stands a recently acquired *yakṣa* (legs missing) in buff stone with red layer (93.37) from Nānakpurā (Mathurā city). It has a peculiar turban fastened through a big projecting ribbon and on back side suspend two scarfs. Torque, necklace and heavy ear rings are his ornaments. While right hand was placed on the waist the traces on the left side suggest a shaft.

The other *yakṣa* statues now installed on two sides of the Parkham Yakṣa were acquired by the Museum in 1987 from village Bharanā Kalān. These are almost in the same style and made in the same buff sand stone as their predecessor Maṇibhadra from Parkham and should be dated in the early 2nd century B.C. Standing majestically straight on the platform inscribed in the countemporary *Brāhmī* script both wear a decorated turban, heavy ear rings with three circles, torque with floral design, and six stringed necklace. Both the neck ornaments are fastened through suspended large knots on back. Both have thin pleats on their lower garment (*dhotī*).

Despite these similarities the notable distinguishing features are as under:

Statue No. 87.145 which is installed on the left side of the Parkham Yakṣa looks slightly upward with no circles (*valayas*) on his neck. Fortunately, both of his arms being intact are adorned with several projecting wristlets and a large armlet (*keyūra*). With his left hand he firmly holds a club type heavy sword (*mudgara* hence called *mudgara pāṇi*) the upper part of which is broken. With his right hand the fingers of which are drawn up he held some object. From the knot of the waistband issue two large and heavy fillets suspending below the knees. The rubbed-off inscription on the pedestal can be read as . . .[10]

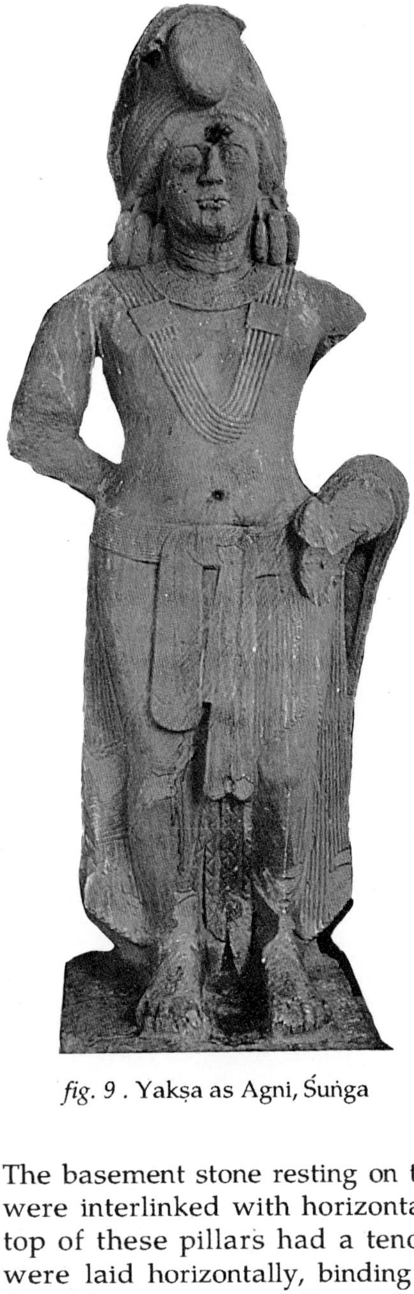

fig. 9 . Yakṣa as Agni, Śuṅga

The statue (No. 87.146; *fig. 9*) installed on the right side of Parkham Yakṣa looks straight with three incised circles (*trivalayas*) on the neck. The arms remain only fragmentary but left hand resting on the left side of the waist shows the traces of thick decorated bangles and support the garment. The waistband is simple and flat. The epigraph on the pedestal is better preserved in this case and it is read as . . .[11]

Śuṅgan

The sculptural art of the Śuṅga period is characterised by flatness of appearance, the wearing of bicornate or one sided turbans on male heads and simplicity of treatment. The figures appear to be the line drawings in stone and the three dimensional effect is wanting. The sculptor seems unconcerned with correct anatomical details and the subtler feelings like solace, sobriety, serenity, surprise, temptation etc. are also not expressive, yet a charm in the overall treatment is noted. The remaining exhibits in Gallery 1 belong to the late Śuṅga period, i.e. end-1st century B.C.

Architectural activity had started at a fairly early stage at Mathurā. The earliest remains so far found belong to the Śuṅga period. These are different constituent parts of the shrines and the *stūpas* made in order to worship a deity and to preserve the holy relics of a saint respectively. From the artistic point of view the railing which surrounded the *stūpa* for its safety, was of utmost significance. It consisted of basement stone (*ālambana piṇḍikā*), upright pillar (*stambha*), cross-bar (*sūcī*) and the coping stone (*uṣṇīśa*). The basement stone resting on the ground level supported the upright pillars which were interlinked with horizontal crossbars inserted in the mortices of pillars. The top of these pillars had a tenon fixed in the sockets of the coping stones which were laid horizontally, binding three or more rail posts. Access to the shrine was through gateways in different directions. Each gate had two big pillars supporting two or three large architraves with balustrades in between and brackets joining the lower beam with the pillars. This whole architectural complex known as *vedikā* (railing) was the centre of attraction for both visitors and sculptors. Religious and secular themes were protrayed on it. The railing now presents a valuable document for the study of various aspects of life in ancient India. The early art of Mathurā followed the artistic trends of Central India and specially those prevalent at Bharhut and Besnagar (Vidiśā). Accordingly, emphasis was laid on various symbols. The Buddha is not yet seen in anthropomorphic form, but is instead represented by sacred symbols which are depicted with due respect.

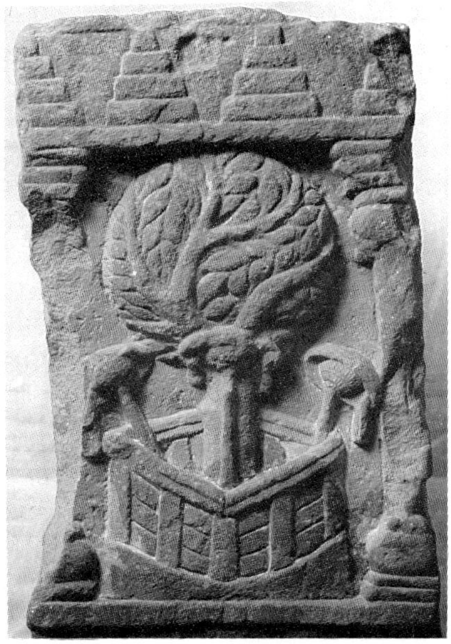

fig. 10 . *Bodhi* tree, Śuṅga

Small rail posts (18.1516 and 14-15-438 both from Mahādevghāṭ; *fig. 10*) showing the *bodhi* tree and *dharma cakra* (Wheel of the Law) aniconically remind of the Master's Enlightenment at Bodhagayā and his first sermon at Sārnāth. The other relief with two flying celestials garlanding a *stūpa* (10.130 from Vrindavan) conveys by the way of veneration the demise of the Buddha. A high vertical slab (I. 11), illustrates different modes of life in separate compartments. Dr. Vogel rightly observes that the relief represents one of the lower heavens (*kāmaloka*) in which sensual element is prominent.[12] The next slab bears a *caurī* bearing male (48.3423 from Kuanwāligalī, Mathurā). The three cross-bars are good examples for the study of floral, creeper and animal motifs. The undulating lotus creeper in the central bar (L. 21) is particularly instresting.

Small sculptures of the Śuṅga period as displayed in a wall case are cross bar (52.3612 from Bhūteśvar), a crossbar from Kaṭrā (36.2601), Kāmadeva (cupid) (18.1448, from Bayana, Mathurā) holding a cluster of bud-shaped arrows, a warrior on a lion (L. 24 from Mathurā Rly. Junction) and a lady playing on *vīṇā* (lyre) under a conventionally treated tree (G. 48 from Gopālpur maṭh, Mathurā city). If the sculpture was intended to make a Sarasvatī figure, the piece then is the earliest representation of this goddess(?). Fragment carved with a young drummer (57.4264 from Mathurā) is a nice specimen of pre-Kuṣāṇa era. The bone plaque depicting a female bust (56.4035 from Caurāsī mound) is a rare antiquity. It should belong to early 1st century A.D. and has close resemblance with ivory plaques from Begrām in Afghanistan which are supposed to be influenced by the early Mathurā art.

Other pieces are fragmentary pillar (29.2041), bust of two males (36.2602 from Kaṭrā), man with folded hands (I. 27), crossbar with a man (47.3363 from Kaṭrā). Some of the other scupltures of the period displayed in the Museum are:

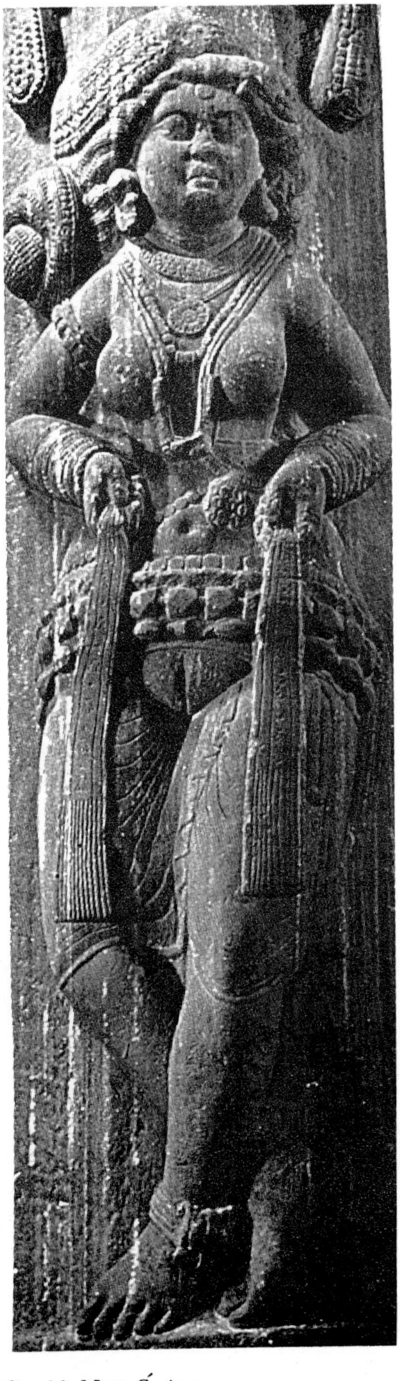

fig. 11. *Naṭī*, Śuṅga

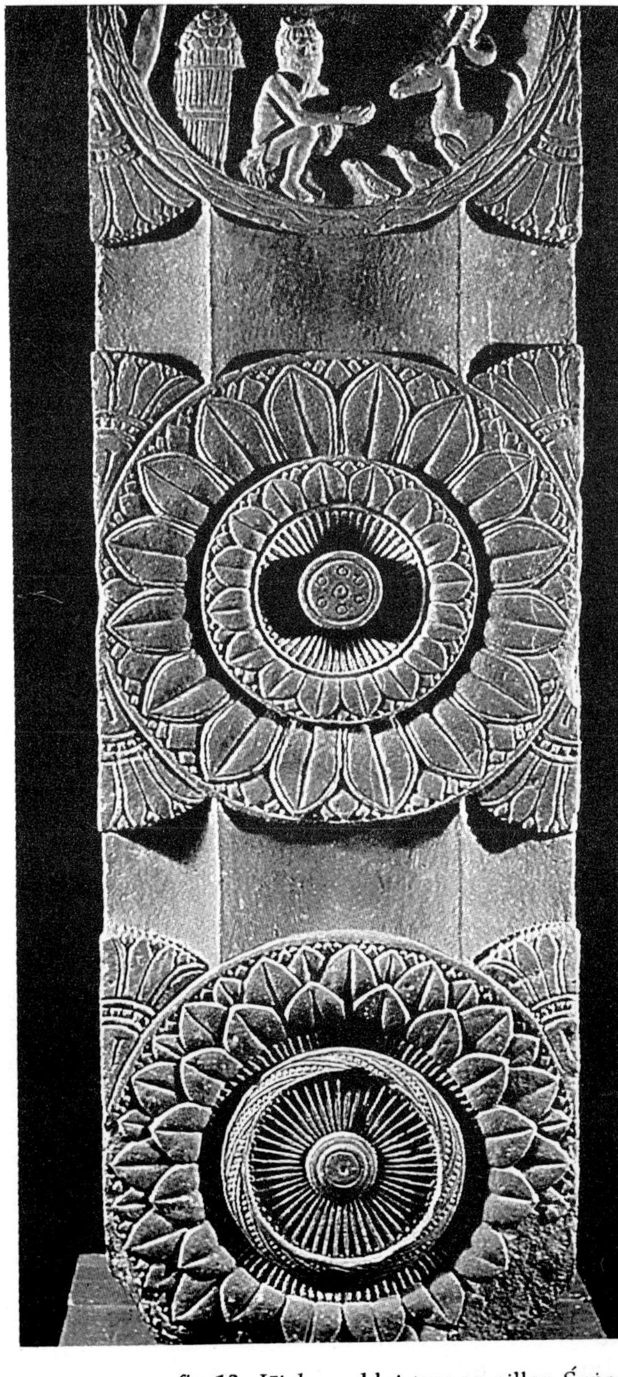

fig. 12 . *Jātaka* and lotuses on pillar, Śuṅga

1. Naṭī (J 2; *fig. 11*)

Beautifully carved on an upright pillar this is seen in dancing pose. The elaborately decorated coiffure, the big *jūḍā* touching her right shoulder and different ornaments impart a rhythmic touch to her graceful action. Although clad in a *sārī* her body is apparently exposed. Crouching a grotesque dwarf under her feet she fastens her waist band. Such dwarfish and grotesque male figures probably represent *yakṣas* whose status was now downgraded. In the present case he appears to be *Śaṅkukarṇa*, an epithet justified by his pointed ears. The medallion above shows a man with umbrella addressing an audience.[13]

2. *Duḥkhopādāna Jātaka* (The *jātaka* of the worst evil 15.586 from Saptarṣī mound; *fig. 12; col. ill. VI*)

The upper panel of the next pillar to right depicts a *jātaka* story. The *jātakas* are the episodes related to the previous births of the Buddha. These were narrated by him as explanations. Once he was requested by four monks of the Jetavana convent to solve their problem regarding the worst evil in the world. The Buddha recalled a similar discussion held in his previous birth between him and the four creatures represented on this pillar. According to the snake the worst evil was hatred, the deer thought it was fear, the crow favoured anger while the dove opined that it was love. They approached an ascetic for judgment. The sage held that the body itself is the worst evil. The Buddha then disclosed that in one of the previous births he was the ascetic and the monks were the four creatures. The pillar has beautiful lotuses of different varieties carved on both sides.[14]

The right corner displays a torso (E. 22 from a well in the village of Morā) supposed to be one of those five Vṛṣṇi heroes who are mentioned in an inscription of the time of Śoḍāṣa (late 1st century B.C.), acquired from the same site. Next is the bust of an attendant (I. 15 from Jamālpur; *fig. 13*) holding a flywhisk in his raised right hand. The

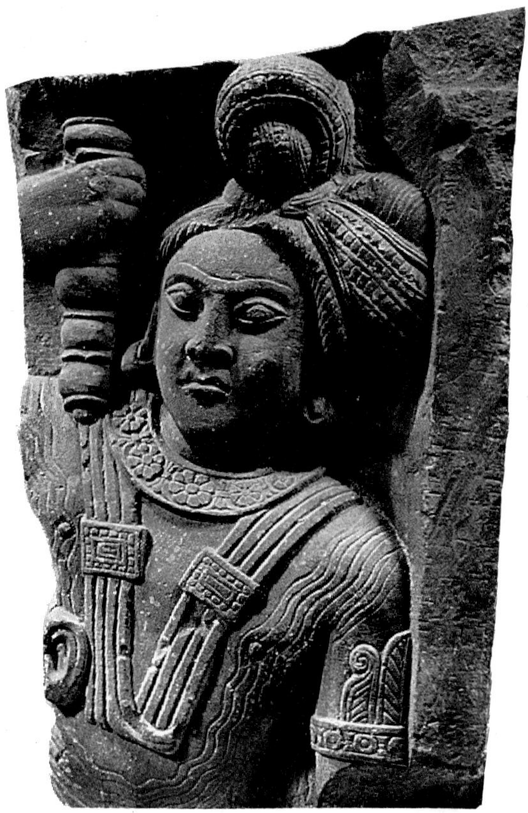

fig. 13. Flywhisk/torch bearer, Śuṅga

fluted headgear torque with rosette motif, and the bulging eyes suggesting a state of helplessness are remarkable.

Doorjamb (13.367 from Janmasthān ?) carved with lovely lotus creeper and other bands consists of a *Brāhmī* epigraph on the adjacent side. It records the erection of a gateway (*toraṇam*) and the railing (*vedikā*) at the great shrine (Mahāsthāna) of god (*Bhagavān* . . .) by certain Vasu in the time of Śoḍāṣa. According to some scholars this refers to the temple of Lord Kṛṣṇa at such an early date. This may, however, be pointed out that the name of the deity (Kṛṣṇa or Vāsudeva) is missing. It reads as follows:

1. . . . (*va*)
2. *sa* (s) *ya*
3. (*vas*)
4. . . . (*ṇa*) *Śiva*
5. *ṣa pu* (*t*) *rena Kauśi* (*kī putrena*)
6. *vasunā bhagavān* (*Vāsude*)
7. *vasya Mahāsthāna* (. . .)
8. *lam toraṇam ve* (*dikā ca prati*)
9. *ṣṭhāpitā prīto* (*bha*) (*Bhagavān Vāsu*)
10. *devaḥ svāmisya* (*mahākṣatra*)
11. *pasya Śoḍāṣa* (*sya* . . .)
12. *saṁvartayatām*

"By Vasu, son of the female descendant of the Kauśika *gotra* a gateway (*toraṇam*) and the railing (*vedikā*) was erected at the great temple (*mahāsthāna*) of *Bhagavān* Vāsudeva. May *Bhagavān* Vāsudeva, being pleased, promote (the dominion or the life and strength) of Svāmin Mhākṣatrapa Śoḍāṣa."[15]

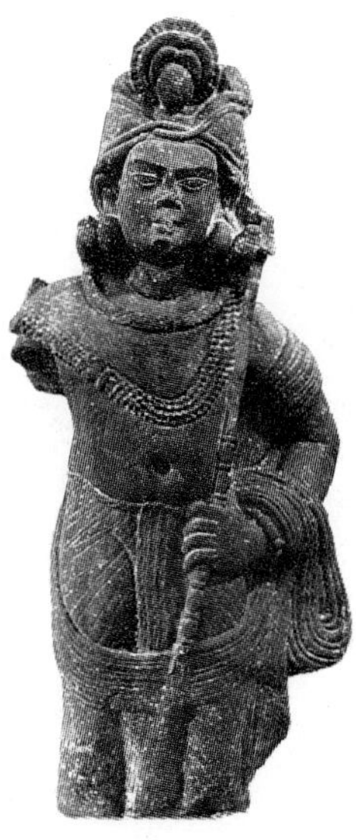

fig. 14. Nobleman, Śuṅga

The bust of a *yakṣa* holding a club in the right and a child in the left hand (I. 18) is a characteristic piece of the Śuṅga period. Such figures are supposed to depict the story of *Mahāsutasoma Jātaka* as will be seen later.

A young man carved in the round (E. 7; *fig. 14*) is a step forward in sculptural development and may belong to a transitional phase between the Śuṅga and Kuṣāṇa periods. The ornaments, high turban, necklace of beaded strings, elegantly worn *dhotī*, the scarf and a decorated sceptre in his left hand suggest for a royal dignity. The deep navel and heavy double ear-ring are archaic in character and remind us of the terracotta figurines of mother goddesses.

Behind placed on the bench pedestal is an interesting frieze (52.3625 from Bhūteśvar) showing worship of *śivaliṅga* by garland bearing centaurs. The *liṅga* is installed inside the railing under a tree. This is an early illustration of a Śaiva shrine.

The lintel more correctly an architrave (M. 1 from Kaṭrā) of the gateway (*toraṇa*) depicts on its obverse the scene of a refectory in a monastery (probably Buddhist) where some monks have assembled for food. One of them pours some boiled stuff (rice ?) from a large vessel and the other is cooling the liquid with a ladle. Some monks are seen with alms bowl while others sit quietly and await their turn. This scene is flanked by a Buddhist *stūpa* on either side and a garlanded tree (*bodhivṛkṣa*) to our right and a mutilated *toraṇa* figure with a female bust to left. Below is a carved railing and row of bells (*ghaṇṭāvalī* or *kiṅkinijāla*) intervened with lotus buds suspended from an ornamental string. The reverse bears a railing and gates surmounted by ogee arches. Several human figures occupy this architectural complex. The importance of the sculpture lies in two points, firstly it contains the earliest depiction of the life of the monks at Mathurā and secondly its acquisition from Kaṭrā proves the existence of a Buddhist *stūpa* on that site at such an early date.[16] Next slab (40.2881) bears probably the scene of the Anotatta lake in which the *Nāga* king Parṇaka was merrymaking with his retinue when he was disturbed by the sudden arrival of Sumana who despite resistence took the water of the lake and flew away. The *Nāga* and the members of the party are seen looking up with surprise, anger and fear. The flowers and twisted buds have been finely chiselled.[17] The beautiful calligraphy of pre-Kuṣāṇa period is evidenced by a slab in *Brāhmī* inscription of the time of Śoḍāṣa (79.29 from Mirjāpur, Mathurā; *fig. 15*).[18]

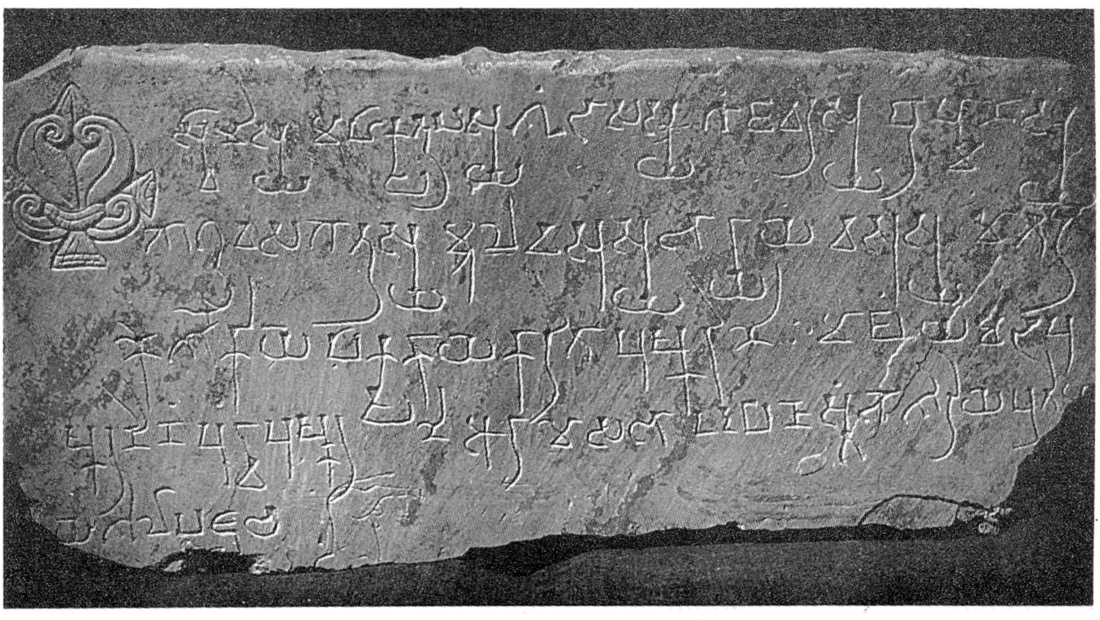

fig. 15. Incription of Śoḍāṣa, pre-Kuṣāṇa

On the other corresponding bench pedestal are placed five important exhibits. The first is a composite figure of lion with elephant head (75.3 from Chaubiā pārā, Mathurā), the second crossbar with human, head inside a beautiful full blown medallion (L. 22) followed by another crossbar (L. 2) showing a lady horse rider.

Architrave (M. 3 from a house in the city; *fig. 16-19*) of a gateway is of outstanding significance from various aspects. Carved on both sides it consists of five compartments on each face. The obverse in the centre shows the *bodhi* tree inside a building (*bodhighara* or *bodhirukkha-pasāda*). The branches of the sacred tree are seen issuing out of a decorated gateway while the stem is noticed in the centre. The shrine on each side is flanked by six devotees carrying garland and one with a water-pot. The compartment to the right represents worship of the 'Wheel of Law' (*dharmacakra*) supported by lions seated back to back. The corresponding scene to left shows the adoration of *stūpa*. These two small square panels are symbolic illustrations of the two great events from the life of the Buddha, i.e. his first sermon at Sārnāth (*dharmacakra pravartana*) and demise (*mahāparinirvāṇa*) at Kasiā respectively. The beam on the two ends bears the figure of the mythical sea monster with fish tailed human bust. The reverse presents the scene of Indra's homage to the Buddha in the Indraśāla (cave of Indra). The Enlightened One sits, cross legged with *abhaya* (posture of protection) in his right hand inside a cave. Outside, to his left Indra wearing a high crown stands with folded hands. He is accompanied by two ladies, probably *apsarās* (nymphs) who are also seen in adoration. Behind them are three elephants of whom the central one with caparison should be identified as Airāvata (Indra's vehicle). On the other side of the cave stands Indra's companion Pañcaśikha Gandharva, divine musician, with a harp. Six celestial nymphs show their respect in different ways. The small square compartment on either side represents a full vase (*pūrṇakalaśa*) decorated with lotus flower, buds and garlands. The sea monster motif as seen on the obverse has been repeated on the two ends of the reverse side.

This exquisitely carved sculpture belongs to the transitional phase, between the Śuṅga and Kuṣāṇa periods, when symbol worship was in vogue and anthropomorphic form of the Buddha was gradually being introduced. This may, therefore, be regarded as one of the earliest representations of the Buddha in human form and should be assigned to the pre-Kaniṣka period.[19] Composition of themes, drawing of motifs and treatment of human and animal figures are quite remarkable. Beside the architrave itself, depiction of gateway with upper railing sloping towards the side bastions and the representation of multi-storeyed *stūpa* with several superimposed decorated bands suggest a high standard of the contemporary architecture.[20] The last object is an arch on the coping stone (14.431 from Pīpalwālā Kuān, Mathurā; *col. ill. VII*) depicts a scene from the *Mahāsutasoma Jātaka*. A man is seen carrying two persons on a *baiṅgī* (baskets hanging from two ends of the pole) towards a tree. As the story goes a king of Varāṇasī had developed the taste for human flesh. When his crime was detected he was removed by his subjects and sent into the forest. There he injured his foot and for its quick recovery he took a vow before a tree deity to offer 101 princes if the wound was healed

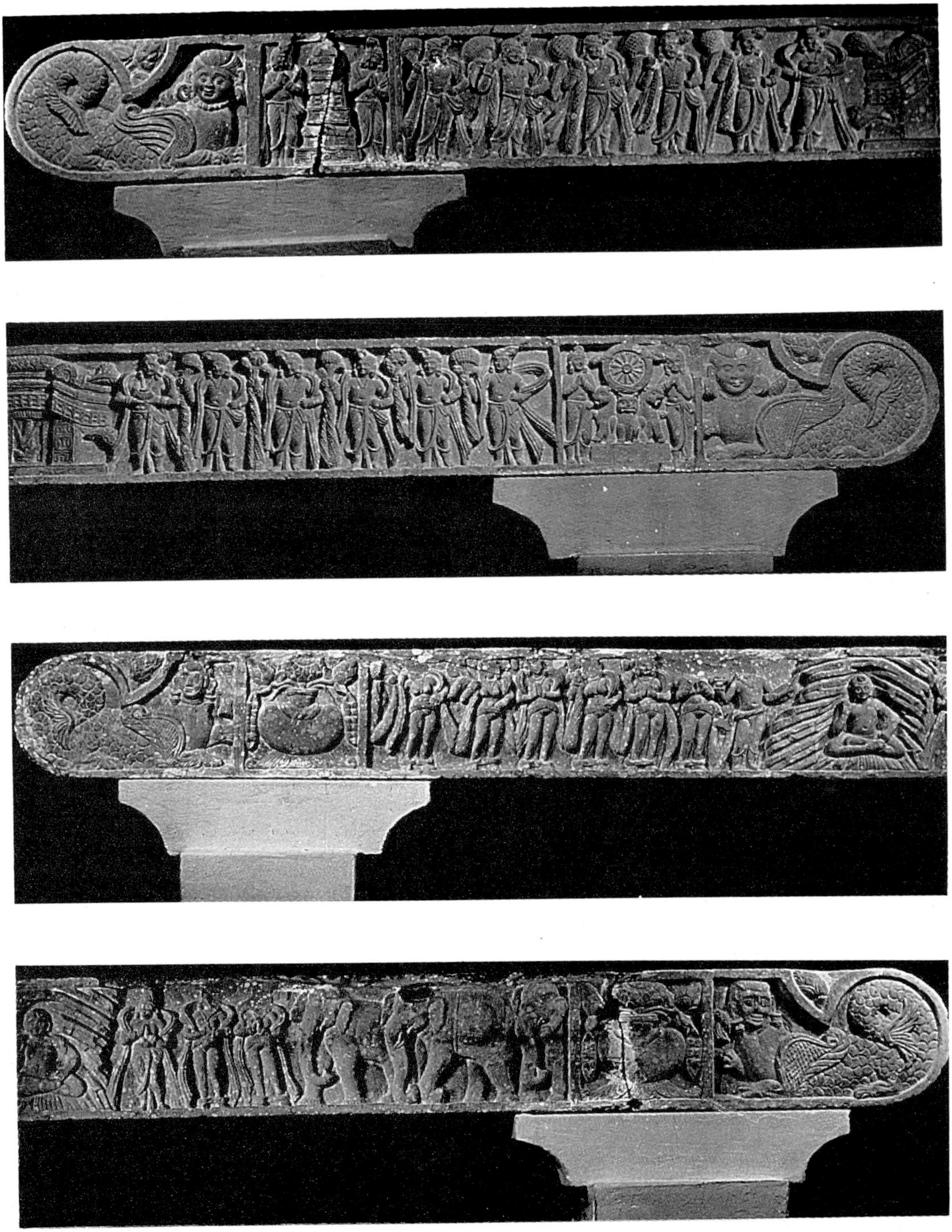

fig. 16-19. Beam with symbols and Buddha, pre-Kuṣāṇa

within a week. After recovery he started capturing the princes and hanging them on the tree. Last of all he caught the Bodhisattva who was prince Sutasoma in that birth. Attracted by the fearlessness and good behaviour of the prince he not only let him free but also began to lead a pious life himself. The episode is conveyed through a different depiction where a giant is shown holding a child in the left hand and a club in the right as if ready to attack. The child is shown with folded hands. R.N. Misra suggests the following story for the identification of such sculptures.

"The *Antagaḍadasāo*, an early Jaina work refers to the Yakṣa Muggarapāṇi who had a temple dedicated to him in a garden outside the city of Rājagṛha. He was the ancestral deity of a gardener-Ajjunaka. Once when he was paying respects to the image of the Yakṣa who held a mace, *mudgar* of 10000 *palas*, five bandits tied Ajjunaka and molested his wife. Ajjunaka fied upon Yakṣa saying what was the use of his worship when Yakṣa could not save him and his wife from bandits. The Yakṣa accepted the challenge and possessed Ajjunaka whereupon, this gardener killed the gangsters and continued to pester the inhabitants of the city with the mace of 10000 *palas* until he was pacified by Sudarśana."[21]

References

1. Agrawala, V.S., *Indian Art*, 1965, p. 111.
2. *Taittīrīya Brāhmaṇa*, 3.12.31.
3. *Kenopaniṣat*, 3.15 and *Jaimīniya Upaniṣad Brāhmaṇa*, IV. 20.
4. *Gītā*, 17.4.
5. *Encyclopaedia of Religion and Ethics*, Vol. II, 1958, p. 809 and Coomaraswamy, A.K. *Yakṣas*, Part II/1.
6. Sivaramamurti, C., *Indian Sculpture*, 1961, p. 2.
7. Vogel, J. Ph., *Catalogue of the Archaeological Museum at Mathurā*, 1910, p. 83.
8. Chanda, R.P., *A.I.S.R.*, 1922-23, p. 165.
9. *Bulletin of Museum and Archaeology in U.P.*, No. 8, Dec., 1971, pp. 71-73.
10. 1. *Amatyena prati (hāra) (e) (na)*
    2. . . . *(Jaya gh (o) (s) (ena) . . . (to) pra*
    3. *(Bh) (āga) (v) (a) to ā (gn) isa prā (t)i (m) (ō)*
11. *(kā) ritā p (ri) yantām (a) ga (ya)*.
12. Vogel, J. Ph., *Catalogue of the Archaeological Museum at Mathurā*, 1910, p. 136.
13. Coomaraswamy, A.K., In *JAOS*, Vol. 51, p. 56, was inclined to identify it as *Mahābodhi jātaka* but Agrawala, V.S., interprets it as the visit of Bāvari, *Mathurā Museum Catalogue, JUPHS*, 1951, p. 4.
14. Agrawala, V.S., *op. cit.*, pp. 38-40.
15. *Ibid.*, pp. 134-36.
16. *Ibid.*, pp. 57-58.
17. Nagar, M.M., *Hindi Guide*, 1947, p. 5.

18. The inscription is read as :
    1. *Svāmisya Mahākṣatrapasya Śunḍāsasya gānjavarasya Brāhmaṇasya.*
    2. *Śegrvasa gotrasya Mūlavasusya bhāryaye Vasusya mātare.*
    3. *Kauśikīye Pākṣakāye kāritā puṣkariṇi imāṣaṁ yameḍa pu-.*
    4. *ṣkaraṇīnām pūrvā puṣkarṇi ārāmo sabhā udapāno stambho siriye pratimā.*
    5. *ye śilāpaṭṭo ca.*

    Kauśiki Pākṣaka, mother of Vasu and wife of Mūlavasu (who was the) treasurer of Swamī Mahākṣatrapa Śoḍāṣa and (who was) a *Brāhmaṇa* belonging to the Śaigrava *gotra*, caused to erect the eastern (water) tank out of the twin tanks, a grove or garden, place for assembly, a well, a pillar and a stone slab of the image of Lakṣmī.

    Sharma R.C., New Inscriptions from Mathurā, In *Mathurā—the Cultural Heritage*, 1989, p. 308.
19. Van Lohuizen, J.E., *The Scythian Period*, 1949, pp. 155-57.
20. Bachhofer, L., *Early Indian Sculpture II*, pp. 27 and 29.
21. *Bulletin of Museum and Archaeology in U.P.*, No. 5-6, June-Dec., 1970, p. 29.

5

Early Kuṣāṇa Art

WITH the rise of the Kuṣāṇa power in Mathurā region in the second half of the 1st century A.D. the pattern of the society began to change. The influx of foreigners mounted but the prevailing peace and prosperity resulted in providing a commensurate atmosphere for development of building and artistic activities. The Kuṣāṇa period is rightly called as the golden era in the history of Mathurā.

Characteristics

Gallery 2 consists of the exhibits of the Kuṣāṇa period when the sculptural art took a new and vital turn. The low relief of the Śuṅga period is replaced by high or bold carving, the male body is shaped straight, firm and stiff with broad and masculine chest. Halo round the head of the deity is plain and often bears scalloped border, the head is shaven or has small curls, the drapery is heavy and covers only one shoulder of the Buddha (*ekānsika sanghāṭī*), lower garment is seen upto the middle of the leg. The right hand is raised in *abhaya mudrā* (gesture of protection) with a decorated filling behind. The face bears round and open eyes with a smiling expression on the face. The attendant figures are mostly large in size. The female beauty has greater charm but sensual delineation is conspicuous. The pantheon of all the three sects viz. Jainism, Buddhism and Hinduism evolved in this period.

Jaina Icons

Keeping to left the visitor stands amidst the Jaina icons. Traditionally, the image worship in Jainism goes back to a hoary past and is associated with Ādinātha, the first Jina. The gap between the 18th (Ādinātha) and the 19th (Mallinātha) *Tīrthaṅkaras* is said to be of one thousand crores of years and about others nothing such has been specified. It is, therefore not possible to account for the origin of image worship on the basis of tradition.[1]

Archaeologically, if the controversial Lohānipur (Patna) torso bearing Mauryan polish is identified as a Jina figure, it becomes the earliest Jaina antiquity, belonging to the 3rd-2nd century B.C.[2] The Hāthīgumphā inscription of king Khāravela (1st century

B.C.) records the installation of a Jina image, which was removed by the king Nanda about 300 years ago (4th century B.C.). A panel in the Rānī Nūr cave at Udayagiri is supposed to represent the life events of Pārsvanātha, the 23rd *Tīrthaṅkara* but the identification is doubtful.[3]

But for these uncertain and indirect illustrations no positive evidence has been found in favour of early origin of the Jina figures. It is only in the late 1st century B.C. or early 1st century A.D. that the Jina figures appear for the first time at Mathurā. The beginning is seen in the *āyāgapaṭṭas* (tablets for worship) which suggest a phase of transition from symbol worship to the human form of the deity. In this gallery the eastern wall displays two such tablets. The first (Q.2 from Maholī; *fig. 20*) is carved with a *stūpa* in worship.

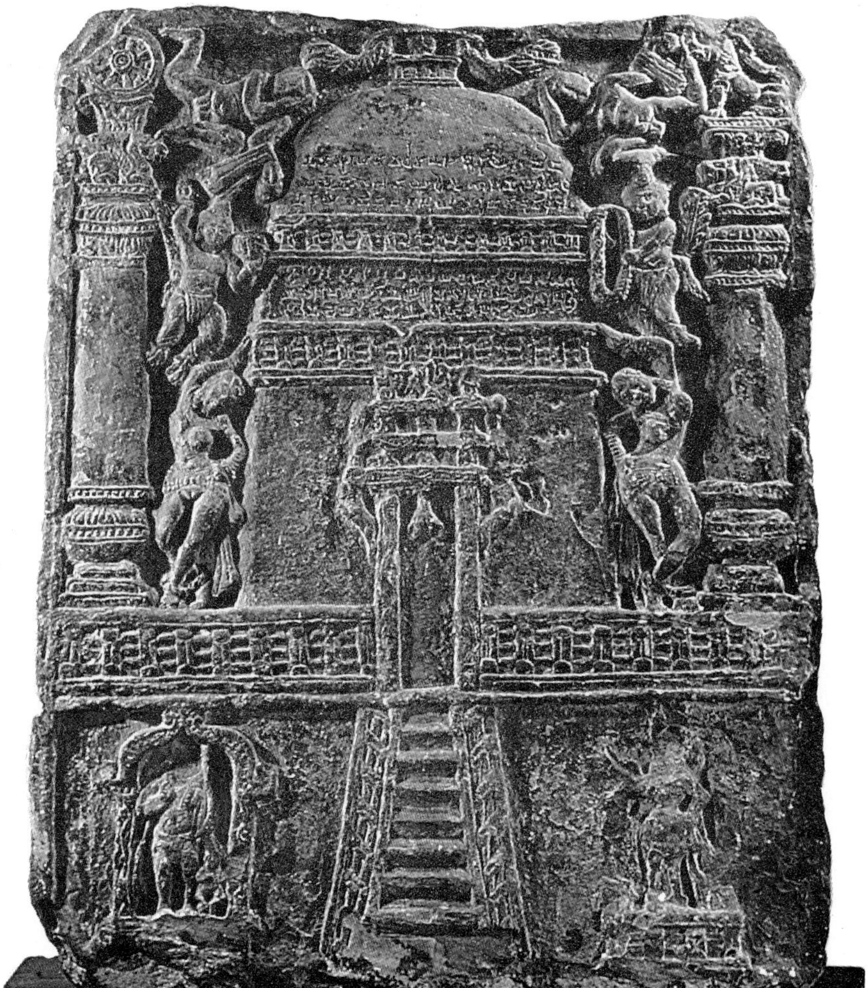

fig. 20. Ayāgapaṭṭa, pre-Kuṣāṇa

The undated inscription records that it was set up by a courtesan Vasu, daughter of *gaṇikā* Lavaṇa Śobhikā. The words 'Arye' (ārya) and 'Nanda' before the names of the two courtesans seem to be epithets and, as Vogel thinks, may represent their ranks among the co-professionals or their status in the society.[4] The sculpture gives a complete idea of the contemporary *stūpa* architecture, with steps, three railings and an ornamental gateway.

The inscription is read and translated as follows:

1. *Namo Ārahato Vardhamānasa Arāye gaṇikā*
2. *ye Loṇaśobhikāye dhitu samaṇasāvikāye*
3. *Nadāye gaṇikāye. Vasu (ye) Ārahato devik (u) la*
4. *Āyāga-sabhā prapā śil(ā) pa (ṭo) pratisṭh (ā) pito Nigathā*
5. *naṁ Araha (tā) yatane sa (hā) m (ā) tare bhaginiye dhitare putreṇa*
6. *Sarveṇa ca parijanena Arahata pujāye.*

"Adoration to the *Arhat* Vardhamāna. The daughter of the matron(?) courtesan Loṇaśobhikā (Lavaṇa-śobhikā), the disciple of the ascetics, the junior (?) courtesan Vasu has erected a shrine of the *Arhat*, a hall of homage *(āyāgasabhā)*, cistern (and) a stone slab at the sanctuary of the *Nirgarantha Arthats*, together with her mother, her daughter, her son and her whole household in honour of the *Arhats*."

In the next slab (48.3426 from, Chaubiāpārā, Mathurā) the *stūpa* is replaced by a meditating figure of the Jina in centre while the symbols have also been conspicuously shown in other bands. There are eight auspicious symbols (*aṣṭamāṅgalika cinhas*) differently listed in the text books. Generally these are : *svastika* (mystic cross), *mīna mithuna* or *matsya yugma* (a pair of fish), *triratna* (three jewels) *bodhi-vṛkṣa* (tree of knowledge), *śarāva sampuṭa* (pair of earthen cups), *bhadrāsana* (caned seat) *śrīvatsa* and *pūrṇaghaṭa* (a pitcher).[5] This slab exhibits the fish symbol in the first semi-circular band while the second band bears *bodhi* tree, *triratna* and a mutilated *bhadrāsana* garlanded by maidens.

The Jina statues are usually seen in two postures viz. standing and sitting. The former is known as *daṇḍa* or *kāyotsarga* in which a *Tīrthaṅkara* is seen standing in austerity, sacrificing even his body *(kāyotsarga)*, and the second in meditation *(dhyānastha)* pose which shows him seated cross legged with soles and palms turned upward. All early Jina figures are without robe *(digambara)*. A mark of *śrīvatsa* (jewel) in the centre of chest is invariably seen. Influence of early *yakṣa* iconography is to be noticed in the formatioin of the body. Sculptures B.12 and B. 32 represent seated and standing poses respectively. Out of 24 *Tīrthaṅkaras* only two can be recognised through their characteristics i.e.

Pārśvanātha with a snake canopy and Ādinātha with locks of hair falling on his shoulders. The stele represents a Jina (B. 63) seated cross legged in meditation and flanked by two devotees. His matted hair is arranged in four-tier strings and the lion throne shows the worship of the *dharmacakra.* Exhibit B. 62 is an interesting Pārśvanātha head with *svastika, śarāva samputa, śrīvatsa, triratna, pūrṇaghaṭa* and *mīna* motifs on hoods. Half of wall showcase No. 4 shows the following interesting Jaina icons:

1. Crowned head of a goat headed male deity Naigameṣa (15.1001 from Mansāwālā well, Pālīkherā).
2. Naigameṣi with children (15.1115 from Yamunā).
3. Naigameṣi as above (34.2482).
4. Spouse of Naigameṣī—Ṣaṣṭhī or Revatī (15.798 from well Shahkazi, Isāpur).
5. Neminātha flanked by Balarāma with snake hood on right and Kṛṣṇa on left (34.2488; *fig. 21*).
6. Small Jina head (18.1536 from Kaṅkālī mound).
7. Shaven Jina head (B. 78 from Mātāmaṭh, Bhūteśvar).
8. Inscribed lion throne with worship of *dharmacakra* (B. 18 from Mātā Maṭh near Holi gate)[6] and lower seated part of Jina.

   The inscription reads as:

   Front : *Kottikato ganato Vachalikato ku*

   1. *lato vadha*
   2. *pratimāye*
   3. *dhitu vacayasya*
   4. *codasya*
   5. *deva saha*
   6. *Ṛṣidāsa*

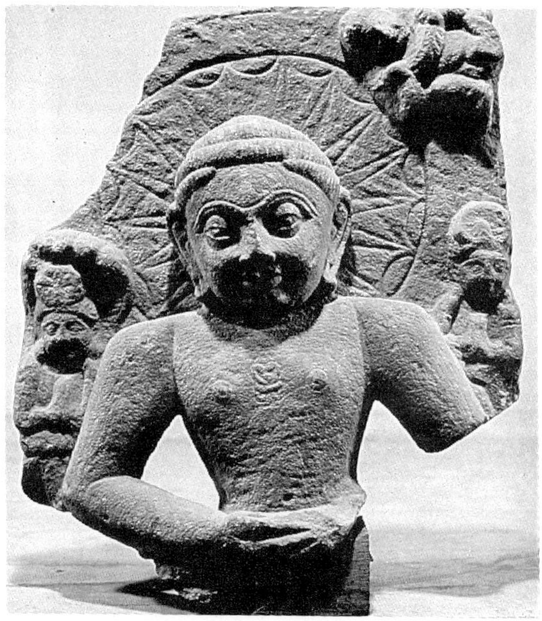

fig. 21. Neminātha, Kuṣāṇa

"Out of the Koṭṭiya gaṇa and of the Vachalika kula, (gift of) the image of Vardhamāna, Coda, the daughter's son, together with Ṛṣidāsa."

The independent exhibit (B. 67) is known as *sarvatobhadrikā* (quadruple) sculpture in which a *Tīrthaṅkara* figure is carved in each direction. The pedestal bears some foreign devotees. Such images were installed in open or in a hall where the people could circumambulate them. Naigameśa (34.2547), a goat headed god associated with the care of infants and his consort (E.2), Revatī or Ṣaṣṭhī with a child on her lap are seen on the bench pedestal in the beginning of gallery No. 2. The frieze (I. 38 from Galī Quanūngoyān, Mathurā) shows from left to right a dragon, city gate or a convent and a procession. In the centre of gallery No. 2 there is an architectural piece (72.7 from Camuṇḍā mound) which is carved with lions, palm and a pot bellied *yakṣa* whose thighs are seen in the alligators' mouths. He also supported two female figures (river goddesses?) with his two hands. The same theme is represented on the other side of the sculpture. There must have been some surmounting emblem which is unfortunately gone now. The whole complex provides a beautiful design for jewellery fabrication.

Buddhist Figures

The other side of gallery 2 shows Buddhist sculptures. The *jātaka* stories continued to be carved. The lower band of the horizontal slab on the bench pedestal (I. 4; *col. ill. VIII*) illustrates the episode of the *Romaka jātaka* which runs as follows : The Buddha in one of his previous births was a pigeon who with his fellow pigeons used to visit an ascetic in the forest. In course of time another ascetic replaced him and he had once an occasion to taste the flesh of the pigeon. Finding it a delicious dish he made up his mind to kill his bird guests. The Bodhisattva, however, guessed the evil intention and warned his companions.[7] The story is also known as *Pārāvata jātaka*. The upper panel is decorated with a heavy undulating twisted garland carried by three *yakṣas*. It may be interesting to note that such garland bearing *atlantes* are frequently met with in the Gāndhāra art and this piece seems to bear that influence at a very early stage.

Origin of the Buddha Image

There is a great deal of controversy among the exponents of the Gāndhāra and Mathurā Schools of Art regarding the origin of the Buddha image. The majority of scholars, however, believes that the Buddha image was made in the beginning of Kaniṣka's reign.[8] The earliest Buddha/Bodhisattva[9] images belonging to the Mathurā School are those of Kauśāmbī (dated in the 2nd regnal year of Kaniṣka)and of Sārnāth (in the third year). Assuming the generally accepted date of his accession as 78 A.D., the two sculptures were installed in 80 and 81 A.D. respectively. Similarly, the undated images in this Museum viz., the Maholī Bodhisattva(38.2798), Kaṭrā Bodhisattva (A. 1; *col. ill. IX*) or Ānyor Buddha (A.2) also stylistically belong to the same period. All these finely executed figures suggest that the practice of representing the Buddha in human form had a long background at Mathurā and the above statues only show a refined and developed stage. The colossal Bodhisattva statues must have been exported to distant places like Kauśāmbī, Sārnāth and also Bodhagayā when the Mathurā school had already earned a good reputation. Considering the slow means of communication in that period a suitable margin should be allowed. It is, therefore, quite natural to suppose that there was a background for evolving the Buddha figure in anthropomorphic form and the above mentioned sculptures did not make a sudden appearance[10].

Rudrāyanavadānam of *Divyāvadānam* refers to the episode recording the preparation of a banner painting of the Buddha in his own time and with his own consent.[11]

As already noticed the Buddha in the Śuṅga period was represented through symbols. But the Brāmanical icons had already evolved at Mathurā. The Parkham *yakṣa,* (C. 1; *fig. 8*) torsos of the Vṛṣṇi heroes (as recorded in Morā well inscriptions Q. 1) Balarāma (G. 215 of Lucknow Museum) are some of the examples. Through image worship, Brāhmanism was gaining popularity and this tempted the other sects too. Mere symbolic depiction of the Master no longer satisfied the urge of the devotee. The prevailing religious rivalry thus compelled the Jaina and the Buddhist churches to introduce icons as media of worship. Jainism was first to adopt it and through the Mahāyānists' efforts Buddhism did likewise. The *yakṣa* image served as a model, hence all early standing Buddha or Bodhisattva figures are in the *yakṣa* style.

In view of the above mentioned religious environment and the advanced style of Buddhist figures in the beginning of the Kuṣāṇa rule, one is naturally eager to know about the sculptures which were made earlier than the Sārnāth, Kauśāmbī, Kaṭrā and Maholī Bodhisattvas. Such figures do exist in Mathurā and Lucknow museums and are very near the old *yakṣa* tradition or the Jina figures in the *āyāgapaṭṭas.* As already discussed the *āyāgapaṭṭas* are to be dated to the end of the 1st century B.C. or early 1st century A.D. hence the Buddhist icons which are close to *āyāgapaṭṭas* may safely be dated to the pre-Kaniṣka period. Out of such sculptures two exist in the Mathurā Museum :

1. Seated Buddha flanked by four *lokapālas;* the second exhibit on the bench pedestal of the Buddhist gallery (H.12 Isāpur, Mathurā; *fig. 22*) The formation of the body of the Buddha and the high pedestal, should be compared with the *āyāgapaṭṭa* figures particularly the Śiṁhanādika tablet in the National Museum, New Delhi (from Kaṅkālī) and the fragmentary *āyāgapaṭṭa* (48.3426 from Chaubiapārā) displayed here on the eastern wall.

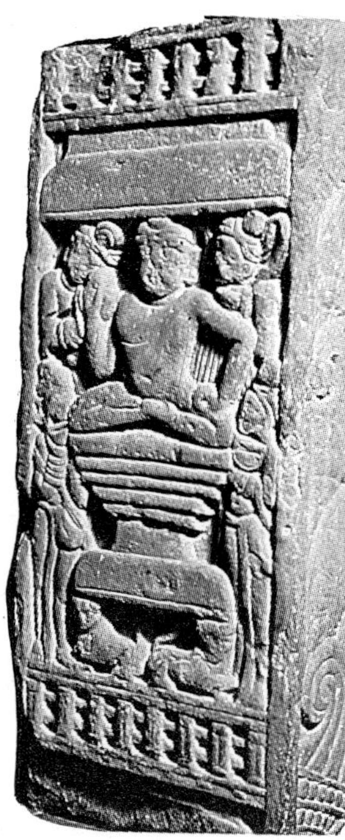

fig. 22. Buddha and *Lokapālas,* pre-Kuṣāṇa

2. Another early seated figure is seen on the *toraṇa* beam (reverse of the architrave M. 3; *fig. 16-19*) already described in the Śuṅga gallery) depicting the Buddha in the Indraśālā cave. On the other side the Master's presence has been conveyed through symbols.

This mode of worship (symbolic representation) was in vogue simultaneously. The vertical slab (39.2868) represents the descent of the Buddha at Saṅkāśya from the *tuṣita* heaven where he had gone to preach the Law after Enlightenment. The *tuṣita* heaven is to be identified by the turban which was thrown by Siddhārtha after renouncing the world. Indra later installed it in the heaven in the *cūdāmahāceitya* which is shown here as a small *stūpa.*[12] The three ladders bridge up the gap between the earth and the heaven. The kneeling devotee if shown below should be identified as nun Utpalavarṇā.

The next slab (56.4239 from Sarai Azampur) shows the cult of *uṣṇīśa* (turban) as described above. The frieze on the western wall (36.2663 from near Mahāban) probably depicts the worship of halo (*prabhā maṇḍala*) placed on a high platform. The background of the halo bears cluster of leaves signifying the *Bodhi* tree. The lower compartment below the railing represents a turbaned male head wearing ear rings. The model Buddha/Bodhisattva in early age is represented by the famous image (A. 1 from Kaṭrā; *col. ill IX* and the front cover). The deity sits in *padmāsana* beneath the *bodhi* tree on a lion throne. The shaven head bearing a snail shell *(uṣṇiśa)* is carved with a scalloped halo. A circular mark between the two eyebrows (*ūrṇā*) represents his Enlightenment. The drapery covers only one shoulder (*ekānsika sanghāṭī*). Symbols indicative of his greatness (*mahāpuruṣa lakṣaṇas)* which have been marked on the body, are, *svastika, cakra, triratna* and auspicious lines in the hand.[13] He is flanked by two flywhisk bearing attendants while two celestials are seen hovering in air and showering flowers. Though clad in monk's dress the inscription on the pedestal labels him as Bodhisattva. This may suggest that the image was set up by the *Sarvāstivādins* who were opposed to represent the Buddha in human form but had no objection in his representation before the attainment of Enlightenment. We are aware of the fact that Mathurā was a stronghold of *Sarvāsthivādin* branch of Buddhism in pre and post Christian centuries. The epigraph reads as follows:

1. *Buddharakitasa mātare amohā-āsiye bodhisaco patiṭhāpito*
2. *sāhā mātāpitihi sake vihāre*
3. *savasatvānā hitasukhāye*

"Budharakhita's mother Amohā-āsī has erected (this) Bodhisattva together with her parents in her own convent (or temple or monastery built by Śakas) for the welfare and happiness of all sentient beings."

It was under worship as Viśvamitra flanked by Rāma and Lakṣmana.[14] This beautiful and intact specimen shows all important stylistic and iconographic developments which took place in the early days of the Kuṣāṇa rule. Probably to avoid conflict between Mahāyānists and Hīnayānists the image although carved as Buddha has been recorded as Bodhisattva. This statue served as model for the subsequent Buddhist images produced in the Mathurā studies.[15]

Image (A.2) from Ānyor is one of the earliest representations of the Buddha in Kuṣāṇa period. Its inscription mentions a monastery, Uttara Hāruṣa Vihāra, where the image was installed. It reads as :

1. *Upādsakasya Suṣasya Hāruṣasya dāna (ṁ) Bu (d) dha prat (i)* mā *Uttarasya H (ā) ruṣa (sya)*
2. *vihāre saha māta pitihi sarva-satvān (a) m hitasukh (ā) rtha (ṁ).*

"Gift of the lay member Susa of Hāruṣa, Buddha image at the convent of Uttara of Hāruṣa together with the parents for the sake of the welfare and happiness of all sentient beings."[16]

The standing Buddha image (71.105 from Govindnagar; *fig.* 23) is an early depiction of the Buddha in the Mathurā style. He has shaven head with top knot, right hand raised in *abhaya* (potection) with wreath decoration behind and the left hand resting on the waist. But for scalloped border the field of the large halo (slightly broken) is blank and the garment covers the left shoulder only. The palm of the right hand bears an auspicious wheel and the finger tips show *svastika* mark. This was the first Buddha image from the site of Govindnagar which

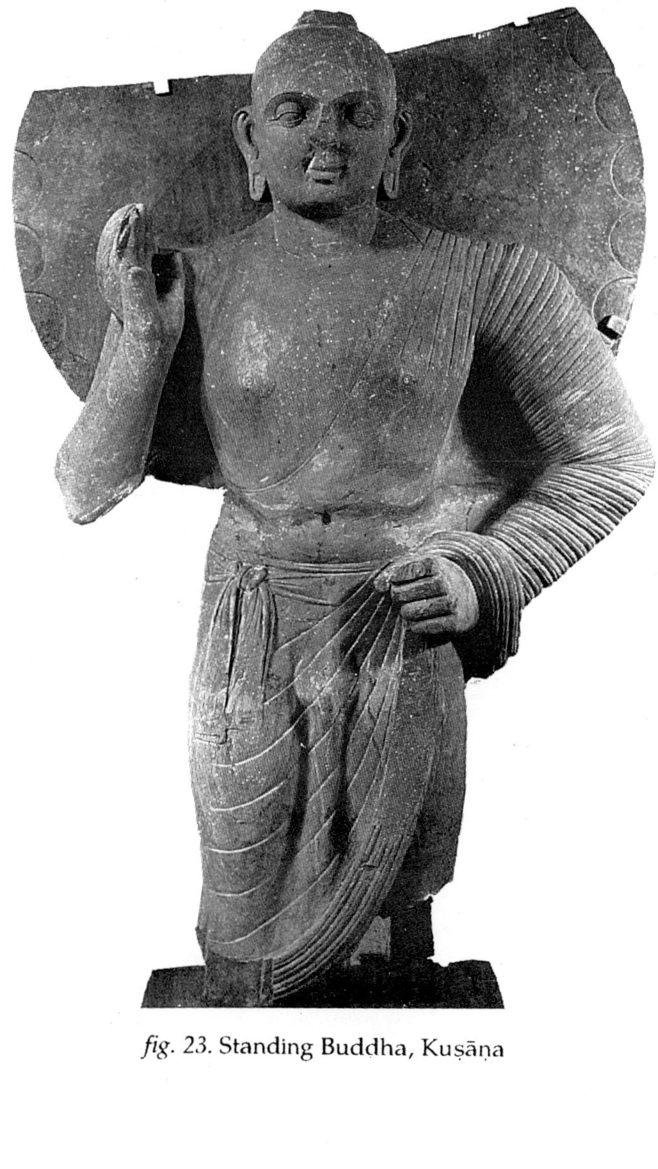

fig. 23. Standing Buddha, Kuṣāṇa

subsequently yielded a large number of sculptures. The next exhibit is the Buddha image (86.148 from Maholī; *fig. 24*) with large halo emerging from the body and wearing a scalloped border. The shaven headed deity held his right hand upraised in protection pose (now broken), the left shoulder is covered with *ekānsika sanghāṭī* and additional thick pleats on the left shoulder. The feet of the cross legged deity are marked with auspicious motifs as *cakra, triratna* and *svastika*. The spotted red sand stone statue should stylistically belong to early second century A.D.

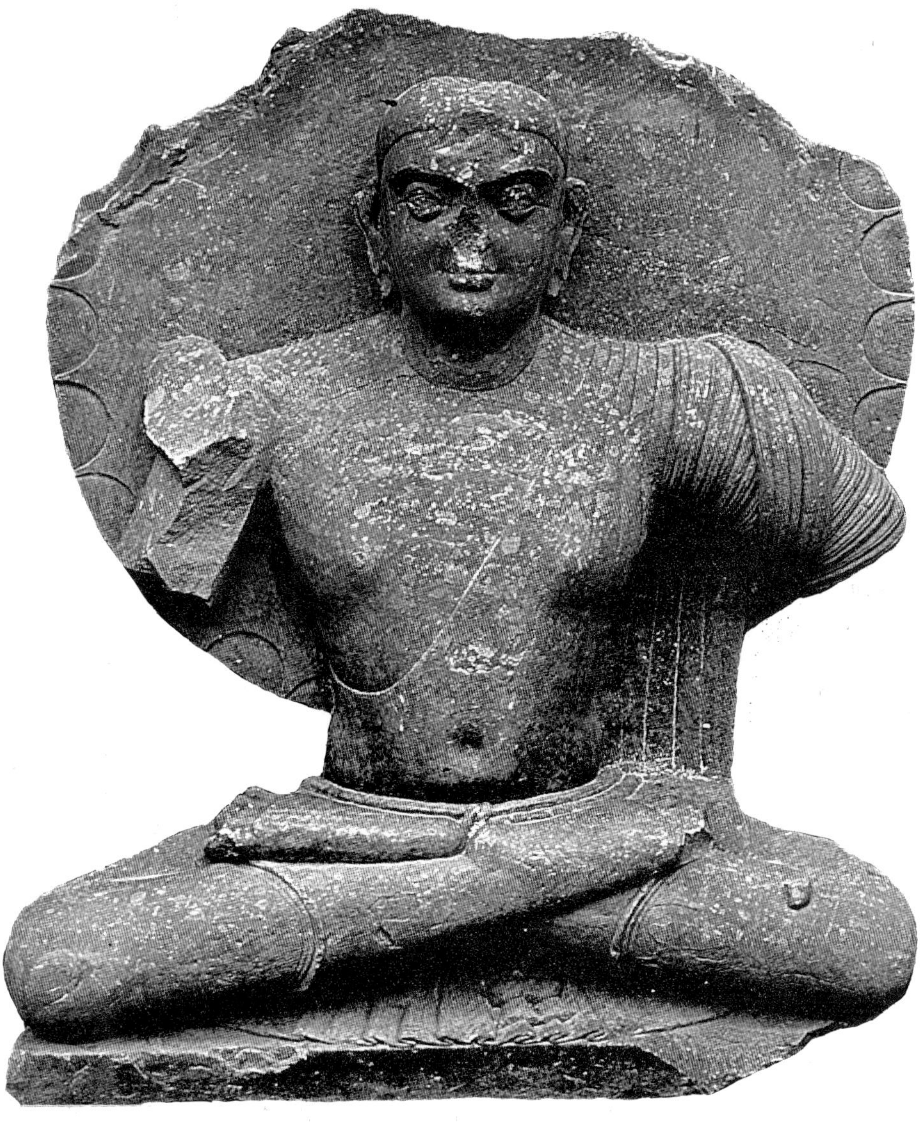

fig. 24. Buddha with large halo, Kuṣāṇa

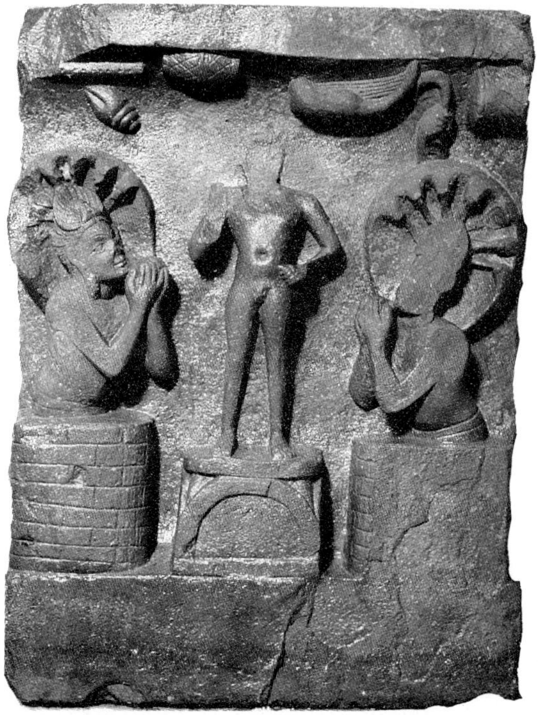

fig. 25. First bath of the Buddha by *Nāgas*, Kuṣāṇa

The bracket on the wall pilaster projects a beautiful Bodhisattva head (16.1239) carved in round and wearing a fluted crown. Turning behind, the second row begins with an independent sculpture (H. 2 from Kaṅkālī mound; *fig. 25*). representing on one side a toilet scene in which a mutilated figure of a lady is seen looking into a mirror and arranging her coiffure, while the man (probably an attendant) holds a basket. But the real interest of the exhibit lies on the other side where the baby Buddha stands on a pedestal. He is worshipped by two *nāgas* who are seen with their hands in adoration. Above, we notice a row of heavenly musical instruments which were played when the Buddha was born. The instruments from right to left are drum, a trumpet being held in the hand (it may be taken as stick for beating the drum), the harp *(pañcatantrī vīṇā)*with five strings, a tabor, a flute and a conch. The colossal Buddha head (A. 27 from Caubārā; *col. ill.* X) bears conspicuous characteristics of the Kuṣāṇa period. viz. the shaven head with an *uṣṇīśa* like a snail shell, round almond shaped open eyes, hollowed mark of *ūrṇā* between the eyebrows; small ear lobe and a smiling expression.

A small square pillar type object put up on a pedestal (P. 67 from Jamālpur) is a rare architectural specimen representing probably a lamp stand *(dīpādhāra)* containing three tiers of niches flanked by Indo-Scythian pilasters. The bottom and top tiers have six niches, the middle one has four, one in each direction. The central tier also consists of standing male figures (devotees) out of the niches and uppermost tier shows ogee arch or *caitya* window motifs on the top of each niche. The piece might have served as *sarvatobhadra* pillar which contained a small figure of deity in each niche and was circumambulated by the devotees. Lower part of a standing male figure (12.214 from Māṭ) with a lion behind and dwarf to his left suggests a bold treatment and a few alien traits. A few small but interesting Buddhist pieces are seen in the showcase 4. Exhibit 34.2367 from Mahādevghāṭ is a crown of some Bodhisattva in which a *dhyānī* Buddha sits in *padmāsana*. On either side he is flanked by two attendants who clasp their hands in adoration. They bear the halo and may be identified as Brahmā and Indra. This composition greatly resembles the famous reliquary of Kaniṣka found at Peshāwar[17]. Stylistically also the two finds are very close. Bodhisattva's head (63.1) wearing a fluted crown and heavy ear-rings is a good specimen, and stele represent the mother goddess Hārītī with children (F. 35 from Bhūteśvar). The small fragment (57.4260 from Gaṇeśara) in the second shelf may represent the decoration of the Rāmagrāma *stūpa*. Slab with nativity scene (15.932 from Rānīwālā well Pālīkherā) where Māyādevī holds the branch of *sāla* tree (from Rānīwālā well Pālīkherā) and Indra's crowned head to right and headless figure of the Buddha turning the Wheel and Law (61.5304). The reverse shows a flute player with two mendicants. The Buddha wearing a chequered drapery (*pānsukūla cīvara* with *pālībandha* and *maryādābandha* (15.514 from Maholī; *fig. 26*) a befitting garment for monk, is also interesting.[18]

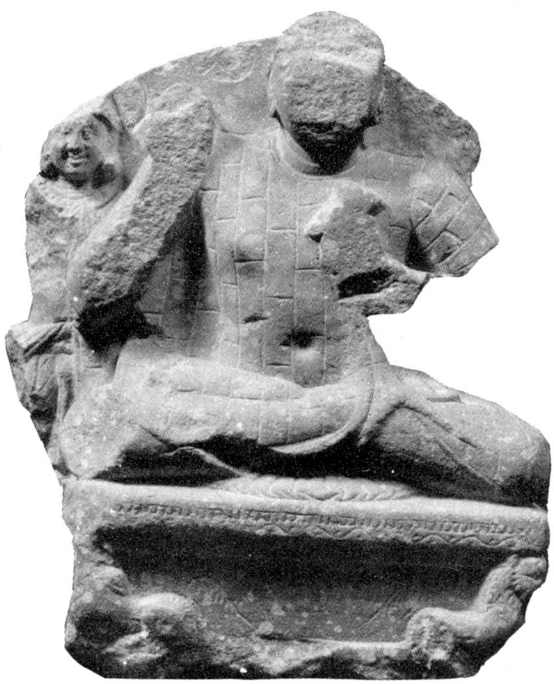

fig. 26. Buddha wearing chequred drapery, Kuṣāṇa

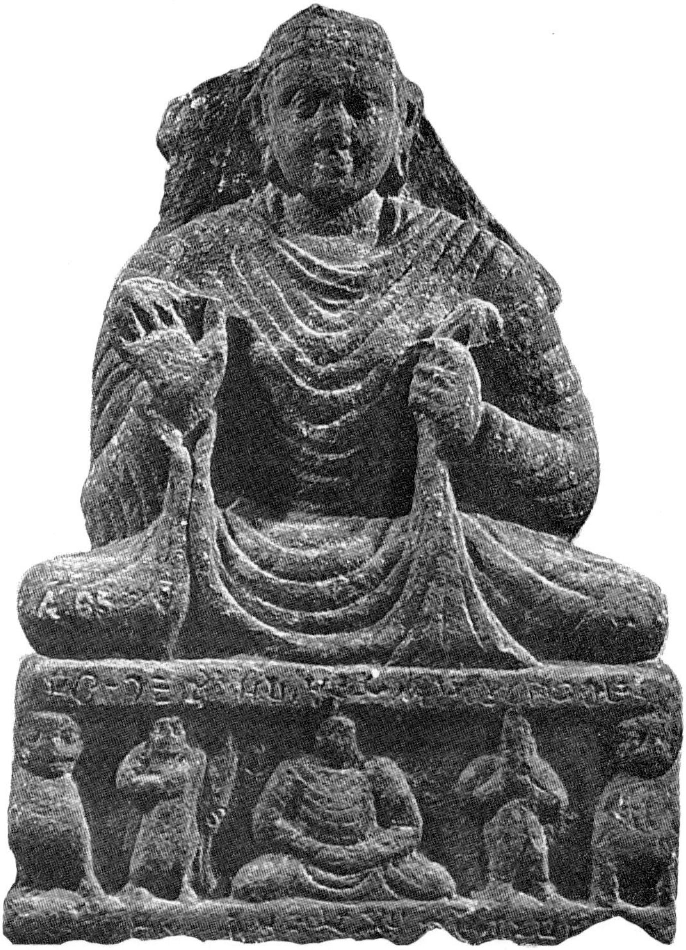

fig. 27. Buddha of the year 51, Kuṣāṇa

The next figure (A. 65 from Anyor; *fig. 27*) bears Gāndhāran influence as seen from the *ubhayānsika sanghāṭī* (drapery covering both the shoulders) with schematic folds.[19] This is one of the most important figures for framing the chronology of the Buddhist iconography in Kuṣāṇa period. It is dated in the year 51 corresponding to 129 A.D. On its pedestal is noticed a small figure of the Buddha in meditating (*dhyāna*) pose, for the first time we come across this attitude in Mathurā art which is known for the protection pose. It appears that the Buddha was represented in the divine form at Mathurā and it was indicated through *abhaya* while meditating posture suggests the human effort. Gāndhāra sculptor derived pleasure in depicting the life cycle of the Buddha. The sculpture bears an inscription which is read as:

1. *Sam 50 gr (i) 3 di (4) asya puvayā...m (a) .. (hāth. grass)*
2. *(sya)..Bo...(t)..a..rya Ma..(nghika)na par(i).(h)-*

In the year 51, in the 3rd (month) of summer on the 4th (?) day, on this date....the Bodhisattva (?). The (gift) of ..,for the acceptance of the teachers (?) the Mahāsāṅghikas.[20]

On the entrance of gallery 3 (consisting of the Gāndhāra sculptures) is a lofty column (Q. 13 from Isāpur). As the epigraph records this sacrificial post (*yajña yūpa*) was installed by certain Droṇala who was *Brāhmaṇa* by caste, in the commemoration of a sacrifice which continued for twelve nights *(dvādaśarātra satra)* in the reign of Vāsiṣka (Śaka era 24-102 A.D.). The antiquity provides an evidence to the fact that beside image worship, the practice of performing the *Vedic Yajñas* was also prevalent.

The inscription is read and translated as follows:

1. *Siddham Mahārājasyas (ā) jat (t) i rājāsya deva (pu)*
2. *trasya Śaher=Vāsiṣkasya rājya-saṁ vatsare (ca)*
3. *turvi śe 24 gri ṣma-māse caturtthe 4 diva (se)*
4. *triṁśe 30 asyāṁ purvvāyāṁ Rudrila putreṇa Droṇa*
5. *lena Brāhmaṇena Bharadvāja-sagottreṇa mā*
6. *ṇa (?) cchandogene iṣṭva satreṇa dvādaśar (ā) trreṇa*
7. *Yūpaḥ pratiṣṭhāpitaḥ Priyantām-agnaya (ḥ)*

"Success in the reign of the King, the King of Kings, His Majesty, Śāhi Vāsiṣka, in the twenty fourth (24th) year, in the fourth (4th) month of summer, on the thirtieth (30th) day-on this date Droṇala, the son of Rudrila, a *Brāhmaṇa* belonging to the *gotra* of Bhāradvāja and a.. chanter of holy hymns, while performing a sacrifice in a (solemn) session of twelve days (lit nights), has set up this sacrifical post. May the (Three) Fires be pleased."[21]

The document is to be compared with the *punyaśālā* inscription No. 29. 1913 in reserve collection from Girdharpur and another inscription in the favour of *Brāhmaṇas* (12.215 A) from Māṭ. Before entering the Gāndhāra gallery in left corner is noticed a fragmentary sculpture (17.1270 from Rāwal) carved with an elephant and a few letters in the *Kharoṣṭhī* script which was used in the northwestern provinces in early India. The letters read as '*sastakhadhātu*' (*śāstā-akṣadhātu*) mean 'the collar-bone relic of the Lord'. The story given in the *Mahāvaṃśa* narrates that Sumana (son of Aśoka's daughter) came to India from Ceylon to take some holy relics of the Buddha as desired by the king of the island. Subsequently, he also went to Indra who handed over the right collar-bone of the Lord (the Buddha). After his return to Ceylon the relic was carried out in a procession on a state elephant. The significance of the sculpture is considerably enhanced to note that this is the only piece outside Ceylon depicting this episode.[22] The stone does not belong to Mathurā and it is quite possible that it was brought from the north-west (now in Pakistan) the ancient region of Kharoṣṭhī inscription. This may be pointed out here that another inscription (17.1271 not displayed) was also acquired from the same spot. It is the copy of an epigraph discovered at Śakardarra well of year 40. The stone is typical which is found in the north-western region. It is a case of forgery

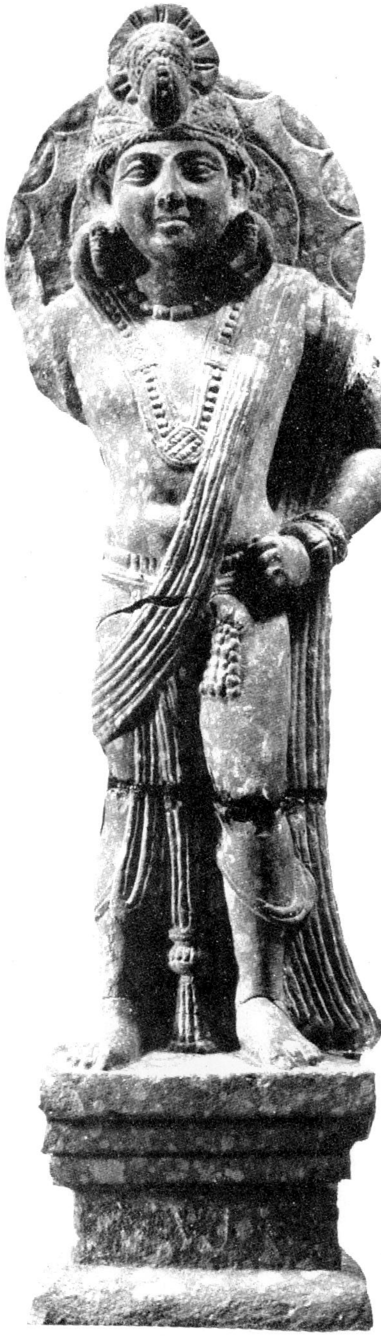

fig. 28. Bodhisattva, Kuṣāṇa

or an attempt to imitate an original record. When it was done cannot be said with certainty but it is very old. The purpose seems to be a magic spell which had its power in the Śakardarra well to secure good water. The same majestic formula was probably applied here. This sheds light on popular concept of lithic record as a kind of magic. These two objects were recovered from Rāwal but in the Museum records the provenance has been mentioned as Barsānā. It seems that the writer who wrote provenance made some confusion between the two places due to the association of Rādhā with both the places. Rāwal was the native place of Rādhā's mother as recorded by Sten Konow also and Barsānā which is more famous is the home town of the father of Rādhā. This tempted some one to write Barsānā for Rāwal. The column of find spot has been filled in at a later stage but it was probably done before Agrawala prepared his catalogue. Still he was not upset by this confusion and based his description on Dr. Sten Konow's paper and gave correct provenance in his catalogue[23].

On the opposite side of the Kharoṣṭhī inscribed slab is seen a small but beautiful standing figure of Bodhisattva (14.485 from Mathurā city; *fig. 28*)wearing crown and other princely ornaments.

References

1. Sharma, R.C., 'Early Phase of Jaina Iconography', In *Chhote Lal Jain Memorial Volume*, 1967, p. 57.
2. Sarasvati, S.K., *A Survey of Indian Sculpture*, 1975, p. 54-55.
3. Ray, N.R., *Maurya and Post Maurya Art*, 1975, p. 52.
4. Vogel, J.Ph, *Catalogue of the Archaeological Museum at Mathurā*, 1910, p. 185.
5. Joshi, N.P. *Mathurā Sculptures*, 1966, p. 17.
6. Agrawala, V.S., *Mathurā Museum Catalogue*, U.P. Historical Society, 1952, pp. 8-9.
7. Agrawala, V.S., *Catalogue of the Mathurā Museum*, *JUPHS*, Vol. XXIII, p. 128.
8. Sharma, R.C., *Buddhist Art of Mathurā*, 1984, ch. 7.
9. Coomaraswamy, A.K., *History of Indian and Indonesian Art*, 1927 p. 56, Footnote No. 5 and 37 and 179.
10. Sharma, R.C., *op.cit.*, p. 173.
11. *Divyāvadānam*, Ed. P.L. Vaidya, 1959, p. 466.
12. Avidūrenidānam, *Nidānakathā*, *Jātaka*, Hindi Sāhitya Sammelan, 1961.
13. The *Lakkhanasutta* chapter of *Divyāvadāna* lists thirty two symbols of great man.
14. Vogel, J. Ph., *Catalogue of the Archaeological Museum* at *Mathurā*, 1910, pp. 47-48.
15. Sharma R.C., *op. cit.*, pp. 176-78.
16. Vogel's *Catalogue*, *op. cit.*, pp. 48-49.
17. Rosenfield, M., *Dynastic Arts of the Kuṣāṇas*, 1967, p. 259.
18. Joshi, N.P., *op. cit.*, p. 83.
19. Van Lehuizen, J.E., *The Scythian Period*, 1949, pp. 188-89.
20. Lüders, *H., Mathurā Inscriptions*, Ed. Janert, K.L. 1961, pp. 170-71.
21. Agrawala, V.S., *op. cit.*, 1951, pp. 136-37.
22. Konow, Sten, *Corpus Inscriptionum Indicarum*, Vol. II. part I, pp. 49-50.
23. Agrawala, V.S., *op. cit.*, p. 151-52.

6

Gāndhāra Sculptures at Mathurā

THE region of Gāndhāran art included north-western provinces of the pre-independent Indian sub-continent and a part of Afghanistan. Its geographical position has made it a meeting place of several cultural currents.[1] Different warrior races viz., Greeks, Scythians, Pārthians and Kuṣāṇas who aspired to conquer the East, first settled here and left their impressions. The fusion of many foreign elements gave birth to a mixed art style known as the Gāndhāra art. It is also called as Greeco-Buddhist, Greeco-Romano-Buddhist and Indo-Hellenistic art. The distinguishing characteristics of this style are: use of dark grey schist stone and stucco in later period, predominance of Greek influence and emphasis on anatomical details. Facial expression and folds of garment of Gāndhāran figures are specially striking features. The art represents Indian themes in foreign style, *yakṣas, garūḍas* and *nāgas* are seen in the guise of Genii, Atlantes, Zens and Herakles. It appears that the non-Indian or Indian sculptors were highly experienced in creating Greek styled art objects.[2] The subject-matter of this art is, however, Indian and mostly Buddhist. It presents mainly figures of Bodhisattva and Buddha, *jātaka* events and the life story of the Buddha. The Gāndhāra School of Art is sometimes credited for creating the first Buddha image although Mathurā has a strong claim.[3]

The dating of the Gāndhāra art is a highly disputed subject. But for a few images dated to an unknown era, no positive evidence has yet come to light. It is rather surprising to note that the Gāndhāra sculptor, who was expected to have a scientific historical attitude due to his association with West, has been so neglectful towards putting date on his product.[4] On the other hand his colleague working in the Mathurā studio is found to be careful. The general consensus about the dating of the Gāndhāra art, however, favours as early 1st century A.D. as the starting point while its blooming phase was the Kuṣāṇa period. The important sites which have revealed the Gāndhāra antiquities are Takhte-Bāhī, Haḍḍā, Jamālgaḍhī, Taxila, Charsaḍḍa, Hotī Mardān, Shabājgaḍī etc.[5] A few sculptures representing this style in the Mathurā Museum are:

Kambojikā (F. 42 from Saptarṣī mound; *fig. 29*)

The central figure shows a well dressed graceful royal lady whose hair arrangement

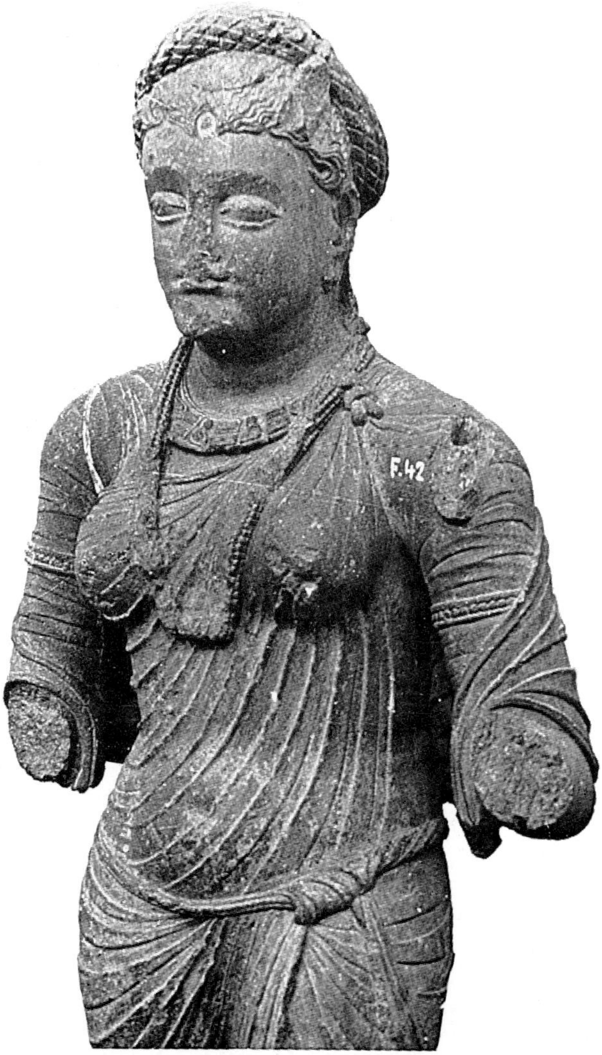

fig. 29. Kambojikā / Hārītī, pre-Kuṣāṇa, Gāndhāra

is remarkable. A wreath is seen fastened with fillets and an ornamental tress showing bead and floral motif suspends on her back. Its local provenance Saptarṣi mound has led some scholars to conjecture that the image might represent Kambojikā, wife of the Kṣatrapa king Rājuvala who has been mentioned in the lion capital found from the same site. Others identify it as Hārītī image brought from Gāndhāra to serve as model for the Hārītī figures, made at Mathurā. Traces of some figure (?) on her left shoulder are also seen. Vogel opined that it was evidently imported from North-west to serve as example for the sculptures of Mathurā.[6]

Small objects are placed in the showcases and we begin from the left.

Dīpaṅkara jātaka (18.1543 from Madhuban)

Fragment from the drum of a *stūpa* depicting mainly the story of *Dīpaṅkara jātaka* which runs as follows:

Dīpaṅkara was the earliest of the twenty-four Buddhas. Once while he was to visit the city of Rammaka, the king had reserved all available flowers to receive the Buddha with due respect. A young ascetic Sumati or Sumedha was also eager to pay homage but he felt distressed in getting no flowers for the purpose. He then saw a young girl carrying a few lotuses. The girl agreed to part with some flowers after a promise from Sumati that she would be his wife in all future births. When Dīpaṅkara arrived Sumati threw flowers over him forming a half circle a round his (Dīpaṅkara's) head instead of falling on the ground. Subsequently, he knelt before Dīpaṅkara and spread his hair requesting him to rest his feet to avoid mud and then he flew in air. Dīpaṅkara later predicted that Sumati would be born as Śākyamuni Buddha.

Here the fourth figure is that of the girl who is offereing flowers to Sumati after the vow. The third figure represents Sumati throwing flowers over Dīpaṅkara who stands with a large halo behind his head. At his feet kneels Sumati spreading his hair and he is again seen hovering in air.

Life Events-Birth (34.2530)

Māyādevī, the holy mother stands cross legged holding the branch of a tree in the Lumbini gardens. To her right Indra is seen receiving the child. Mahāprajāpati, sister of the queen, is assisting. The last figure is of a female attendant holding a waterpot in her right hand and a palm branch in the left.

At the school (34.2531)

It portrays the prince Siddhārtha at the school. His teacher sage Viśvāmitra, astonished to note the extraordinary wisdom with which the student was already equipped, helplessly clasps his hands in adoration before the prince who is seen explaining something. The top of the panel consists of a fragmentary railing with lotus carving.

Meditation (34.2537)

The Buddha sits in meditation under the *bodhi* tree symbolised by a canopy of four big leaves. He wears *ubhayānsika sanghāṭī* (upper garment covering both shoulders). Plain halo, wavy hair, schematic parallel lines of drapery and projecting acanthus leaves represent typical Gāndhāra features.

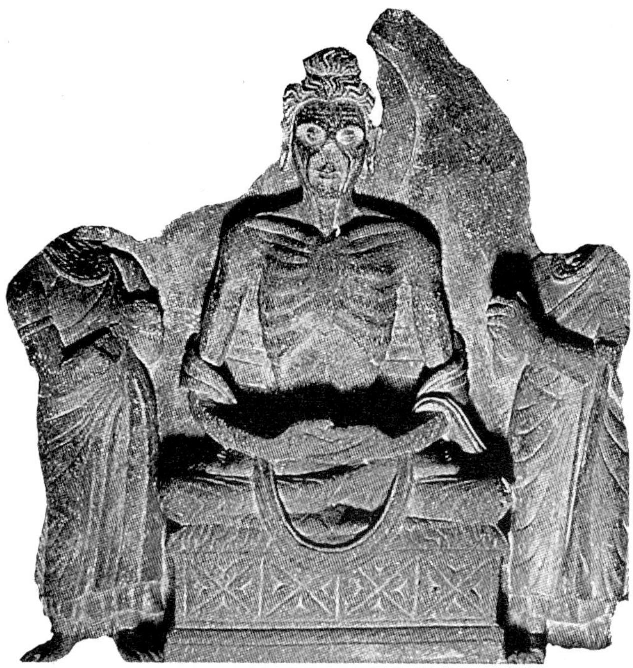

fig. 30. Fasting Buddha, Kuṣāṇa, Gāndhāra

Penance (18. 1550 from Madhuban, Maholī; *fig. 30*)

It is a remarkable sculpture representing the Buddha in penance. The Gāndhāra artist was much careful in carving the body details to show forceful realism. Here the fasting Buddha's physical condition has been shown by ribs and bones, emaciated belly and sunken facial expression. He is flanked by Trapuṣa and Bhallika, two wealthy merchants who offered him food subsequently.

Meditation (34.2536)

This sculpture shows Buddha under the *bodhi* tree. From the position of broken hands it appears that he was in the *vyākhyāna* (preaching) attitude. The conventionalised treatment of leaves and particularly moustache-bearing face of the Buddha is the result of Hellenistic influence. The *uṣṇīśa* (bump of hair) on his head is unusually large. The attendant with folded hands may be Indra as can be gathered from the traces of his high crown.

Gods Pay Homage (11. 161)

The Buddha after Enlightenment is requested by the gods to preach the Law. Indra and Brahmā are seen to the right and left respectively. Their superior position has been conveyed by carving of halo round their heads.

Jyotiṣka (27-28. 1685; *fig 31*)

When the Buddha was camping at Rājagṛha, he for his alms reached the house of Subhadra who was a follower of the *Nirgrantha* (Jaina) sect. On an enquiry about the child which his wife was expecting, the Buddha made a prophecy that it would be a

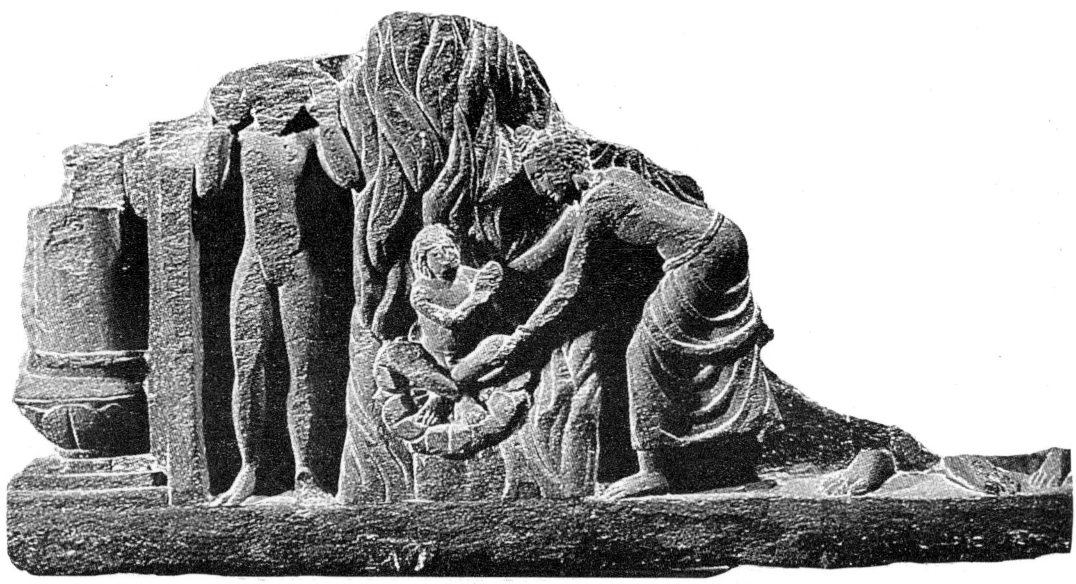

fig. 31. Birth of Jyotiṣka, Kuṣāṇa, Gāndhāra

son and an asset to the family. Subhadra was very happy to hear this and offered suitable alms. This greatly upset the followers of the other sect who declared that the child would be inauspicious bringing misfortune to him. Subhadra's wife thereupon took some medicine which instead of causing abortion proved fatal. When her body was being cremated, delivery was caused through the efforts of Jīvaka (Buddha's physician). As the child was born and taken out of the flames he was known as Jyotiṣka and was later brought up by king Bimbisāra. Here Jīvaka is seen receiving the child. From the traces of feet it is certain that two persons were standing nearby. Out of them one must have been the Buddha.[7]

Apalāla (34.2540)

The upper panel bears figures of three standing devotees while the lower concentric arch represents the episode of Nāga Apalāla. Once when the Buddha was touring the Swāt Valley region, he was informed about the evil deeds of the *Nāga* king Apalāla who used to cause flood in the area for his selfish motives. Being asked by the Buddha to set him right, Vajrapāṇi began to strike on the mountain so furiously with his thunderbolt that Apalāla had to come out and stand in adoration before the Buddha for compromise. Here Vajrapāṇi is seen smitting the mountain while Apalāla with a five headed serpent hood stands frightened. The figure of the Buddha is missing.

Buddha Refuses Anupamā (18.1545 from Madhuban, Maholī)

A *Brāhmaṇa* ascetic Mākandika who was highly impressed with Buddha's personality (physical beauty) aspired to offer him his charming daughter Aunpamā in marriage. But the Enlightened One, who had renunciated all worldly pleasure, declined the proposal. Here the *Brāhmaṇa* ascetic is shown with a water pot in his upraised right hand indicating his determination for the gift. On the right side of the Buddha the beautiful young girl stands in suspense.

A Discourse (34.2538)

A panel with group of four persons listening to some discourse, above is the headless bust of a lady on a railing. It may possibly represent the interpretation of Māyā's dream or horoscope reading.

Bimbisāra's Welcome (34.2541)

In the upper panel the frieze consists of garland bearing *yakṣas*. Each loop of the garland bears a five petalled projecting flower. Below four persons are seen marching forward with lotuses in their hands perhaps to receive some dignitary. This should portray the visit of the Buddha at Rājagṛha at the invitation of king Bimbisāra after Enlightenment. The idea of the town has been communicated through the city gate. The next slab (34.2542) seems to be another version of the same episode. Here the king has been shown with a halo round his head.

Buddha (34.2543)

The Buddha sits in meditation wearing an *ubhayānsika sanghāṭī*, the hair is arranged in wavy lines forming a central knot *(uṣṇīśa)* and *urṇā* in relief is marked between the two eyebrows. Expression of the face is very youthful. The pedestal shows five meditating Buddhas under *pīpala* leaves.

Ornamental frieze (18.1553 from Madhuban, Maholī)

Frieze showing three ornamental niches containing a boy with bunch of flowers, a man sitting in commanding attitude and the Buddha in meditation respectively. The other friezes (34.2534 and 34.2535) from the drum of a *stūpa* show human figures in compartments separated by Indopersepolitan pilasters. The lower band has latticed window motif. Another (18.1556 from Madhuban Maholī) is a panel carved with two garland bearing erotes. One is nude and probably takes out a thorn from his right foot. The loops of the wreath also bear human busts holding some object in the right hand.

Other Bodhisattvas

The Gāndhāra sculptor has portrayed the figures of other Bodhisattvas of whom two are seen here. As already pointed out royal attire differentiates a Bodhisattva from the Buddha who is shown in the monk's dress. The present sculpture (27-28. 1689) represents Siddhārtha in meditation. The next two exhibits (16.1255, from Barsānā and 27-28.1686) show Bodhisattva Maitreya (Buddha to be born) wearing amulets and holding a flask (*amṛta ghaṭa*). These two features are generally not seen with Siddhārtha.

Atlantes (11.160)

The small stele bears an atlantes (giant) in the load bearing attitude. Heavy muscular body clearly suggests Greek influence. Depiction of such figures was a favourite theme of the Gāndhāra artists.

Stuccos head (49.3476 from Taxila)

In later period (3rd century A.D.) stucco started to be used more often as medium of sculpture making. It was sometimes painted with colour. This meditating Buddha figure bears traces of red colour.

Therefore, to conclude, the Gāndhāra art could not make significant contribution to the development of Indian plastic art. It, however, influenced the contemporary art of Mathurā which adopted some motifs on the exchange basis. The acanthus leaf decoration, wavy hair, drapery covering both shoulders, Bacchanalian scenes, moustaches, Maitreya with crescent mark, garland bearing erotes, Atlantes shaped *yakṣas* sandalled feet of Bodhisattva, round pillars with Corinthian capital, figures in niches as separating units, Vajrapāṇi, Pañcika and Hārītī or Kubera with Hārītī, foreigners with conical caps, woman victimised by Garuḍa, drapery with schematic fold in bold relief etc. are the notable Gāndhāran features which have occasionally appeared in the Kuṣāṇa art of Mathurā. But these elements began to disappear after the Kuṣāṇas and almost completely washed away during the Indian renaissance in the Gupta age.

The Gāndhāra sculptor on the other hand borrowed the following motifs and themes from the Mathurā artist: drapery covering one shoulder, wheel on palms (rare), notched hair, lion throne, lotus seat, lotus, creeper, *vedikā* design for dividing a panel, four or five rectangles of diminishing size, lady with parrot, woman and tree *(śālabhañjikā)*, deities emancipating from the body of the main figure, lion supporting the door jamb, elephants, peacock etc.[8]

References

1. Rowland, Benjamin, *The Art and Architecture of India* 1967, p. 100.
2. Nehru, Lalita, *Origins of the Gāndhāran Style*, 1989, pp. 59-65.
3. Sharma R.C., *Buddhist Art of Mathurā*, 1984, ch. 7.
4. Agrawala, V.S., *Indian Art*, 1965 p. 237.
5. *Ibid.*, p. 26.
6. Vogel, J.Ph., *Catalogue of the Archaeological Museum at Mathurā*, 1910, p. 118.
7. *Divyāvadānam* (19th episode) ed. P.L. Vaidya, 1961, pp. 162-79.
8. Joshi, N.P. and Sharma, R.C., *Catalogue of Gāndhāra Sculptures in the State Museum, Lucknow*, 1969, pp. 27-37.

7

Diversity of Kuṣāṇa Art

THE Mathurā School of Sculptural Art not only evolved and grew further in the Kuṣāṇa period but it also fructified in different forms.[1] Pantheon developed manifold, folk and traditional deities assimilated with the newly emerging divinities of whom some hailed from foreign lands. With high demand the number of ateliers increased and the town became an important centre of manufacturing and export of images and architectural components to be consecrated and used in distant quarters. It also had a good deal of interaction with the Gāndhāra School of which some specimens were found in and around the city.

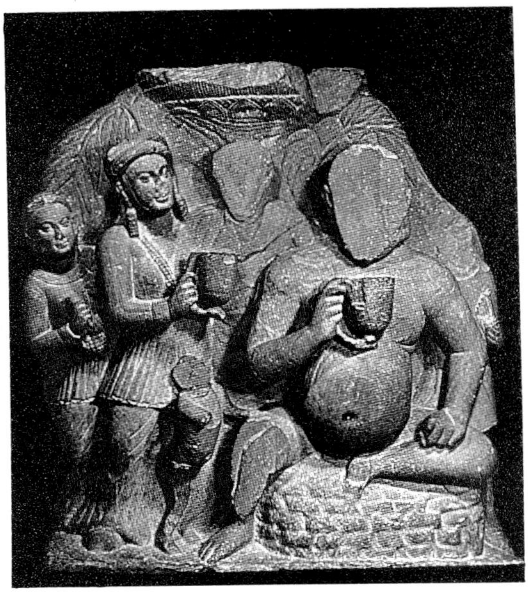

fig. 32. Kubera enjoying drink, Kuṣāṇa

Leaving the bay the visitor looks at a pot bellied man enjoying wine (*āsava*) served by a lady in the ornamental cups (C. 2 Pālīkherā; *fig.* 32). The adverse effect of excessive drinking is to be noticed on the other side where he is portrayed in a helpless state supported by two attendants. The identification of this scene poses a problem. Three such drinking scenes have been acquired from Mathurā (now one in Calcutta and the other in New Delhi) and are called as Bacchanalian (*apānagoṣṭhī*) scenes. The dress of the attendants, facial features and nudity of children show considerable Greek influence. But the pot bellied man figure clad in Indian style and sitting on a rocky platform can be identified as Kubera on the mountain Sumeru/Kailāśa.[2] This shows that contemporary Mathurā art was influenced by the Greek traditions which percolated through Gāndhāra.[3]

The next figure (C. 3 from Maholī)[4] placed on the wall side shows a corpulent man with pot belly and large head. A scarf is tied to balance the stomach. Although the image is disproportionate yet an expression of happiness is noticed on the face. The arms (now missing) were probably raised up to hold a vessal (*pātravāhaka*)[5] and the complete figure must have resembled an Atlantes from Gāndhāra region. Such fat and dwarfish statues have generally been called as Kubera (the god of wealth), a term which etymologically means a bad figure. (*Ku+bera*).[6]

Behind the Kaṭrā Buddha are seen some other Bodhisattva images. Seated image of Bodhisattva Maitreya (future Buddha) is adorned with a large number of ornaments (A. 45 from Ganeśarā). This *Brāhmaṇic* association is understood through the wearing of amulated sacred thread. Garuḍa motif suggesting light and knowledge is marked on the armlets. Behind is seen the Buddha image (head missing) with inscribed pedestal (78.34, from Govardhan bypass, Mathurā; *fig.* 33) seated cross legged in *padmāsana*, wearing *cakra* and *triratna* on soles, right hand raised in *abhaya* with webbed features, bearing several auspicious marks on palm and finger tips. Elbow of the left arm is missing and the hand rests on the knee. The *ekānsika sanghāṭī* has an additional covering of pleats, while the head is missing. The fragmentary large halo is decorated with several bands. The inscription informs that it was installed by *Kāyastha* Bhaṭṭipriya. The spotted red sandstone statue belongs to the second century A.D.

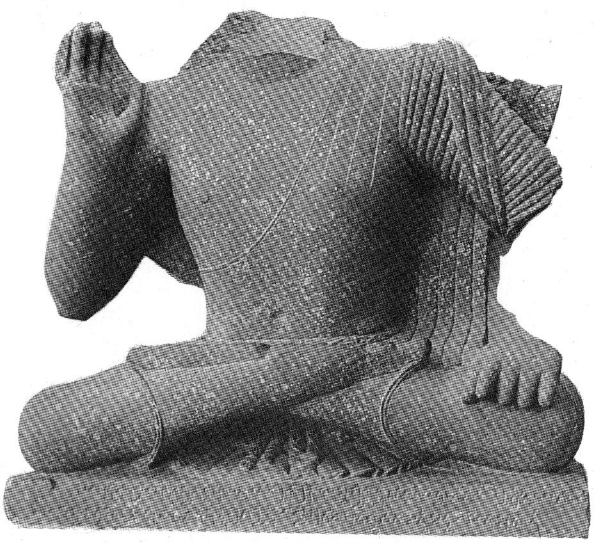

fig. 33. Inscribed Buddha image, Kuṣāṇa

The two line inscription is read as under :

1. *(Bha) ṭṭisena putrasya Bhaṭṭihasti pautrasya Bhaṭṭipriyasya hemakare kayasthasya kutunibiniya grahadīnasya pitu yaśāye*
2. *Hatisya Dattasya ca mātare Bhagavato Buddhasya Sākyamunisya pratimā pratiṣṭhāpitā sarvasattvānām hitasukhārthaṁ*

> The image of Śākyamuni Buddha was set up for the welfare of all beings by Yaśā, daughter (?) of Grahadīna, mother of Hasti and Datta and housewife of goldsmith (?) *Kāyastha* Bhaṭṭipriya who is the son of Bhaṭṭisena and grandson of Bhaṭṭihasti.

The colossal Bodhisattva (38.2798 from Maholī) through its volume, drapery and pose reminds the early *yakṣa* traditions. Wearing an *ekānsika sanghāṭī* he rests his left hand on the waist. A cluster of lotus is placed between his feet. If Prof. Härtel's inclination to identify this object as Siddhārtha's turban is upheld, its position below feet suggests the inferiority of kingship before the Buddhahood, a feature often noticed in the contemporary images. This sculpture belongs to the early Bodhisattva figures of Kauśāmbī and Sārnāth dated in the second and third regnal year of Kaniṣka. Just near this image an inscription (No. 38.2801 not displayed) was found. It is read as :

1. *Saṁ 90 2 he. di 5 asyapūrvvayaṁ*
2. *Khaṇḍa vihāre vasthavya bhikṣusa graha*
3. *dāsikasa sthuve pratishṭhapayati sa*
4. *rva satvanaṁ hitasukhāye*

> "In the year 92 the first month of *hemanta*, on the fifth day, on this date in the *stūpa* of monk Grahadāsika a resident of Khaṇḍavihāra monastery, establishes for the welfare and happiness of all sentient beings".[7]

On the basis of this inscription, Agrawala dates the Maholī Buddha to 170 A.D. But this is not acceptable to Van Lohuizen who thinks that Kapardin type figures should be dated only in 1st century A.D. preferably to pre-Kuṣāṇa period. Moreover, the inscription notes the part of the image and it does not specify the purpose for which the document was written. Hence the inscription should not be associated with the image which betrays earlier features.[8]

Buddha's Life-Events

Behind, against the wall are displayed some friezes representing the life-events of the Buddha.

The slab (H. I from Rājghāt, Mathurā) represents main life-events of the Buddha. From the right the first is his birth where Māyādevī stands under a *śāla* tree assisted by Mahāprajāpati, her sister, to left and to right Indra receives the baby. Below is seen his first bath by the two *Nāgas* — Nanda and Upananda. The birth scene is followed by his penance at Bodhgayā below the *pīpal* tree. Daughter of Māra is trying to disturb him and Māra himself is seen below shooting with his flower-arrow. But the earth touching attitude (*bhūmisparśa mudrā*) of the (would be) Buddha confirms his firm determination. Next is noticed his descent from heaven after preaching the Law to his mother. The Buddha in centre is accompanied by Brahmā and Indra on different ladders. The next scene depicts the Buddha in *abhaya* pose but from the lower scene, showing worship of the Wheel of Law on a pillar (*dharma-cakrastambha*) it appears that the sculptor intended to represent the first sermon at Sārnāth. The last scene portrays the demise of the Buddha (*mahāparinirvāṇa*) at Kuśīnagar.

The architectural fragment on the wall H. 8 is a forceful depiction of the great demise of the Master who with a large halo is seen lying on a cot resting his head over a pillow. In the background three mourners express their grief through different actions. One of them places his hand over the head while the other raises his arms, the third weeps and covers his face with a scarf. Towards the Buddha's feet stand three persons of whom one wearing the monk's chequered dress is Mahākaśyapa. The man on the opposite side looks a devotee. Below the couch are carved three more figures. From the left the first is Vajrapāṇi who on the sad event placed his *vajra* (thunderbolt) on the ground. The second is a simple worshipper while the third meditating ascetic is Subhadra, the last disciple of the Buddha. His earlier association with the *Brāhmaṇa* sect *tridaṇḍa*, has been conveyed by a triple pronged staff seen to his left. The Buddha breathed his last between the two *śāla* trees out of which only one with the figure of a celestial showering flowers, is extant.

The Bodhisattva's meditating posture (46.3231 from Maholī; *fig. 34*) suggests that

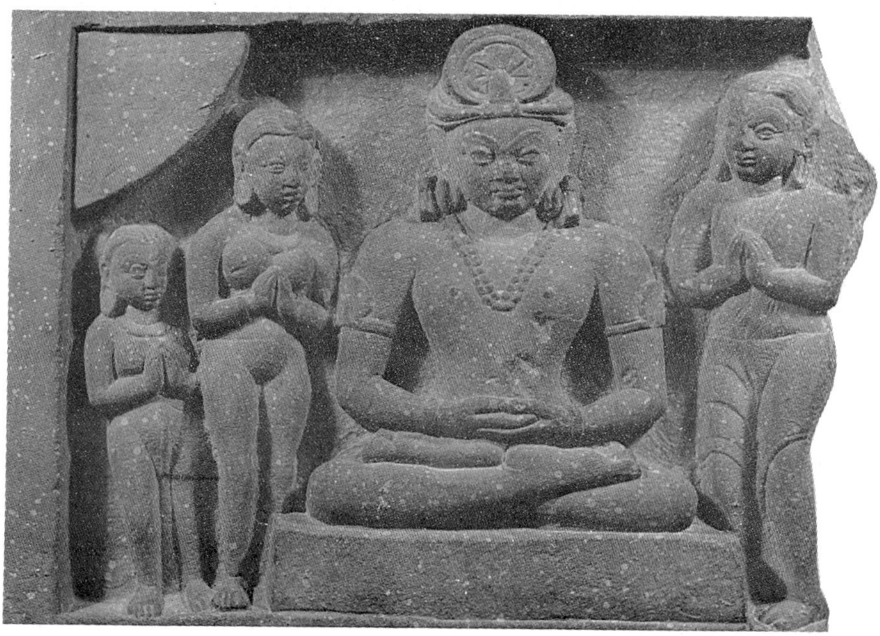

fig. 34. Siddhārtha in meditation, Kuṣāṇa

attainment of the highest goal (*nirvāṇa*) was not the monopoly of ascetics. This is what the great contemporary Buddhist poet Aśvaghoṣa also remarks.[9]

The pedestal in foreground displays three architectural components of a votive *stūpa* as under:

1. Square pedestal (20.1605 from Gokaṇeśvar, Mathurā) representing the Buddha in several compartments separated by heavy pilasters. Flanked by devotees he is seen either meditating or preaching or touching the earth or imparting protection. It belongs to about 4th century A.D.
2. Circular drum of a *stūpa* (N. 2) depicting different life events of the Buddha separated by Indo-Corinthian pilasters. These are birth, first anointment by the two *nāga* chiefs Nanda and Upananda, penance and vow, first sermon, the demise, *gandhakuṭī*, descent from heaven, offering of alms by the four guardian deities, homage of Indra and Pañcaśikha gandharva inside a cave. This should belong to the 2nd century A.D.
3. Votive *stūpa* (N. 1 from Jamālpur) carved with the figures of the Buddha seated in the *abhaya* (protection) pose facing four directions. These are intervened by blank arches. The plain *aṇḍa* emerges upon a decorated frieze showing the garland bearing erotes. The inscription on top records: *Nusapriyāye Śuranasya ditu*-(gift) of Nuśapriyā, the daughter of Śurana. This early sculpture belonging to late 1st century A.D. probably came from the Jamālpur mound near the Collectorate. The piece is not only weather worn but also vertically split up in two parts.

Another pedestal in this gallery (4) on one side displays a corpulent *yakṣa* carrying a bowl over his head (77.31 from Govindnagar; *fig.* 35). Bearing a mysterious smile he has a large head but small arms. The eyes are wide open and the ears are also big *śūrpakarṇa*.

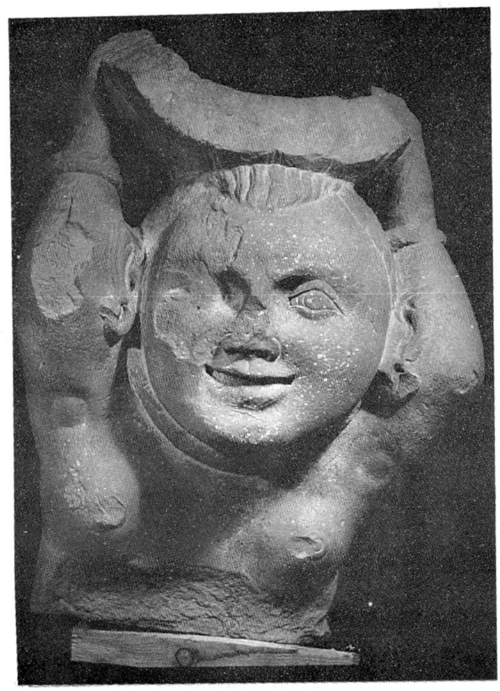

fig. 35. Yakṣa with bowl, Kuṣāṇa

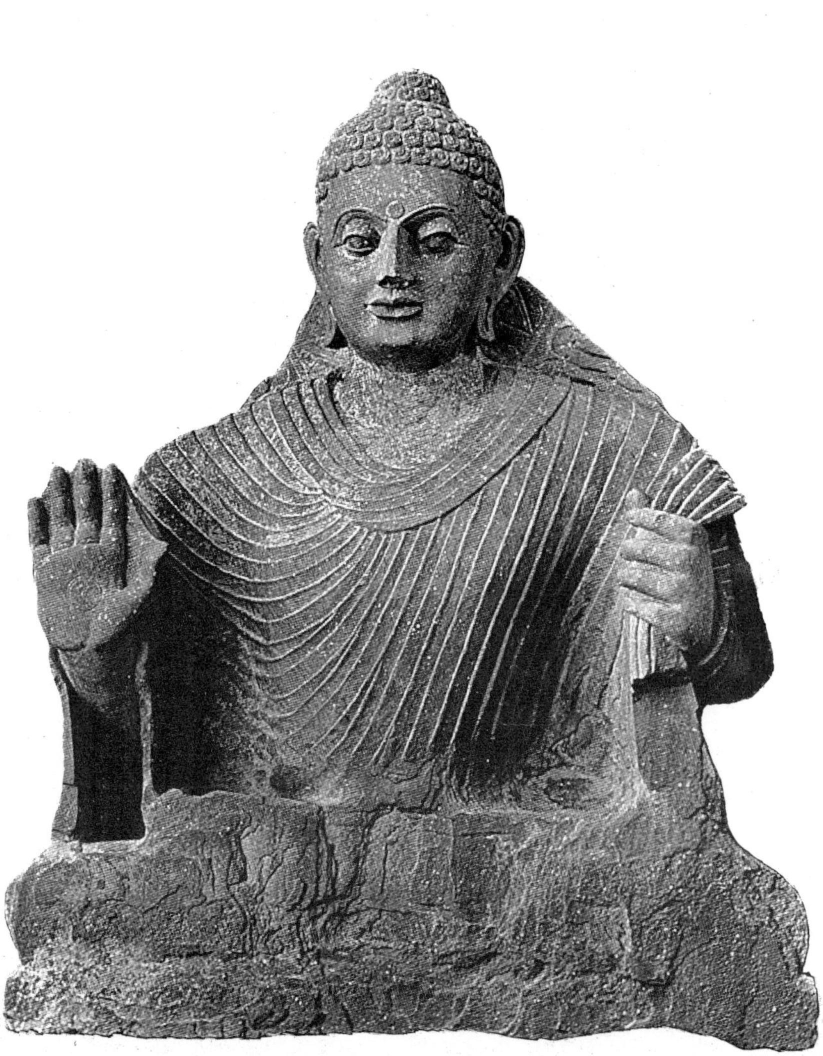

fig. 36. Buddha with thick garment, Kuṣāṇa

On the other side is the seated Buddha (76.17 from Govindnagar; *fig. 36*). It belongs to the late Kuṣāṇa phase when the Gāndhāra idiom had overwhelmingly dominated the Mathurā School. This is particularly reflected by thick pleats in the garment, one overlapping the other, and making a master pleat on the elbow. The curly hair is tied in a tuft and the eyebrows are drawn up with a circular (*ūrṇā*) mark projecting from the forehead. The frontal *abhay* posture of the right hand shows a net behind the fingers (*jālagrathitāṅguli*), a feature of the 'Great Man' (*mahāpuruṣa lakṣaṇa*). The half raised left hand holds the hem of the drapery. There are traces of halo behind the head. It bore full blown lotus, scalloped and beaded bands and arrows.

The wall side towards east displays the following exhibits from left to right:

1. A double sided buff sand stone seated small yakṣa with a tenon above (C. 25 from Vināyaka ṭīlā, Mathurā).
2. Lion throne (76.167 from Govindnagar) with four pegs and row of projecting lion heads supporting a band of niches with human heads, another band of ornamental railing and battlements repeated in four directions. This is a unique discovery from the site.
3. Stele carved with the figure probably of Maitreya holding a pitcher and wearing a sacred thread (76.24 from Govindnagar).
4. A small umbrella again from Govindnagar (76.172).
5. Headless bust of Maitreya (A.46 from Jamālpur) with locks of hair falling on both the shoulders. He wears a beaded necklace, flat necklace, another neck and shoulder ornament and a large and heavy necklace with eight pearl strings issuing from crocodile head on top and bottom. Finally, a large rosette designed medal with nine vertical heads suspends on the chest. An amulated sacred thread hangs to the right side.
6. Buddha seated in meditation (76.19 from Govindnagar) wearing shutter type thick *sanghāṭī* bespeaking of heavy Gāndhāra impact.

The fore part of lion (O. 4) either served as corner slab to protect a building or stood on the entrance. The anatomy reflects vigour and force.

The Māṭ Portraits

On either side of the main entrance of the Museum are some royal statues. Acquired in 1912 by late Pt. Radha Krishna from Iṭokri mound in village Māṭ 16 km. north of Mathurā (as the crow flies), the statues of the Kuṣāṇa/Śaka rulers have a significant place in the history of the Museum collection. Inception of portrait figures was a unique experiment of the Mathurā sculptor. An inscription on the pedestal of the Vema image records that a *devakula* which in all probabilities can be taken as a Śaiva temple or shrine was constructed in the beginning of the Kuṣāṇa rule. This may further be pointed out that the Kuṣāṇa rulers often used the title '*devaputra*' and some scholars opine that the term *devakula* should be interpreted as a gallery presenting the statues of *devaputras* (Kuṣāṇa Emperors). The mighty rulers aimed at enjoying a divine status and propagated this idea by installing these images which were probably worshipped also.[10] But the word '*devīkula*' occurring in an *āyāgapaṭṭa* (Q. 2 described in ch. 5) means a shrine.

Vema Kadphises (12.215 from Māṭ; *col. ill. XI*)

Seated on a lion throne the king wears a long coat, trousers and boots. Embroidery on the drapery is noteworthy. From the position of the right hand it appears that he held a sword. Through this majestically enthroned monarch the sculptor has conveyed the idea of the might and prowess of the Kuṣāṇa kings. This quite agrees with the high sounding epithets known from the legends of his coins as '*sarvalokaīśvara*' (the lord or the whole world). As already indicated, the space between the feet of the king bears an inscription which records the construction of a *devakula* (temple or gallery), a garden (*ārāma*), tank (*puṣkariṇi*), a well (*udapāna*) etc. by Bakapati Hum . . .(?)

Considering different aspects, Prof. Mitterwallner furnishes the relevant information alongwith the rendering of epigraph as under :

1. *Mahārājo rājātirājo devaputra*
2. *Kuṣanaputra* (*o*) (*sa*) *hi-V* (*e*) *ma Ta* (*kṣu*) *masya*
3. *bakanapatina Humanṣphalena devakula* (*ṁ*) *kāritā*
4. *ārāmo puṣkariṇi udapāna* (*ṁ*) *ca sa* (*bh*) *ā dāra koṭhaka*

"(This is) the *mahārāja*, the *rājādhirāja*, the *devaputra*, the Kuṣāṇa *putra* (=the son of the Kuṣāṇa). The *devakula* of the Ṣāhi—V (e) ma-takṣuma, the garden, lotus tank and well, the assembly hall (and) the gateway were caused to be made (*kāritā*) by the *bakanapati* Humasphala."

Vema was the predecessor of Kaniṣka and ruled from about 40 to 78 A.D. He is also mentioned as Māheśvara in his coins, a fact which hints that he had adopted Śaivism. Śiva with Nandī (bull) is seen frequently portrayed on his coins. In the light of the discovery of a stone inscription (Mathurā Museum No. 71.8 from near Caurāsī) *devakula* appears to be a popular term for a Śaiva shrine. The present inscription giving his name as Vema Takṣama hints that the Kuṣāṇas probably belong to Śaka tribe from Iran where Tassama meant owner of strong horses.[12]

Kaniṣka (12.213 from Māṭ; *col. ill. XII*)

Facing Vema stands his successor Kaniṣka, the most powerful king of the Kuṣāṇa dynasty and one of the most important figures of Indian history. He was a great patron of art and literature. The famous poet and philosopher Aśvaghoṣa and scholars like Pārśva, Vasumitra, Saṅgharakṣaka and the renowned physician and chemist Nāgārjuna, exponent of Mahāyāna doctrine, are believed to have flourished in this period and enjoyed Kaniṣka's favour.[13] Both Mathurā and Gāndhāra Schools of Art were at the zenith of glory in his time. In historic India Mathurā never received greater importance than in Kaniṣka's reign when it became an important headquarter of Kuṣāṇa Empire. He favoured Buddhism and the 4th Buddhist Council was held under his patronage. According to the Buddhist traditions Kaniṣka has been mentioned to have possessed the supernatural power also. This justifies his title of *devaputra* and also suggests a deep impression of his personality. Kaniṣka's reign was the golden period of Mathurā School of Art.

He is represented as a warrior wearing long tunic, trousers and heavy boots. The right hand supports a big mace (?) which has five ornamental bands and a *makara* (?) motif below. A sword with decorated scabbard hangs to his left side. The grip of the left hand holding the hilt is conspicuous. The folds of the drapery are indicated through incised lines. The inscription in the *Brāhmī* characters reads: '*Mahārājā Rājātirājā Devaputro Kaniṣko*'-'the great king, king of kings *Devaputra* (the son of god) Kaniṣka'. The portrait may be assigned to the early days of the Emperor as his costume is seen on the coins of his predecessor Vema only.

The coins of Kaniṣka or his successor do not show this style. The fashion was probably discarded just after the accession of Kaniṣka.

Caṣṭana (12.212)

Torso next to the statue of Vema represents Caṣṭana or Ṣaṣtana, or Maṣṭana as known from the *Brāhmī* letters inscribed on his tunic or overcoat above the right knee. His dress shows minute and fine embroidery work. The folds of the trousers (*salvāra*) are very schematic and the belt consists of several square and round medallions carved with different decorative motifs and the traces of sword seen to his left. A simple necklace with a drum shaped bead is worn round the neck. Stylistically, this life-size slim figure has been executed very realistically and displays great skill of the sculptor in making human portraits.

Caṣṭana was the founder of the Śaka-Kṣatrapa dynasty of Western India with his capital at Ujjain. The installation of his image in the *devakula* of Māṭ may hint to some relationship between the Śakas and Kuṣāṇas, probably a contemporary of Kaniṣka.[14]

The torso of another prince (43.3085) facing Caṣṭana was acquired from Gokarṇeśvara. Like the other Śaka-Kuṣāṇa chiefs, he also wears a long coat and trousers. This type of stitched dress which became a typical fashion in northern part of the country is mentioned as *udīcya veṣa* (Northern Style).[15] The deity under worship on the spot also appears as a Kuṣāṇa king.

Sūrya images

The Sūrya (sun) images were greatly influenced by the northern style of dress. The early figures of this deity look like a Scythian prince. The specimens on the right wall of gallery 5 show the inconography of Sūrya in three centuries. The first (12.269 from Kaṅkālī; *col. ill. XIII*) is one of the earliest figures in the collection of the Museum. Wearing a tunic with embroidery work, trousers and plump boots and holding a dagger in the left hand, the deity looks like a Kuṣāṇa king. The necklace with a central bead quite resembles the ornament worn by Caṣṭana. He wears a helmet, earrings (*kuṇḍala*) and the locks of hair fall on both the shoulders. *Ūrṇā* mark is noticed between the eye-brows and traces of halo behind. The pair of moustaches and facial expression remind of foreign ethnic features. Drawn in a chariot of two horses (sometimes explained as lions) he sits in squatting posture.[16]

The pedestal is carved with an Indian fire altar. This feature suggests the association of Sun and Fire worships introduced by the Magi priests who migrated into India in early centuries of the Christian era and were known as *Śākadvīpī Brāhmaṇas*.[17]

The next sculpture (61.16 from Jaint) also represents the sun god of the Kuṣāṇa period although due to mutilation many of its features are missing. The third figure (D. 46 from Saptasamudri Well) shows a developed stage. The number of horses in the chariot has increased to four and the rigidity of the Scythian attire is also relaxed. The helmet is missing and the facial features do not look foreign.

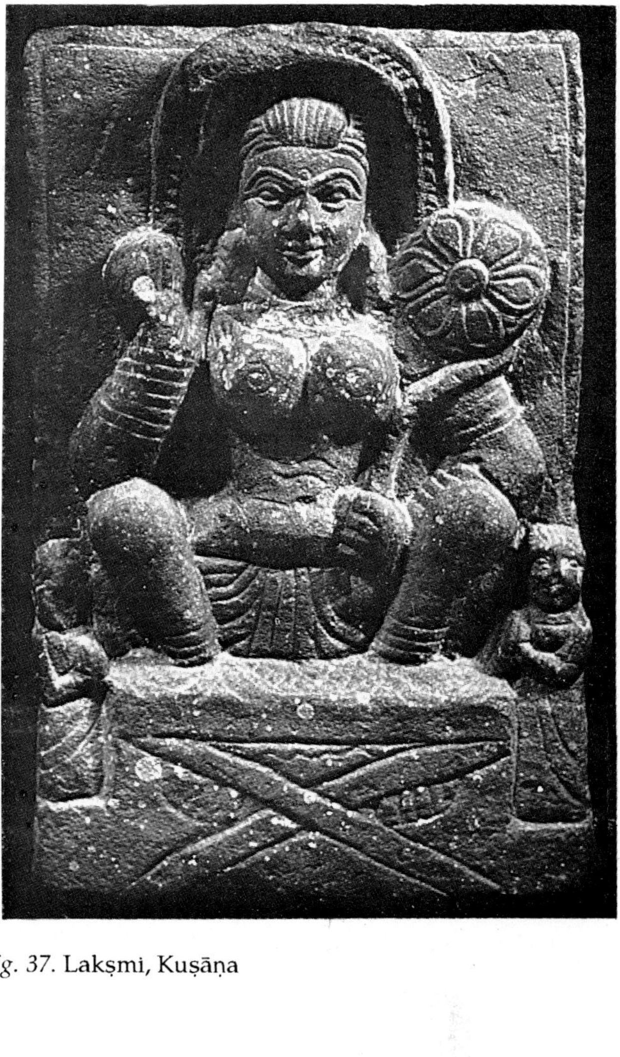

fig. 37. Lakṣmi, Kuṣāṇa

Inside the showcase is shown goddess Lakṣmī (80.2 from Janmasthān; *fig.* 37) holding stalked lotus in left hand and posture of *abhaya* in the right. The figure once stolen from the spot returned through the good offices of Prof. H. Härtel of Berlin.

Turning to left after a double faced figure showing a garland bearing Scythian devotee on both sides (G. 13 from Isāpur) one sees a slab (F. 1 from Jamālpur) carved on both sides with a centauress (*kinnarī*) composed of a female bust and elongated gallopping horse body. Her left hand holds the reins and with the right hand she sets her necklace right.

On her back is seen a rider (her husband) holding a mirror. Below his foot and also on one side the space is decorated with acanthus leaf. Depiction of composite figures or mythical beings was a favourite subject of ancient Indian and Central Asian artist. References to such figures are met with in early Indian literature also.[18]

The railing pillar (J. I from Bhūteśvar, Mathurā city; *col. ill. XXV*) on the wall side shows a lady with a parasol. A compartment on the top depicts an interesting and humorous scene of an eye ward of an animal hospital where two monkeys examine the eyes of a corpulent *yakṣa* and a bird respectively. Letter '*h*' on one side may denote the figure 100 or 30.[19] The very idea of carving such sculpture is quite intelligent. The vertical slab. (P. 79 from Maholī Kī Paur) from some door frame contains three full and one half compartments. These are separated by a railing and arch occupied by a female figure whose right hand is raised in *abhaya*. One arch is, however, devoid of the human figure but the object may be recognised as casket (?). One side of the frame is carved with scroll decorated with honeysuckle, *triratna* and lotus motifs. The other side is shaped as a vertical string with a cluster of pointed upward leaves intercepted by reels.

The first compartment shows a drinking scene in which two ladies exchange their goblets and a waiter serves them with a fan. The second compartment represents a music scene in a palace where a lady plays on an eight-stringed harp, another is busy with flute and the third one tries probably the castanets. The third compartment depicts a toilet scene where a lady on seat is being served by her two female attendants of whom one carries a basket and the other holds the left leg of the mistress for ornaments. The lower compartment now consists of a male bust who was holding some object and the other figures are now missing. The wicker seats bespeak of fine quality of furniture.

Horizontal slab (71.8 from near Caurāsī) is inscribed in the early *Brāhmī* characters and belongs to some *Śaiva* complex it reads as follows.

1. *Goti putrasa Rāhilasa (pau) trasa Vāsi (ṣṭi) putrasa (Pra) bastasa putrasa Ko (tsī putrasa (Magakasa Kula* (?) *(toṭasa)*/
2. *(Piskī) ri ni ārāma sabhā śilāpatte devakula ni piyatāṁ bhaga (vān) (Ma) heśvaram.*

'A water tank, garden, assembly hall, stone tablet (and) temple were erected (by) the son of Goti grandson of Rāhila, son of Vāsiṣṭi, son of Prabasta, son of Kotsī of Magaka (and) of Kulatota ? May god Maheśvara be pleased.'[20]

The word *devakula* appears to be a standard term for a *Śaiva* shrine. It also occurs on the pedestals of two royal portrait figures from Māṭ (12.215 and 12.215A). To right, shown independently, is a bracket (M. 4 from Deegh Gate, Mathurā) part of a *toraṇa* carved with a lady holding a branch of an *Aśoka* tree. A bracket used to join the beam of the gate-way with the upright pillar. The other independent female figure (F. 6 from Akrūr) carved in round illustrates fine coiffure and ornaments. The hair arrangement on the back side is also noteworthy.

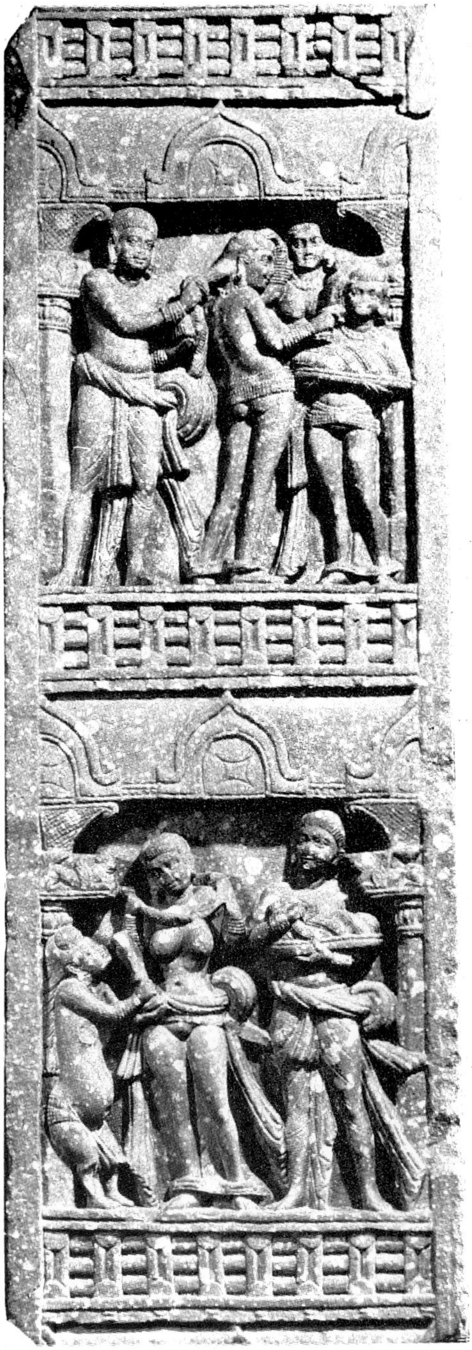

fig. 38. Harem (*Saundarānanda*) scene on doorjamb, Kuṣāṇa

Behind on the wall side the central railing pillar (12.186 Guḍgāon; *fig. 38*) shows two toilet scenes. In the upper panel a man is seen arranging the hair (*Veṇī prasādhana*) of a lady who looks into a mirror. A female attendant holds a toilet basket (*utpalamāla dhāriṇīkanyā*). In the lower compartment the lady puts on a necklace looking into the mirror (*maṇḍanadarpaṇa*) which is held by a corpulent dwarf. To her left stands a man carrying a toilet basket. The sculpture is supposed to represent the palace life of Nanda and Sundarī as described by the contemporary poet Aśvaghoṣa in his epic *Saundarānanda*.[21] The right corner bracket bears a female bust (17.1324 from Girdharpur) with voluptuous bosoms intervened by a pearled string. Besides a fine necklace she has an attractive hairdo with two braids falling on front and touching her breasts. The remaining hair is combed back and tied with a tress which is tastefully studded with various jewels and gems.

The bracket on the other side displays a female head (13.363 from Bairāgpurā) wearing an elaborate six stringed chaplet on the head and a large circular ornament suspends on the forehead. Facing south-east to the *nāga* gallery one finds a beautifully carved female torso (43.3099 from Kaṅkālī) wearing several ornaments. This faces a faceless bust of a female deity (F. 2) out of which five other female figures are seen emerging. Till now it was taken to represent a *nāgī* but there is hardly any *nāga* (serpent) feature. She may either represent a cosmic form of Female Energy or as R.C. Agrawala opines, may be an image of Ṣaṣṭhī, mother of Kārttikeya.[22] His title Ṣānmātura suggests that he was born of six female energies. The back of the sculpture is tastefully decorated with a tree consisting of stylistic leaves and fruits. The presence of the squirrel has imparted a realistic touch to the sculpture. Behind, on the entrance of the bay (gallery 6) a pillar (57.4447 from Caurāsī) bears beautiful vegetal motifs. Lotus and *aśoka* creepers are seen springing from the full vase on the two sides.

Nāga (Snake) Deities

The bay (gallery 6) displays some *nāga* and associated sculptures. The snake worship (*nāgapūjā*) was prevalent in India in a fairly early period. They are common to all the three sects. Supārśvanātha and Pārśvanātha figures bear a snake canopy, the Buddha in one of his previous births (*Campeyya jātaka*) was a *nāga, nāga* Mucalinda protected the *samādhi* of the Buddha, Śiva wears a garland of *nāga* (snake), Viṣṇu sleeps on the coils of the cosmic serpent Śeṣanāga who also supports earth on his hoods and Balarāma is supposed to be his incarnation. An independent *nāga* shrine was discovered at Sonkh in Mathurā District as a result of excavation by Härtel.

The central dominating life size figure (C. 13 from Chargāon) shows a *nāga* deity whose right hand was raised in the attitude of protection (*abhaya*) while the left hand held a cup. The head is surmounted by the spirited serpent hoods and coils are prominently shown. The back bears an inscription in the Kuṣāṇa *Brāhmī* which records that this image of snake deity (*bhagavān nāga*) was installed by Senahasti and Bhoṇuka (?) in the 40th year of Huviṣka.

The epigraph is given below :

1. *Mahārājasya rajāttirājasya Huviṣkasya savatsara chat* (*u*) *risa 40*
2. *Hematta-mase 2 divase 23 etta purvāyyā*
3. *Senahasti* (*ca*) *Piṇḍapayya-putra Bhoṇuka* (or *Bhoṇḍake ?*) *ca*
4. *Viraviridhi-putro etti vayyasya ubhayye*
5. *Nāgā* (or *Nagaṁ ?*) *Prattistāp* (*e*) *tti pushkaraniyy* (*am*)
6. *svakayyam priyyati Bhagavā Nāgo*

"In the fortieth year (40) of the king, the king of kings, Huviṣka, in the 2nd month of winter, the 23rd day. On this (date specified as) above Senahasti (n), the son of Piṇḍapayya and Bhoṇuka the son of Vīravṛddhi, these two comrades, erect (ed) both(this) Nāga at their own tank. May the Lord Nāga be pleased".[23]

The Balarāma statues were also represented in the similar way except that a big garland (*vanamālā*) and sometimes a lion staff (*siṁhalāṅgala*) also appear. The earliest Balarāma image of the Śuṅga period (G. 215 in the Lucknow Museum, acquired from Junsuṭī, Mathurā) shows him with serpent hoods and holding a club and plough. In

Kuṣāṇa period the more common depiction was the wine cup and *vanamālā*. Here to the left Balarāma (C. 15 from Kukargrām) is seen with same features.

The *nāga* deities are sometimes seen holding a pot of nectar (*amṛtaghaṭa*). The next sculpture (12.211 from Rāl-Bhadār) consists of a *nāga*, flanked by *nāgī* on either side. Both *nāga* and *nāgī* hold an *amṛtaghaṭa* but lower part of the third figure is chipped off.

The inscription on the pedestal records the following:

1. *Mahārājasya rāj (ā) tirājasya (Śāhi) Kāṇikkhasya sa 8 gri 4 di 5*
2. *as (yā)ṁp (ūrvv) āy (ā) ṁ bhagavataḥ Bhūmināgasya puskiri ṇni ār (ā) mo ca prati*
3. *(ṣṭhāpito . . .) turasya niya . . . kasya sa . . . sata hi . . .*

"In the year 8 of the great king, the king of kings, Śāhi Kanikkha, in the fourth (month of) summer, on the 5th day, on this date specified as above, a tank and a garden were dedicated to the divine lord Bhūmināga. . ."[24]

The next figure (14-15.439 from Kacehrighāṭ well) is sharply chiselled and has much resemblance with Maitreya Bodhisattva who also holds an *amṛtaghaṭa*. As noticed from exhibits 14-15.435 from Jamnābāgh and 36.2665 from Bhikcand Kā Naglā, the *nāga* figures continued to be carved in subsequent periods.

It is interesting to note that the icons of *Garuḍa* (bird deity who is the deadly enemy of *nāga*) are also found at Mathurā in the Kuṣāṇa period. Here a *Garuḍa* (41.2915) is seen carrying away a *nāgī*.

The next torso (40.2889 from Vrindāban) represents him with a pair of snakes in the clutch of his fist.

A lofty doorjamb (57.4446 from Caurāsī) to the left as one leaves the Nāga gallery, consists of eight compartments on both sides. The uppermost shows the Buddha flanked by a devotee on either side while the remaining panels contain male and female worshippers with garlands. The front side bears a projecting semi-circular band showing numerous finely executed motifs.

The large spotted red sand stone bowls displayed here were installed in the monastery for collection of alms and gifts and distribution of the same among the monks. These are carved with full blown lotus and decorative bands like scroll. The one (No. 10.97 from Sadar Bazar) projects from the base and other (80.4 from Dhaulī Piāū) has a flat base. The rim of the latter although badly rubbed off by sharpening of blades of agricultural implements still a few letters are intact and read as '*Bhadrasya sa*'.

The small bowl behind (12.260 from Sadar Bazar) carried on a human head (*yakṣa*) was set up by Ayala for adoration of all the Buddhas. The place where it was installed is mentioned as *Suvarṇakāra vihāra* (monastery of the goldsmiths).

The inscription is read as :

1. *'Iṁdrasama-pūtasa Ayalasa dana sava Būddhanam pūjāya Suvaṇakāra (vihāre) ācariyana (ma) hopad (e) ṣakana*
2. *parighae*

"(This bowl is) the gift of Ayala, the son of Iṁdrasama (Indrasarman) in the Monastery of Goldsmiths for the adoration of all the Buddha (and) for the acceptance of the teachers who were great preachers".[24]

Brāhmanical Icons

The Pillar installed on the pedestal represents *ekamukha* (one faced) *Śivaliṅga* from Akbarpur (81.19). The head of the deity showing teeth is in *aghora* form. His matted hair is tied in a big knot with some locks falling below the neck. He bears moustache and the eyebrows are somewhat drawn up. The necklace is probably stringed with the *rudrākṣa* beads. Behind the nut the *liṅga* is fastened with a flat decorated band. Below the plain shaft are seen two devotees carrying garland. Stylistically, the *śivaliṅga* should be assigned to the post-Kuṣāṇa period. The next pedestal displays two standing male deities on both sides. Elegantly standing Kārttikeya (42.2949 from Kaṅkālī mound; *col. ill. XIV*) holding long lance (*śakti*) in left hand and wearing a crown, ornaments and scarf is a good example of Kuṣāṇa art. Its importance is further enhanced by the inscription on the pedestal which labels the deity as Kārttikeya. Acquired from the Kaṅkālī mound well the statue was set up in the 11th year corresponding to 89 A.D. The epigraph is read as:

1. *Saṁ 11 he 4 di 1 etasya pū vuāyām Kārttikeyasya pratimā*
2. *pratiṣṭhāpitā Viśvadevana Viśvasomena (Viśva) bhavena Viśvavastuna*
3. *ca bhratubhirvviśvila putrehi Kṣatriye hi svake (asa) vsthe paṣitthika* (?)

"In the year 11, in the fourth month of winter on the first day, on this date (as specified above) was installed (this) image of Kārttikeya by Viśvadeva, Viśvasoma, Viśvabhava, Viśvavaśtu, the four brothers, the sons of Viśvila, *Kṣatriyas* in their own temple (house) at Pauṣthika (?)."

On the other side is framed an architectural piece, part of a doorjamb (85.163 from Dewānā Kalān) with a band of undulating creeper and male guard holding a long spear with left hand and the right one placed on the waist. Like a royal guard he wears several ornaments including one over his head.

Brāhmanical Deities

Showcase No. 6 in gallary 7 contains small sculptures which show early forms of Brāhmanical deities. They are :

1. Viṣṇu: Four armed (15.956 from Isāpur) holding mace, *abhaya*, disc and *amṛtaghaṭa;* seated in *lalitāsana* (39.2858) on a lotus seat and eight armed (15.1010 from Mansāvālā well, Pālīkherā).
2. Balarāma: (39.2856) four armed with a club and a lion staff (*siṁhalāṅgala*).
3. Kāmadeva with Rati: The plaque (19.1563 from Yamunābed, Mathurā) with a male and female may represent Kāmadeva (god of love) with his consort Rati. The long stick looking like a sugarcane bow (*ikṣukodaṇḍa*) helps in its identification.[26] Can it be identified as Rāma with Sītā ?
4. Durgā: Four armed (33.2317) holding a spear and trident (*triśūla*) and strangulating the buffalo demon (Mahiṣa). This form is popularly known as Mahiṣāsuramardinī. Appearance of her vehicle lion, seen below, is a rare feature in Kuṣāṇa periods, but in subsequent period it became an essential characteristic. Six armed (42.2947) deity is seen with different attributes.
5. Gajalakṣmī: (15.985 from Pālīkherā) Lakṣmī being bathed by two elephants.
6. A goddess (Pārvatī ?): (15.879 from Pālīkherā well) between flames.
7. Divine Mothers (*mātṛkās*): (33.2331) with animal or bird face and each carrying a child.
8. Kubera: (15.613 from Gośnakherā) a pot bellied deity with *abhaya* in right and a purse in the left hand, club shaped object is held in the left armpit.
9. Śiva-Pārvatī: (34.2495) with mutilated figure of Nandī behind.
10. Arddhanārīśvara: (15.874 from Pālīkherā well) male and female aspect combined as indicated by one breast.
11. Another form of Arddhanārīśvara: (15.800 from Isāpur) showing the lower part standing against the bull Nandī. The female part wearing anklet.
12. Four deities: (34.2520; *fig. 39*) Arddhanārīśvara, Viṣṇu, Gajalakṣmī and Kubera shown in one stele. It points to the efforts made towards eclecticism in the early Kuṣāṇa period.
13. Varāha (?) : Whether or not the theory of incarnation can be dated back to such an early date but we have a slab (65.15 from Yamunābed) showing probably Varāha lifting earth on his tusk. Although the face is damaged

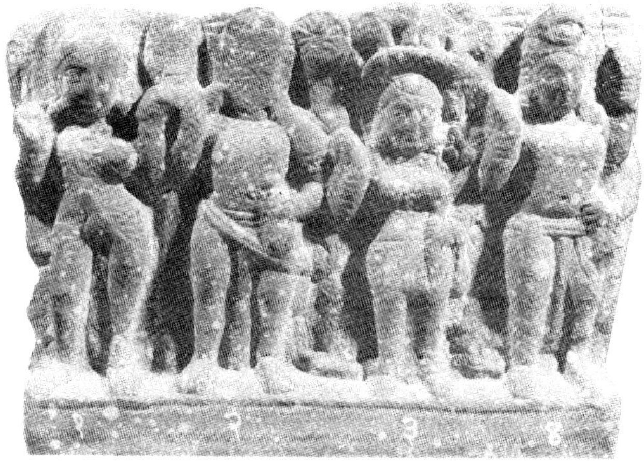

fig. 39. Four deities on stele, Kuṣāṇa

yet the position of legs, formation of body in load bearing pose and female figure above his neck seem to corroborate this identification.

The four armed deity with his legs apart rests his two hands on the waist while the upraised hands hold two separate discs carved with sun seated on a two-horse chariot. To his left stands a devotee with folded hands probably below a mountain. The right side is occupied by a reclining male and another standing. The one line inscription of which the meaning is rather obscure reads as "*ṭā sāmika pratiṣthāpita kaṭi priyataṁ bhagavā*.[27]

14. Skanda: The slab (40.2883 from Kaṭrā) shows Skanda with *abhaya* in upraised right hand and spear in left and Agni or Viṣākha with *abhaya* in right and pot in the suspended left hand. He bears an aureole of flames behind his shoulders and the long hair is fastened in knot to left. While the portion below same is badly corroded, a human head probably of a devotee is extant on the right side of Skanda.

    On the bench pedestal are placed some other figures of Brāhmanical pantheon.

15. Torso of Balarāma: (17.1325 from Girdharpur) Balarāma wears a garland of flowers and leaves (*vanamālā*) and has a *musala* (pestle or a club like weapon).

16. Image of Agni: (40.2880) shows the fire god with aureole of flames round his head and a pot of *ghee* (butter) in the left hand. The deity with a pot belly wears a sacred thread.

17. Indra (?) Torso: (E. 24 from Tarsi) wearing a long garland and holding a thunderbolt (*vajra*) with triple prong in the left hand appears to represent Indra.

18. Kubera: (46.3232 from Kaṅkālī mound; *col. ill. XV*) holding a cup of lemon fruit (*bijaurā*) is interesting as the epigraph on the pedestal mentions it as

an image of *yakṣa*. The face features, lips, ear rings and serenity on face suggest that the sculpture was in the end of 3rd century or the beginning of the 4th century A.D.

The inscription reads as :

1. *Mihiragṛh Yakṣaḥ dharma n (i) ty (o) vi*
2. *jna (pa) yati kare devaprasāta (dah)*

The sculpture was originally recovered from a well at the Kaṅkālī site. This suggests that there existed a Sun shrine (*mihiragṛha*) in the Kuṣāṇa period at the place and its provenance. The Museum has already acquired a sun image from this site (12.269) clad in northern style-*udīcya veṣa* and looking like a Kuṣāṇa king. Agrawala also favoured the reading as *Mihiragṛha* but interpreted it as *Mihiravihāra* which is not correct.[28] *Mihiravihāra* existed at Kāmvan as recorded in an inscription of Bodhisattva pedestal and referred to in Lüders list (No. 12), the whereabouts of this sculpture are not known.

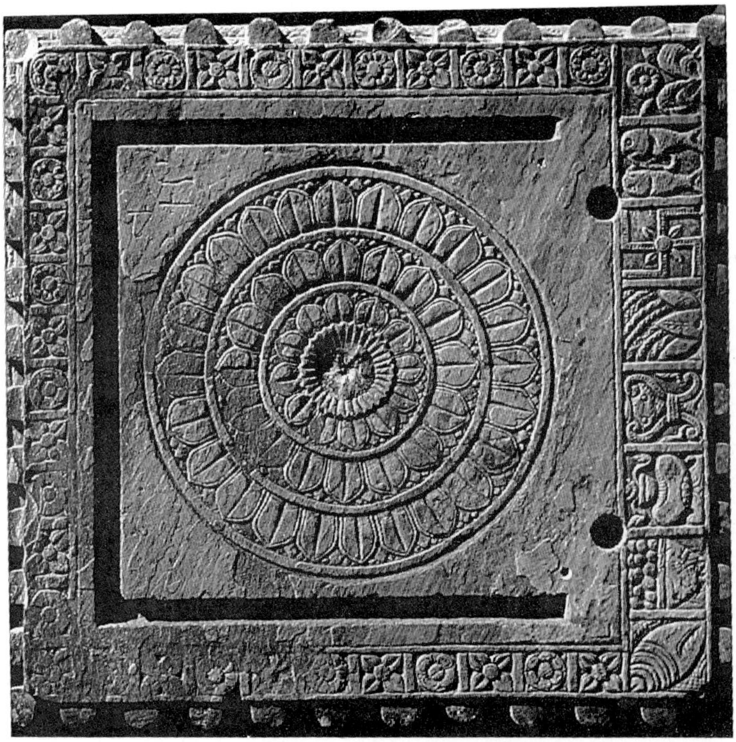

fig. 40. Square parasol, Kuṣāṇa

The last exhibit on the wall pedestal represents a parasol (*chattra* 76.12; *fig*. 40) decorated with full blown lotus in centre and three sides carved with rosette and lotus bands. The broader frieze on one side displays conch (*śaṅkha*), basket of fruits or gems (*ratnapātra* or *phalapātra*), full vase (*maṅgalakalaśa*), *srīvatsa*, basket of garlands (*puṣpadāma*), *svastika*, a pair of fish (*matsyayugma*) and three jewels (*triratna*). The three undercut grooves and two postholes explain that the sculpture served as roof of a small shrine.

The right upper corner is marked with five Kuṣāṇa period *Brāhmī* letters reading: *'dārukārasa'*. The exhibit is important for the development of temple architecture and it belongs to the pre-*śikhara* phase.

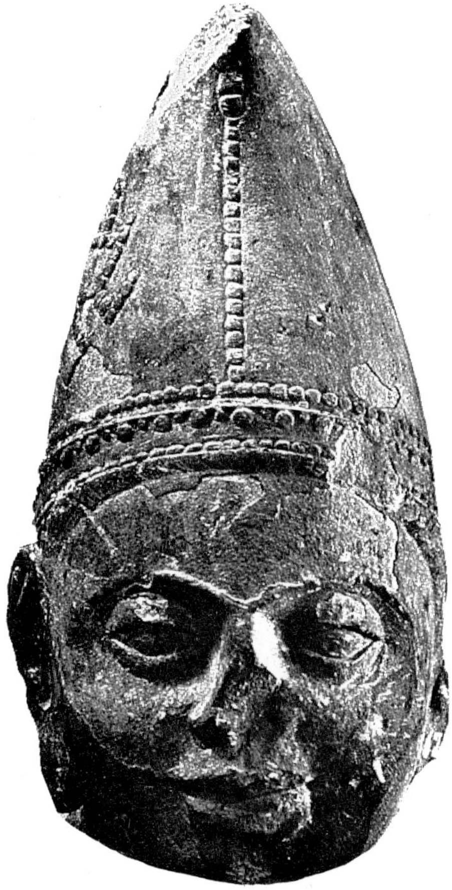

fig. 41. Head with conical cap, Kuṣāṇa

The wall projects three interesting male heads each wearing a peculiar headdress. The first one (11.57 from Bhūteśvar) shows a headgear with a pair of ram's horns. The features are very expressive and demonstrate the capability of Mathurā artist in shaping the foreign faces also with a high degree of workmanship. The second head (16.1252 from Māṭ; *fig. 41*) again represents a foreigner with a conical hat bearing a monogram on the right side which reads *'Nāyasa'* in the Kuṣāṇa *Brāhmī* alphabets. Its provenance is the same site of *devakula* at Māṭ which revealed the famous royal portraits of the Kuṣāṇa dynasty. The third head (19.1586 from Asgarpur) is conspicuous for the pair of moustaches and turban which ends in the large loose knot to right.

The showcase no. 12 at the end of gallery 7 displays a variety of male and female heads with different hairstyles and headdresses which were in vogue in the Kuṣāṇa period. Some of them are typically foreign in style. These are: male head wearing crown (56.4059 from Kaṭrā), female head (39.2832), another female head (15.785 from Isāpur), a male head with turban (42.43.2987 from Maholī), male head with moustache (15.673), male head with large turban (40.2902), Buddha head with *uṣṇīśa* (A. 28), crowned head with third horizontal eye on forehead and figures of *Garuḍa* on the right side of the head gear, Indra (17.1297 from Sūrajghāṭ), Scythian head with helmet type ornamental turban (31.2123 from Yamunābed, Mathurā), and an alien head horned headgear (35.2564 from Mahādevghāṭ). Inside the wooden railing (14.392-395 from Saptasamudrī well; *col. ill. XVI*) is seen Kṛṣṇa or Viṣṇu, with crown, mace, *vanamālā*, and *śaṅkha* as his attributes. From his right shoulder emerges Balarāma with snakehood and a cup of wine in his left hand. A headless bust is seen over his head. The third figure which was on his left shoulder is now missing. The traces of flames in the crown of the main deity suggest that one of the twelve Ādityas is Viṣṇu. According to *Vāyu Purāṇa*, five Vṛṣṇi heroes are: Saṅkarṣaṇa, Vāsudeva, Pradyumna, Sāmba and Aniruddha.[29]

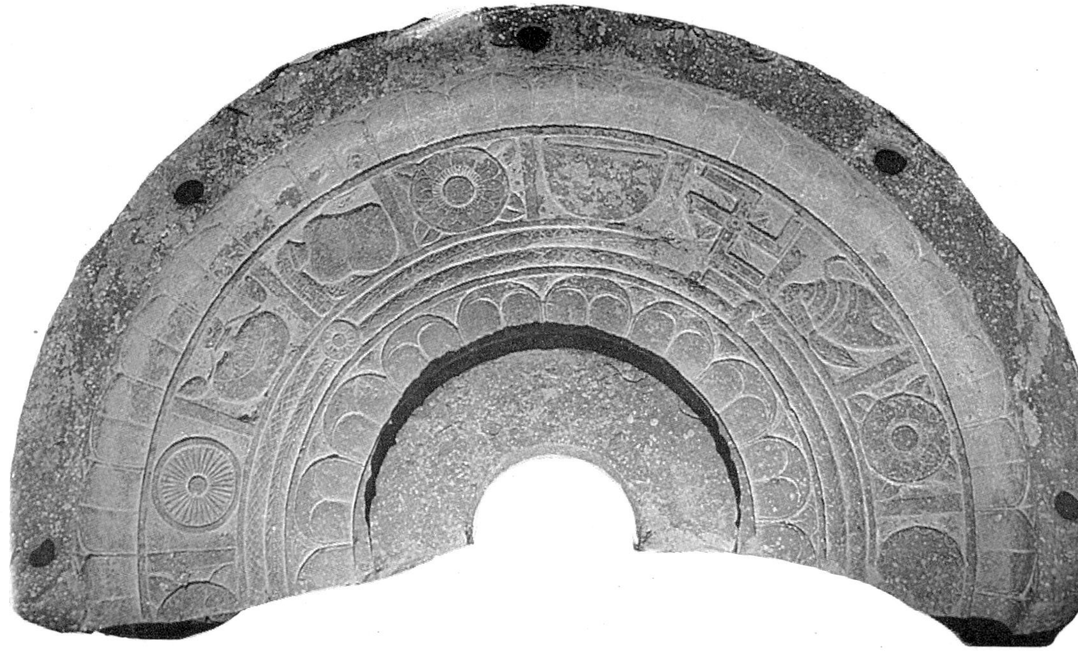

fig. 42. Part of umbrella, early Kuṣāṇa

The back portrays a tree with branch. This form is known as *Caturvyūha* and is a step towards the cosmic representation of Viṣṇu which became a popular theme in the later period. It has also been identified as Indra by Coomaraswamy and Agrawala.[30]

Now if one turns and proceeds to the bench pedestal where he first views a small standing figure of Kubera in *abhaya* pose holding a purse (18.1506 from Rāmghāṭ). It is followed by a large semicircular stone umbrella (72.5 Govindnagar; *fig. 42*) rest with the wall. It is carved with various decorative bands and auspicious symbols. The main circular panel consists of lotus, wheel, full vase winged pot oozing square coins, lotus, bowl, *svastika*, winged conch emitting wealth (*śaṅkhanidhi*), lotus and lastly a halo with scalloped border. The smaller but marvellous specimen (75.32; *fig. 43*) is complete and displays eight auspicious motifs viz., full vase (*maṅgalakalaśa*), mystic cross (*svastika*) three jewels (*triratna*), conch (*śaṅkha*), basket with rosary (*mālāpātra*), basket with fruits (*phalapātra*), the central jewel (*śrīvatsa*) and a pot pouring the wealth in shape of square coins (*nidhipātra*). Each of these motifs is flanked by a full blown rosette on the side and a ten grooved simple design on the other. Lotus carving is also remarkable. The third umbrella is again a beautiful specimen (91.34 from Saraniāzampur) of early Kuṣāṇa sculptural art of Mathurā carved with full blown lotus and four auspicious motifs viz. full vase (*pūrṇa gaṭa*) *śrīvatsa* (symbol of prosperity), *svastika* (anticlockwise cross) and

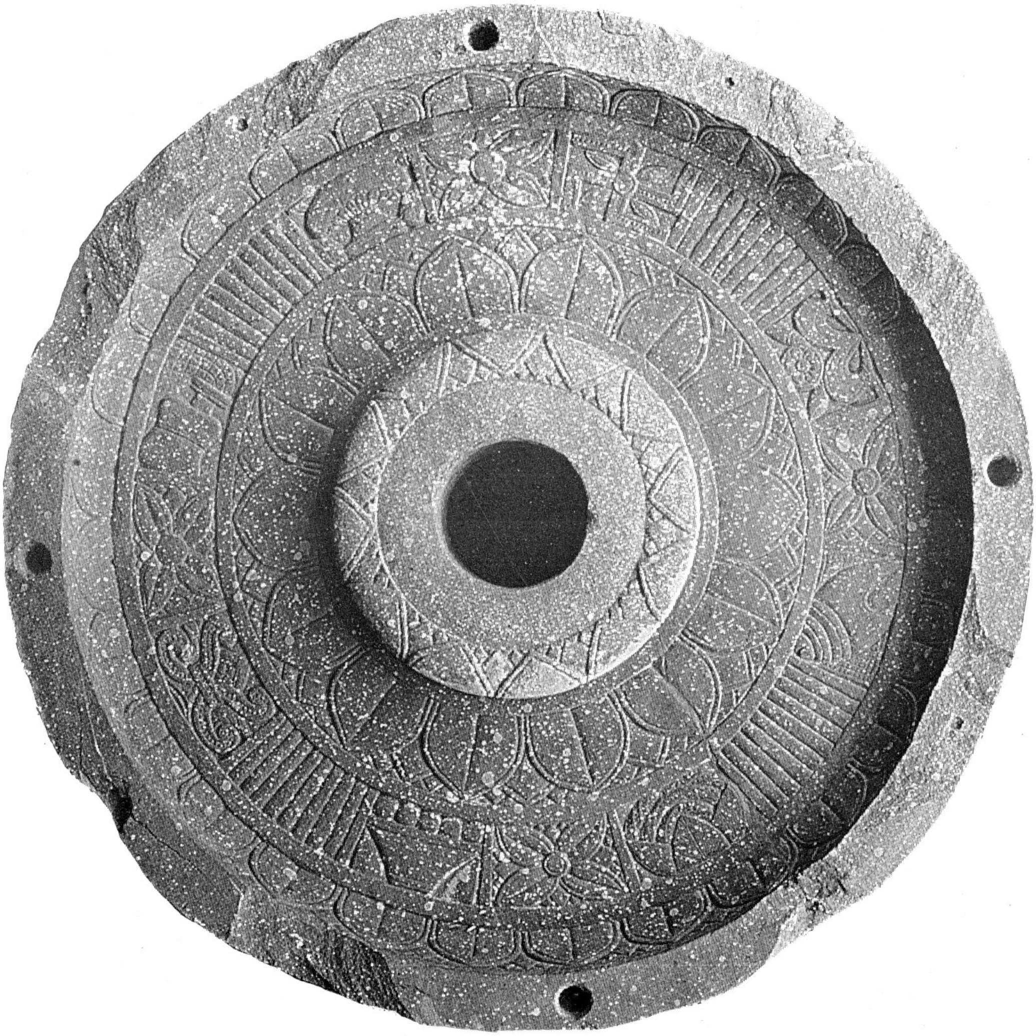

fig. 43. Umbrella, Kuṣāṇa

triratna (three jewels). The central large hole contained a shaft for its installation.

The bench pedestal on the other side of the door houses the following sculptures:

(a) Ṣaṣṭhī, female deity associated with birth and child care (F. 3) flanked on either side by a male spear holder and right hand in *abhaya* (protection). These should be identified as Skanda and Viṣākha.

(b) Vasudhārā, another female deity associated with abundance (89.62 from Sonkh Road near Maṇḍi Samiti, suburb of Mathurā city) stands with the posture of *abhaya* in right hand and flanked by female attendants of whom one holds an umbrella. The deity wears a *stanahāra* (necklace suspended between the breasts), ear rings, bangles and girdle. The hair arrangement shows several braids and the smile on the face is remarkable. Divine celestials hover with wreath and flowers on top corners. This belongs to third century A.D.

(c) Pot bellied Kubera wearing moustaches and curly hair (C. 6 from Kaṅkālī, Mathurā city) has raised his arms (now broken) in load supporting pose. This should be assigned to 3rd-4th century A.D.

(d) A female flute player (F. 22 from Jamālpur, Mathurā Collectorate) pearched on the wall must have been the part of a bracket figure of a gateway.

(e) A big male head (34.2519) which belonged to some colossal *yakṣa* statue. The thick eyebrows are drawn up and the forehead bears three straight horizontal lines one over the other suggesting the practice of *tripuṇḍa*. The heavy garland type necklace and blossoming *aśoka* flower ear pendants are noteworthy. The arrangement shows frizzled locks in paralleled rows.

(f) The Buddha head (18.1390 from Bājnā, Mathurā district) bears the heavy Gāndhāra impact as indicated by moustaches and notched hair terminating into a decorated tuft.

Railing Pillars

The culmination of the Kuṣāṇa art is, however, seen in the railing pillars, which present feminine beauty with great care and charm. The obverse carved in bold relief generally shows a lady busy in one action or the other while the reverse in low relief depicts different scenes. Even the dwarf below her feet feels happy and enjoys the kicks of her delicate feet.

While various interpretations have been offered for the nude, amorous or erotic figures appearing on the religious monuments the real purpose still remains obscure. Some of the views advanced by the scholars are[31] the sculptures protected the monument from lightening and thunder; signify the cult of love and fertility; taught the lessons on sex to the adolescent youth who led a chaste student career in the forests and had no experience of worldly pleasures; represent the ritual practices of the followers of the *tāntric* cult; displayed the world of *māyā* which surrounds the Divine; attracted the layman to the abode of God. Some accept them as *yakṣīs* (super human spirits), *vanadevatās* (forest deities), *vṛkṣikās* (tree goddesses), nymphs, dryads and dancing girls etc.[32] Female figures under trees have been explained as the garden sports (*udyāna krīḍā*). According to some these remind of the mother of the Buddha, Māyādevī who gave birth to the child in the gardens of Lumbinī. Whatever interpretation they may bear but it seems quite probable that such figures were derived from the early terracottas representing nude goddess. On Bharhut railings these are labelled as *yakṣīs* and *devatās*. Although carved on Buddhist or Jaina *stūpas* they hardly convey any religious significance. They may possibly represent the taste of the donors who, even without following a particular sect used to donate for the construction of a religious building. Similarly, the artists who were employed for execution were not essentially religious minded. In order to make the building popular both the donor and the sculptor wanted to shape it attractive.

Even after adopting the Buddhism, the Kuṣāṇas did not accept its pessimistic view of life. They were in tune with Aśvaghoṣa who declared that it was not necessary to renounce the world to seek salvation. Dr. Mulk Raj Anand's observation is a correct assessment of the values of the Kuṣāṇa people, 'Apart from the compassion of the Buddha, they seem to have discovered the grace of women, both mother and object of arching desire in the fullness of her big breasted, large hipped and delicately adorned presence.[33] The church whether Buddhist, Jaina or Hindu probably had no alternative but to adjust itself with the urge of the contemporary society.

Galleries 7 and 8 show some representatives in three rows. The stair railing pillar (33.2348), first piece in the first row to left, bears a lady under the *aśoka* tree holding a stalked lotus (*līlākamala*), and kicking the trunk of the tree with her foot. The back shows full blown lotus medallion. Such illustrations are termed as *aśokadohada* as according to the poetic imagination the *aśoka* tree blooms when a damsel kicks it with her foot. The leaves of the tree are finely executed. The next pillar (11.149) represents a woman in *namaskāra mudrā* (folded hands) under a tree. The hack consists of lotuses. The third pillar (F. II) shows two ladies playing with the parrot (*śukakrīḍā*), a favourite pastime of early days. The back of the sculpture bears tasteful depiction of *aśoka* tree. The last pillar (J. 63) on this bench pedestal on one side depicts a beautiful young lady with a large bulging tuft of hair on head and holding a sword in the right hand. The sculpture from knees is broken. The back which contained full flown lotuses is rubbed off.

The first pillar in the middle row (J. 5 from Bhūteśvar) shows a graceful young woman standing on a dwarf (*guhayaka*) looking at the nail marks or adjusting her pendant. The hair, making a central knob, is tastefully combed back. The girdle of five rows of crescents is also remarkable. Although looking nude she wears a *sāṛī* as seen from the folds to her right and below anklets. In most cases the figures are clad but the physical beauty is exposed through the transparent muslin. Above, two persons are seen on the balcony. One of them offers something but the other refuses. The reverse is carved with three compartments. The lowermost shows a lion attacking a man. It possibly represents *vyāgrhī jātaka* when the Boddhisattva offered his body for a hungry tigress. The uppermost panel shows Buddha flanked by two attendants. The next rail post (J. 6) which is rather crude work displays a lady standing crosslegged under a tree. The back bears three compartments illustrating from top to bottom (a) worship of *bodhi* tree (b) large bowl probably consisting of relics worshipped by the devotees and

(c) the Buddha in *abhaya* pose attended by a devotee. The third pillar (11.152 from Bhūteśvar) in this row represents a lady with noteworthy bob hair holding a sword but in dancing attitude (*khaḍga-nṛtya*). The weather worn and corroded back shows the worship of the *dharmacakra*.

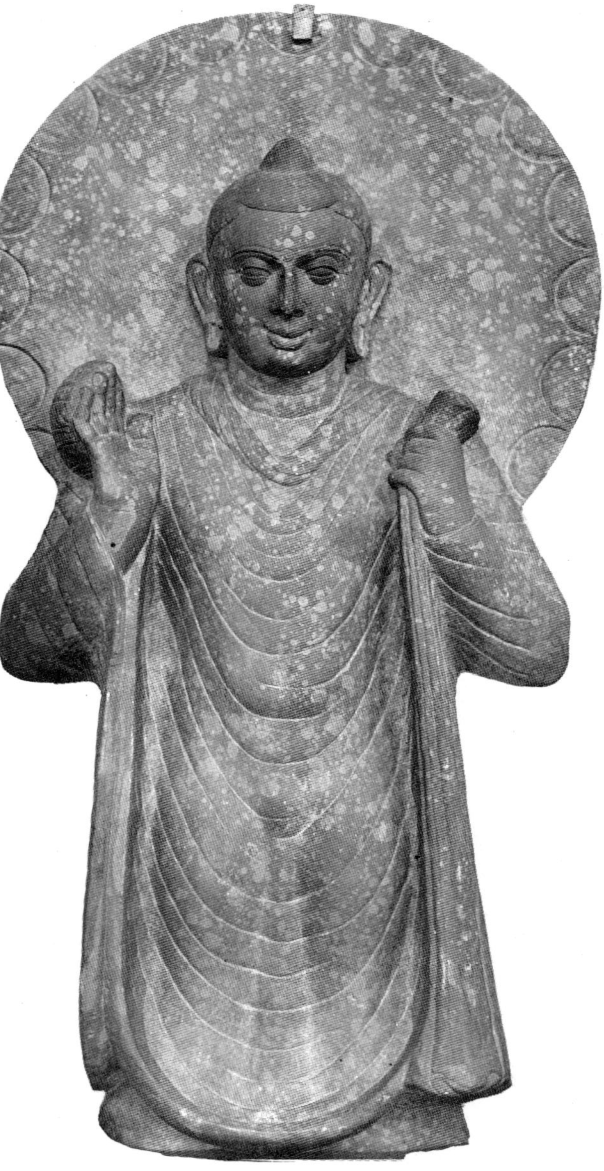

fig. 44. Buddha in *abhaya*, Kuṣāṇa

The front object of the third row (76.39 from Govindnagar; *col. ill. XIX*) bears a lady holding a mirror (*darpaṇadhāriṇī*) and seated on the beautiful wicker seat. She probably points to the nail or teeth marks on her cheek while a youngman from the balcony enjoys the fun. The large horizontal slab over the pillars is a coping stone (57.4448 from Caurāsī), carved with a human couple and palmette in decorative arches. The supporting rail posts show a lady wearing ornaments (17.1277), lady under tree standing over the dwarf (10.119 from Vrindāban and another mutilated *śālabhañjikā* upto the knees (J. 17). The back of the last pillar shows the coffin box of the Buddha on the couch, nobleman and a wreath carrying dwarf and a devotee with garland.

The continuity of the railing pillars is broken by a colossal parasol (*chatra* 10.86 from Ganeśarā), which must have protected a *stūpa* or a deity. Its ceiling bears lotus decoration. Exhibits below the parasol are a handsome bust of the *nāga* or Balarāma (14.406 from Katcerighāṭ well; *col. ill. XVII*), Buddha standing in *abhaya* pose (A. 4; *fig. 44*) which is simple but beautiful piece, a Jina head (B. 46 from

Kaṅkālī mound) and a warrior or a royal portrait (28-29.1726 from the Museum building foundation Dampier Park).

The central row of the charming rail posts again shows some of the classical products of the master artist.

The Lady (J. 4 from Bhūteśvar; *col. ill. XX.*) appears after bath (*sadyasnātā*) in the act of putting on her garment. The perfect anatomy, nicely chiselled curves and contours and her rhythmic action have imparted a subtle grace and charm to this young lady. Above, on the balcony a young flute player is being dragged by a man of gigantic physique. The back depicts the story of *Vessantara jātaka* which has been given by Agarwala as follows:

> "Prince Vessantara (Sanksrit Viśvantara) had married Mādrī and their children were Jāli and Kṛṣṇājinā. The prince had a peerless elephant which he gave away in charity in order to relieve a great drought in Kaliṅga since the elephant was credited with the power of making rain to fall. The citizens of his own capital were upset at this and demanded banishment of prince Vessantara and their will prevailed. The prince, his wife and two children took to a forest. Here he passed through a breath-taking ordeal of charity giving away first the four horses and the chariot, and ultimately his own children to an old *Brāhmaṇa* called Jūjaka at a time when the mother of the children was away in the forest".

On the pillar, in the top panel Vessantara is living as a hermit and giving his children away to Jūjaka. In the central panel he makes the children over to the *Brāhmaṇa* notwithstanding their supplication. In the lower panel his wife is shown returning to the hermitage.[34]

The railpost represents graceful treatment of the body and a subtle smile infusing life in stone (J. 12 from Jaisinghpurā). Looked from different angles it appears more mysterious. Above, a man rests her head on the right hand perhaps in grief. The back shows lotus carving. The third pillar (J. 10 from Jaisinghpurā) depicts a young woman standing under a railed terrace with a wreath.

The fourth pillar (11.151 from Bhūteśvar; *col. ill. XXI*) represents a lady holding grapes (*drākṣā*) or little mango fruits (*āmramañjarī*) in her right hand and a jar covered with a mug on the left hand. It is received by a man seen on a balcony with his beloved. The reverse represents the episode of Ekaśṛṅga or Ṛṣyaśṛṅga who was the son of sage Vibhāṇḍaka and owing to a horn over his head, he was known as Ekaśṛṅga or Ṛṣyaśṛṅga. He was an ascetic by birth and nature and had never seen a woman. Once the territory of king Lomapāda was hard hit by drought. He was advised by the *Brāhmaṇas* to invoke the young ascetic Ṛṣyaśṛṅga whose arrival to the capital would cause rains. He immediately sent the princess with other beautiful women to attract the ascetic. They prepared a house boat and reached the hermit. In the absence of sage Vibhāṇḍaka they succeeded in tempting the adolescent hermit through their sensuous overtures. The love sick ascetic left the forest for the capital in the joyous company of those women. Just after his arrival to the king's palace it began to rain heavily and the happy king married his daughter Śāntā to Ṛṣyaśṛṅga.[35]

Here the top panel shows the ladies undertaking the boat journey to the hermitage of Ṛṣyaśṛṅga. In the centre the innocent ascetic enjoys the music and plays on a harp, the last compartment shows him in union with the princess who plays a more active role. In two panels the hermit can be recognised with a horn over his head.

The other four pillars on the central bench pedestal depict a crudely formed woman with a branch of lotus flowers under a balcony on which two human heads are seen (J. 11 from Jaisinghpura), a lady under tree looking into the mirror and mounting over the dwarf (J. 64 from Maholī, Mathurā), lady under a tree feeding a parrot (12.258 from Mahāban) side door pillar with a lady standing against the pillar which has vase base, lion abacus and four tiered projecting top; (17.1329 from Girdharpur mound).

The bench pedestal behind presents some other interesting rail posts. It begins with Ṛṣyaśṛṅga episode (76.40 from Govindnagar; *col. ill. XXII*) discarded in four compartments. The top one depicts the worship of the Bodhisattva's turban placed on a high pedestal. This is followed by a scene in which a sage and dove are seen near the hut and the fire altar. The third compartment illustrates the birth of the baby Ṛṣyaśṛṅga from the dove and last niche represents the wedding of the hermit Ekaśṛṅga with the daughter of the king of Varāṇasī. Each compartment is divided by a railing below and arch above. The heels is damaged but the traces of illustration are extant. The rail post should be assigned to the 1st century B.C.

The other pillars are: a man with Scythian cap holding a bunch of flowers. The *Brāhmī* letters are read as *Deyahu* probably the name of the sculptor, a lady with stalked flower under balcony and the back showing *gandhakuṭī* (11.154 from Bhūteśvar).

The maiden experience of the company of woman has been well conveyed on the opposite pillar (J. 7 from Caubārā; *col. ill. XXIII*) which shows the young *brahmacārī* lost in deep thought ecstasy, putting the index and middle fingers below his chin. The poor fellow did not know what a woman was and he mistook her for another *brahamacārin.* When she left for a few days he became very sad and was not able to reconcile himself. The horn over his head is quite conspicuous in two panels. The reverse in the upper panel shows the worship of the *bodhi* tree, the next panel probably represents birds' fight. Two persons (owners of the birds) are seen in a challenging posture while the other two are witnessing. The one line inscription reads as:

'*Abhyaṁtaropastāyakasa Kaṭhikasa dānaṁ*

gift of Kaṭhika, the servent of the interior.[36]

The two rail posts on either side of a basement stone (P. 27 recording the gift of the two friars Bhadra and Bhadraghoṣa (Siddhaṁ) *Daja* (*dānaṁ*) *bhikhuno Bhadrasya Bhadragh* (*o*) *ṣasyaca*)[37] and a small lion capital (17.1328 from Girdharpur) also need mention.

To right a lady (14.369 from Kaṅkālī mound) standing under the beautifully carved *campā* flowers carries a toilet or worship basket over her left hand while in the suspended right hand she holds an incense burner. Last but not the least important among the railing pillars is seen on the other side of the lion capital. The lady after bath (18.1509 from Narhaulī; *col. ill. XXIV*) is seen drying her hair. The drops of water falling through squeezing and looking like pearls are being swallowed by a tempted swan (*muktālobhīhaṁsa*). Another curious feature is the short petticoat worn by the young woman, it looks like a modern skirt. The top of the post bears a drinking scene. The two objects exhibited in the small vertical glass case; a celestial flying with garland (58.4479 from Kaṭrā; *fig. 45*) and the stylistically carved female bust playing on flute (F. 17) were selected for the issue of Mathurā Museum Centenary Commemorative postage stamps, released in the Museum on October 9, 1974.

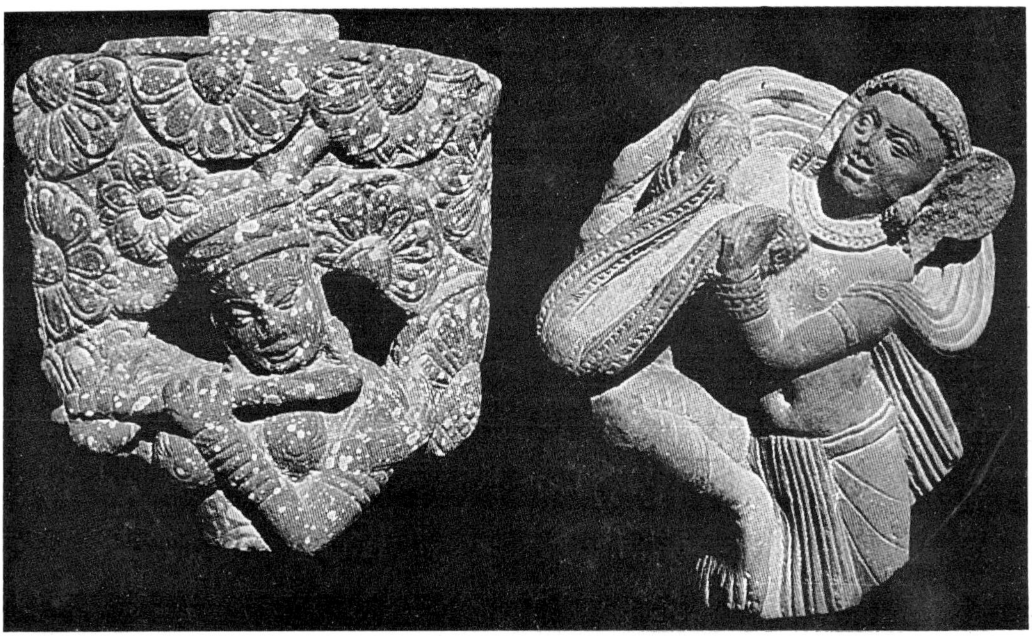

fig. 45. Lady playing on flute and Celestial, Kuṣāṇa

The next pillar (J. 43 probably from Jamālpur) on front shows a pot bellied Scythian wearing a long coat and *salwār* type lower garment. He carries a bunch of flowers in his upraised right hand and stalked flower in the left one. The head and feet are gone.

The damaged upper compartment on the reverse depicts the Buddha seated inside the *indraśāla* (cave) and the lower one shows with a man probably examining the ailment of a bird. Both the man and the bird are seated on stools. In the background is to be seen the *bodhi* tree. The exhibit is to be compared with large rail post (J. 1 from Bhūteśvar, Mathurā city; *col. ill. XXV*) an eye ward of a veterinary clinic has been humorously shown.

As gathered from their fabrication on top the next four rail posts belonged to stairs. The first (55.3876 from Dhaulīpiāū) is carved with the figure of the Buddha standing on a high lotus seat under an umbrella. He wears an *ubhayānsika sanghāṭī* (garment covering both shoulders). The back depicts the lotus medallion. The next pillar (17.1275) bears a male devotee with garland clad in the Scythian dress. The back shows lotus carvings. The next post (J. 56 from Koṭā) again represents foreign devotee in the *udīcyaveṣa* (long coat, *salwār*, high cap and boots) with flowers in hands. The reverse shows full blown lotuses. The last fragmentary stair post shows (J. 33) the bust of some royal devotee carrying a garland. The background probably represents *kalpavṛkṣa* with flowers oozing garments. The back shows full blown lotus pattern.

The third bench pedestal displays nine railposts carved with various themes.

Many female figures are seen under a tree either holding its branch, or plucking the flowers or with a bunch of flowers. A corpulent male dwarf under the feet is the common site. These are variously known as '*śālabhañjikā*' or *puṣpapracāyikā* (J. 57 from Koṭā, J. 8, J. 9 and J. 58 from Koṭā). The other rail posts show a woman under the tree putting on a necklace (J. 14), Yawning lady (J. 61 from Koṭā) playing with ball with back side carved with *bodhi* tree and probably the relic casket (*dhātupātra*), lady playing with a parrot (19.1595 from Nar-haulī), attendant or a *yakṣa* with a flywhisk (J. 25) and a lady (head missing) standing against a pillar and playing with a *vīṇā* (J. 62 from Koṭā). The back is invariably carved with full blown lotuses unless described otherwise.

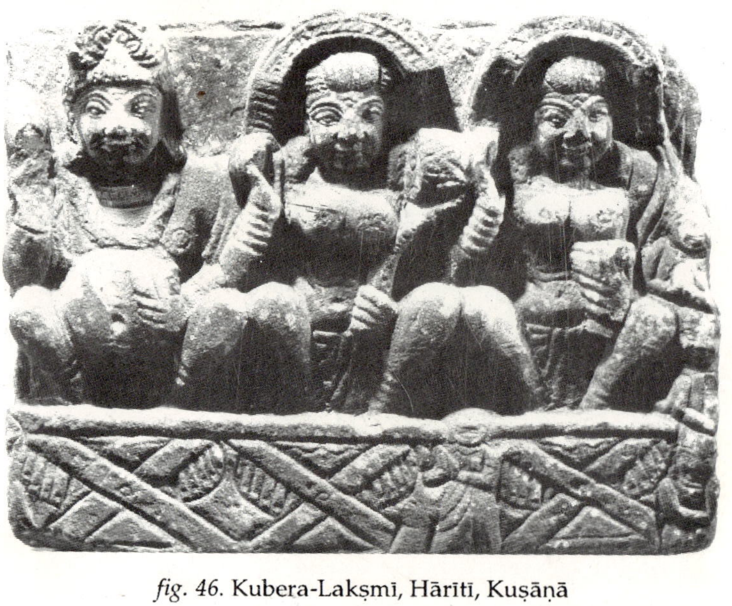

fig. 46. Kubera-Lakṣmī, Hārītī, Kuṣāṇā

Small objects of Kuṣāṇa period to be viewed in wall showcase No. 7 are: standing Vasudhārā with an umbrella (29.1965), bust of Vasudhārā (42.2943), a standing royal lady (33-2334), *Yakṣa* Vaiṣravaṇa or Agni with an aureole of flames and pot of *ghee* (42-43.3048), one faced *Śivaliṅga* (18.1533), standing *nāga* with snake hood and coils (*c.* 21) bearing an inscription dated in the year A.D. 52-130. The inscription is read as '*saṁ 52 va 3 di 25 bhagava* (*ta*)'. Kubera with Lakṣmī and Hārītī on a stele with their feet fastened on pedestal (*c.* 30 from Manoharpura mound; *fig. 46*), Lakṣmī with stalked lotus (17.1301), Indra's head with crown probably showing eyes (15.1178 from Yamunā river, Mathurā), relief with worshippers and musicians (17.1276), Brahmā with four heads or cosmic form of a deity (14.382 from Saptasamudrī well, Museum compound) and a panel showing five women feasting and dancing (14. 405 from Kaṭhoti Kuān).

The wall side bench pedestal contains a slab identified as scene just after the birth of Kṛṣṇa when Vāsudeva carries child Kṛṣṇa in a basket over his head and crosses the flooded Yamunā in which are seen crocodiles, tortoises, fish and a *nāga* deity Śeṣa (17.1344 from Kaṭrā; *col. ill. XVIII*). The exhibit belonging to the Kuṣāṇa period is the earliest sculptural remain showing the birth of Kṛṣṇa. The next is Gajalakṣmī (36.2660 from Śītalāghāṭī) with trunks of elephants anointing the canopied head of Lakṣmī, on wall a beautiful bracket figure with mother and child where the mother pampers the weeping and angry child who had caught the locks of the lady motif (F. 16; *fig. 47*) a bracket capital with

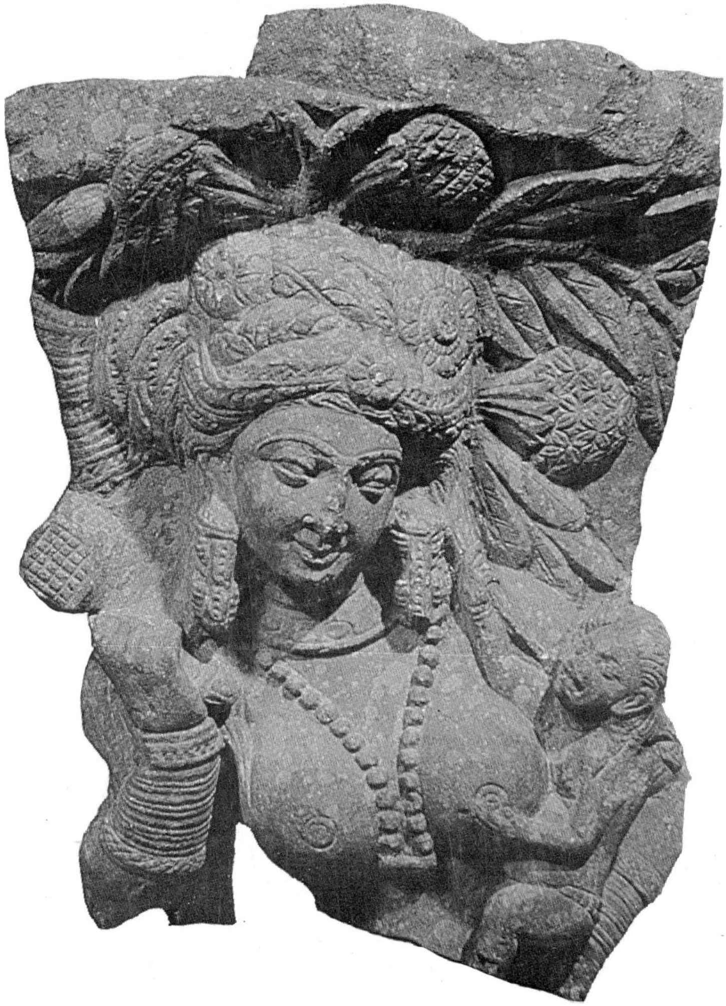

fig. 47. Mother and child, Kuṣāṇa

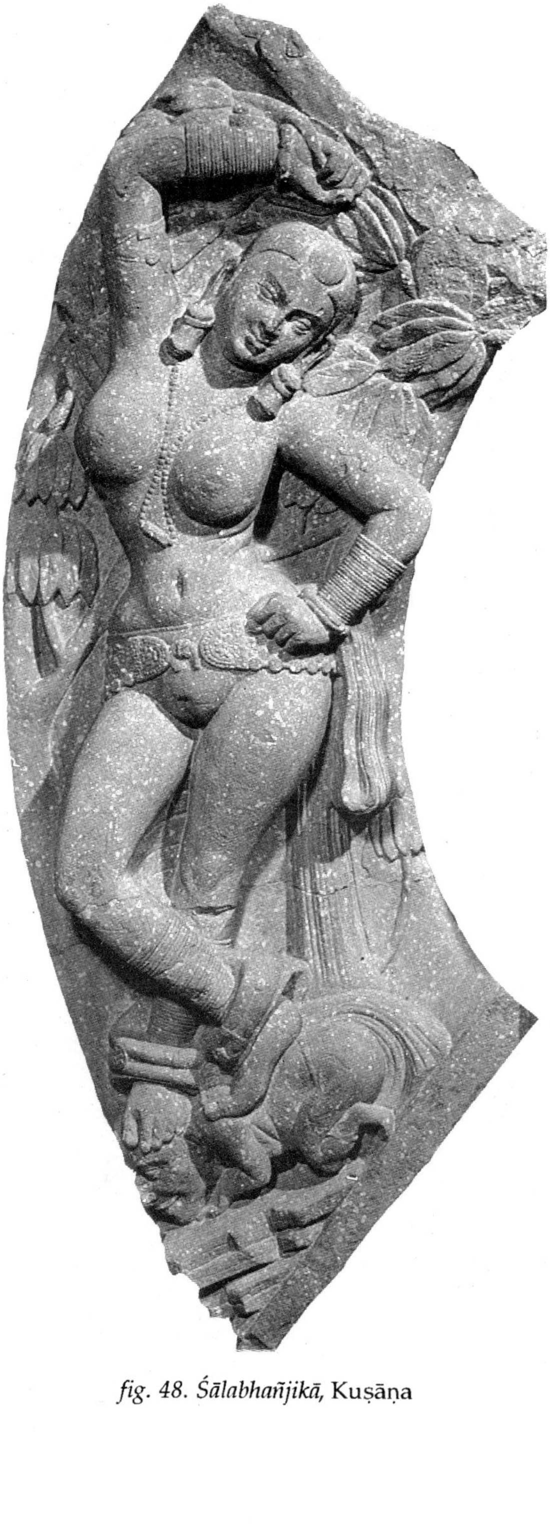

fig. 48. Śālabhañjikā, Kuṣāṇa

Buddha's life scenes and decorative motifs (44.3118-19 from Swāmighāṭ) slab projecting busts, a couple feeding a parrot and branch of a blossomed *campā* tree below (10.99 from Isāpur; *col. ill. XXVI*). The fragmentary doorframe depicts the scene of worship of *Śivaliṅga*, placed on a high pedestal, by Scythians clad in northern style (*udīcaveṣa*). A celestial is seen hovering in the sky and the border shows a vine scroll with peacock (36.2661 from Seth Bhikhcand kā naglā, Dampier Park).

Sonkh Sculptures[38]

The wall on the southern side of gallery 8 of the Museum represents some of the outstanding art treasures of Kuṣāṇa age, revealed in Jan. 1972 from Sonkh as a result of the campaign undertaken by the German archaeologists under the direction of Prof. H. Hartel from 1966 to 1974. These architectural gems formed the part of a gateway of the railing of a *nāga* shrine which was originally put up in the 1st century B.C. but rebuilt in the Kuṣāṇa period. Interestingly enough, small shrine on the spot still consists of a *nāga* deity which is worshipped as Camardevī.

Śālabhañjikā

The first exhibit from the beginning of gallery 8 (SO IV 27; *fig. 48*) is a bracket part of the gateway representing a young lady standing on a postrate dwarf and holding a branch of a tree (*śālabhañjikā*). Wearing different ornaments and diaphanous drapery she presents her real beauty through her slender body, fine curves and contours, charming features and graceful posture. Her association with the *nāga* family is ascertained by a serpent hood in her ankle.

Nāga Panel

The lintel (SO IV 36; *fig. 49*) is another wonderful creation of the Mathurā studio of sculpture in the Kuṣāṇa period. The panel illustrates some scene of a *nāga* court in which the king is majestically sitting on couch (throne) with a seven hooded snake conopy. He is busy in fastening a long turban, presented by a group of four children probably forming part of a delegation to his court. A lady with equal number of serpent hoods in her canopy occupies a place to his right with much grace and elegance. She has stretched her right arm towards a young lady who is inclined to the delegation. She wears a single hooded snake scalp, and holds a small necklace-type ornament. To the left side of the king are seen two female and three male attendants each marked with a snake hood on top. In view of the commanding position of the lady Hartel is not inclined to identify her as the wife of the *nāga* king but opines that the royal *nāga* pair represents *nāgarāja* Vāsuki and his sister Jaratkāru.[39] The story is narrated in detail in the *Mahābhārata*.[40] Whatever may be the interpretation of the scene it is a superb specimen of plastic art.

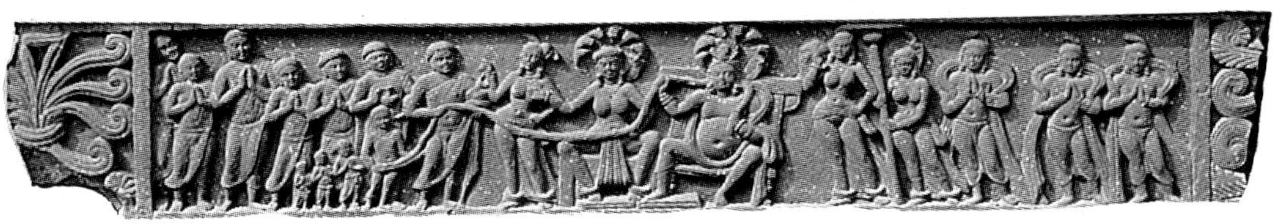

fig. 49. Nāga lintel, Kuṣāṇa

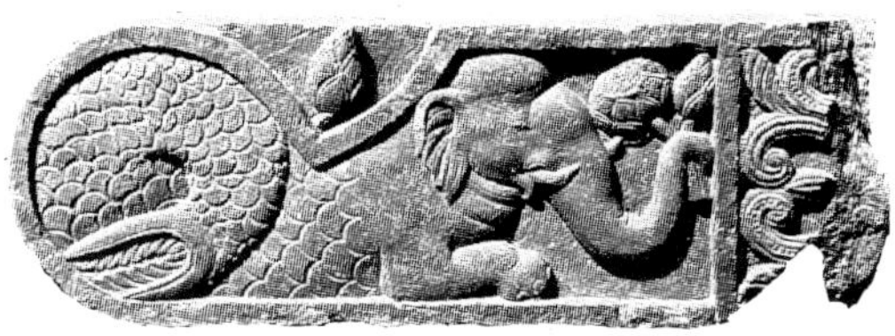

fig. 50. Fish-tailed elephant, Kuṣāṇa

The fragmentary coping (SO IV-37) showing *nāga* nobleman coming out of the wide open jaws of a fish tailed crocodile. The depiction might be indicative of some critical moments through which the *nāga* dynasty passed and ultimately emerged triumphant. The next beautifully chiselled fragment (SO IV 39; *fig. 50*) shows a fish-tailed elephant in a delightful and pleasurable mood holding two stalked lotus buds in his half upraised trunk. The last item (SO IV 35) is a square baluster from the *toraṇa* beam carved with an intricate floral design.[41]

References

1. Sharma, R.C., 'Kuṣāṇa Idiom in Mathurā', In *Prāchī Prabhā* (Essays in honour of Prof. B.N. Mukherjee), 1989, pp. 225-26.
2. Rosenfield, M., *Dynastic Arts of the Kuṣāṇas*, 1967, pp. 247-48.
3. Mukherjee, B.N., *Mathurā and its Society—the Śaka-Pallava Phase*, 1981, p. 127.
4. Agrawala, V.S., *Mathurā Museum Catalogue, JUPHS*, 1949, p. 179.
5. Asthana, Shashi, 'A unique *Patravāhaka yakṣa* image from Abichchhata, In *Purātattva* ', no. 11, 1982, pp. 74-77.
6. Sharma, R.C., *Buddhist Art of Mathurā*, 1984, p. 191, ft. nt. 63.
7. Agrawala, V.S., *Mathurā Museum Catalogue, JUPHS* XIX, 1948, pp. 79-80.
8. Van Lohuizen, J.E., *The Scythian Period*, pp. 181-82.
9. *Prāpto gṛhasthairapi mokṣa mārgaḥ, Buddha Carita*, IX. 10.
10. Mukherjee, B.N., *The Rise and Fall of the Kuṣāṇa Empire*, 1988, pp. 313-22.
11. Mitterwallner, G.V., *Kuṣāṇa Coins and Sculptures*, 1986, pp. 53.
12. Jayaswal, K.P. *JBORS*, 1920, p. 15 and Keith, A.B., Aryan Names in Early Asiatic Records, In *IHQ*, 1936, p. 574.
13. Agrawala, V.S., *Mathurā Museum Catalogue*, In *JUPHS*, 1950, p. 72 Bhattacharya, B., 'Statue of Caṣṭana', *JBORS*, Vol. VI, 1920, p. 51.
14. *Ibid.*, p. 76.
15. *Bṛhatsaṁhitā* of Varāhamihira, 58.46.
16. Chaturvedi, S.N., *Bulletin of Museum and Archaeology in U.P.*, No. 15-16, p. 76.
17. *Mahābhārata, Bhiṣmaparva*, XI, 35-36.
18. Agrawala, V.S., *Indian Art*, 1965, p. 46.
19. Agrawala, V.S., *Mathurā Museum Catalogue*, 1951, p. 3.
20. Sharma, R.C., New Inscriptions from Mathurā, In *Mathurā—the Cultural Heritage*, 1989, p. 312.
21. Agrawala, V.S., *Mathurā Museum Catalogue*, 1951, pp. 32-33.
22. *Bulletin of Museum and Archaeology in U.P.*, No. 4, Dec. 1969, pp. 4-5.
23. Agrawala, V.S., *op. cit.*, 1949, pp. 199-200.
24. *Ibid.*, p. 204.
25. *Ibid.*, p. 193.
26. *Ibid.*, 1952, p. 51.
27. Joshi, N.P., *Mathurā Sculpture*, 1966, Appendix II.
28. Agrawala, V.S., *Poddāra Abhinandana Grantha*, p. 798.
29. संकर्षणो वासुदेवः प्रद्युम्नः साम्ब एव च।
    अनिरूद्धश्च पंचैते वंशवीराः प्रकीर्तिताः।।
    Vāyu Puraṇa, LXXXIX, 1.2.

30. Agrawala, V.S., *Mathurā Musuem Catalogue, JUPHS*, 1949, p. 144. Joshi, N.P., identified it as Viṣṇu, *op. cit.*, pl. 38.
31. Prakash, V. *Khajuraho*, 1967, pp. 153-54.
32. Coomaraswamy, A.K., *History of Indian and Indonesian Art*, 1927, p. 64.
33. *Marg*, Mathurā Number, March 1962, p. 3.
34. Agrawala, V.S., *Handbook of the Sculptures in the Curzon Museum of Archaeology*, 1939, p. 42.
35. *Mahābhārata, Vanaparva*, ch. 110-13.
36. *Indian Antiquary*, Vol. XXXIII, p. 152, No. 29.
37. Vogel's *Catalogue, op. cit.*, pp. 177-68.
38. Härtel, H. 'A Kuṣāṇa Nāga Temple at Sonkh', In *Bulletin of Museums and Archaeology in U.P.*, No. 11-12, 1973, p. 166.
39. *Ibid.*, pp. 5-6.
40. *Mahābhārata, Ādiparva*, 14.2-7, 46.2-13.
41. For detailed study of Sonkh sculptures see H. Härtel, *Excavations at Sonkh*, 1993, Berlin, pp. 428-36.

8

Gupta Sculptures

WITH the advent of the Gupta rule the entire country and particularly the Northern India witnessed revival in every sphere of life. The foreign traditions imported by the Kuṣāṇas were either discarded or Indianised. The intellectual resurgence gave birth to new ideals establishing a few set formulae. Beauty had a different concept now. The great contemporary poet Kālidāsa hints in his epic *Kumārasaṁbhavaṃ*, that beauty is not meant for sin (*narūpam pāpavṛttaye*). The projection of *mārakanyās* (daughter of cupid) with charming and inviting gestures must have been necessary in the preceding era when the Buddha was frequently shown busy in practicing meditation to overpower the passions. Now the stage had passed and he had overcome the evils hence the exposition of physical beauty was restrained and the womanhood appeared in form of *devakanyās* or devotees.[1] This greatly affected the formation of figures. The female nudity which gave sensuous impression was outdated and restrained. In fact the mental discipline reflected in the contemporary products of art. The sculptor concentrated on combining the inner feelings of the saint with his outer expression. He did not care much to give body details but aspired for a higher goal, i.e. to convey the immortal bliss which a heavenly figure enjoyed.

The spiritual values underwent a great change. The concept of Bodhisattva in the Kuṣāṇa period was to promote the feelings of living for all and sacrificing for the welfare of others (*sarvasattvānām hitasukhārtham*). But now the Buddha stood for the attainment of the highest knowledge as the chief objective (*anuttarajñānāvāpti*).[2] Consequently, the smiling expression on the Kuṣāṇa figures gave way to serene calmness. The wide open eyes were half shut in meditation, looking inward under heavy and drooping eyelids. The face is now lit up with the supreme knowledge (*kevalajñāna* or *anuttarajñāna*). As Agrawala observes the permanent spiritual values of life had been cast into an aesthetic mould.[3]

The figures are no more overburdened with ornaments but appear relaxed. A subtle grace, movement and life were infused in them. The vigour was substituted by delicate treatment and linear rhythm. The youthful and slim body symbolises the flow of energy. The elaborate halo behind the head of the deity signifies the radiation of knowledge.

The animal and vegetal world finds less importance as these were no more treated as essential media for conveying the presence of a divinity, which travelling from symbols to minifigures had now developed a perfect form. Drapery with diaphanous treatment and rich folds is suggestive of lightness, ease and comfort. The divine figures were differentiated from those of mortal beings by carrying out small curly hair, elongated ear-lobes, long arms which were supposed to be the symbols of great man (*mahāpuruṣa lakṣaṇas*). To sum up, the Gupta artist strove to show the triumph of spiritualism over materialism. No doubt he imparted the best form of beauty to his piece but the figure despite its highly attractive features looks so disciplined that it does not appear mundane in characteristic. This is true of almost all sculptures produced in this golden age of Indian history.

Buddha Icons

Gallery 9 of the Museum shows the development of the Buddha image from the 1st to the 5th century A.D. The dominating front sculpture (A. 5 from Jamālpur mound; *col. ill. XXVII*, and black and white *fig. 51*) is one of the finest examples of Indian art. All

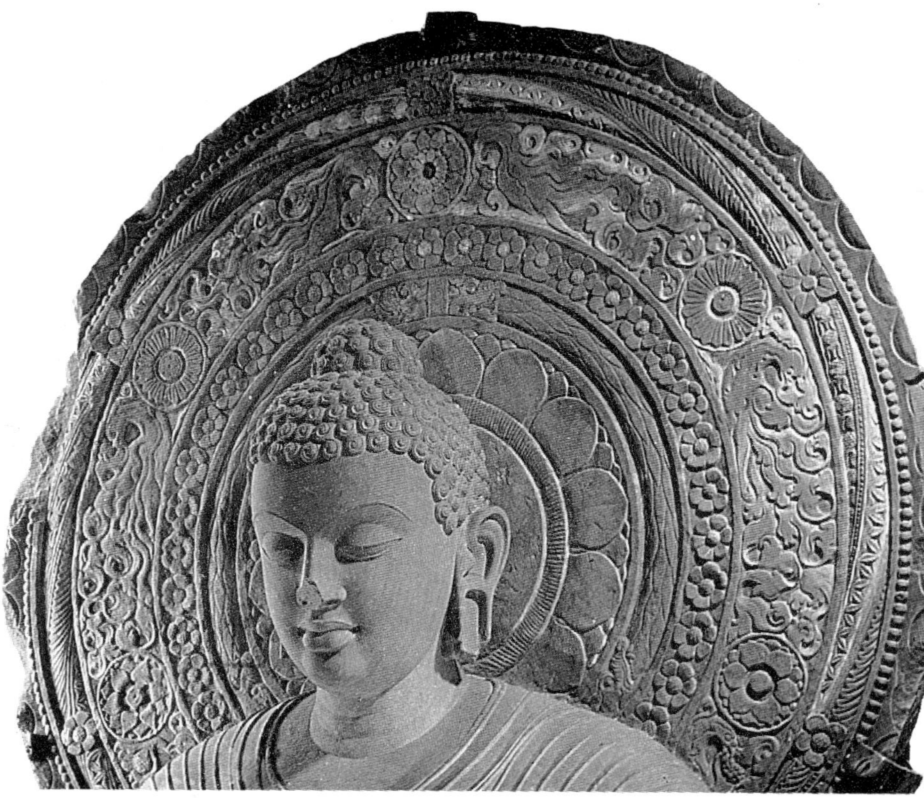

fig. 51. Buddha's bust part, Gupta

essential characteristics of the blooming Gupta art are reflected in the piece. Fine curls in hair, large ears with elongated lobes, big lotus shaped eyes closed half and looking inward, the diaphanous *ubhayānsika sanghāṭī* (drapery covering both shoulders) looking like a thin muslin cloth, the richly carved nimbus depicting several decorative bands and above all a serene contemplation are remarkably shown. He stands enjoying a super human bliss after burning all passions of life in the fire of knowledge. *Anuttarajñānāvāpti* (attainment of supreme knowledge) the chief objective in installation, as described in the inscription, must have been fully achieved through this divine creation. Standing before this classical piece one feels delighted and inspired. On the other hand the physical beauty has been nicely shown through a perfect linear rhythm, shaping the youthful body with utmost care and delicacy. The sculpture thus presents a harmonious combination of outer forms with inner feelings. This pious gift of Yaśadinna is undoubtedly a pride piece of the Mathurā School of Art. The epigraph on the pedestal reads:

1. *Deyadharmoyaṁ, Śākyabhikṣo (r) Yaśadinnasya yadatra puṇyaṁ tad bhavatu mā*
2. *tā pittro ācāryopāddhyā (dhyā) yānāṁ ca sarvva-satvā (ttvā) nuttara-jñāna (nā) vāptaye.*

This is the pious gift of the Buddhist monk Yaśdinna. Whatsoever merit (there is) in this (gift), let it be for the attainment of the supreme knowledge of (his) parents, teachers and preceptors and of all sentient beings".[4]

This may be pointed out here that it took five centuries to reach such perfection. The gradual process of evolution can be explained through the sculptures on show. The seated Buddha figure (12.188 from Guḍgāon, Haryana) first to left of the gallery belongs to the early Kuṣāṇa period, the characteristics of which have already been discussed in detail.

The exhibit below the showcase (76.I; *fig.* 52) represents the lower half of the Buddha image standing on the inscribed pedestal. The deity is flanked by devotees on both sides. The drapery is unusual and does not bear folds. The sharply incised three line *Brāhmī* epigraph is read as follows:[5]

1. *Siddhaṁ Mahārājasya deva putrasya Vāsudevasya saṁ 90 (+) 3 he 4 di 20 (+) 5 asya (yaṁ) pūrvvayaṁ bhāga (va) to pi*
2. *tāmahasya svamatasya avirudhasya pratimā chattraṁ ca pratiṣṭhapitaṁ Aryya Dharmeśvaram Arya Māgha*
3. *Arya Dhanaṁ pitaraṁ ca Sarvanandi māttaraṁ ca Jīva (śi) ri puraskṛtya sramaṇeāṁ Kāyastenaṁ*

'In the 93rd year (A.D. 171) of *Mahārāja Devaputra* Vāsudeva, in the 4th month of *hemanta* as on the 25th day, an image of the Buddha, who has full grasp of knowledge and whose faith cannot be shaken, was set up along with a parasol by a Buddhist monk who was Kāyastha (?) after paying due respect to his father Sarvanandī, mother Jīvaśrī and Ārya Dharmeśvara, Ārya Magha and Ārya Dhana.'

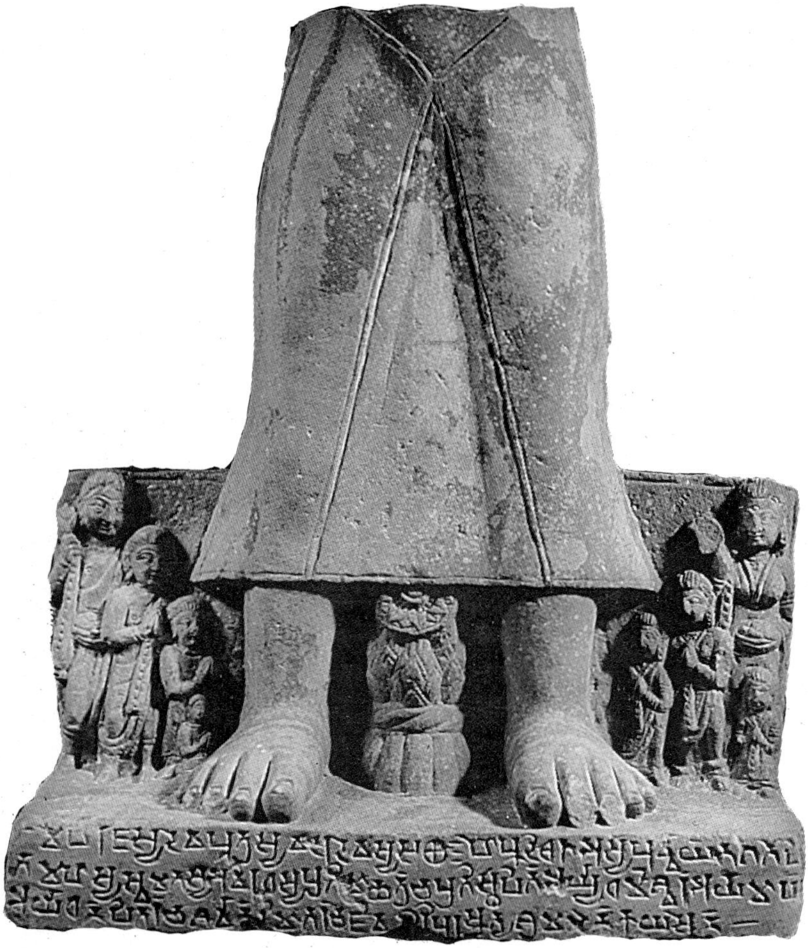

fig. 52. Buddha's lower half dated in Kuṣāṇa year 93

The wall showcase through three Buddha heads (A. 29, 41.2908 and A. 38) shows the development of the Buddha image features from Kuṣāṇa to the Gupta age. The buff stone headless statue of the Buddha (76. 16 from Govindnagar) represents him in protection imparting (*abhaya*) pose in upraised right hand the fingers of which show a web behind (*jālagrathitāṅguli karaḥ*). The palm is carved with wheel. The left hand supports the hem of the drapery which covers both the shoulders (*ubhayānsika sanghāṭī*). Between the feet of this standing figure is placed the crowned hair of Siddhārtha suggesting the superiority of the Buddhahood over the kingship. The *sanghāṭī* towards the right side bears the traces of red paint which must have been applied to harmonise the image with other statues. The next pedestal displays the torso of a Buddha image (A. 9) in the Gupta transparent folded drapery. Similar statue is seen on the other side (A. 10 from Jamālpur).

The next exhibit, an inscribed pedestal of a Buddha image (64.12 from Jamālpur) is a precious document specially for three reasons. Firstly it is the only dated inscription of Kumāragupta from Mathurā, secondly it records the name of the city, and thirdly it came from the collectorate compound (Jail or Jamālpur mound) where once stood the Buddhist monastery of Huviṣka in the Kuṣāṇa period and later in the Gupta period existed another monastery known as Yaśāvihāra in which an important Buddha image (B. 10 of Lucknow Museum) was installed by the nun Jayabhaṭṭā. The famous Mathurā Buddha (A.5) was also recovered from the same site. The present inscription has been read and translated by Srivastava as follows[6]:

1 . . . *Śrī Kumāra guptasya va (i) jaya r (ā) a (m) vva (tsare) 100 (+) 20 (+) 5 (A) śvayuja māsé di 9 asya (āṁ) diva sa (pūrvvā)yā (m) Māthurasya*

2 . . . *Māra Dasa Daṇḍa vijñāyamānasya* (i) *yadatra Puṇyam tadbhavatu mātā pitroh sarva satvānāṁ dānuttara*

3 . . . II.

. . . In the victorious year 125 of (the reign of the Gupta Emperor) Śrī Kumāragupta, in the month of *Āsayuja* (September-October) on the 9th day, on that date specified as above (resident) of Mathurā . . .Who is known as . . . Māra Daśa Daṇḍa. Whatever religious merit there is (in the gift) let it be for the welfare of mother, father and all sentient beings.

The next red sand stone figure on a stele (15-578) is a standing Buddha raising his right hand in protection pose and the left hand holding the garment. As gathered from the large eyes, elongated ears and curly hair the sculpture should belong to the 4th century A.D. The garment is very thin and the folds are just incised. The deity is devoid of halo. The last buff sand stone Buddha statue with fragmentary halo (76.26 from Govindnagar; *col. ill. XXVIII*) is important for the fact that it shows the wet (foldless) drapery at Mathurā although it is peculiar to the Sārnāth School. This may indicate that the Sārnāth idiom had taken birth at Mathurā in the 4th century A.D. but since it did not gain popularity the sculptor switched over to the customary schematic folds.[7]

Leaving this bay of the Museum next are two important inscribed pedestals of Buddha images displayed against the front pilasters. The piece to the right records the installation of the statue of Amitābha Buddha in the 26th year which corresponds to 104 A.D. (77.30 from Govindnagar; *fig 53*). The importance lies in the fact that this is the earliest archaeological evidence to prove the prevalence of the cult of *dhyānī* Buddha at Mathurā. With the accession of Huviṣka, the Buddhist art at Mathurā took a distinct turn in the beginning of the 2nd century A.D. and this included the presentation of different forms of the Master. The exhibit under consideration is the pedestal of

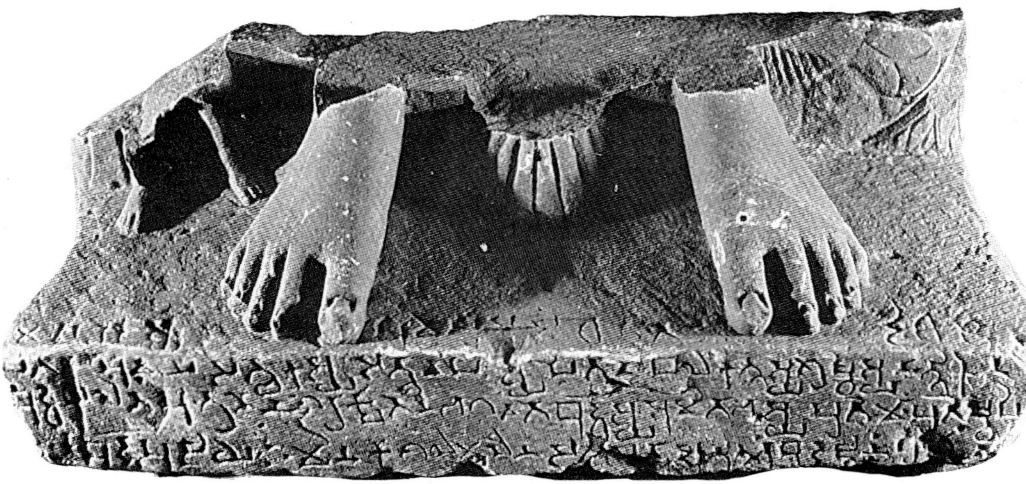

fig. 53. Pedestal of Amitābha Buddha of Kuṣāṇa year 26

Amitābha whose only the feet are extant. An attendant figure is traced by his feet and lotus carving on the other side. The latter was recognised as a figure of the Amitābha in the subsequent age. The inscription is as under:[8]

1. *Mahārājasya Huviṣkasya saṁ 20 (6) va de 20-6*
2. *etasya purvaya Satvakasya Sārthavāhasya pautreṇa Bala k (ī) ratasya śreṣṭhisya nāttikena*
3. *Buddhabalena putreṇa Nāgarakṣitena bhagavato Buddhasya Amitābhasya pratimā pratiṣṭhāpi (tā)*
4. *(sarva) Buddha pūjāye imena kuśalamūlena sarva (sattvā) anuttara Buddha jñāna (śrāvitaam)*

'On the 26th day of the second month of rainy season in the year 20 (6) (i.e. 104 A.D.) on this occasion the image of Amitābha Buddha was installed by Nāgarakṣita son of Buddhabala grandson of the merchant Satvaka and grandson (daughter's son) of the trader Balakīrti for the worship of all Buddhas. Whatsoever merit in this charity let it be for listening to the supreme knowledge of the Buddha.'[9]

Huntington on this discovery observes, 'Those who wish to see the cult as a non-Indian development or a movement that never was very popular in India will need to explain the implications of this image.[10]

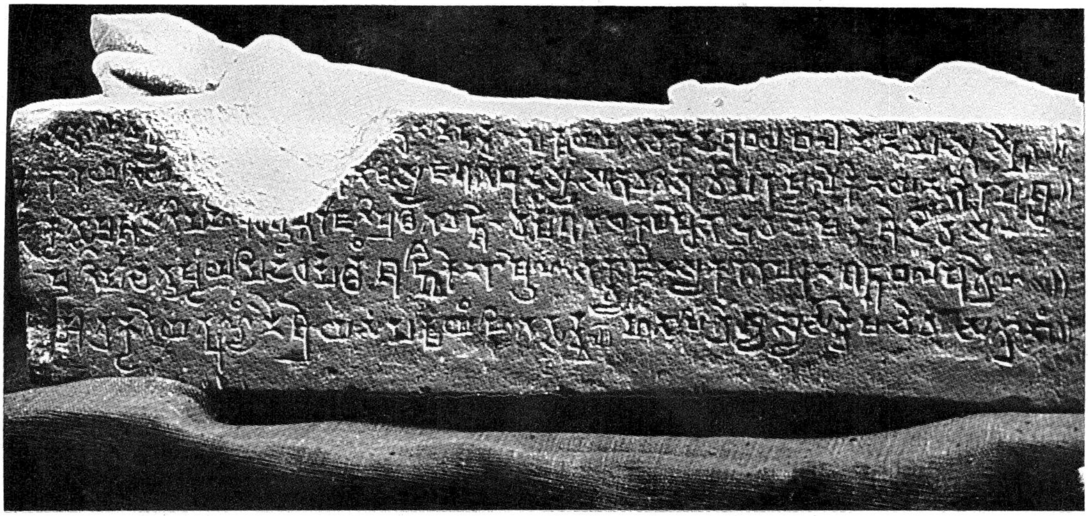

fig. 54. Buddha's pedestal of Gupta year 161

The epigraph on the corresponding jamb belongs to the Guptȧ age (82.240 from Govindnagar; *fig. 54*). While the image of the Buddha can be conjectured by the traces of feet only the inscription dated in the Gupta era 161 (A.D. 480) is of considerable importance for the fact that this is the only document discovered at Mathurā mentioning the name Budhagupta. It is read as :

1. *Siddha (ṁ) yo (?) va (ndya) . . . (ba) ndhana niruddha (?) (ja) nma kṣaya mataṁ cakre daśa bala baline namastasmai*
2. *Kārayati yah (pratimāṁ lo) kanāthasya jagati Buddhasya sa bhavati sukhī Mārasya loke nayanābhiramaśca*
3. *Kṛtsnāṁ praśāsati mahīṁ Budhagupta rājani prathita vanśe varṣaśata eka ṣaṣṭhe bhādrabade śoḍaṣe divase*
4. *Pratimā catushtayamidaṁ dharmārathaṁ Śaṅkhikena Rāṣṭreṇa bhaktyā jinasya kāritamadhunā Gangabala putreṇa*
5. *Atrakṛte yatpuṇyaṁ naiśreyasamakṣayaṁ hi tatsarvvaṁ*

mātāpitroścāsya sarvveṣāmca (a) vani satvānām (nām)

1. Success—salutations to one who preached the doctrine of destroying births (*nirvāṇa*) who is powerful by virtue of possessing the ten powers.

2. He who on earth installs an image of the Buddha, 'the Lord of the world' he becomes happy in the next birth and (is born with) a pleasing personality.

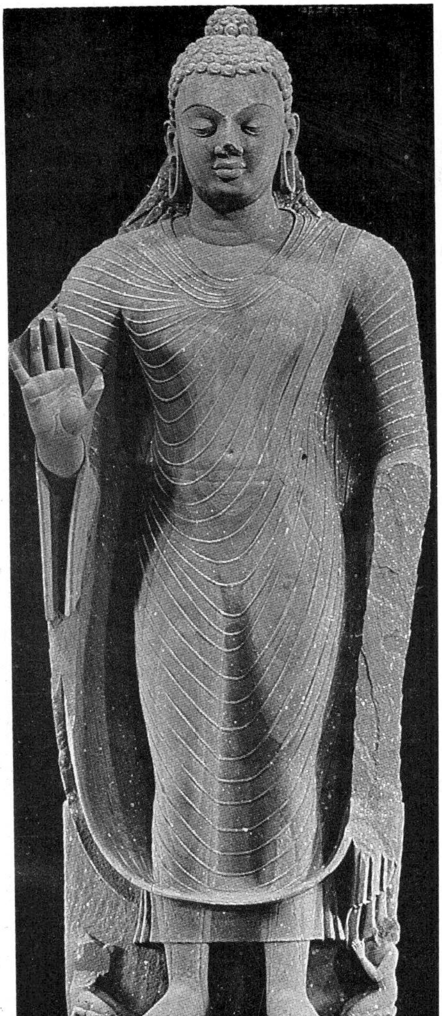

fig. 55. Buddha image carved by Yaśadinna, Gupta year 115

3-4. Today (when) king Budhagupta of the famous dynasty is administering the whole earth, in the year one hundred and sixty one, in the month of *Bhādrapada* on the sixteenth day, a set of four images of Jina (literally the conqueror i.e., the Buddha) is installed with devotion by Śaṅkhika (of Rāṣṭra family?) son of Gangabala for the sake of religions (merit).

5. Whatever merit be there in this act, may that be for the complete *nirvāṇa* of his (i.e. donor's parents and all sentient beings on the earth.[11]

The two big heads attract the attention through their notable features. The first head (49. 3510 from Camuṇḍa mound; *col. ill. XXIX*) representing the Buddha is one of the rare specimens of the Gupta art. Fine curls in hair, elongated earlobes and lotus shaped large eyes under heavy eyelids imparting serene contemplative attitude are nicely chiselled. From the colossal head (B. 61) one can imagine the exceptionally large size of the complete *Tīirthaṅkara* figure.

On the wall space between gallery 8 and 9 is seen one of the superb creations of the Gupta period (76.25; *fig. 55-56*). The standing Buddha image has lovely curls in hair, elongated ear lobes, lotus bud shaped half open eyes and a very subtle and serene expression on the face. Traces of broken halo are marked by lotus petals. The *sanghāṭī* has beautiful rippling folds through which the waist band is also seen.

The inscription on the pedestal reads as:

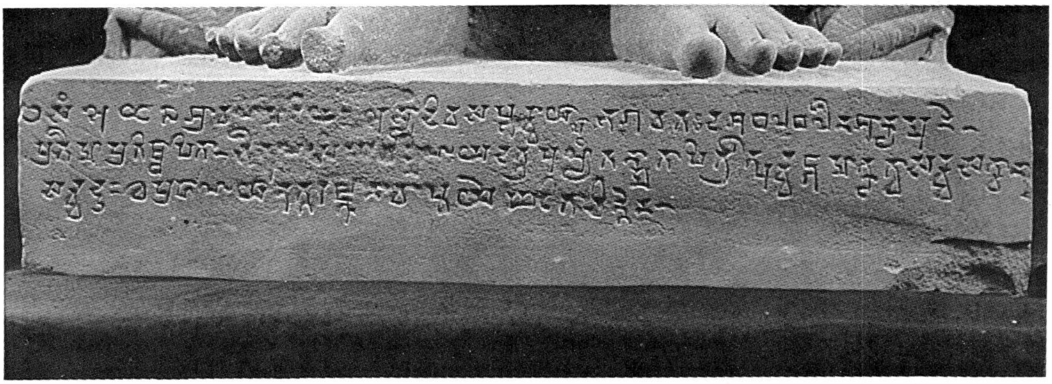

fig. 56. Inscription on the pedestal of Buddha image carved by Yaśadinna, Gupta year 115

1. *(Siddhaṁ) saṁ 100+10+5 śrāvaṇa mā di (sa 10) 3 asyāṁ divasa pūruvāyaya Bhagavataḥ daśabalabalina śākyamune*
2. *pratimā pratiṣṭhāpitā bhikṣuṇā Saṅghavarmaṇā yadatra punyaṁ tanmātā pitrāpūrvvangamat kṛtvā sarvva satvana (ṁ)*
3. *sarvva dduḥ kha praharaṇāyanuttara jñānāvāptaye ghaṭitā Dinnena*

Success! In the year 115, in the month of *Śrāvaṇa* (July-August) on the 13th day, on the day (specified) above, an image of Lord Śākyamuni, the conqueror of ten faculties (possesor of ten powers) was installed by Friar Saṅghavarman, after paying due respects to parents. Whatever merit (there is) here (i.e. in this act), let it be for the removal of the sufferings of and for the attainment of Supreme Knowledge by all sentient beings.[12]

The importance of the image is that it records beyond doubt the name of artist as Dinna who was responsible for making several masterpieces as the one in gallery 9 (A.5), and another famous *mahāparinirvāṇa* image at Kuśīnagar.[13] The image rests on a stone pedestal (78.11) which was also recovered from the same site (Govindnagar). The cavity of the pedestal received the tapering tenon of the image. It is a fine example of the technique of installation of images in early India. Such installation remained generally concealed under earth hence left uncarved.

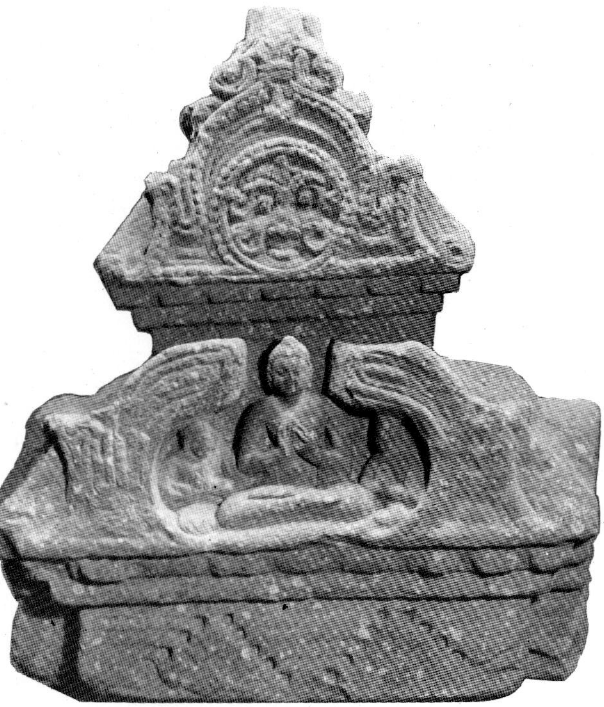

fig. 57. Buddha and *Caitya* window, Gupta

At the beginning of gallery 10 is an architectural fragment (87. 251; *fig 57*) representing Buddha in *upadeśa mudrā* (preaching pose), flanked by a devotee on either side and a conical *kīrttimukha* on top. The spotted red sandstone sculpture belonging to *c.* 5th cent. A.D. was gifted by Sri Sambho Mal Sarraf, Mathurā. Behind is seen Kubera enjoying drink (C. 5. from Jamālpur, Mathurā Collectocate), belonging to post Gupta period.

Transition Kuṣāṇo-Gupta

The death of Vāsudeva in *c.* 176 A.D. resulted in the disintegation of the Kuṣāṇa rule and there prevailed a disruption for more than a century till the Guptas came to the political scene of India in 319 A.D. The art of the transitional period (between the Kuṣāṇa and Gupta period) is sometimes termed as Kuṣāṇo-Gupta art which shows the continuity of Kuṣāṇa features and a process of refinement. Foreign features start vanishing. No separate gallery has been earmarked for the sculptures of the period of transition and they are displayed along with the specimens of the Kuṣāṇa and Gupta periods. Exhibits on the bench pedestal on the opposite side in gallery 10 of the Museum are representatives of the transitional phase.

Female Deities

To continue the view of Gallery 10 one can turn behind. A beautiful door jamp (79.120) from Janmasthān on the independent pedestal shows river goddess Gaṅgā on crocodile holding a water pot under an umbrella. Above is a full blown lotus and rosette decoration. This is followed by other floral motifs latticed decoration, wreath and *kīrttimukha* on top. The adjacent sides bear full blown lotus rosette and a stylised peacock on the top. The projecting jamb contains an attendant with shaft inside the niche. The spotted red sand stone architectural component belongs to *c.* 5th cent. A.D. On the bench pedestal he witnesses the female deities from Kuṣāṇo-Gupta to Gupta period. The eight armed Durgā (D. 12 from Kaṅkālī mound) clasping the tail of the buffalo demon (Mahiṣāsura) combines both Kuṣāṇa and Gupta features. The dating of this sculpture is disputable but on the stylistic ground it should be assigned to the early fourth century A.D. (transitional phase). The next figure (10.104) shows lower portion of Kaumārī, the female counterpart of Kumāra, (Kārttikeya or Skanda). She wears a long skirt, a beaded girdle bracelet and anklets. Sitting on a small couch she rests her feet on the plumage of her vehicle peacock (*mayūra*) who has been elegantly carved. It must belong to about 5th century A.D. The hair style and ornaments of the next figure (14.487 from Sarasvatī Kuṇḍ) are remarkable. The headless female bust (F.13) with her half exposed breasts, despite a close fitting bodice, is yet another beautiful piece of the early Gupta art. The deity pressing her breast represents Śrī Devī, goddess of abundance (19. 1600 from Hīzronwālā ṭīlā). The *yakṣī* hoding cup (50. 3549 from Mahāvidyā mound) displays graceful simplicity. This is followed by a fragmentary sculpture (35.2571) showing spirited Kārttikeya playing with cock which is perched on the thigh of Pārvatī. It may also be identified as Hārītī figure. The head (F. 33 from Azāmpur), is noted for the beautiful coiffure with looped dress and an unusually large ear-ring.

The exhibit after the bench pedestal (12.261 from Mathurā city; *col. ill. XXX*) has very charming features. The big ornamental wreath stylistically fastening the coiffure largely enhances the grace and serenity of the face. I find in agreement with H. Hartel's suggestion that the head represents Durgā garlanding herself after her victory over the demon Mahiṣa. This is corroborated with some terracotta figurines in the Museum and the famous Mahiṣāsuramardinī sculpture of Udayagiri. The next sculpture on the wall side (54. 3810 from Kaṭrā; *col. ill. XXXI*) is a unique *śālabhañjikā* (bracket) figure or a river goddess. Despite the absence of her vehicle Mulk Raj Anand describes it as Yamunā. "The slender grace of the figure flowing almost like a gentle river might easily have been called Yamunā for the quiet movement it suggests.[14] While moving to the other side of gallery 10 one passes through two pillars (R. 35 and R. 36, both from Kaṅkālī) carved with full vase, foliage and bell motifs.

Trideva Icons

The Gupta emperors no doubt were staunch Bhāgavatas but they followed the policy of religious tolerance. This can be known from the high quality of sculptures belonging to all the three sects: Buddhism, Jainism and Brāhmanism. The last of the three had, however, considerably developed due to royal patronage. Concept of trinity (*trideva*) i.e. Brahmā, Viṣṇu and Śiva (generally known as the presiding deities of creation, protection and destruction) had evolved and they were given a superior rank among the divinities. While Brahmā did not find popular depiction in art, Viṣṇu and Śiva were represented with great zeal. As appears from the scriptures undue sectarian rivalry was not prevalent. Co-existence and harmony were their ideals. The message of eclecticism has been nicely conveyed by the great contemporary poet Kālidāsa that one God has been manifested into different forms (*Ekaiva mūrtistrividhā bhidesā.*).[15]

Viṣṇu Images

Different aspects of Viṣṇu (the protector) have been presented in the gallery. At a little distance between the two pillars is Viṣṇu wearing an elaborate crown showing a lion emitting festoons of pearls (59. 4838). The figure on the bench pedestal to right (34. 2525) shows the Nṛsiṁha-Varāha-Viṣṇu form as seen from the lion (Nṛsiṁha) and boar (Varāha) heads carved on the shoulder of the deity. The elaborate crown shows two rampant lions issuing festoons in opposite directions (*siṁhasyodgīrṇa mauktikajāla*). The *vaijayantīmālā* (garland of victory) and armlets (*bhujabandha*) are very conspicuous. A long *yajñopavīta* (sacred thread) hangs down from his left shoulder to the knee. This form of Viṣṇu (Nṛsiṁha-Varāha-Viṣṇu) commenced and became a popular depiction in the Gupta period.[16] The large head (44.3112 from the Yamunā bed, Mathurā) identified as Bodhisattva may also be interpreted as Viṣṇu head. In former case the figure emitting pearled strings should be Garuda and in latter case it may be lion (*kīrttimukha*).

Viśvarūpa Viṣṇu

The next exhibit (42-43. 2989 from Bhāṅkhri, Aligarh; *fig. 58*) represents Viṣṇu in cosmic form (*viśvarūpa*) which has been described in detail in the 11th chapter of *Bhagvadgītā*. Different heavenly figures are carved in the background while the main deity majestically dominates. The universal aspect of this deity first evolved in the Gupta period and was followed as a favourite subject by the later artist. The vertical sculpture (54. 3837 from Kaṭrā) is a fragment from the *viśvarūpa* Viṣṇu image. The central deity is missing and the Rudra aspect is seen conspicuous in two large heads. The terrific look in the upper head has been well

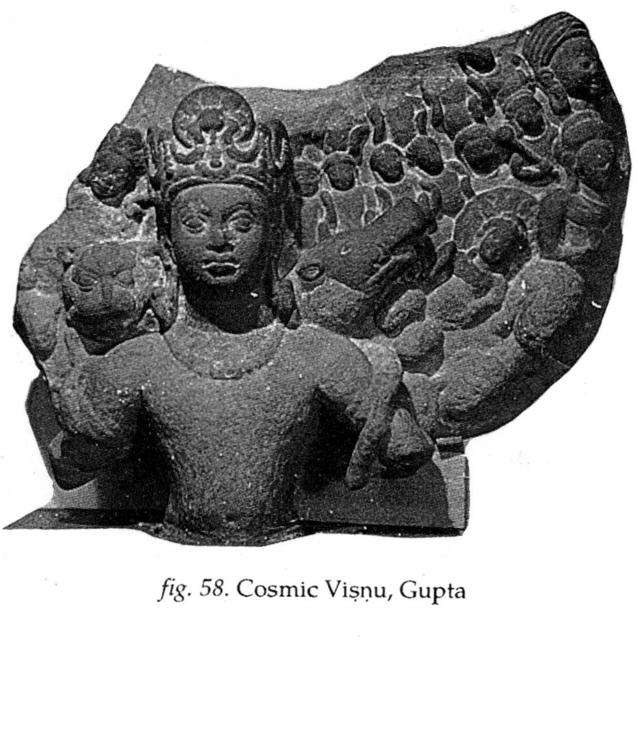

fig. 58. Cosmic Viṣṇu, Gupta

expressed through bulging eyes, wide open mouth with two sharp teeth and beard. The next torso (50. 3532 from Jaisinghpura; *col. ill. XXXII*) is a superb specimen of the age. Its suppleness, light treatment of drapery and fine curls falling on the shoulders are indicative of the high skill of the craftsman. The delicately depicted jewellery is equally significant. The first ornament round the neck is *ekāvalī* (a single-lined string of round beads). The next is the crescent shaped necklace (*candrahāra*) consisting of several pearled strings, jewels and a big square gem studded in the centre. The third ornament shows twisted cluster of pearl festoons issued from two crocodile heads may be called *makarī.* The belt or waist band (*kardhanī*) is also tastefully shown with alligator heads and other motifs. Below his knees are seen the traces of *vanamālā* or *vaijayantīmālā* (garland of victory) on the basis of which the torso may represent a Viṣṇu figure. Architectural component from a temple door representing a beautiful figure of Gaṅgā (OA 8/7; *fig. 59*) standing on her mount *makara* (crocodile). A divine musician couple is seen on its stylised tail. The holy river goddess under a tree has been shaped like a *śālbhañjikā.* The buff sand stone sculpture should belong to 6th-7th cent. A.D. (from the collection of Sri Sambho Mal Sarraf). Kṛṣṇa (incarnation of Viṣṇu) is seen quelling the *nāga*

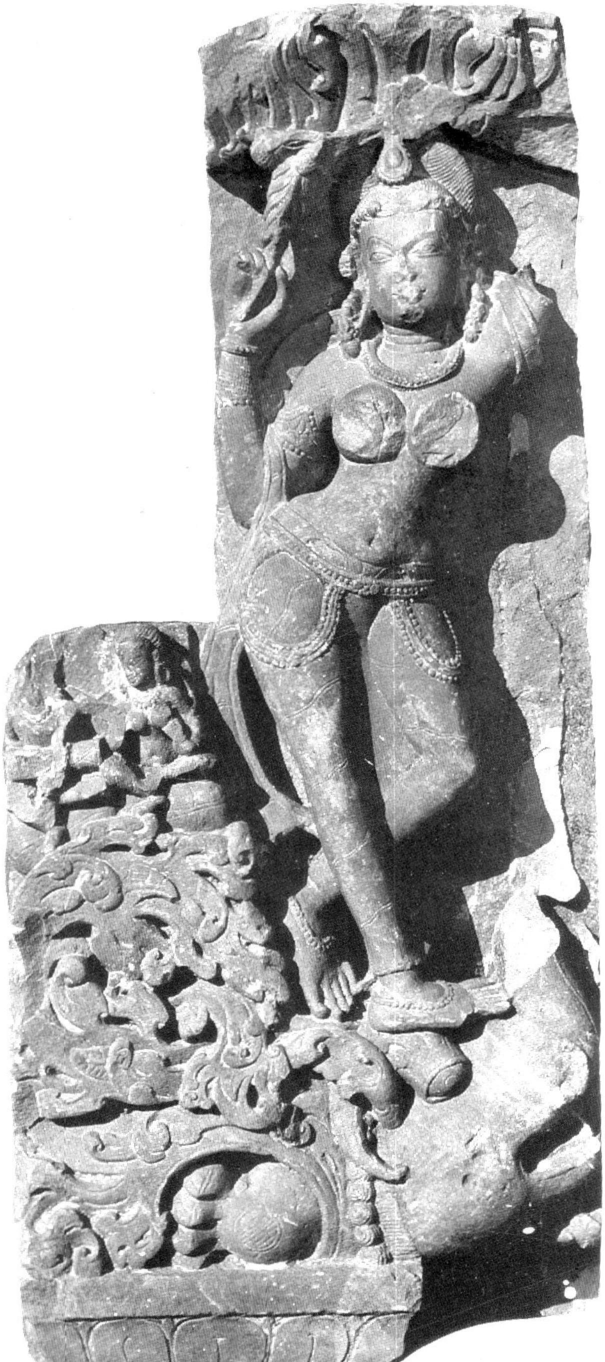

fig. 59. Gaṅgā, late Gupta

Kāliya who had made his abode in the Yamunā near Vrindāban (47.3374 from Kaṅkālī, Mathurā city). The people of the locality were much afraid as sometimes he used to take human and cattle life. The boy Kṛṣṇa in order to punish him once jumped into the river. But the five hooded huge cobra (Kāliya) and his retinue caught him in their deadly clutches. After a long dual Kṛṣṇa was victorious and the subdued *nāga* was forced to leave the river. In the sculpture, Kṛṣṇa is mounting over the hoods of the serpent who has been tied with a rope (*pāśa*). The third figure below is the consort of Kāliya, helplessly clasping her hands and praying for the release of her husband. The lady with high tuft of hair has a sad face.

Behind, another event from Kṛṣṇa's life has been represented on the stele (D. 47 from Gataśram ṭilā; *col. ill XXXIII*). As the story runs the people of Vraj worshipped Indra (god of heaven) with great pomp and show. Kṛṣṇa persuaded the people to discontinue this practice and to start the worship of mountain Govardhana. This humiliated Indra who caused heavy rains in order to frighten the people. But his evil intentions were not fulfilled due to the efforts of Kṛṣṇa who offered shelter to each person and animal after miraculously lifting the mountain (Govardhana) like an umbrella. The cows and people rest under protection. The sculpture stylistically should belong to post-Gupta period,[17] although Coomaraswamy assigned it to late Kuṣāṇa (*c.* 3rd cent.) period.[18]

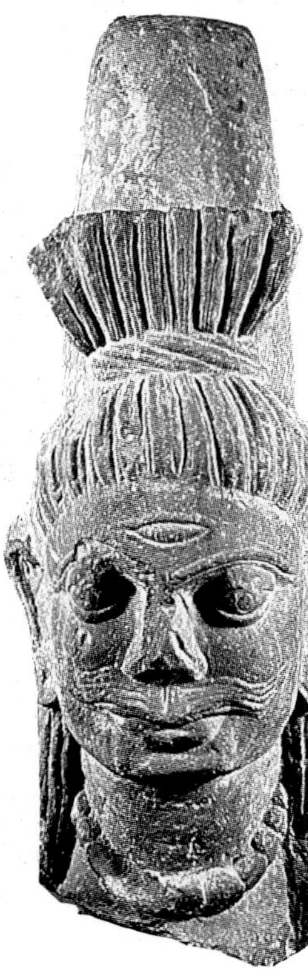

fig. 60. Śivaliṅga, post Kuṣāṇa

On the next pedestal is placed a *caitya* window (*kīrttimukha* 51. 3607) showing a beautiful female head with tastefully arranged coiffure in different wavy plaits. The border of the arch is carved with foliage which is issued from another face seen on the top. Such architectural pieces decorated the exterior walls of the temples and palaces. The frieze behind (76.7 from Mogarra P.S.) displays the dancing celestials.

Śiva Images

Śiva, an important god of the Hindu trinity (Brahmā, Viṣṇu and Śiva) is represented in several forms. He is the only god whose symbolic worship has continued simultaneously with anthropomorphic form. This unmanifest form is shown through a *liṅga* (phallus). Sometimes the *liṅga* aspect is combined with his human form and the figure is called as *mukhaliṅga* (*liṅga* with face).

The sculpture (14-15.462 from Mātāmaṭh, Arīng; *fig. 60*) in gallery 10 is a double faced *Śivaliṅga* belonging to *c.* 3rd century A.D. Matted hair, third eye on the forehead and a garland of human skulls (*muṇḍamālā*) or *akṣamālā* (garland of *rudrākṣa*) are some notable characteristics on one of the faces. It rests on a capital (R. 11 from Kansa ṭīlā, Mathurā) of Gupta period showing *kīrttimukha* and other motifs. It is followed on the junction of gallery 10 and 11 by a single faced *Śivaliṅga* with a band (19.1588 from Asgarpur). Below is a square base of some *stūpa* (47.3266) at Gokarṇeśwara with lions seated back to back and a human head on four directions. It must belong to 3rd-4th century A.D.

An independent octagonal pillar in gallery 11 (29.1931 near from Raṅgeśvar temple) with square base and top is carved with a big trident (weapon of Śiva known as *triśūla*) and a corpulent figure with third eye (*trinetra*) and a shaft in the right hand. His lower part seems naked and may represent the *lakulīśa* cult which had a strong hold at Mathurā. The inscription records that some Uditācārya set up two *Śivaliṅgas* (Upamiteśvara and Kapileśvara) in the 61st year of the Gupta Era (A.D. 380).

The epigraph is read and translated as follows:

1. *Siddhaṁ (l) Bhaṭṭāraka-Mahārāja (rājādhi) rāja-Śrī-Samudra- gupta-sa*
2. *(tpu) trasya bhaṭṭāraka-ma (hārāja)-(rājādhi) rāja-Śrī-Candra- gupta*
3. *sya vija (ya) rājya-samvatsa (re) (Gupta)-kāl-⁻ānuvarttamāna- saṁ*
4. *vatsare eka-ṣaṣṭhe 60 I . . . (pra) thame śukla-divase pam-*
5. *camyāṁ (I) asyām pūrvvā (yaṁ) (bha) ga (vat-Ku) sikad daśamena bhagava*
6. *t-Parāśarāc=catur (th) e (na) (bhagavat-Ka) pi (la)-vimala-śi-*
7. *ṣya-śiṣyeṇa bhagavad (-Upamita)-vimala-śiṣyena*
8. *āryy-odi (tā) cāryye (ṇa) (sva)-pu (ny-ā). pyāyana-nimittaṁ*
9. *gurūṇāṁ ca kīrtya (rtham=Upamiteśva) ra Kapileśvarau*
10. *Gurvv-āyatane guru . . . pratiṣṭhāpitau nai-*
11. *tat=khyāty-arthamabhili (khyate) (atha) māheśvarāṇām vi-*
12. *jñaptih kriyate sambodhanam ca yathā-kā (li) n=ācāryyā*
13. *ṇāṁ parigraham=iti matvā viśanka (m) pūjā-pura*
14. *skāra (m) parigraha-pāripālyaṁ kuryyād=iti vijñaptir=iti (1)*
15. *yaś ca kīrty-abhidrohaṁ kurry(ā) d=yaś=c=ābhilikhitamu-paryyadho*
16. *vā (sa) pamcabhir mahāpātakairupapātakaiśca samyuk-tas-syāt (1)*
17. *jayati ca bhagavā (ndanḍah) rudra-danḍogra-(nā) yako nitya (m)*

1-5. Accomplished! In the . . year-of the victorious reign of the *Bhaṭṭāraka Mahārāja Rājādhirāja,* the illustrious Candragupta, the good son of the *Bhaṭṭāraka Mahārāja Rājadhirāja,* the illustrious Samudragupta on the fifth of the bright half of the first (Āṣāḍha) of the year 61 following the Gupta era.

5-10. On this aforesaid (*tithī*), the *liṅgas* Upamiteśvara and Kapileśvara (comprising the portraits of) the teachers 'were installed in the Teacher's Shrine. Ārya Uditācāryya, tenth from the Bhagavat Kuśika, fourth from the Bhagavat Parāśara, a stainless disciple's disciple of the Bhagavat Upamita (and) a stainless disciple of the Bhagavat Kapila, for the commemoration of the preceptors and for the augmentation of the religious merit of self.

10-16. (It is) not written for my own fame, but for beseeching the worshippers of Maheśvara. And it is an address to (those who are) the *Ācāryas* for the time being. Thinking them to be (their own) property, they should preserve, worship, and honour (them) as (their own) property. This is the request. Whosoever will do harm to these memorials or (destroy) the writing above or below, shall be possessed of the five great sins and the five minor sins.

17. And may divine *daṇḍa* be always victorious, whose staff is terrific and who is the foremost leader.[19]

The pedestal in the centre displays on one side three faces of Brahmā with head (48. 3433 from Mathurā city) of 4th century and on other a sunken niche (19.1570 from Yamunā bed, Mathurā) with Śiva with matted hair holding *triśūla* and rosary seated in *lalitāsana* on his mount bull. The buff sand stone sculpture should belong to *c.* 6th century A.D. The next pedestal shows a *Śivaliṅga* (15.516) from the Museum well, with four human heads each projecting in different directions. From the traces of the fifth head it appears that the sculpture was intended to be a *pañcmukhī* (five faced) *liṅga* representing the *pañcānana* aspect of Śiva. These heads are called *tatpuruṣa, aghora, vāmadeva* and *sadyojāta* facing the east, south, west and northern directions respectively. The top face which looks upward is known as *Īśāna.* The sculpture may belong to late Kuṣāṇa or early Gupta period on the basis of the thick projecting band fastened round the four heads.

Behind is seen a beautiful *Śivaliṅga* of Gupta period with four faces, one facing each direction and wearing garland of skulls (85.161). On the central pedestal, Śiva and his consort Pārvatī stand with their vehicle Nandī (bull) (30. 2084). The sculpture which is carved on both sides shows Śiva with matted hair (*jaṭā*), third eye (*trinetra*) and phallus in erect position. His garment is made of tiger's skin (*vyāghrājina* or *vyāghrāmbara*) as indicated by the paws, marked on the ends. The bull wears a garland of skulls (*muṇḍamālā*). The sculpture with Śiva and Pārvatī is commonly known as

Umāmaheśvara. Umā probably holds a lily in her left hand. The gallery has two Gupta period *ekamukha Śivaliṅgas* with matted hair (66.5 and 34.2528). The third eye on the forehead in conspicuous in the latter case.

A round stele figure of Kārttikeya (14.466; *col ill. XXXIV*) on his vehicle peacock holding a spear (*śakti*) in the left hand is exhibited while turning to the wall of gallery 11. Peacock is added only in Gupta period as the Kuṣāṇa figures do not show this vehicle. Kālidāsa mentions this form as-*Mayūra pṛṣṭhāśriya guha*.[20] The depiction is met with in the gold coins of Kumāragupta Mahendrāditya.[21]

He is anointed by Brahmā (right) and Śiva (left) (?) who pour sacred water from the jars. The sculpture represents a significant event when Kārttikeya was requested by the gods to become the commander of the divine army and to defeat the mighty demon Tāraka. After his consent anointment ceremony (*abhiṣeka*) was performed. The deity is known through several names viz. Svāmī Kārttikeya, Skanda, Kumāra, Ṣaḍānana, Mayūravāhana, etc. In the southern parts of the country he is popularly known as Subramaṇya.

The next exhibit (71.23; *fig. 61*) shows Śiva with matted hair, garland and *rudrākṣa* and phallus in erect position (*ūrdhvaretas*).

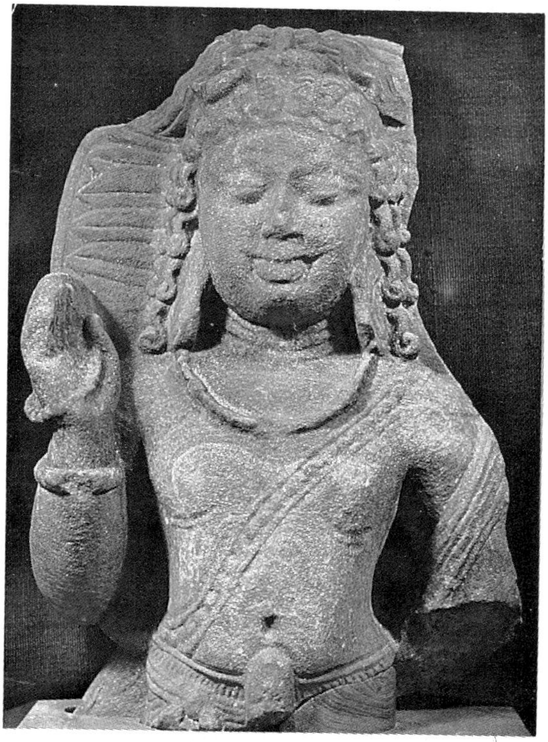

fig. 61. Śiva, Gupta

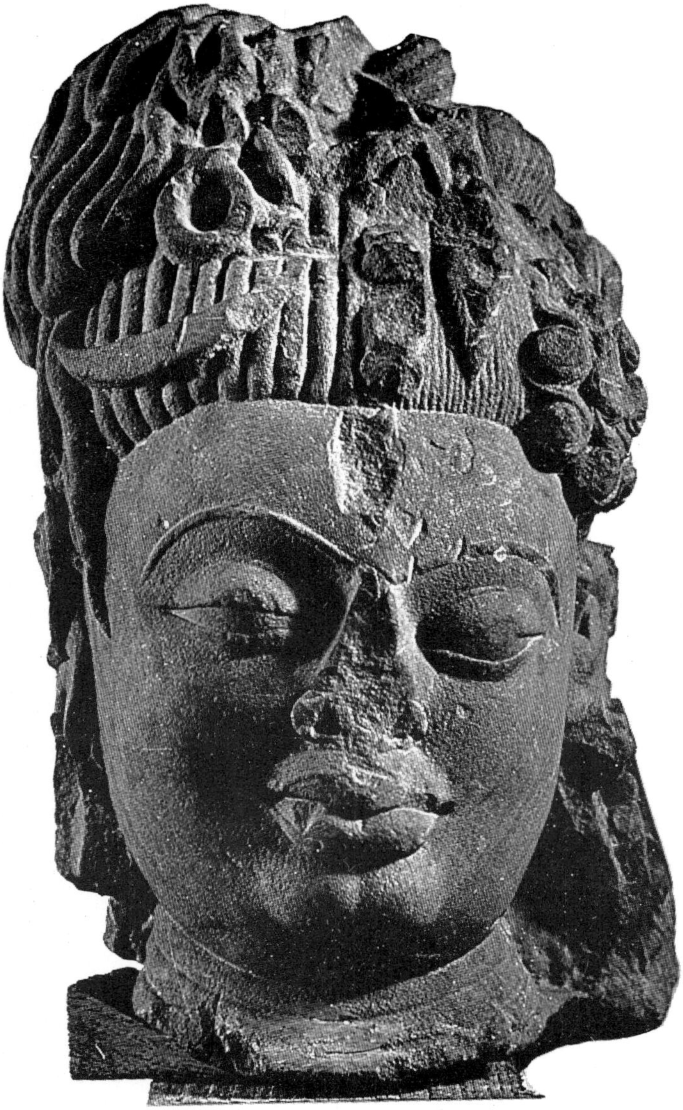

fig. 62. Arddhanārīśvara head, Gupta

The showcase on the adjacent wall presents five heads of the Gupta period showing different hair styles. (K T 242, 54.3770, 13.362, 68.15 and rare head of Harihara 17.1336). The central piece Arddhanārīś-vara head (13.362 from Mathurā city; *fig.* 62) displays high workmanship of plastic art of Gupta age. The male and female aspects are seen quite distinct. The right side shows high matted hair and a crescent while the left side is adorned with beautiful coiffure and a large round ear-ring with a vertical pearled string. The very look differentiates the masculine and feminine features. Śiva's eyebrow is drawn up while the female portion has been delicately handled. Only a master artist could have brought this perfect synthesis.

The story of the merger of Śiva and Pārvatī aspect has been differently narrated in the *Purāṇas.* According to *Kalki Purāṇa* once Pārvatī saw her own reflection on the chest of Śiva which shone like a crystal. Mistaking it for some other woman she felt jealous and requested Śiva not to leave her for a single moment. The popularity of Arddhanārīśvara aspect is evidenced by the fact that Kālidāsa begins *Raghuvaṁśa* by offering prayer to Pārvatī- Parameśvara who remain inseparable.[22] Metaphysically, the *arddhanārīśvara* form suggests the union of *prakṛti* and *puruṣa.* Pārvatī and Parameśvara (Śiva) are eternally united (*sampṛkta*) like speech (*vāk*) and meaning (*artha*). This hints to the approach of eclicticism.

The bench pedestal on the opposite side of gallery contains a fragment from the exterior wall of temple (45.3211 from Swāmighāṭ, Mathurā) showing god Śiva, seated cross legged, in preaching attitude, (*vyākhyāna mudrā*). He is in *ūrdhvaretas* form, organ in erect position. In the left arm he holds a staff (*lakula*) on the basis of which he may be identified as *lakulīśa*. A scarf (*yogapaṭa*) is fastened to his knees. He is flanked by two persons who are probably his disciples as confirmed by the book like object held by the figure to the right and Śiva's preaching pose. But these flanking figures have also been described as Brahmā and Viṣṇu. The frieze is further decorated with beaded garland (dentils) and fine scroll work. An architectural fragment of Gupta period from Mathurā now in the State Museum, Lucknow (No. V. 550) also represents a similar *lakulīśa* Śiva in preaching pose but the disciples are missing.

Other Significant Images

The showcase on wall side between gallery 11 and 12 consists of sculptures of varied interest.

Gaṇeśa: The first sculpture (15. 758; *fig.* 63) is an early (probably the earliest) representation of the elephant headed deity Gaṇeśa who is popularly known as the younger son of Śiva. The story of his birth is variously described in the texts.[23] He is supposed to have been created by Pārvatī as her personal attendant. Once when she was in the toilet, Gaṇeśa refused the entry of Śiva to the house. The angry god cut off the head of the impertinent servant. Hearing this news, Pārvatī became very sad and felt annoyed. To please her, Śiva promised to restore the head and ordered his *gaṇas* (attendants) to bring the head of the first available creature. A single tusked (*ekadanta*) elephant was seen first and his head was placed on the body of Gaṇeśa. He was also bestowed with several boons.

In the present statuette the deity is seen as a nude and corpulent dwarf resembling the *yakṣa* figures. He wears the sacred thread of serpent (*vyāla yajñopavīta*).[24] On his left hand he carries the balls of sweet (*laḍḍū*) which he eats with his trunk.

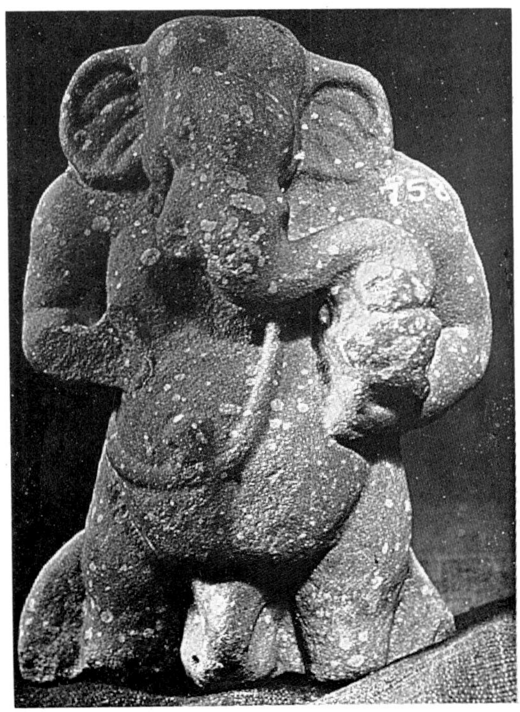

fig. 63. Gaṇeśa, early Gupta

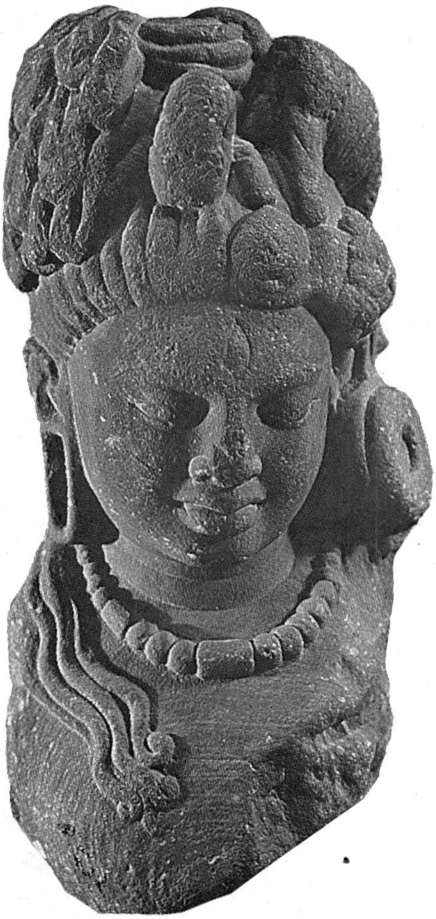

fig. 64. Arddhanārīśvara bust, Gupta

The next exhibit is an exceptionally beautiful bust (15.772 from Gosna; *fig. 64*) illustrating the Arddhanārīśvara aspect of Śiva, a composite form of Śiva and Pārvatī indicating the fusion of male and female energies. The right side with high matted hair (*jaṭājūṭa*) represents Śiva while the remaining half with tastefully combed hair and tuft bedecked with flowers, large and heavy ear-ring, is that of Pārvatī. The forehead bears a vertical third eye and an *ekāvalī* (pearled necklace) is worn round the neck. The beautiful lips, half closed eyes and a subtle grace have further enhanced the attraction of composite features.

Viṣṇu figure (D. 28) is significant to note as the deity has been shown with *āyudhapuruṣa* (personified arms), a distinct feature which evolved in the Gupta period and was followed subsequently.[25] Here the mace has been shaped as a lady (*gadādevī*) while the disc assumes the male form (*cakrapuruṣa*).

The vertical stele (46.3226) represents Indra with a crown, horizontal third eye on the forehead and his vehicle divine elephant Airāvata. The next slab (70.58) illustrates Viṣṇu in Trivikrama form measuring the whole universe in three steps.

The sculpture, Rāvaṇānugraha carved in relief (35. 2577) depicts the episode of Rāvaṇa lifting the mountain Kailāśa on which Śiva and Pārvatī are sitting. As the story goes when Rāvaṇa was passing through Kailāśa his chariot was stopped by Nandikeśvara, an attendant of Śiva. On inquiry Rāvaṇa was informed that the area was prohibited as Śiva and Pārvatī were sporting. The angry demon king of Laṅkā then started lifting the mountain in order to frighten Śiva and his retinue. Knowing the cause of disturbance Śiva pressed the mountain and Rāvaṇa with his foot. The load became unbearable and the mighty demon began to weep. As he wept he was called Rāvaṇa. He was relieved of the heavy burden when Śiva was pleased after many prayers. In the present sculpture the prowess of Rāvaṇa is shown through his strong physique, heavy head and terrific look. At the same time his anxiety is noticeable from the bulging face. Pārvatī clings to her husband who is seen in *ūrdhvaliṅga* form (organ erect) and pressing Rāvaṇa with his right foot.

The showcase is flanked by two doorjambs from a temple and depicts two chief river goddesses viz. Gaṅgā (73.26) with a small figure of crocodile below the pedestal and Yamunā (73.27) with tortoise. Holding full bloomed stalked lotus they stand in the central niche and one of their female attendants holds a waterpot. The upper parts of jambs show mainly the undercut scroll work. These pilasters with twelve other sculptures were presented to the Museum by the management committee of Caurāsī Khambhā temple, Mahāban.

The next exhibit (38.2797 from Gopālpur, Mathurā) is a doorjamb carved on two adjacent sides representing a dwarf playing on a small drum and another blowing the conch. The pillar is fully decorated with half lotus medallion, *kīrttimukha* (festoons issuing from the lion's face) and *pūrṇakumbha* (full vase) motifs. The other exhibit (17. 1343 from Gāyatrī Ṭīlā) which again seems to be a fragment from the doorjamb represents an amorous couple while the border is carved with a fine scroll. The upper compartment depicts an apsidal shrine. It must belong to the Kuṣāṇa period. Another architectural fragment which looks like a pillar or sidejamb (I.13; *col. ill. XXXV*) shows a rampant lion with a rider holding the reins. The animal is shaped like a leogryph (*śārdūla*) and depiction of such rider figures (*śārdūlārohī*) was a favourite subject of the Gupta artist. The next sculpture (76.23 from Govindnagar) bears an attendant with a long shaft and scroll motif. The last piece (38.2793 from Isāpur) represents a nicely carved pediment with a figure of warrior on either side. The central medallion consists of a lion's face. The lower horizontal niche is left blank. The creeper and floral motifs are noteworthy.

Jaina Icons

A part of gallery 11 on the other side is devoted to the Jaina sculptures the evolution of which has already been discussed while explaining gallery 2 (chapter 5). The specimens displayed here carry from Gupta to medieval period. The *Tīrthaṅkaras* are either seated in meditation (*dhyānastha*) or stand in penance (*kāyotsarga* or *daṇḍa*). It is interesting here to make a distinction between a Buddha and a Jina (*Tīrthaṅkara*) image. The Jina, particularly in Mathurā bears a religious mark (*śrīvatsa*) on his chest while the Buddha figure is devoid of it. The Buddha head is provided with an *uṣṇīśa* (bump of hair) which is not seen with the Jina figure upto the Gupta period. While the Buddha statues can be seen in various poses e.g. protection (*abhaya*), earth touching (*bhūmisparśa*), turning the Wheel of Law (*dharmacakra pravartana*), preachaing (*vyākhyāna* or *upadeśa*), meditation (*dhyāna*), the Jina is found in sitting or standing posture. The independent pedestal on one side represents the 22nd Jina, Neminātha (37. 2738 from Caurāsī mound) head flanked on right by four armed figure of Balarāma holding cup and plough and on the other side by four armed Kṛṣṇa, whose attributes are now gone.[26] The Jina sits in meditation on the lion throne in the centre of which a wheel is carved. Neminātha being considered as a cousin brother of Kṛṣṇa is sometimes shown with Balarāma and Kṛṣṇa.

The other side displays another Jina Candra-prabha (86.150) seated in meditation on the lion throne on which a crescent is also marked as his cognizance. Both the sculptures belong to the early medieval period.

The bench pedestal shows a meditating Jina of Gupta period (B. 1) followed by a headless but beautiful image of the first Jina Ṛṣabhanātha (B. 6) as noticed by the matted hair falling on the shoulders. He is attended by a flywhisk bearer on each side. Halo which is partly preserved on the back stele, depicts several decorated bands.

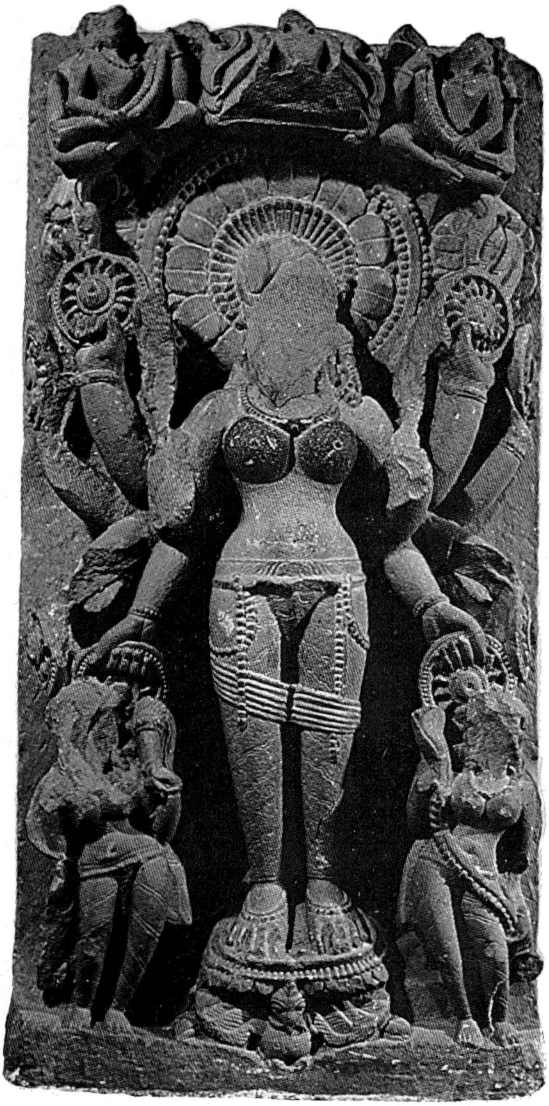

fig. 65. Cakreśvarī, Medieval

The vertical stele in buff stone (12.268 from Kaṭrā; *col. ill. XXXVI*) is of great significance for the fact that its pedestal records the Jina as *Ṛṣabha.* It became easy to identify such images (locks of hair falling on shoulders) as that of Ādinātha or Ṛṣabhanātha. The pedestal which also bears a *dharmacakra* placed on a pedestal in centre reads as :

1. *Siddham Ṛṣabhasya pratimā Samudra*
2. *Sagarābhyām Sangarakasya*
3. *datta Sāgarasya pratimā*

> "Success! This image of Ṛṣabha was dedicated by Samudra. The image (belonged to) Sāgara"

Dr. Agrawala is inclined to assign it to the early 4th century A.D.[27] but it appears to belong to the 6th century A.D. The next statue (18.1505 from Kosī Kalān) shows Supārśvanātha or Pārśvanātha with a serpent canopy seated in meditation.

On the adjacent bench pedestal are seen two female Jaina deities, Cakreśvarī, *Yakṣī* of Ṛṣabhanātha (D. 6 from Kaṅkālī mound; *fig. 65*) with a Jaina version of Vaiṣṇavī with ten arms holding a disc in each (head missing). She stands on a lotus seat supported by her mount *Garuḍa*; below stand female attendants with garland and flywhisk. A canopy also shows celestials with garland. The buff sand stone statue belongs to *c.* 10th century A.D.

The next is Ambikā (*Yakṣī* of Neminātha) a Jaina counterpart of Pārvatī (D. 7) mounting on lion with a child on her left lap. Several deities like Gaṇeśa, Kubera, Viṣṇu and Balarāma are also seen beside the *caurī* bearing attendants. In the centre of top is seen a meditating Jina and the background shows beautifully chiselled flowers. The pedestal bears eight female devotees in adoration. The buff sand sculpture is of *c.* 9th-10th century A.D.[28]

On the independent pedestal in centre of Jaina complex is installed a *sarvatobhadra* (quadruple) with image meditating seated Jina in each direction (B. 65; *fig. 66*). These may be identified as Ādinātha with hair falling on shoulders, Supārśvanātha or Pārśvanātha with snake canopy, Neminātha with his attendant as Gomedha and Padmaprabha with lotus mark on seat. The red sand stone statue should belong to *c.* 7th-8th century A.D.

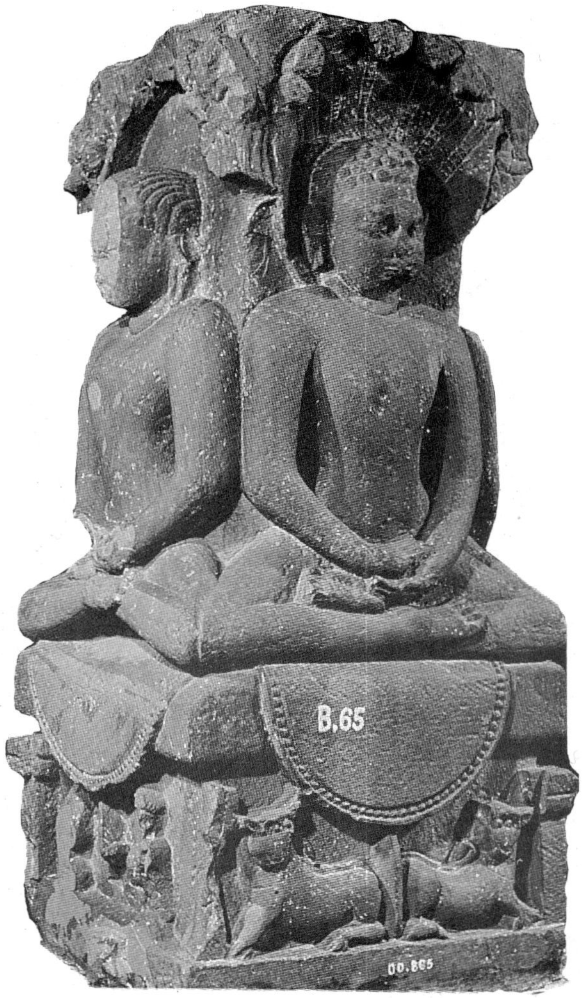

fig. 66. Quadruple Jaina image, post-Gupta

References

1. Sharma, R.C., 'Buddhist and Brāhmanical Sculptures from Mathurā', In *The Golden Age*, Marg, 1991, p. 22.
2. *Ibid.*, p. 21.
3. Agrawala, V.S., *Studies in Indian Art*, 1965, p. 199.
4. Vogel, J. Ph., *Catalogue of the Archaeological Museum at Mathurā*, 1910, p. 50.
5. Srivastava, V.N., *Epigraphia Indica*, XXXVII, Part IV, pp. 151-54 and *Bulletin of Museum and Archaeology in U.P.*, No. 4, December 1969, pp. 19-22.

6. Srivastava, V.N., *Bulletin of Museum and Archaeology in U.P.*, No. 1, March 1968, p. 16.
7. Sharma, R.C., *Buddhist Art of Mathurā*, 1976, pp. 218-19.
8. *Ibid.*, pp. 231-32.
9. Sharma, R.C., New Buddhist Sculptures from Mathurā, In *Lalit Kalā* No. 19, p. 26.
10. Huntington, J.C., 'Mathurā Evidence for the Early Teaching of Mahāyāna', In *Mathurā—the Cultural Heritage*, 1989, p. 89.
11. Thaplyal, K.K. and Srivastava, A.K., *Journal of the Epigraphical Society*, No. 9.
12. Sharma, R.C., *Buddhist Art of Mathurā*, 1984, p. 223, footnote 148.
13. *Ibid.*, pp. 223-24.
14. *Marg*, Mathurā Number, 1962, p. 51.
15. *Kumārasambhavam*, VII, 44.
16. Agrawala, V.S., *Mathurā Museum Catalogue, JUPHS*, 1949.
17. *Ibid.*, p. 119.
18. Coomaraswamy, A.K., *History of Indian and Indonesian Art*, 1927, pp. 66, 235, fig. 102.
19. Bandarkar, R.D., *Egipgraphia Indica*, Vol. XXI, Part I, Jan. 1931, pp. 8-9.
20. *Raghuvaṁśam*, XI. 4.
21. Mukherjee, Chanda, *Gupta Numismatic Art*, 1991, pp. 92-93.
22. *Raghuvaṁśam* I. 1.
23. Agrawala, V.S., *Mathurā Museum Catalogue, JUPHS*, 1949, p. 138.
24. Gopiṅatha Rao, T.A., *Hindu Iconography*, Vol. I, Pt. 1, pp. 50-51.
25. *Raghuvaṁśam*, X. 60.
26. Agrawala, *op. cit.*, 1950, pp. 64-65.
27. *Ibid.*, pp. 56-57.
28. *Ibid.*, p. 65.

9

Mathurā Through Coins

COINS have played an important role in the reconstruction of cultural and political history of India. When the barter system failed to fulfil the requirement of trade and commerce of the developing economy, necessity was felt of issuing the coins for exchange. In India and also at Mathurā the currency seems to have commenced in the 6th century B.C. and the earliest coins are known as Punch Marked (*āhata mudrā*) found in different irregular shapes mostly in silver.[1] The names of early currency as known from literature are *paṇa, pāda, kasaka, śāṇa* and *śatamāna*. These bear a number of stamped symbols on obverse and reverse. These were followed by cast coins produced through moulds and bear several symbols. Balarāma and Kṛṣṇa have been noticed by P.L. Gupta on some of these specimens.[2] The coins were also issued by the local kings of small states and their names are in the early *Brāhmī* letters and on other side the figure of the deity. The coins from Mathurā bearing the names of Hindu kings Mitra, Datta and Śaka coins belong to *c.* 1st century B.C.[3]

The bay of gallery 12 houses a small gallery of coins displayed in five showcases arranged in the chronological sequence. The first showcase shows the coins from the punch marked type to the local currency.[4] Besides, some moulds which were used for fabricating the cast coins are also seen.

The second showcase displays the coins issued by the foreign invaders as the gates of the land were open to the foreigners since the invasion of Alexander in the 4th century B.C. Several Indo-Greek, Parthian and Scythian rulers infiltrated into India to exercise their sway in the 2nd-1st century B.C. and they issued coins in their names even in a short duration. The important kings as known through currency are Diodotus, Demetrious, Menander, Apolodotus, Maues, Azes and Gondophernes.[5] Their coins show a marked improvement in shape and quality. The currency was in gold, silver and copper with Greek/Kharoṣṭhī/ Brāhmī legend and the deity of their choice. The coins were called as *stator* (gold), *dracom* (silver), *chelkon* (copper) and *obel* (alloy).

These were followed by the Kuṣāṇa rulers who established a mighty kingdom and ruled for about two hundred years. The important names are Vema Kadphises, Kaniṣká, Huviṣka and Vāsudeva.[6] They issued generally gold and silver coins bearing the figure of the king on obverse and a deity on the reverse. The name of the king and deity is also recorded.[7] A good number of foreign features are noticed in these coins.

The third case contains the coins belonging to the Gupta and Medieval Hindu rulers who reigned between the 4th and the 6th centuries. The names of the Gupta kings are Candragupta I, Samudragupta etc.[8] The gold coins or tokens (known as *dināra*) were issued on different important events. These are rich in variety and metal contents. Foreign features were discarded and Indian conventions were revived. This is testified by the numismatic (coins) as well as the plastic art.

After disintegration of the Gupta rule regional kingdoms were established and several currencies came into existence but the aesthetic significance was lost.[9] Half of the third showcase shows coins of different Hindu rulers of Medieval India.

With the advent of Muslim rule in the 11th century the coins were issued in different fashion. These are displayed in the 4th showcase. The figure of deity and king was eliminated and stress was laid on calligraphy in Arabic. Beside the name of the ruler, year and mint were also recorded. The other side contained the Quaranic citation (*qalamā*). The early issues bear the figure of Lakṣmī and a horse rider. Quality of Mughal coins improved and figure of the king was also added. Jahāṅgīr issued the zoadiac currency also. The gold coins were known as *mohar*, silver as *rupia*, copper as *dam/faloos* and alloy as *kani* or *gani*. The coins of Śāh Ālam II record the name of Mathurā as Islāmābād and that of Vrindāban as Muminābād.[10]

The last showcase contains some post Mughal coins of Native States, East India Company, British rule and the post Independence issues.

The Museum houses a large number of coins in its reserve. Some hoards were examined by the State Museum, Lucknow.[11]

References

1. Srivastava, A.K., Mathurā as known through the coins, In *Bulletin of Museums and Archaeology in U.P.*, June-December, 1993, p. 30.
2. Gupta, P.L., 'Early Coins of Mathurā Region', In *Mathurā — the Cultural Heritage*, 1989, p. 127, Pl. 13.1.1.
3. Allan, J., *British Museum Catalogue, Ancient India*, Intro, p. cix-x.
4. *Journal of the Numsimatic Society of India*, XV, Pt. I, p. 61.
5. Minutes of the Managing Committee, April 1888 to March 1889, Provincial Museum N.W.P. and Oudh, Curator's Report for March 1888, Apk. A, p. 7.
6. Narain, A.K., 'Ancient Mathurā and the Numismatic Material', In *Mathurā — the Cultural Heritage*, 1989, p. 117.
7. Mitterwallner, G.V., *Kuṣāṇa Coins and Sculptures*, 1986.
8. Srivastava, A.K., *op. cit.*, p. 33.
9. *Ibid.*
10. *Ibid.*, p. 34.
11. *Ibid.*, Treasure Trove Finds from Mathurā District, pp. 37-41.

10

Medieval Sculptures

THE sculptures of the Medieval period (*c.* 7th to 12th century A.D.) belong to an era when the quality of art started descending. The art in the Gupta age had reached its zenith achieving the highest aim in harmonising the beauty with spirit. The Medieval artist for some time strived hard to follow the Gupta idiom but could not successfully handle the chisel.[1] The spiritual expression, slimness, suppleness, grace and elegance start gradually vanishing. National disintegration reflected itself in the domain of artistic creations also. The treatment is rather coarse and formal. The human figure continues to dominante and emphasis is laid on ornament, high crown, multiplication of arms of the deity and increase in the number of attendant figures which symbolize process. The deity is gradually transformed into a *tantra*. The high stylisation is noticed by the carved figures (*tribhaṅga* pose). Depiction of amorous and erotic scenes on the exterior walls of the temple and particularly on the doorjamb is a distinct feature of the age. The presiding deity is flanked by other divinities of the family (*parivāradevatās*).[2] The red sandstone is generally replaced by buff colour as is evident from most of the exhibits in gallery 13. Several remarkable specimens of the sculptural art of the Medieval period have seen their way from Rataul, Meerut district to the Mathurā Museum. Besides a few outstanding sculptures were installed in Mathurā and its adjoining region. All these finds prove that even after the fall of Mathurā city and the School of Plastic Art the chisel did not stop and the sculptors migrated to safer places and practised the art with same zeal.

The gallery commences with some interesting Sūrya (sun) images ranging from the late Gupta period to the late Medieval phase and hailing from different places. The first sculpture on the independent pedestal (92.1 from near the Museum premises) represents a damaged but rare and very interesting Sūrya pillar in red sand stone. The main deity (head missing) sits under a big decorated balcony and he is drawn in a high and magestic chariot of seven horses. Below, a panel represents the demons of darkness covering their face and sinking into the ocean. The bottom panel also shows some seated figures but their mutilation does not permit the identification. The side jambs show Piṅgala with an inkpot, Vāyu (god of winds) with blowing scarf, Kārttikeya, Kubera, and others. The sculpture belongs to the late Gupta period, *c.* 6th century A.D.

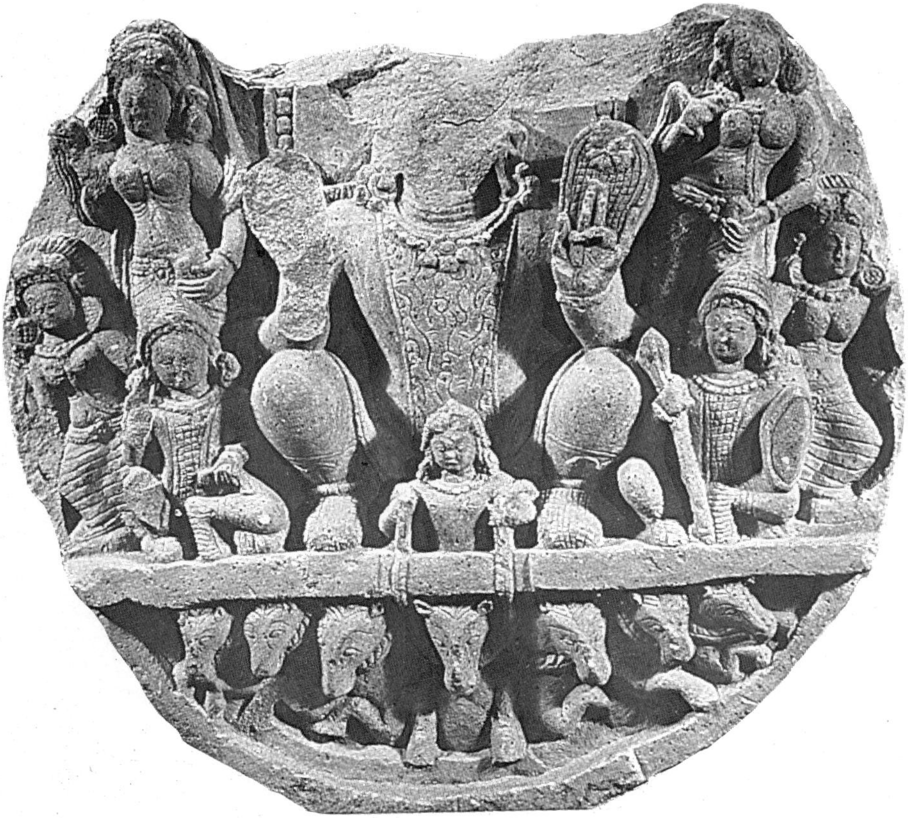

fig. 67. Sūrya, Medieval

A circular plaque on a high wooden pedestal (68.1 from Cūrīwālīṭek, Mathurā; *fig. 67*) carved on both sides illustrates the sun god with his retinue. He is drawn in a chariot of seven horses whose reins are held by the charioteer Aruṇa. His two attendants Daṇḍa and Piṅgala are seen seated near his legs holding a staff and inkpot respectively. Like their master they also wear boots. Above, the deity is flanked by two females holding flywhisk. The other two ladies are seen with bow. These female figures are indentified as consorts of Sūrya under different names viz. Uṣā, Pratyūṣā, Chāyā, Nikṣubhā, etc. Depiction of Sūrya with boots and armoured drapery is northern variation, which was known as *udīcyaveṣa*, a style prevalent in the northern part of the country. It shows that the influence of the foreign art tradition in Indian pantheon continued through ages. The wall side displays the bust of Sūrya (86.147 from Bicaulā, Ṣhahjahanpur, U.P.) with two full blown lotuses, high crown, large ear rings, coat of mail, lotus halo and flying celestials. The buff sandstone statue belongs to *c.* 10th century A.D.

The Sūrya image from Madaura, Sādābād (88.18; *fig. 68*) inside a decorated pillared

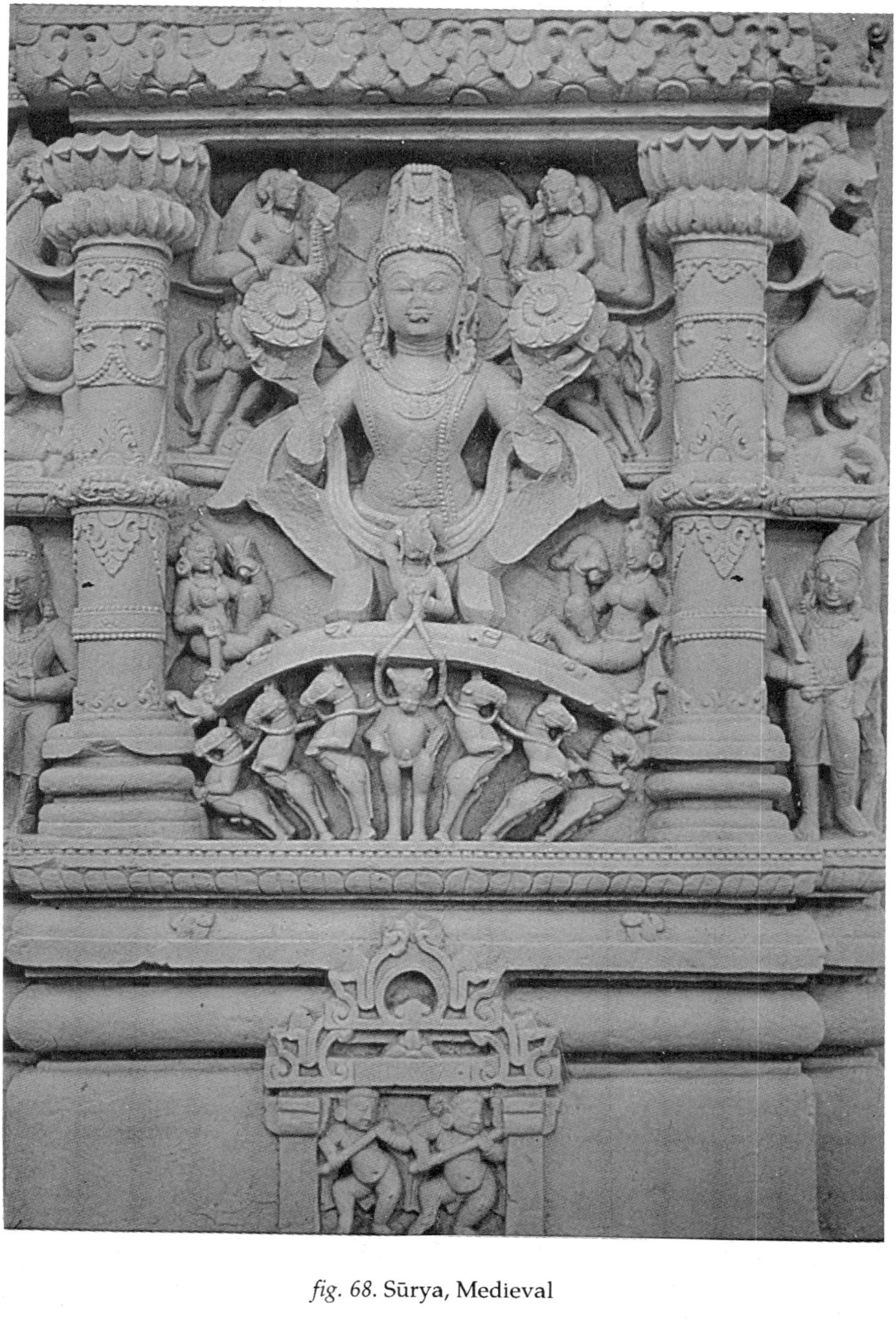

fig. 68. Sūrya, Medieval

niche is a superb citation of Medieval sculptural art. The deity sits in the squatting posture wearing crown, ear rings and other ornaments, armour and boots. In his upraised two hands he holds two stalked lotuses. Halo also bears lotus decoration behind the head. He is drawn in the chariot of seven horses whose reins are held by the lame charioteer Aruṇa while Uṣā and Pratyūṣā are seen with bow near the shoulders. The other two female attendants Chāyā and Nikṣubhā rest with flywhisk. The top corners bear two hovering celestials with garlands. Daṇḍa and Piṅgala with their usual attributes i.e. staff and inkpot respectively outside the pillars and above them is seen couchant leogryph. Beside the richly carved decorated pillars showing several mouldings, the niche also has a top frieze of rosette scroll. The bottom is carved with a niche surmounted by a *caitya* window showing two musicians. The entire compostion bespeaks not only the superb aesthetic workmanship but also reflects an atmosphere of calm and joy after a big accomplishment, i.e. rising of dawn after subduing the darkness. The buff sand stone statue belongs to *c.* 10th century A.D.

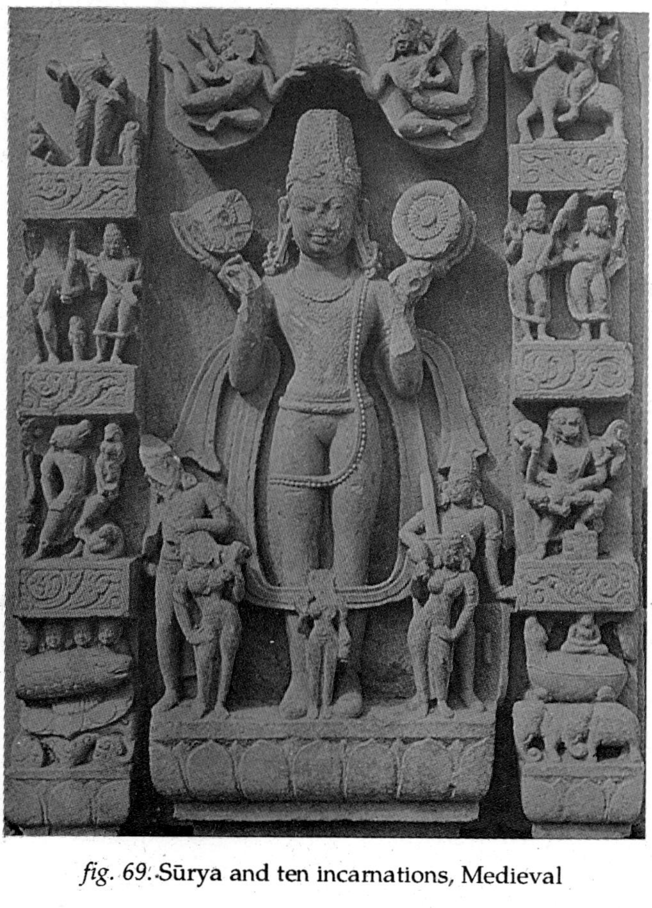

fig. 69: Sūrya and ten incarnations, Medieval

The pedestal to our right on one side shows standing Sūrya (88.19 from Madaur, Sādābād; *fig. 69*) with usual attributes, i.e. stalked lotus, large earring, high crown, armour and boots. He is flanked by his attendants Piṅgala (defaced) and Daṇḍa with a sword and shield and Chāyā and Pratyūṣā on both sides and Bhūdevī between the feet. All these deities stand on lotus pedestal. On top are seen two flying *gandharvas* holding a crown above the head of Sūrya. The rarity of the sculpture is that two side jambs represent the ten incarnations. It begins from Matsya on lotus in water to our left, Kūrma on elephants to our right, Varāha lifting earth to the left Nṛsiṁha slaying Hiraṇya-kaśiup to right, Vāmana with umbrella and Rāma with arrow to our left, Paraśurāma with battle axe and Balarāma with snake hood and cup to right, Buddha in *abhaya* (head missing) to left and finally the four armed Kalki on the horse back to the right. The buff stone sculpture should belong to *c.* 10th century A.D.

The bust of Sūrya (86.147) with two full blown lotuses, high crown, large earrings, coat of mail, lotus halo and flying celestials. The buff sandstone statue belongs to *c.* 10th century A.D.

The beautiful and intact image of Sūrya (88.9 from Rataul, Meerut; *col. ill. XXXVII*) which represents him standing on lotus pedestal with high crown, earrings, rich ornaments, armour indicated by beaded line and boots. He holds two large stalked lotuses in the two hands. The halo of the deity is intricately carved with full blown lotus and a disc of rays. In the centre of his feet stands Bhūdevī having pot and bearded Piṅgala with a pen, inkpot and writing plank and on other side Daṇḍa with a long staff. The other deities are two horse headed Aśvini-kumāras and two female deities with lotus. In the centre of the side jambs are seen Uṣā and Pratyūṣā in charging posture. Above one notices four armed Brahmā, Śiva and Viṣṇu on two sides and the top semi circular band represents in the centre a seated meditating four armed figure of Sūrya holding two stalked lotuses flanked by garland bearing celestials and two divinities on elephants carrying pitchers. The buff sandstone statue belongs to *c.* 11th century A.D.

A small sculpture (68.2) on the wall shows the son of sun, Revanta on the horse back under the umbrella. The buff sandstone scultpure belongs to *c.* 9th century A.D.

The small showcase consisting of a beautiful four armed Viṣṇu (78.1; *fig. 70*) is seen on the wall side. In his *vāmana* (dwarfish) form, he

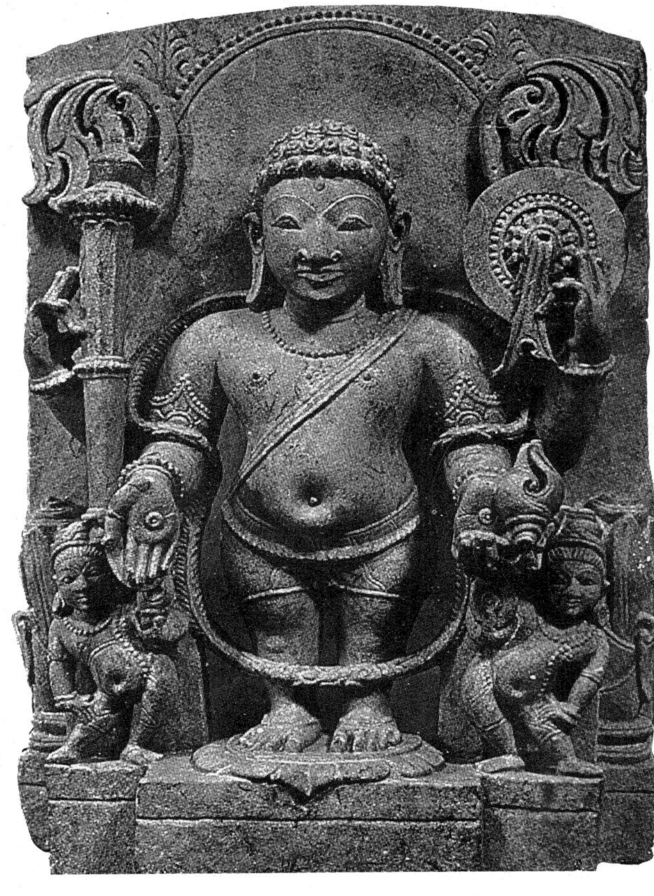

fig. 70. Vāmana Viṣṇu, Medieval

holds a club *cakra* (disc) conch and boon bestowing posture. The two attributes (*cakra* and *śaṅkha*) are personified. The stele in buff sandstone belonging to *c.* 10th century A.D. was acquired from Meerut.

The two doorjambs behind (R. 57 and 10.137) are the example of amorous poses, a notable feature of the Medieval sculptures. The bottom of the jamb generally represents river deities (Gaṅgā and Yamunā) standing on their vehicles, crocodile and tortoise respectively. They stand carrying full vase (*pūrṇakalaśa*) in their hands and are generally accompanied by the parasol holding attendants.

Brahmā Icons

To follow the sequence one may turn to left and walk to the zig-zag wall showing the icons of Brahmā (god of creation) and his family. The first (13.285) is the bust of this deity with three heads and matted hair. It has already been explained that his heads represent the four *vedas*. There is a small beard on the chin of the central head. The second sculpture (16.1258) represents Sarasvatī (goddess of wisdom and learning) playing on a *vīṇā* (lyre).[3] The next dominating image is another version of Brahmā (D. 20 from Sarasvati Kuṇḍ, Mathurā) who is shown on a lotus seat and holding two ladles, *sruk* and *sravā*.[4] The last exhibit on this small wall is Brahmāṇī (40.2874/7), the consort of Brahmā, with three heads. She is often represented as one of the seven divine mothers.

Viṣṇu Icons

On the adjacent main wall are seen the figures of Viṣṇu and his family. The first sculpture (14.379 from Pannāpur wall near Satohā) is a beautiful creation of Medieval age. Here the god sits in *padmāsana* in the posture of meditation (*dhyānamudrā*). His attributes are mace (*gadā*) and wheel (*cakra*) in the two upraised arms, while the other two hands are placed one over the other befitting the posture of meditation. The conch is seen below. The deity wears an elaborate halo beside other jewellery and the figures of Brahmā and Śiva appear above. The meditating Viṣṇu sculptures are influenced by the Buddhist inconography and are sometimes known as Viṣṇu in the Buddha incarnation (*Buddhāvatāra*).[5]

An elaborate version of the above sculpture (D. 37 from Gataśram temple, Mathurā; *fig. 71*) can be viewed where the main deity bears almost the same characteristics. Below the lotus seat is seen Bhūdevī (goddess earth) with folded hands and flanked by the snakes deities (*nāgas*) and other devotees or donors. The two attendant figures holding conch and wheel are his personified weapons (*āyudhapuruṣas*), *śaṅkhapuruṣa* and *cakrapuruṣa*, respectively. The background above consists of several divinities.[6]

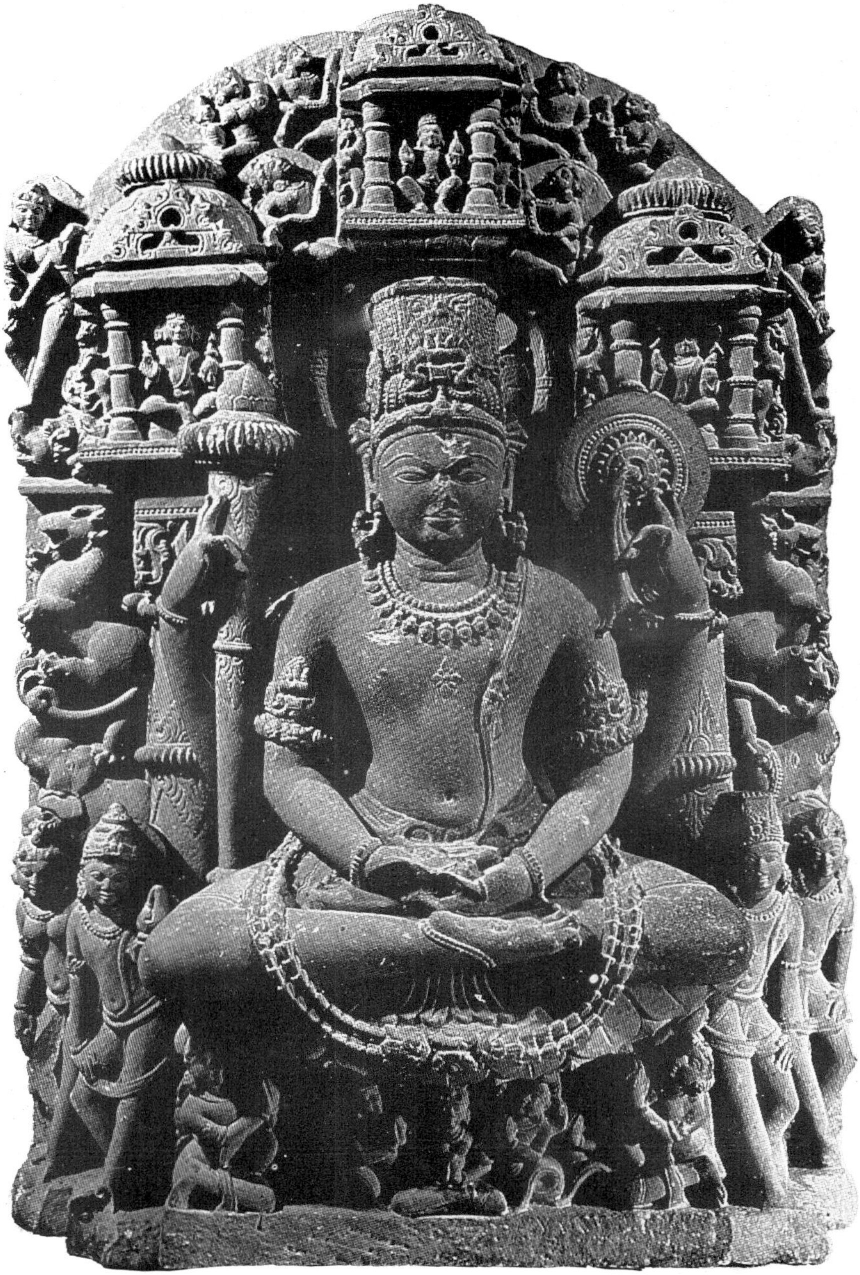

fig. 71. Meditating Viṣṇu, Medieval

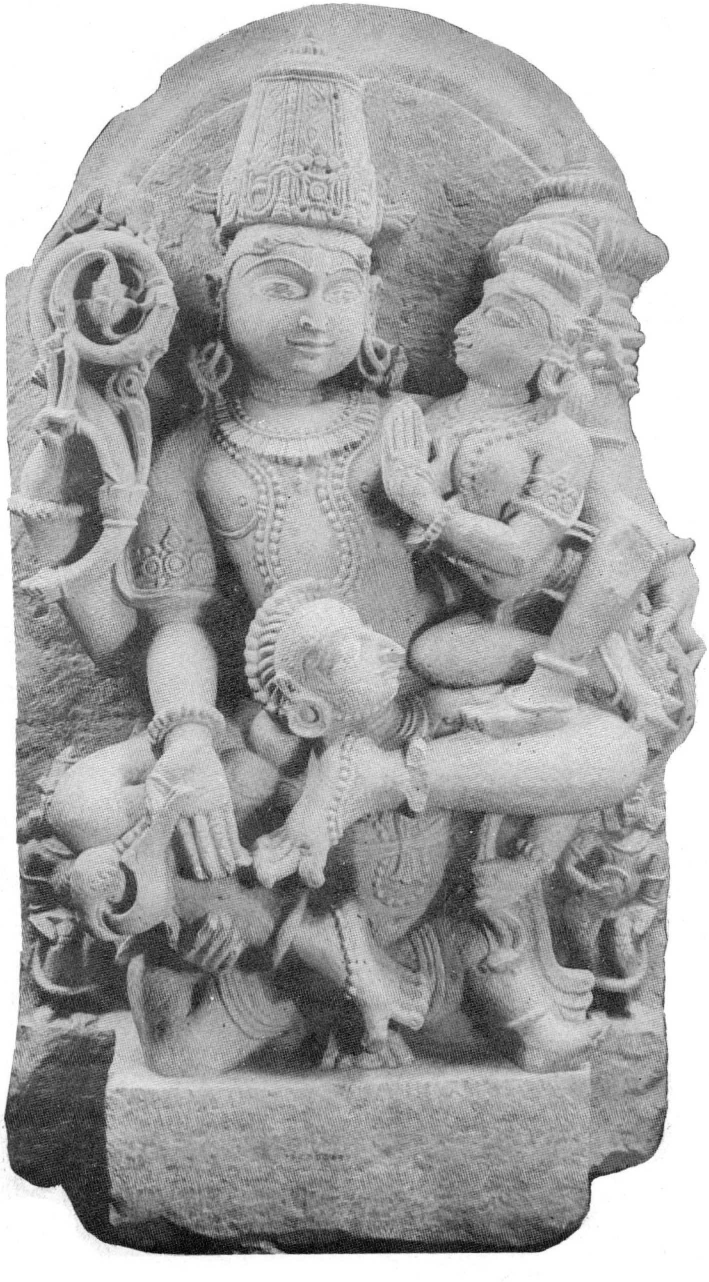

fig. 72. Lakṣmī-Nārāyaṇa, Medieval

The next sculpture on the wall side (85.185; *fig. 72*) represents Viṣṇu and Lakṣmī mounting on their vehicle Garuḍa—personified eagle. The deity holds stylised lotus, conch, club and disc. His spouse Lakṣmī claps her hands in adoration. The back stele on lower side shows personified attributes—the buff sandstone image belonging to *c.* 10-11th century A.D. was acquired through the courtesy of local police. In the black basalt stele (D. 35 from Vrindāban) the deity stands on a lotus seat wearing a high conical diadem and holding mace, wheel, conch and boon bestowing (*varada*) feature. Lakṣmī and Sarasvatī are seen as attendants.[7]

The stele (93.31 from Gokul Barrage; *fig. 73*) representing two standing Viṣṇus is a rare iconographic specimen for the fact that both the deities have identical features. Each stands on a scroll pedestal with four arms holding mace, disc, conch and boon bestowing posture. Below the

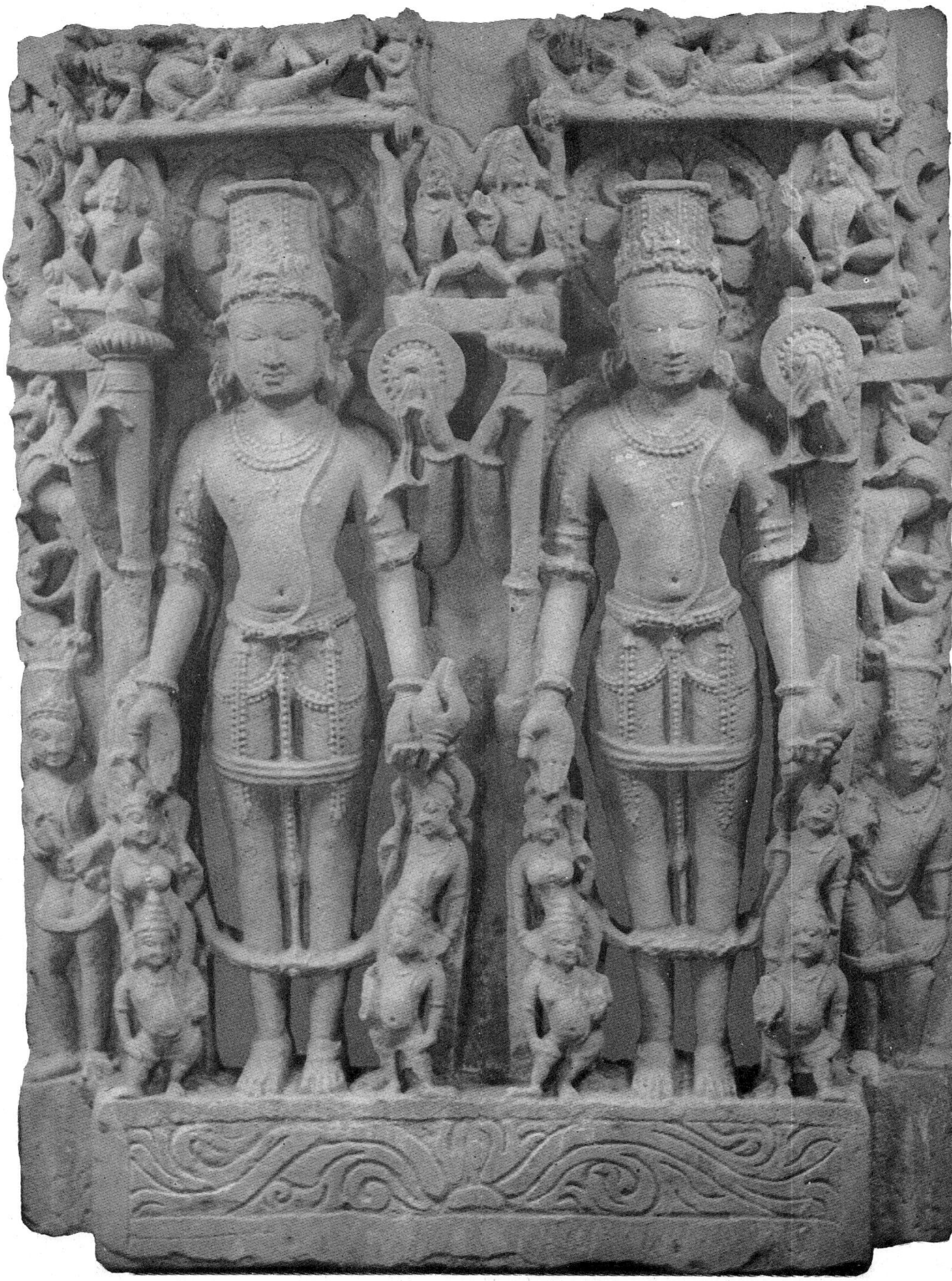

fig. 73. Double Viṣṇu, Medieval

suspended two hands stand Lakṣmī with lotus on one side and personified Garuḍa holding snake and a crest on head (*śaṅkha cūḍa*). In front of these are noticed two personified attributes. i.e. *śaṅkhapuruṣa* and *cakrapuruṣa.* Above on the side jambs are seated four headed Brahmā and probably Śiva. On the top is seen *Śeṣaśāyī* Viṣṇu (sleeping on the cosmic serpent) and Lakṣmī is shampooing his feet. The extreme side jambs on one side projects an attendant with a decorated staff or sceptre, while his counterpart on the other side holds a vase type object. The other decorative motifs are leogryph on elephant, crocodile with trunk and foliage. The buff sandstone beautiful sculpture belongs to *c.* 10th century A.D.

The next wall sculpture (88.10 from Rataul, Meerut; *fig. 74*) represents standing four armed Viṣṇu, which is a beautiful specimen of medieval plastic art. The deity holds the usual attributes i.e. club, disc, conch and protection in an upraised hand. He is flanked by personified weapons i.e. *śaṅkha-puruṣa* and *cakrapuruṣa,* Bhūdevī and Śrīdevī, Balarāma and devotees. Upper side jambs bear the figures of bearded Brahmā and Śiva with matted hair and *triśūla.* The halo shows lotus and disc of rays.

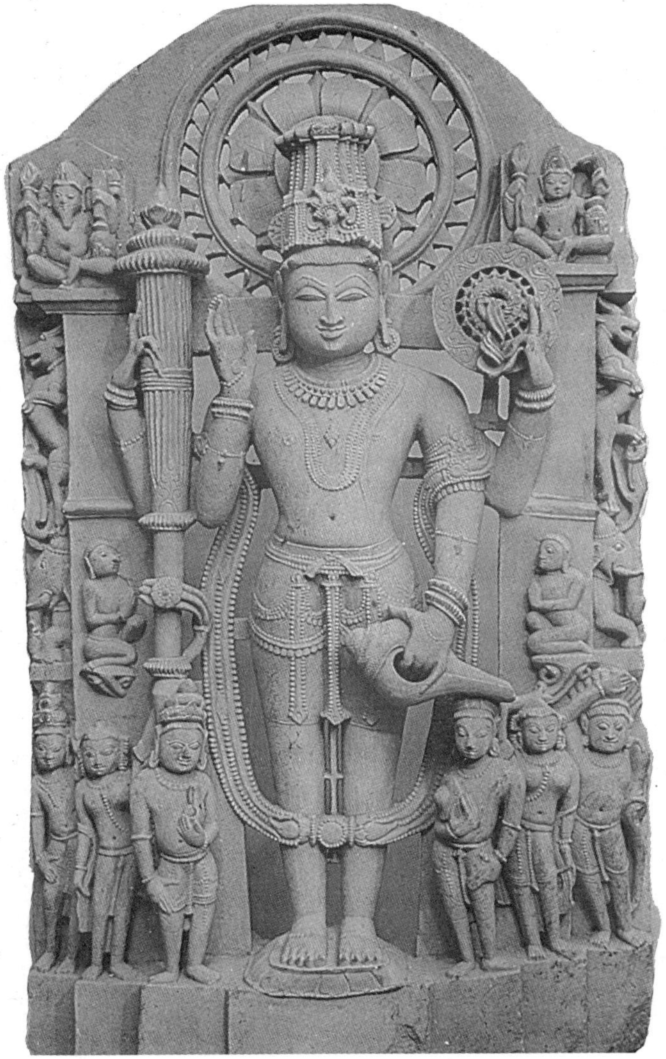

fig. 74. Viṣṇu with other deities, Medieval

The last image on the wall side (OA.8/3) represents a standing *Vaikuṇṭha* Viṣṇu with three heads, central being human and the side heads are of the lion and boar. The deity wears usual crown and other ornaments beside a large garland of victory (*vaijayantī-mālā*). Out of his attributes in his broken four arms only suspended mace is extant. He is flanked by the *āyudhapuruṣas* (personified weapons). The back slab is carved with a plain nimbus. Buff sandstone. *c.* 8-9th century A.D. It is from the collection of Sri Sambho Mal Sarraf.

Incarnations

Viṣṇu descends himself in the form of incarnations (*avatāras*) to recreate congenial atmosphere and to protect pious people. To the right and in the opposite row are seen different incarnations.

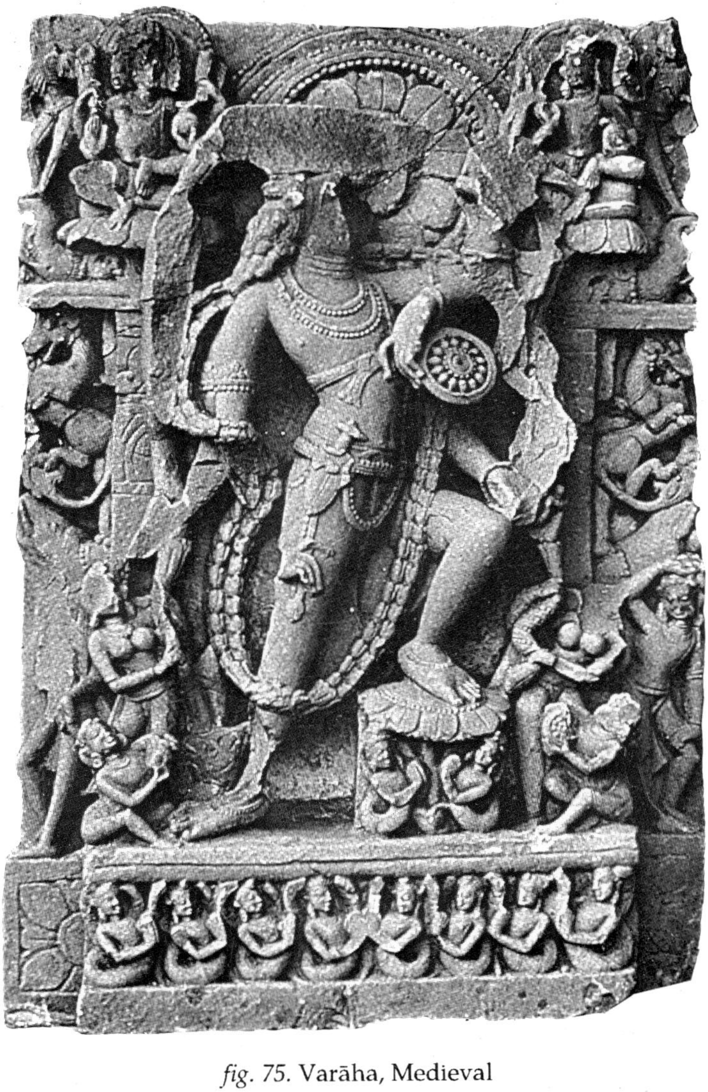

fig. 75. Varāha, Medieval

The standing deity (45.3210 from Swāmīghāṭ, Mathurā) inside an arch to the right is Balarāma with snake canopy wearing a number of ornaments and holding a cup in the left hand which is now mutilated. The top of the slab is carved with an elephant and a young man. This may probably be identified as the scene of subjugation of elephant Kūbalyāpīḍa by Kṛṣṇa.

The first sculpture to the right is of Varāha (87.6 from Mānasigaṅgā, Govardhan; *fig.* 75) the third incarnation in sequence lifting goddess earth on one of his four arms. He is boar headed but the major part of head is missing. Only one of his attribute, *cakra* remains intact. The *vaijayantīmālā* (garland of victory) is quite conspicuous. The posture and vigour in lifting the personified earth (now mutilated) is remarkable. He is flanked by male and female attendants and the pedestal bears eight *nāga* figures, representing *nāga-loka.* Above are seated Brahmā on right and Śiva on left. The buff sand stone statue belong to *c.* 10th century A.D.

The next (D. 39) is the dwarf form of Viṣṇu (*vāmana*) when he measured the whole universe in less than three steps and punished the demon king Balī. The third sculpture (D. 21 from Gantyauli near Govardhan) shows Viṣṇu with his usual attributes. But the interesting part is the top panel which represents ten incarnations of Viṣṇu flanked by two sages on either side. They are Sanaka, Sanadana, Sanātana and Śanatkumāra. The incarnations from left to right are: 1. Matsya (fish), 2. Kūrma (tortoise), 3. Varāha (boar), 4. Nṛsiṁha (man-lion), Vāmana (dwarf), 6. Paraśurāma, 7. Rāma, 8. Balarāma (not Kṛṣṇa as identified by Dr. Agrawala).[8] 9. Buddha and 10. Kalki, riding on horse (future incarnation). The next is a fragmentary panel (68.3) in which only four incarnations are extant. Rāma stands with a bow, Balarāma with a snake canopy holding a cup of wine, Buddha sits in meditation (*dhyāna*) on a lotus seats (*padmāsana*) and lastly Kalki on the horse back. The last pedestal shows Balarāma (R. 46) with a large snake canopy holding a *musala* (club), *hala* (plough) and a cup of wine. He is flanked by the *nāga* below and flying celestials (*gandharvas*) above.

Śiva Icons

The row behind incarnations presents Śiva and his family.

The first sculpture (88.12 from Rataul, Meerut; *col. ill. XXXVIII*) is one of the most beautiful specimens of medieval plastic art representing a dancing Gaṇeśa with ten arms holding several attributes like *paraśu* (battle axe), *pāśa* (noose), club, snake, sweet balls and the pose of *abhaya*. Below are seen figures of *kinnaras* playing on musical instruments. The mount of deity, mouse, is incised on the pedestal. The buff sandstone sculpture should belong to *c.* 10th century A.D.

The next piece (D. 41) is a Śiva head with high matted hair lotus halo behind verticle, third eye on forehead and upper part of trident above which is seen Brahmā—on his vehicle goose (*haṁsa*). The skeleton figure of Bhṛngī is noticed in dancing posture, on the crocodile head with trunk, below is a female bust with *caurī*. The buff sandstone, fragment of a big image belongs to *c.* 10th century A.D.

The next sculpture (88.16 from Rataul, Meerut; *fig. 76*) represents Durgā (in Ambikā form) holding a child below her breasts. The other eight hands carry *asi* (sword), *vajra* (thunderbolt), *cakra* (disc), *bāṇa* (arrow), *tūṇīra* (quiver) *triśūla* (trident) *pāśa* (noose), *khaḍga* or *ḍhāla* (shield) and *dhanuṣa* (bow). She stands on lotus seat, placed on lion throne. There are several flanking female attendants carrying garland, flywhisk, etc. Two female deities are perched on the top. The buff sandstone stele belongs to *c.* 10th

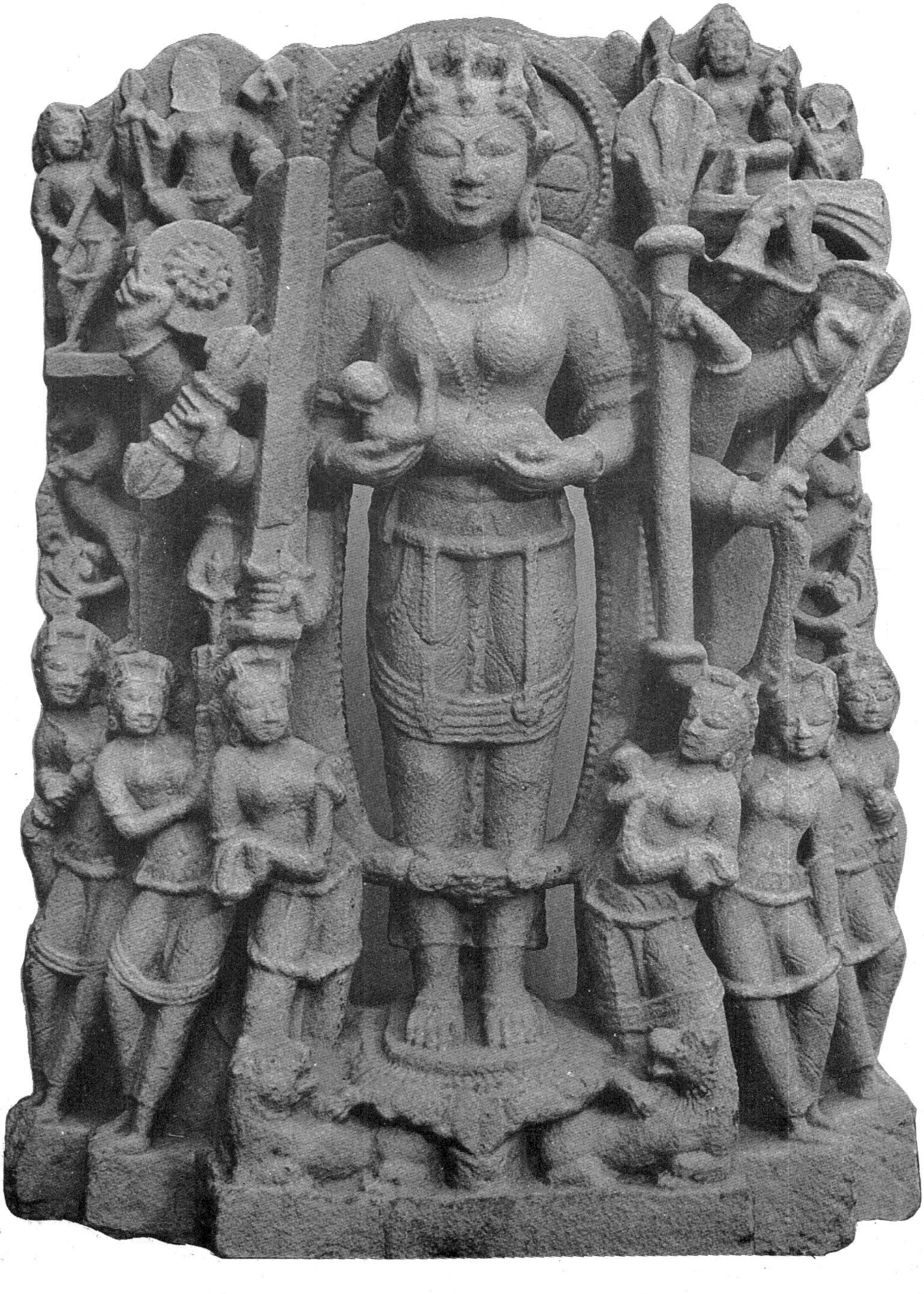

fig. 76. Durgā / Ambikā, Medieval

century A.D.

The next sculpture (88.15 from Rataul, Meerut) shows Śiva and Pārvatī seated on mount Nandī (bull). The four armed Śiva holds *triśūla* (trident), a flower, large snake and with the fourth hand presses the breast of Pārvatī, who holds a mirror in her hand and sits on the left thigh of Śiva. Below are seen the figures of Kārttikeya on peacock with spear and Gaṇeśa with pot of sweets and Bhṛṅgī in dancing attitude. The buff sandstone stele belongs to *c.* 10th century A.D.

The last sculpture illustrates the scene of marriage of Śiva (87.8 from Mānasīgaṅgā, Goverdhan; *fig.* 77) known as *kalyāṇa-sundara* form, where Śiva stands to the left of Pārvatī. Both the deities are beheaded. Betweeen Śiva and Pārvatī is seen Brahmā performing the *yajña* for wedding. The flanking acolytes holding pitcher are to be identified as Viṣṇu and probably Varuṇa or Vāyu. The top panel shows a row of *aṣṭadikpālas* (eight guardian deities). The background has been carved to give a glimpse of mountain Kailāśa. The lotus pedestal has tall vase (an auspicious motif for the occasion) on each side. The buff sandstone sculpture belongs to *c.* 10th century A.D.

The centre of the gallery houses a doorframe of red sandstone (17.1353 from Parkham) with river goddesses and attendants below and row of nine planets above. This belongs to *c.* 10th century A.D. On the top of this is placed another lintel (73.32 from Caurāsīkhambhā temple, Mahāban) carved with nine planets and figures of Brahmā, Viṣṇu and Śiva inside the niches. The three compartments are seen on the back also but probably wrongly carved upside down. It belongs to *c.* 10th century A.D. On each adjacent of this gate is seen buff sandstone temple pillar carved with scroll, full vase, foliage etc. (R. 3 and R. 4 from Sahar, Chātā).

Through the above gate is seen a miniature shrine (12.247 from Daulta, Mathurā District) carved with *caitya* window, *kīrttimukha* motifs and several other decorated mouldings. The figures of the deities (mutilated) are seen around. Inside the shrine is placed a stele, representing '*Śeṣaśāyī* Viṣṇu' (12.248 from the same spot as the preceding one). Both the exhibits should belong to early medieval period, and are carved in buff sandstone which has become weather worn.

Behind is placed a large storage terracotta jar (54.3719) acquired from Shergarh, Mathurā.

Inside the Central arch of the gallery is displayed a stele (88.17 from Rataul, Meerut; *col. ill.* XXXIX) showing Ambikā, probably a Jaina version of Durgā, holding several weapons in her ten arms and carrying a child on her left, she is flanked by two female attendants on either side. This beautiful buff sandstone image is of 10th century A.D.

On the pedestal to right is installed a quadruple (*sarvatobhadra*) image (58.4720) carved with Brahmā, Viṣṇu, Sūrya and Śiva facing in different direction. It is followed by a sculptural relief representing Rāhu—one of the nine planets—(*grahas*) in offering

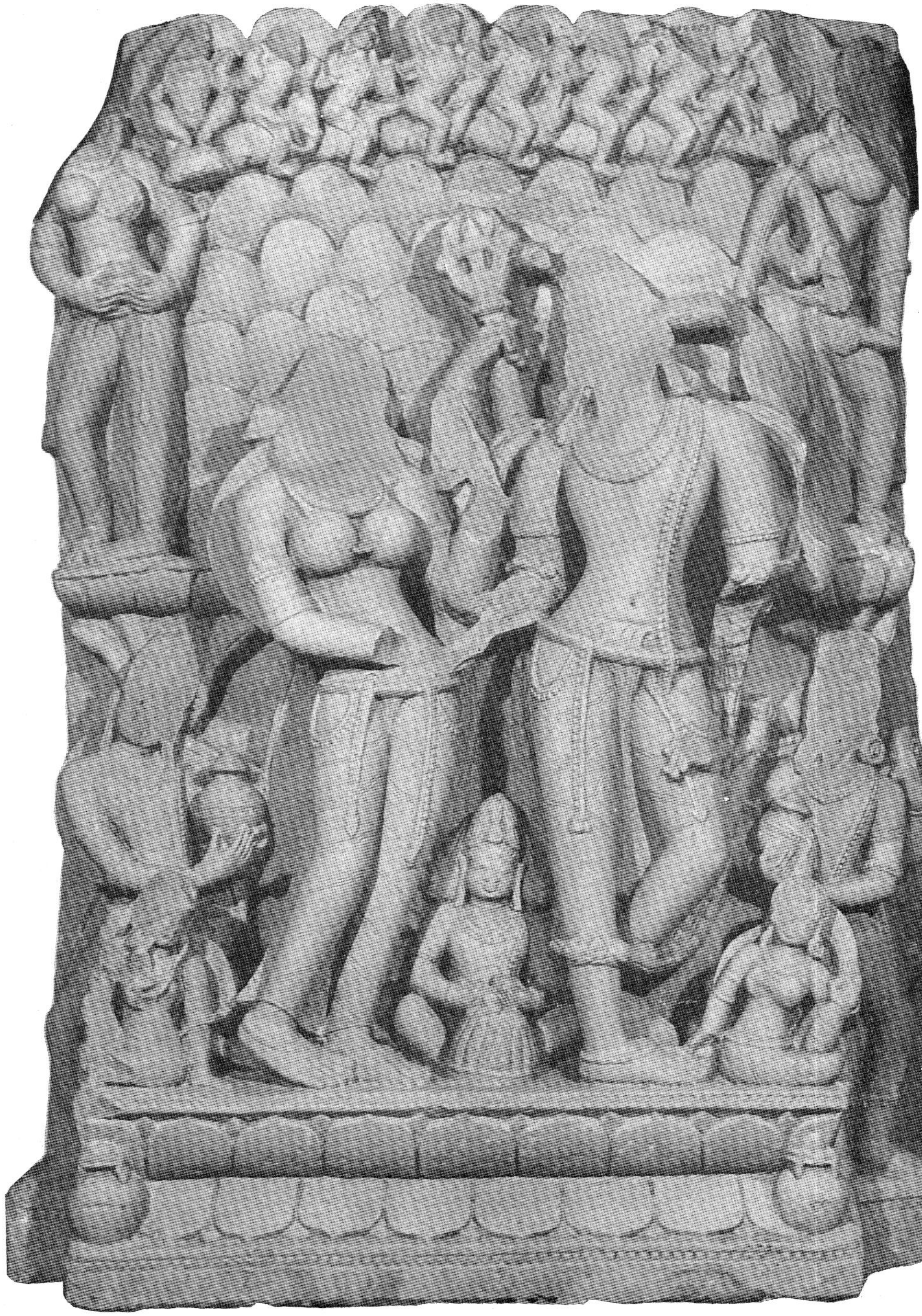

fig. 77. Kalyāṇasundara, Medieval

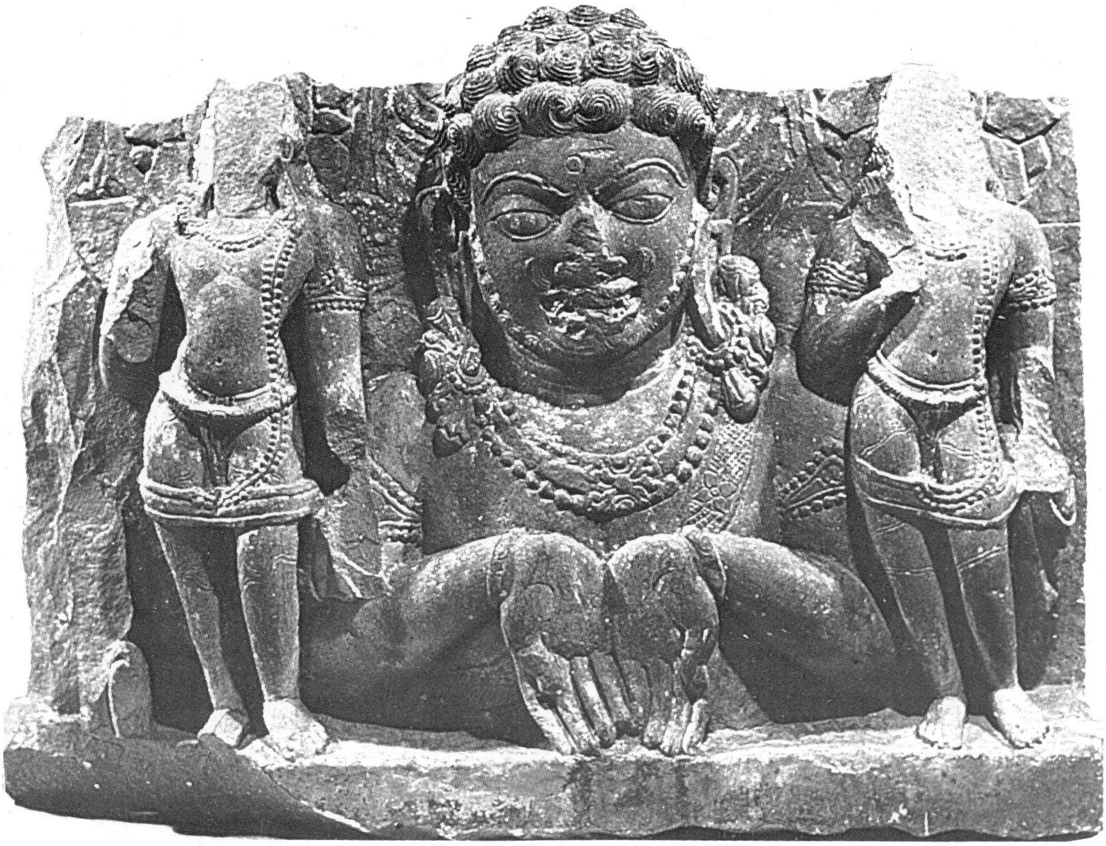

fig. 78. Rāhu, Medieval

(*tarpaṇa*) pose (39.2836 from Satoha, Mathura District; *fig. 78*).

The next pedestal on both sides shows fragmentary buff sandstone, early medieval, door jambs representing Gaṅgā. The bigger piece (16.1205 from Bharnā Khurd) contains beside the river goddess and attendant, four verticle panels carved with foliage, flying celestials and amorous couples. The smaller piece (R. 56; *fig.* 79) in the same fashion contains in its four verticle panels Kārttikeya on peacock, Cāmuṇḍā, full vase, *caurī* bearer etc.

The stele on the independent pedestal displays 'Umā-Maheśvara' (85.167 Hāzipur, Hāthras; *fig. 80*) seated on lotus seat with their mount bull and lion respectively and attendant Bhṛṅgī in skeleton on the pedestal. Another attendant is seen behind Nandī. The four armed Śiva holds lily, trident and with his two hands touches the chin and breast of Pārvatī, who holds a mirror in her left hand. On the top of the back slab are seen garland bearing celestials hovering in air and the stylised *kīrttimukha* with horn,

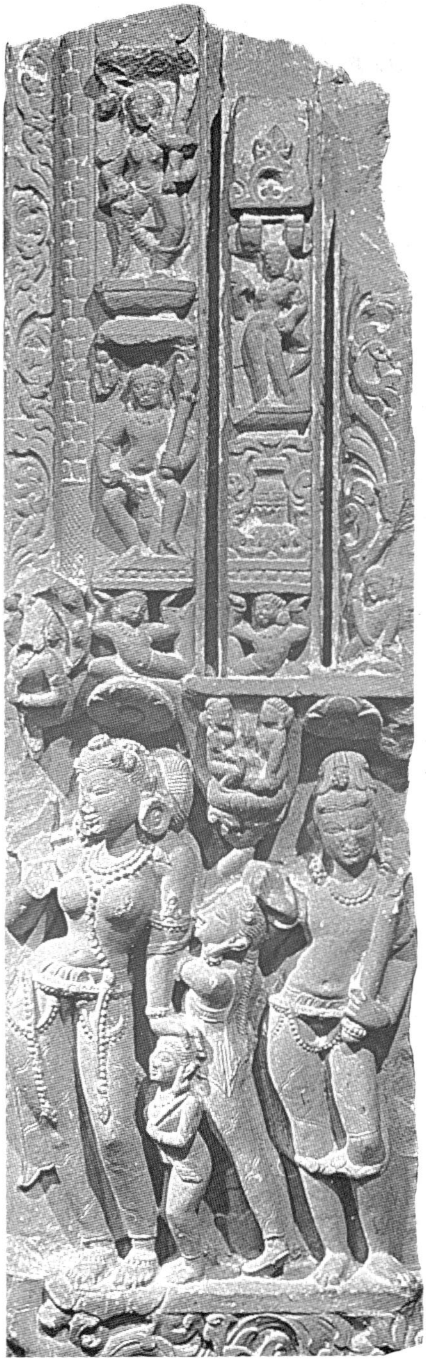

fig. 79. Gaṅgā on doorjamb, Medieval

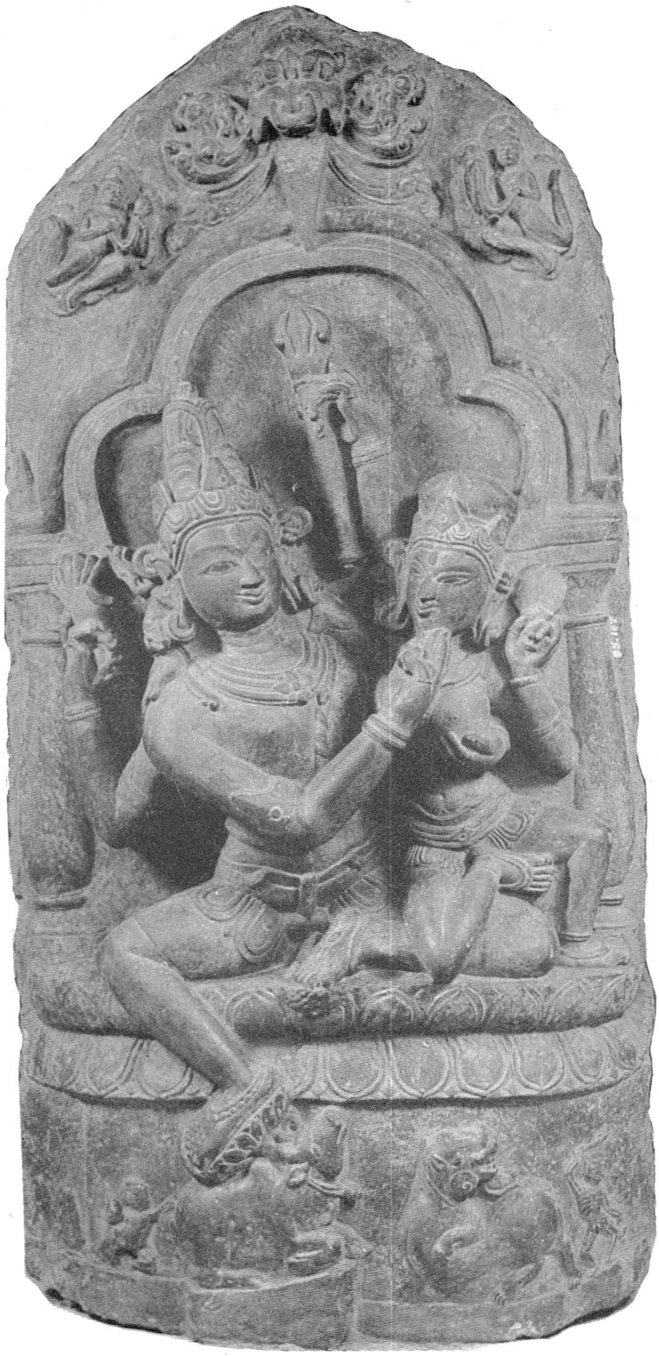

fig. 80. Umā-Maheśvara, Medieval

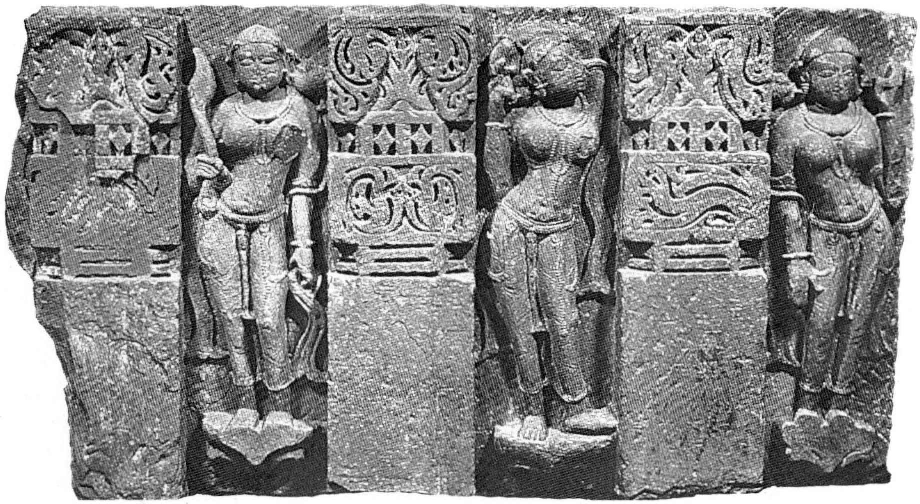

fig. 81. Damsels, Medieval

lion head and protruding large tongue. Dark basalt sculpture belonging to Pāla style of Eastern India is to be placed in the *c.* 11th century A.D.

The independent pedestal on one side displays Agni, fire God (D. 24 from Nāradakuṇḍa near Rādhākuṇḍa) with aureole of flames and flanked by personified figure of his vehicle 'goat' and a pot of *ghee* (butter) which is a rare iconographic feature. This buff stone image belongs to *c.* 10th century A.D.

On the bench pedestal, rest two red sandstone architectural components. The first (73.28 from Mahāban; *fig. 81)* is carved with three damsels and the other is a large lintel of a temple doorway (80.23) now broken into two parts. The central figure, which is now badly mutilated represents four armed Viṣṇu who was probably seated on his mount Garuḍa. To his left is row of ten incarnations i.e., fish (Matsya), tortoise (Kūrma), boar (Varāha), Man-lion (Nṛsiṁha), dwarf (Vāmana), Paraśurāma, Rāma, Balarāma, Buddha and lastly Kalki on the horse back. To the right of Viṣṇu is seen another row consisting of nine planets beginning from Sūrya (sun), Candra (moon), Bhauma or Maṅgala (mars), Budha (mercury), Bṛhaspati (jupiter), Śukra (venus), Śani (saturn), Rāhu and Ketu. The projecting figure to the right of Sūrya, is a lady squeezing her hair and a swan collects the drops in the guise of pearls. The last sunken compartment to her right shows Śiva and Pārvatī in amorous pose. On the other side, behind Kalki is another projecting figure of a lady flanked by the attendants and to her left is probably Śiva and Pārvatī in amorous pose. Pārvatī holds a mirror in her left hand. The spotted red sandstone sculpture belongs to *c.* 9th-10th century A.D.

Mother Goddess Panels

The bench pedestal on the other side of the door displays three architectural fragments illustrating the divine mother goddesses (*mātṛkās*). The first is a slab (68.18) with foliage, *kīrttimukha* and lotus bands containing six mother goddesses between Gaṇeśa and *Vīṇādhara* Śiva. The goddesses from left to right are as follows: Indrāṇī with *vajra* on elephant, Vārāhī with boar head on buffalo, Vaiṣṇavī with club on personified Garuḍa, Kaumārī with braids on head, spear and mounting on peacock, Māheśvarī probably with trident on bull, Brahmāṇī with a water pot on goose. The first figure of Gaṇeśa is not very clear and may also be identified as Cāmuṇḍā with a staff, bowl and probably human corpse below. The buff sandstone sculpture belongs to *c.* 9-10th century A.D. The divine mothers were created to help Śiva or Durgā to fight against demons.[9]

This is followed by horizontal slab (15.552) which shows seven mothers (*saptamātṛkās*) between *Vīṇādhara* Śiva (Śiva playing on a *Vīṇā*) and the elephant headed god Gaṇeśa. The mothers from left to right as identified from their vehicles, attributes and features are (1) Brahmāṇī on goose (haṁsa) holding a ladle, (2) Māheśvarī on bull with trident (*triśūla*) in her hand, (3) Kaumārī on peacock with a spear (*śakti*) , (4) Vaiṣṇavī on Garuḍa with a mace, (5) Vārāhī with a boar head on his vehicle probably buffalo, (6) Indrāṇī on elephant (Airāvata) with her weapon *vajra* (now missing) and lastly, (7) Cāmuṇḍā with sunken belly, garland of human skulls (*muṇḍamālā*) and riding over human corpse (*pretavāhana*). Each of the female deities holds a child on her left side. The last (40.2874/1; *fig. 82*) is the fragment from a large sculptural frieze of which only three mother godesses Kaumārī, Vaiṣṇavī and Vārāhī are extant.

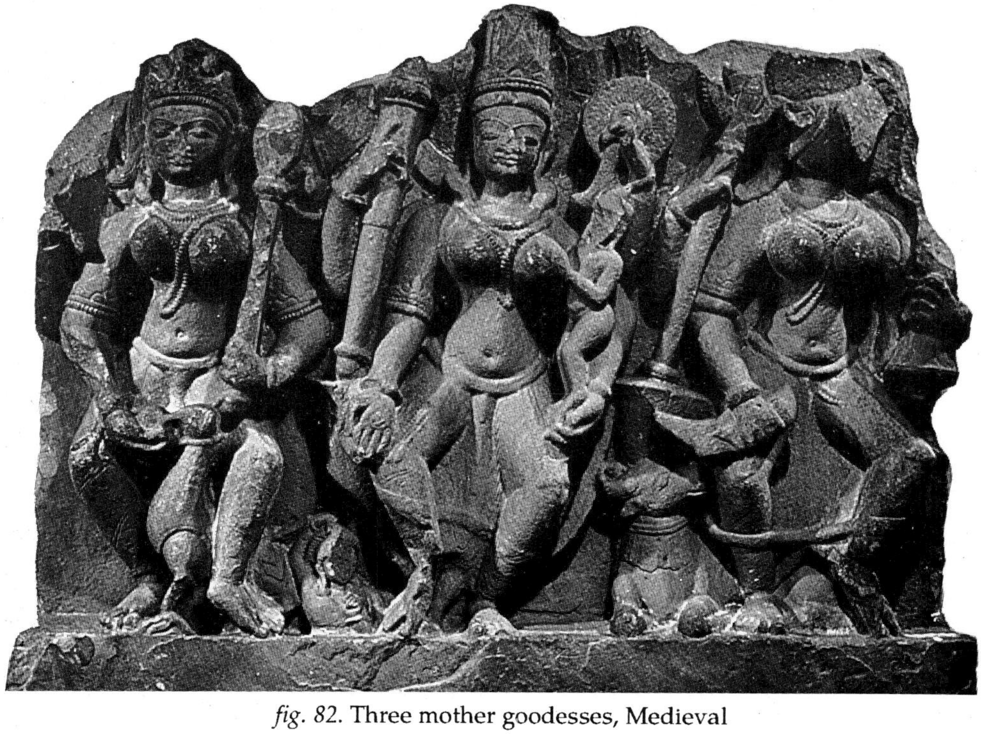

fig. 82. Three mother goodesses, Medieval

The smaller sculptures are to be viewed inside the two showcases and some of them are quite interesting from iconographic point of view (from Barsānā *c.* 7th century A.D). These exhibits are Sūrya (16.1256) in Gāndhāra style with Daṇḍa and Piṅgala, grey stone, having close resemblance with a Sassanian ruler, Balarāma (U. 98), Umā Maheśvara on Nandī (15.1080), Sūrya (16.1208), Govardhan, Kṛṣṇa (15.1113), Varāha (15.1114), Māheśvarī (15.1108), Kabera (12.254), Brahmā (15.1098), Gaṇeśa with his consort (15.1112) couple with *Tīrthaṅkara* (15.1111) and Māheśvarī (15.1093).

References

1. Kramrisch, St. *Indian Sculpture,* p. 77.
2. Saraswati, S.K., *A Survey of Indian Sculpture,* 1975. pp. 182-84.
3. Dr. V.S. Agrawala is inclined to identify it as Pārvatī: *A Catalogue of the Images of Brahmā, Viṣṇu and Śiva in Mathurā Art, JUPHS,* 1949, p. 156.
4. Dr. J. Ph. Vogel was inclined to identify it as the image of Dattātreya and assigned it to the Muslim period (*Catalogue of the Archaeological Museum at Mathurā,* 1910, p. 20).
5. Agrawala, V.S., *op. cit.,* p. 120.
6. *Ibid.,* p. 116.
7. Dr. Agrawala thinks that it is a specimen of South Indian style (*Ibid.*) but it should be accepted as a product of Pāla Style of Eastern India.
8. *Ibid.,* p. 114.
9. Gopinath Rao, T.A., *Hindu Iconography,* Vol. 1, pp. 381-82.

Select Bibliography

Agrawal, O.P., 'Conservation Problem of Mathura', In *Journal of Indian Museums*, Vol. 29, 1973, pp. 43-49.

Agrawala, P.K., *Mathura Railing Pillars*, Varanasi, 1966.

— *Gupta Temple Architecture*, Varanasi, 1981.

— 'Iconoplastic Beginnings of Multi-headed and Multi-armed Images at Mathura', In *Journal of the Indian Society of Oriental Art*, New Series, Vol. 15, 1985-86, pp. 21-28.

Agrawala, R.C., 'Some Kusana Sculptures in the National Museum, Delhi and Allied Problems', In *Bulletin of Museums and Archaeology in U.P.*, No. 3, June 1969, pp. 6-24.

— 'Goddess Sasthi in Mathura Sculptures', In *Bulletin of Museums and Archaeology in U.P.*, No. 4, December 1969, pp. 1-6.

— 'Matrka Reliefs in Early Indian Art', In *East and West, New Series*, Vol. 21, Nos. 1-2, March-June 1971, pp. 79-89.

— '*Videśī Saṅgrahālayon Men Mathurā Kalā Kī Advitiya Mahiṣamardinī Pratimāyen*', In *Bulletin of Museums and Archaeology in U.P.*, Nos. 41-42, 1988, pp. 57-58.

Agrawala, V.S., 'Mathura Terracottas', In *Journal of the U.P. Historical Society*, Vol. 9, Pt. 2, July 1936, pp. 6-38.

— 'Brahmanical Images in Mathura', In *Journal of the Indian Society of Oriental Art*, Vol. 5, 1937, pp. 122-130.

— 'Dhyani Buddhas and Bodhisattvas', In *Journal of the U.P. Historical Society*, Vol. II, Pt. 2, December 1938, pp. 1-13.

— 'A New Bodhisattva and a Bacchanalian Group from Mathura', In *Journal of the Indian Society of Oriental Art*, Vol. 6, 1938, pp. 68-72.

— *Handbook of the Sculptures in the Curzon Museum of Archaeology*, Muttra, Allahabad, 1939.

— *A Short Guide-book to the Archaeological Section of the Provincial Museum*, Lucknow, Allahabad, 1940.

— 'A Catalogue of the Images of Brahma, Vishnu and Siva in Mathura Art', In *Journal of the U.P. Historical Society*, Vol. 22, Pts. 1-2, 1949, pp. 102-210.

— 'Catalogue of the Mathura Museum', In *Journal of the U.P. Historical Society*, Vol. 23, Pts. 1-2, 1950, pp. 35-147.

— 'Catalogue of the Mathura Museum: Architectural Pieces', In *Journal of the U.P. Historical Society*, Vols. 24-25, 1951-52, pp. 1-160.

— 'A Catalogue of the Brahmanical Images in Mathura Art', In *Journal of the U.P. Historical Society*, 1951.

— (*ed.*), *Seṭha Kanhaiya Lāl Poddār Abhinandana Grantha* (Hindi), Akhila Bhāratiya Braj Sāhitya Maṇḍal, Mathura, 1953.

— *Jaina Tirthankaras and Other Miscellaneous Figures*, Varanasi, 1963.

— *Masterpieces of Mathura Sculpture*, Varanasi, 1965.

— *Studies in Indian Art*, Varanasi, 1965.

— *Pre-Kushana Art of Mathura*, Varanasi, 1984.

— *Mathura Terracottas*, Varanasi, 1984.

Anand, Mulk Raj, 'Origin of the Buddha Image', In *Marg*, Vol. 15, No. 2, March 1962, pp. 8-14.

Asthana, S., 'A unique *Patravahaka Yaksha* Image From *Ahichchhatra*', In *Purātattva*, No. 11, 1982, pp. 74-77.

— 'The Kushana Art of Mathura', In S.P. Gupta's ed. *Kushana Sculptures From Sanghol (1st-2nd Century A.D.): Recent Discovery*, New Delhi, 1985, pp. 25-36.

— 'The Kusana Art of Sanghol', In *Lalit Kalā*, No. 24, 1990, pp. 9-13.

— 'A Mahaparinirvana Panel in the National Museum', In *Purātattva*, No. 16 (1985-86), New Delhi, 1987, pp. 35-38.

— *Catalogue of the Mathura Sculptures in the National Museum* (under Publication).

Bacchofer, L., *Early Indian Sculpture*, Vol. I, New Delhi, 1973.

Bajpai, K.D., '*Mathurā Kī Jaina Kalā*' (Hindi), In *Śrīmad Rājendra Surī Smāraka Grantha* Ahor, Sri Sandharmabrihatpagachchiya Jain Svetamber Sri Sangh, 1957, pp. 608-11.

— 'Some Problems of the Kushana', In *Journal of the U.P. Historical Society, New Series*, Vol. 9, Pt. 1, 1961, pp. 1-5.

— 'The Kusana Art of Mathura', In *Marg*, Vol. 15, No. 2, 1962, pp. 28-42.

— *Mathura*, New Delhi, 1980.

Banerjee, J.N., *The Development of Hindu Iconography*, Calcutta, 1956.

Banerjee, P., *The Life of Krishna in Indian Art*, New Delhi, 1978.

Banerjee, R.D., 'The Scythian Period of Indian History', In *IA*, Vol. 37, 1908, pp. 25-75.

— 'New Brahmi Inscriptions of the Scythian Period', In *Epigraphia Indica*, Vol. 10, 1909-10, pp. 106-121.

Basham, A.L. (ed.), '*Papers on the Date of Kaniska*' Submitted to the Conference on the Date of Kaniska, London, 20-22 April 1960, Leiden, 1968.

'Bricks in the Archaeological Museum, Mathura, No. 2', In *Annual Report on Indian Epigraphy*, 1972-73, pp. 116 (*c*. 3637).

Buhler, G., 'Epigraphic Discoveries at Mathura', In *Journal of the Royal Asiatic Society of Great Britain and Ireland*, 1896, pp. 578-581.

— 'New Jaina Inscriptions from Mathura', In *Epigraphia Indica*, Vol. I, 1892, pp. 371-393.

— 'Jaina Sculptures from Mathura', In *Transactions of the International Congress of Orientalists*, 9, 1982, pp. 219-221.

Bussagli, M. 'The Problem of Kaniska as Seen by the Art Historian', In A.L. Basham's ed. *Papers on the Date of Kaniska*, Leiden, 1968, pp. 39-56.

Chanda, Ramaprasad, 'The Mathura School of Sculpture', In *Archaeological Survey of India, Annual Report*, 1922-23, pp. 164-170.

Chanda, Ramaprasad, 'The Hair and the *Usnisa* on the Head of the Buddhas and the Jinas', In *Indian Historical Quarterly*, Vol. 7, No. 3, September 1931, pp. 669-673.

— 'The Mathura School of Sculpture', In *Indian Museum Bulletin*, Vol. 10, No. 1, January 1975, pp. 35-40.

Chattopadhyay, Bhaskar, *The Age of the Kushanas*—A Numismatic Study, Calcutta, 1967.

Chattopadhyaya, B.D., 'Mathura from the Sunga to the Kusana Period: An Historical Outline', In Doris Meth Srinivasan's ed. *Mathura: The Cultural Heritage*, New Delhi, 1989, pp. 19-28.

Chaturvedi, Sarojini, *Foreign Influx and Interaction with Indian Culture*, Delhi, 1985.

Codrington, K. de B., 'Mathura of the Gods', In *Marg*, Vol. 9, No. 2, pp. 41-49.

Cole, Henry Hardy, *Illustrations of Buildings near Muttra and Agra showing the mixed Hindu-mohamedan Style of Upper India*, London, 1873.

Coomamswamy, A.K., 'Early Indian Sculptures: Six Reliefs from Mathura', In *Bulletin of the Museum of Fine Arts*, Boston, Vol. 24, No. 144, August 1926, pp. 54-60.

— *History of Indian and Indonesian Art*, New York, 1965.

— *The Origin of the Buddha Image*, New Delhi, 1972.

Cunningham, A., *Archaeological Survey of India*, Vol. I: Four reports made during the year 1862-65, pp. 231-244; *ASR*, Vol. III, 1871-72, pp. 13-46; *ASR*, Vol. XI, pp. 75-76; *ASR*, Vol. XVII, 1881-82, pp. 107-12; *ASR*, XX, 1888-89, pp. 30-54.

Czuma, Stanislaw, *Kushana Sculpture: Images from Early India*, New York, 1985.

Damsteegt, Theo, *Epigraphical Hybrid Sanskrit*, Leiden, 1978.

Dehejia, Vidya, '*Stupas* and Sculptures of Early Buddhism', In *Asian Art*, Vol. 2, No. 3, 1989, pp. 7-31.

Deo, S.B., 'Expansion of Jainism', In A. Ghosh's ed. *Jaina Art* and *Architecture*, Vol. I, New Delhi, 1974, pp. 22-34.

Dowson, J., 'Ancient Inscriptions from Mathura', In *JRAS, NS*, Vol. V, 1871.

Drake-Brockman, D.L. ed., *Muttra: A Gazetteer*, Allahabad, 1911.

Dwivedi, V.P., 'Mathura Art in the Museums of United States of America', In *Journal of Indian Museums*, Vol. 29, 1973, pp. 22-29.

'Excavations at Mathura', *Annual Progress Report of the Archaeological Survey-Circle, North Western Provinces and Oudh for the year ending, 30th June 1896*, pp. 1-2.

'Excavations at Sonkh, Distt. Mathura', In *Indian Archaeology: A Review*, 1966-67, pp. 40-43.

'Excavations at Sonkh, Distt. Mathura', In *Indian Archaeology: A Reivew*, 1968-69, p. 40.

'Excavations at Sonkh, Distt. Mathura', In *Indian Archaeology: A Review*, 1969-70, pp. 42-43.

'Excavations at Sonkh, Distt. Mathura', In *Indian Archaeology: A Review*, 1970-71, pp. 39-40.

'Excavations at Sonkh, Distt. Mathura', In *Indian Archaeology: A Review*, 1971-72, pp. 47-48.

'Excavations at Sonkh, Distt. Mathura', In *Indian Archaeology: A Review*, 1972-73, pp. 33-35.

'Excavations at Mathura, Distt. Mathura', In *Indian Archaeology: A Review*, 1973-74, pp. 31-32.

'Excavations at Mathura, Distt. Mathura', In *Indian Archaeology: A Review*, 1974-75, pp. 48-50.

'Excavations at Mathura, Distt. Mathura', In *Indian Archaeology: A Review*, 1975-76, pp. 53-55.

'Excavations at Mathura, Distt. Mathura', In *Indian Archaeology: A Review*, 1976-77, pp. 54-56.

Fabri, Charles, L., 'Mathura of the Gods', In *Marg*, Vol. 7, No. 2, pp. 8-22.

Fleet, J.F., *Corpus Inscriptionum Indicarum*, Vol. 3, Inscriptions of the Early Gupta Kings and their Successors, Varanasi, 1963.

Foucher, A., *The Beginnings of Buddhist Art and Other Essays in Indian and Central-Asian Archaeology*, Paris, 1917.

Fuhrer, A., 'Indo-Scythic Architecture and Sculpture of Mathura School', In *Journal of Indian Art*, Vol. 5, 1894, p. 58.

Fussman, Gerard, 'The Mat *Devakula*: A New Approach to its Understanding', In Doris Meth Srinivasan's ed. *Mathura: The Cultural Heritage*, New Delhi, 1989, pp. 193-199.

Gai, G.S., 'Mathura Jaina Inscriptions of the Kushana period — A Fresh Study', In U.P. Shah and M.A. Dhaky's ed. *Aspects of Jaina Art and Architecture*, Ahmedabad, 1975, pp. 81-85.

Gordon, D.H., 'Early Indian Terracota', In *Journal of Indian Society of Oriental Art*, Vol. II,

1943, pp. 136-195.

Growse, F.S., 'The Country of Braj', In *Journal of the Asiatic Society of Bengal,* Vol. 40, Pt. I, No. 1, 1871, pp. 34-45.

— *Mathura: A District Memoir,* Second Edition, 1880.

— 'Mathura Inscriptions', In *Indian Antiquary,* Vol. 6, 1877, pp. 216-219.

Gupta, P.L., *Coins,* New Delhi, 1969.

— 'Early Coins of Mathura Region', In Doris Meth Srinivasan's ed. *Mathura: The Cultural Heritage,* New Delhi, 1989, pp. 124-139.

Gupta, S.P., *The Roots of Indian Art,* Delhi, 1980.

Gupta, S.P. (ed.), *Kushana Sculptures from Sanghol,* (1st-2nd Century A.D.): *A Recent Discovery,* New Delhi, 1985.

— 'Sanghol: The Meeting Place of Works of Art of Gandhara and Mathura Schools', In *Investigating Indian Art,* Berlin, 1987, pp. 89-104.

Harle, J.C., *Gupta Sculpture: Indian Sculpture of the Fourth to the Sixth Centuries* A.D., Oxford, 1974.

— 'Mathura Sculpture in the Ashmolean Museum', In *Bulletin of Museums and Archaeology in U.P.,* Nos. 15-16, June-December 1975, pp. 15-17.

Härtel, Herbert, *Indische Skulpturen* (German), Berlin, Museum fur Volkerkunde, 1960.

— 'A Kusana Naga Temple at Sonkh', In *Bulletin of Museums and Archaeology in U.P.,* Nos. 11-12, June-December 1973, pp. 1-6.

— 'Aspects of Early Naga Cult in India', In *Journal of the Royal Society of Arts,* 1976, pp. 663-683.

— *Excavations at Sonkh,* Berlin, 1993.

Härtel, Herbert & Lobo, Wibke, *Schatze Indischer Kunst* (German), Berlin, Staaiche Museen Preussischer Kulturbesitz Museum fur Indische Kunst, 1984.

Havell, E.B., *Ideals of Indian Art,* 1911.

— *Indian Sculpture and Paintings,* 1928.

Hirananda Sastri, *Jaina-Shilālekh Saṅgraha* (Hindi), Vols. 2-3, Bombay, 1952-57, Vol. 4, Varanasi, 1961.

Ingholt, H., *Gandhara Art in Pakistan,* New York, 1957.

Jain, Jyoti Prasad, *The Jaina Sources of the History of Ancient India* (100 B.C.-A.D. 900), Delhi, 1964.

— *'Mathurā Kī Jaina Kalā'* (Hindi), In *Jain-Sandesh,* Vol. 20, 1964, pp. 338-340.

Janert, K.L., *Mathura Inscriptions,* 1961.

Jayaswal, K.P., 'Problems of Saka-Satavahana History', In *Journal of the Bihar and Orissa Research Society,* Vol. 16, Pts. 3-4, September-December 1930, pp. 227-316.

Jitendra Kumar, '*Bharṇa Kalā kī Śuṅga Kālīna Yakṣa Aura Mānasī Gaṅgā Kī Madhyakālīna*

Prastara Pratimāen: Mathura' (Hindi), In *Dhyānam*, Vol. 56, 1985-86, pp. 51-54.

— *Masterpieces of Mathura Museum*, 1989.

Joshi, M.C., 'Mathura as an Ancient Settlement', In Doris Meth Srinivasan's ed. *Mathura: The Cultural Heritage*, New Delhi, 1989, pp. 165-170.

Joshi, M.C. & Nargbandhu, C., 'Some Terracottas from Excavations at Mathura', In *JISOA, N.S.*, Vol. 8, 1976-77, pp. 16-32.

Joshi, N.P., '*Mathurā Kalā Men Māṅgalika Cinha*' (Hindi), In *Pt. Suratinārāyaṇa Maṇi Tripāṭhi Abhinandana Grantha*, Varanasi, 1965, pp. 32-37.

— *Mathura Sculptures*, Mathura, 1966.

— *Matrikas, Mothers in Kusana Art*, New Delhi, 1986.

— *Brahmanical Sculptures in the State Museum*, Lucknow, Pt. 2, Vols. 1-2, 1989.

— 'Early Jaina Icons from Mathura', In Doris Meth Srinivasan's ed. *Mathura: The Cultural Heritage*, New Delhi, 1989, pp. 332-367.

Konow, Sten, *Corpus Inscriptionum Indicarum*, Vol. II, Pt. 1, 1919.

— 'Rawal Spurious Inscription of the Year 40', In *Epigraphia Indica*, Vol. 19, 1927-28, pp. 206-209.

Kramrisch, Stella, *Indian Sculpture*, Calcutta, 1933.

— 'Indian Terracottas', In *Journal of the Indian Society of Oriental Art*, Vol. 7, 1939, pp. 89-110.

— *The Art of India*, London, 1965.

Kreisel, Gerd, *Die Siva — Bildwerke der Mathura-Kunst* (German). Stuttgarh, 1986.

Krishan, Y., 'The Origin of the Buddha Image', In *Marg*, Vol. 15, No. 2, March 1962, pp. 15-16.

— 'The Emergence of the Buddha Image, Gandhara Versus Mathura', In *Oriental Art, New Series*, Vol. 34, No. 4, 1988-89, pp. 255-275.

Krishna Deva, 'Pan-Indian Style, North India *c*-250 B.C.-A.D. 400: Mauryas, Sungas, Kanvas, Kusanas, Ksatrapas', In Michael W. Meister and others' ed. *Encyclopaedia of Indian Temple Architecture: North India, Foundations of North Indian Style, c.* 250 B.C.-A.D. 1000, Vol. 2, Part I, 1988, pp. 3-17.

Lal, B.B., 'Mathura: A Re-assessment of the Chronology of the Crucial Northern Black Polished Ware Horizons', In *Man and Environment*, Vol. 9, 1985, pp. 109-112.

Law, B.C., 'Mathura in Ancient India', In *Journal of the Royal Asiatic Society of Bengal, Letters*, Vol. 13, No. 1, 1947, pp. 21-30.

Lohuizen De Leeuw, J.E. Van, *The Scythian Period*, Leiden, 1949.

— 'Gandhara and Mathura: Their Cultural Relationship, In Pratapaditya Pal's ed. *Aspects of Indian Art*, Leiden, 1972, pp. 27-43.

Luders, H., 'A List of Brahmi Inscriptions from the Earliest Times to About A.D. 400 with the exception of Those of Asoka', In *Epigraphia Indica,* Appendix, Vol. 10, 1909-10, pp. 1-25.

— 'A List of Brahmi Inscriptions from the Earliest Time to About A.D. 400', In *Epigraphia Indica,* Vol. 10, 1909-10.

— *Mathura Inscriptions,* ed. by Klaus L. Janert, Gottingen, 1961.

— 'Seven Brahmi Inscriptions from Mathura and its Vicinity', In *Epigraphia Indica,* Vol. 24, 1937-38, pp. 194-210.

Margabandhu, C. & Gaur, G.S., Some Fresh Evidence from Sanghol Excavations, 1986, In *Purātattva,* No. 16 (1985-86), New Delhi, 1987, pp. 73-78.

— 'Sanghol Excavations 1987: Some New Evidences', In *Purātattva,* No. 17 (1986-87), New Delhi, 1988, pp. 1-4.

Marshall, J.H., 'Archaeological exploration in India, 1909-10', In *Journal of the Royal Asiatic Society of Gr. Britain and Ireland,* 1911, pp. 127-158.

Maxwell, T.S., *Visvarupa,* Delhi, 1988.

Misra, R.N., *Yaksha Cult and Iconography,* New Delhi, 1981.

Misra, Shivadhar, 'Mathurā Kalā Me Jātak Kathāen' (Hindi), In Radhey Shyam Dwivedi's ed. *Braj Vaibhav,* Mathura, Bharati Anusandhan Bhawan, 1972, pp. 191-198.

Mitra, R.L., 'Notes on Sanskrit Inscriptions from Mathura', In *JASB,* Vol. XXXIX, 1870.

Mittal, K.K. & Agrawal, A. (ed.), *Buddhist Art and Thought,* New Delhi, 1993.

Mittal, Prabhu Dayal, *Braj Kī Kalāon Kā Itihās*a (Hindi), Mathura, 1975.

— *Braj Kā Sāṃskṛtika Itihāsa* (Hindi), Delhi, 1966.

— *Braj Ke Dharma-Sampradāyon Kā Itihāsa* (Hindi), Delhi, 1986.

Mitter wallner, Gritle V., The Kusana Type of the Goddess Mahishasuramardini as Compared to the Gupta and Medieval Types', In *German Scholars of India,* Vol. 2, Bombay, 1976, pp. 196-213.

— 'Two Stupa Basements of Mathura of the 4th and 5th Centuries A.D.', In Anna Libera Dallapiccola and Stephanie Zingel-ave Lallemant's ed. *The Stupa: Its Religious, Historical and Architectural Significance,* Wiesbaden, 1980, pp. 72-89.

— *Kusana Coins and Kusana Sculptures from Mathura,* Mathura, 1986.

— *Munzen der spaten Kusanas des Munnen Kirda/Kisaka, undder furhen Guptas Tail I,* Munich, 1983.

— 'Yaksas of Ancient Mathura', In Doris Meth Srinivasan's ed. *Mathura: The Cultural Heritage,* New Delhi, 1989, pp. 368-382.

Moti Chandra, *Sārthavāha* (Hindi), 1953.

Mukherjee, B.N., *The Kushana Genealogy,* Calcutta, 1967.

— *Disintegration of the Kushana Empire,* Varanasi, 1976.

— *Mathura and its Society: The Śaka-Pahlava Phase*, Calcutta, 1981.

— *The Rise and Fall of the Kushana Empire*, Calcutta, 1988.

— 'Problems of dated Images of the Mathura School of Sculpture of the Kushan Period', In *Central Asia in the Kushan Period: Proceedings of the International Conference of the History, Archaeology and Culture of Central Asia in the Kushan Period*, 1968, Vol. 2, UNESCO, 1975, pp. 346-362.

— *Kushana Coins of the Land of the Five Rivers*, Calcutta, 1978.

— *Kushana Silver Coinage*, Calcutta, 1982.

Nagar, M.M., 'Some New Terracottas from Mathura', In *Journal of the U.P. Historical Society*, Vol. 17, Pt. 2, December 1944, pp. 73-75.

— *Purātattva Saṅgrahālaya Kī Paricaya Pustikā* (Hindi), 1947.

Narain, A.K., 'Ancient Mathura and the Numismatic Material', In Doris Meth Srinivasan's ed. *Mathura: The Cultural Heritage*, New Delhi, 1989, pp. 115-118.

Nehru, Lolita, *Origins of the Gandhara Styles*, New Delhi, 1989.

Pal, Pratapaditya, *The Sensuous Immortals: A selection of the sculptures from the Pan-Asian collection*, Los Angeles, 1978.

— *Indian Sculpture: A Catalogue of the Los Angeles County Museum of Art collection*, Vol. I, Los Angeles, 1986.

Palast Gotter (Palace of Gods), Exhibition Catalogue organised in Berlin, 1992.

Pandey, Raj Bali, *Historical and Literary Inscriptions*, Varanasi, 1962.

— 'Prakrit and Sanskrit Inscriptions, Mathura', In *Indian Archaeology: A Review*, 1958-59, pp. 63-64.

Parimoo, Ratan, *Life of Buddha in Indian Sculpture, Ashta Maha Pratiharya*, New Delhi, 1982.

Poster, Amy G., *From Indian Earth: 4,000 years of Terracotta*, New York, 1986.

Prakash, Pratibha, *Terracotta Animal Figurines in the Ganga-Yamuna Valley* (*600 B.C. to 600 A.D.*), Delhi, 1985.

Pramod Chandra, *Stone Sculpture in the Allahabad Museum*, New Delhi, 1970.

Puri, B.N., *India Under the Kushanas*, Bombay, 1965.

Ray, Niharranjan, *Maurya and Sunga Art*, Calcutta, 1965.

— *Maurya and Post-Maurya Art*, New Delhi, 1975.

Ray, Sunil C., 'Stratigraphic Evidence of Coins from Excavations at Mathura', In Doris Meth Srinivasan's ed. *Mathura: The Cultural Heritage*, New Delhi, 1989, pp. 140-145.

Ray Chaudhari, Hem Chandra, *Political History of Ancient India*, Calcutta, 1953.

Rosenfield, John M., *The Dynastic Art of the Kushans*, Berkeley and Los Angeles, 1967.

Rowland, Benjamin, *The Art and Architecture of India: Buddhist, Hindu, Jain*, Middle-sex, 1956.

— 'Gandhara, Rome and Mathura: The Early Relief style', In *Archives of the Chinese Art Society of America*, Vol. 10, 1956, pp. 8-17.

Roy, U.N. *Salabhanjika in Art, Philosophy and Literature*, 1979.

Sahni, Daya Ram, 'Seven Inscriptions from Mathura', In *Epigraphia Indica*, Vol. 19, 1927-28, pp. 65-69.

Saraswati, S.K., *A Survey of Indian Sculpture*, Calcutta, 1957.

Satya Shrava, *The Kushana Numismatics*, New Delhi, 1985.

— *Dated Kushana Inscriptions*, Delhi, 1993.

Sawoo Mangala, 'Some Interesting Mathura Terracotta Figurines in the Indian Museum', In *Indian Museum Bulletin*, Vol. 14, 1979, pp. 91-94.

Shah, U.P., 'A Note on Stone Umbrellas from Mathura', In *Journal of the U.P. Historical Society*, Vols. 24-25, 1951-52, pp. 205-208.

— *Studies in Jaina Art*, Banaras, 1955.

Shan, U.P. & Bender, Ernest, 'Mathura and Jainism', In Doris Meth Srinivasan's ed. *Mathura: The Cultural Heritage*, New Delhi, 1989, pp. 209-213.

Sharma, B.N., 'Kusana Siva-Lingas from Mathura', In *Journal of the Oriental Institute*, Vol. 27, Nos. 1-2, Septemeber-December, 1977, pp. 33-39.

Sharma, I.K., *The Development of Early Saiva Art and Architecture*, Delhi, 1982.

Sharma, R.C., 'The Early Phase of Jaina Iconography', In *Chotte Lāl Jain Smrti Grantha*, Calcutta, 1967, pp. 57-61.

— 'Pre-Kaniska Buddhist Iconography at Mathura', In *Bulletin of Museums and Archaeology in U.P.*, Nos. 5-6, June-December 1970, pp. 16-27.

— *Mathura Museum Introduction*, 1971.

— 'New Inscription from Mathura', In *Bulletin of Museums & Archaeology in U.P.*, No. 8, 1971, pp. 24-28.

— 'Terracotta Art of Mathura', In *Lalit Kala Akademi Independence Jubilee*, 1972.

— 'New Rare Sculptures in Mathura Museum', In *Bulletin of Museum and Archaeology in U.P.*, No. 8, December, 1971, pp. 71-75.

— *Mathura Museum and Art*, Second Edition, Mathura, 1976.

— 'Hundred years of Mathura Museum', In *Journal of Indian Museums*, XXIX, 1973, pp. 1-8.

— 'Buddha as Appears in Mathura Art', In *Journal of Indian Museums*, Vol. 29, 1973, pp. 18-21.

— '*Mathurā Saṅgrahālaya Kī Kuṣāṇa Jaina Mūrtiyāṅ*' (Hindi), In Jyoti Prasad Jain's ed. *Bhagvāna Mahvāvīra Smṛti Grantha*, Lucknow, 1975, pp. 119-125.

— 'Kusana Idiom in Mathura', In D.C. Bhattacharya and Devendra Handa's ed. *Prāci-Prabhā: Perspective in Indology*, New Delhi, 1980, pp. 225-233.

— 'Gupta Sculptures from Mathura' In *Bulletin of Museum & Archaeology in U.P.*, Nos. 27-28, June-December 1981, pp. 89-109.

— *Buddhist Art of Mathura*, Delhi, 1984.

— 'Early Phase of Buddhist Icons at Mathura', In *Bulletin of Museums and Archaeology in U.P.*, Nos. 33-34, June-December 1984, pp. 57-66.

— 'Archaic Terracotta Divinities—A Case Study of Mathura', In *Indian Museum Bulletin*, Vol. 21, 1986, pp. 34-37.

— 'Mathura as School of Sculpture', In Lokesh Chandra and others' ed. *Dimensions of Indian Art Pupul Jayakar Seventy*, Vol. I, Delhi, 1986, pp. 407-416.

— *Album of Art Treasures: Mathura Sculptures*, Calcutta, 1987.

— 'New Inscriptions from Mathura', In Doris Meth Srinivasan's ed. *Mathura: The Cultural Heritage*, New Delhi, 1989, pp. 308-315.

— 'Buddhist and Brahmanical Gupta Sculptures from Mathura', In Khandelwala's ed. *The Golden Age*, Marg Publications, 1991, pp. 15-24.

— 'New Buddhist Sculptures from Mathura, Pre-Gupta epoch', In *Lalit Kalā*, No. 19, pp. 19-26.

Sharma, R.C. & Misra, Shivadhar, 'Kusana Acquisitions in the Mathura Museum During the Last Decade', In *Bulletin of Museums and Archaeology in U.P.*, No. 4, Dec. 1969, pp. 46-65.

Shashi Kant. 'Some Unique Jain Images', In *East and West, New Series*, Vol. 26, Nos. 3-4, 1976, pp. 435-438.

Shukla, S.P., 'Sanghol: Kusana Buddhist Stupa and Sculptures', In K.K. Mittal & A. Agrawala's ed. *Buddhist Art and Thought*, New Delhi, 1993, pp. 131-136.

Sircar, D.C., 'Brahmi Inscriptions from Mathura', In *Epigraphia Indica*, Vol. 34, 1961-62, pp. 9-13.

— *Select Inscriptions*, Calcutta, 1965.

— *Studies in Indian Coins*, Delhi, 1968.

Sivaramamurti, C., *Indian Sculpture*, Bombay, 1961.

— *The Art of India*, New York, 1977.

— *Sculpture Inspired by Kalidasa*, New Delhi, 1984.

Smith, Vincent A., 'Graeco-Roman Influence on the Civilization of Ancient India', In *Journal of the Asiatic Society of Bengal*, Vol. 58, Pt. I, No. 3, 1889, pp. 107-198.

— *The Jaina Stupa and Other Antiquities of Mathura*, Allahabad, 1901.

— 'Kushana Inscriptions', In *Journal of the Asiatic Society of Great Britain and Ireland*, 1905, pp. 151-152.

Snellgrove, David L. ed., *The Image of the Buddha*, Paris, UNESCO, 1978.

Srinivasan, Doris Meth, 'Early Krishna Icons: The Case of Mathura', In *Bulletin of*

Museums and Archaeology in U.P., Nos. 21-24, June 1978-December 1979, pp. 1-18.

— '*Early* Vaisnava Imagery: Caturvyuha and Variant forms', In *Archives of Asian Art*, Vol. 32, 1979, pp. 39-54.

— 'Early Krsna Icons: The case at Mathura', In Joanna G. Williams' ed. *Kalādarśana*, New Delhi, 1981, pp. 127-136.

Srinivasan, Doris Meth (ed.), *Mathura : The Cultural Heritage*, New Delhi, 1989.

Srivastava, A.K., 'Mathura as known through the Coins', In *Bulletin of Museums and Archaeology in U.P.*, Nos. 11-12, June-December 1973, pp. 30-36.

— *Coin Hoards of Uttar Pradesh*, Lucknow, 1980.

Srivastava, A.L., 'Mathura: The Cradle of Indian Cult Images', In Devendra Handa's ed. *Indological Studies: Essays in Memory of Shri S.P. Singhal*, Delhi, 1987, pp. 49-66.

Srivastava, C.S., 'Kusana Hoards of Treasure Trove Coins from Uttar Pradesh' (1941-42 to 1969-70), In *Bulletin of Museums and Archaeology in U.P.*, No. 3, June 1969, pp. 48-67.

Srivastava, Rani, *Mathurā Kalā Ke Do Naye Abhiprāya*, In *Bulletin of Museums and Archaeology in U.P.*, Nos. 33-34, 1984, pp. 19-24.

— *Kuṣāṇa Prastara Mūrtiyon Men Samāja Evam Dharma* (Hindi), Delhi, 1992.

Srivastava, V.C., 'The Kushanas and the Sun Cult', In *Journal of the Gaṅgānātha Jhā Kendriya Sanskrit Vidyāpīṭha*, Vol. 35, Pts. 3-4, July-December 1979, pp. 115-146.

Srivastava, V.N., 'Gupta Sculpture at Mathura', In *Marg*, Vol. 15, No. 2, March 1962, pp. 50-58.

— '*Braj Kī Vastu Kalā*', In Radhey Shyam Dwivedi's ed. *Braj Vaibhav*, Mathura, 1972, pp. 173-178.

Srivastava, V.N. & Joshi, M.P., 'The Mathura Inscription of Yavana Era 116', In *Bulletin of the Museums and Archaeology in U.P.*, Vols. 41-42, 1988, pp. 103-106.

Srivastava, V.N. & Misra, S., 'Inventory of Mathura Museum Sculputres Since 1934', In *Bulletin of Museums and Archaeology in U.P.*, Vol. 11-12, 1973.

Stacy, L.R., 'Note on the Discovery of a Relic of Grecian Sculpture in Upper India', In *Journal of the Asiatic Society of Bengal*, Vol. 5, 1836, pp. 567-570.

Thakural, Pushpa, 'Yavana Inscription from Mathura', In *Indian Museum Bulletin*, 1991, pp. 23-25.

Thakhural, Pushpa & Mishra, Pyare Lal, *Mathurā Saṅgrahālaya Kā Navaprāpta Abhilekh*' (Hindi), In *Bulletin of Museums and Archeology in U.P.*, Nos. 41-42, 1988, pp. 109-113.

Thapar, B., 'The Kushan Civilization in India: An appraisal of the Component Elements', In *Central Asia in the Kushan Period: Proceedings of the International Conference on the History, Archaeology and Culture of Central Asia in the Kushan Period*, 1968, Vol. I, UNESCO, 1974, pp. 90-94.

Thaplyal, Kiran Kumar, *Studies in Ancient Indian Seals*, Lucknow, 1972.

Thaplayal, K.K. & Sharma, R.C., 'Mathura Buddhist Image Inscription of Jiva dt. Years 121 and 15', In *Bulletin of Museums and Archaeology in U.P.*, Nos. 29-30, 1982, pp. 17-24.

Tiwari, M.N.P., *'Mathurā Me Jain Dharma Aur Kalā'* (Hindi), In *Uttar Pradeṣh,* Vol. 10, No. 7, December 1981, pp. 28-31.

Trivedi, R.D., 'Vishnu and His Incarnations in the Works of Kalidasa', In *East and West, New Series,* Vol. 22, Nos. 1-2, March-June 1972, pp. 51-62.

Trivedi, S.D., 'Masterpieces of Mathura Museum', In *Journal of Indian Museums,* Vol. 29, 1973, pp. 30-32.

— *'Mathurā Saṅgrahālaya Me Ṛṣabhanāth Kı Pratimāeṅ'* (Hindi), In Neel Kantha Purushottam Joshi's ed. *Jaina-nibandhmālā,* Vol. I, Rampur, 1977, pp. 26-28.

— 'Fresh light on some Icons of Mathura Museum', In A.M. Shastri and others' ed. *Vajapeya: Essays on Evolution of Indian Art & Culture, Prof. K.D. Bajpai Felicitation Volume,* Vol. 2, Delhi, 1987, pp. 211-215.

Upadhyaya, B.S., *Bhāratiya Kalā Aur Saṃskṛti Kī Bhumikā* (Hindi), Delhi, 1965.

Uttar Pradesh District Gazetters, Mathura, Lucknow, 1968.

Verma, T.P., *'The Palaeography of Brahmi Script in North India' (from c. 236 B.C. to c. 200 A.D.)*, Varanasi, 1971.

Vogel J. Ph., 'The Mathura Sculpture', In *Archaeological Survey of India: Annual Report,* 1906-07, pp. 137-160.

— 'The Mathura School of Sculpture', In *Archaeological Survey of India: Annual Report,* 1909-10, pp. 63-79.

— 'Naga Worship in Ancient Mathura', In *Archaeological Survey of India: Annual Report,* 1908-09, pp. 158-163.

— *La Sculpture de Mathura Ars Asiatica,* Vol. 15, 1930.

— *Archaeological Museum at Mathura* (Reprint), Delhi, 1971.

— *Buddhist Art in India, Ceylon and Java,* New Delhi, 1977.

The Way of the Buddha, New Delhi Publications Division, 1956.

Yadav, Jagdish S., *Cultural Heritage of Mathura: A Bibliography,* Delhi, 1991.

Zimmer, H., *The Art of Indian Asia,* 2 Vols, New York, 1960.

Zwalf, W. (ed.), *Buddhism: Art and Faith,* London, 1985.

Index to the Exhibits

General Index

Coloured Illustrations

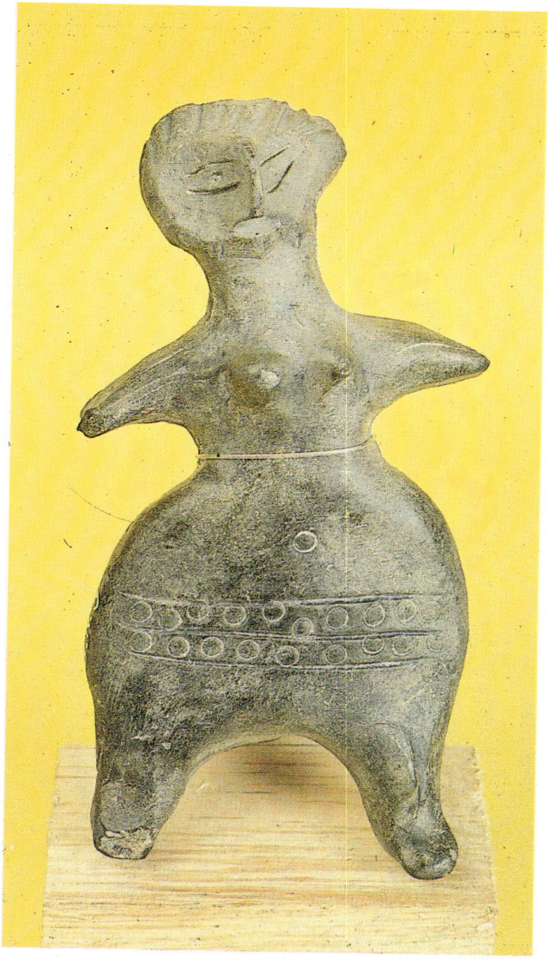

I. Terracotta mothergoddess, Archaic

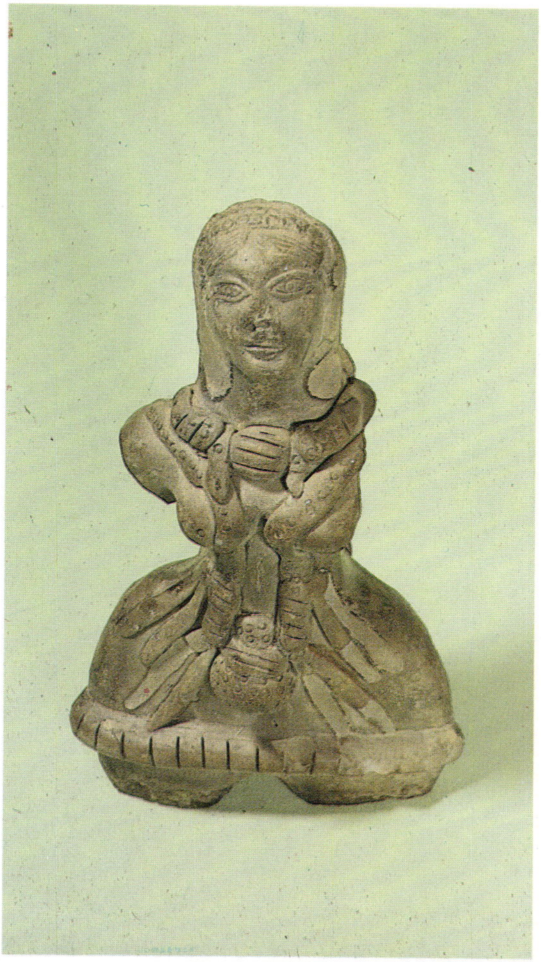

II. Terracotta mothergoddess, Maurya

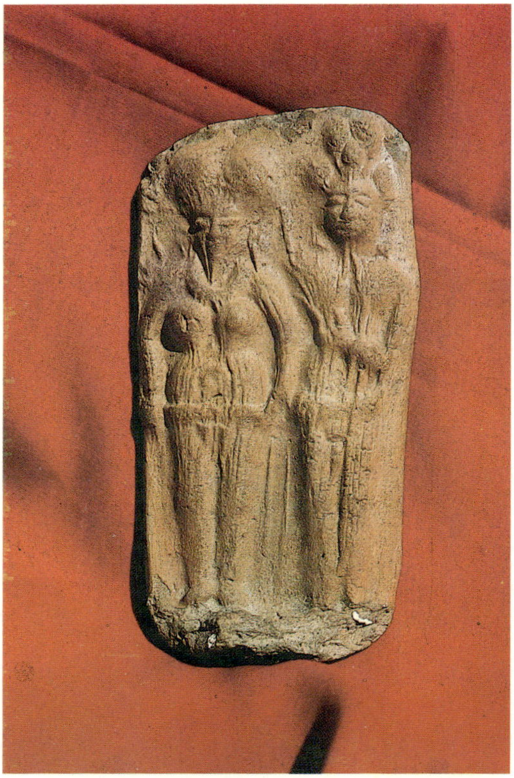

III. Terracotta plaque, Śuṅga

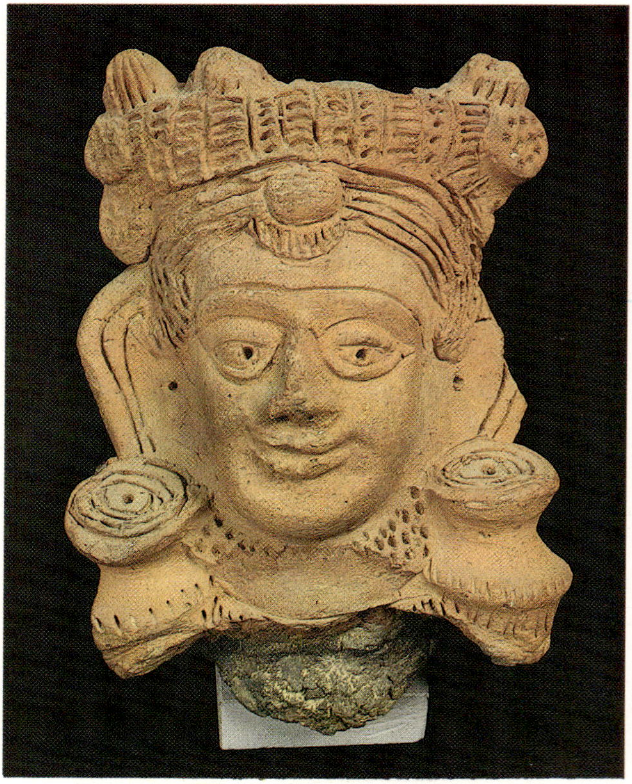

IV. Terracotta female head, Kuṣāṇa

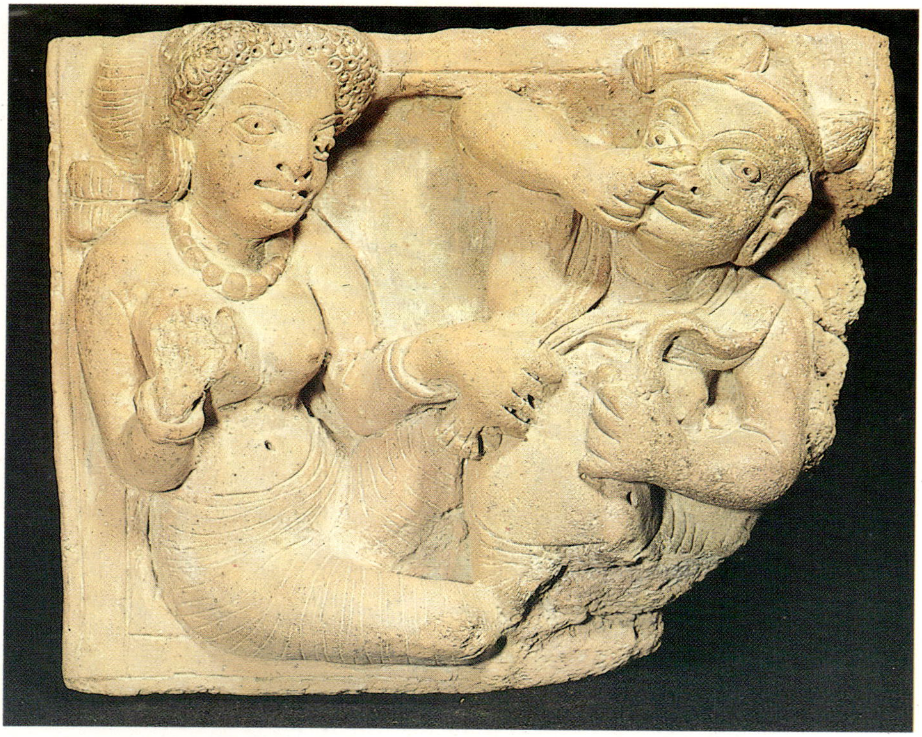

V. Terracotta brick - lady and jester, Gupta

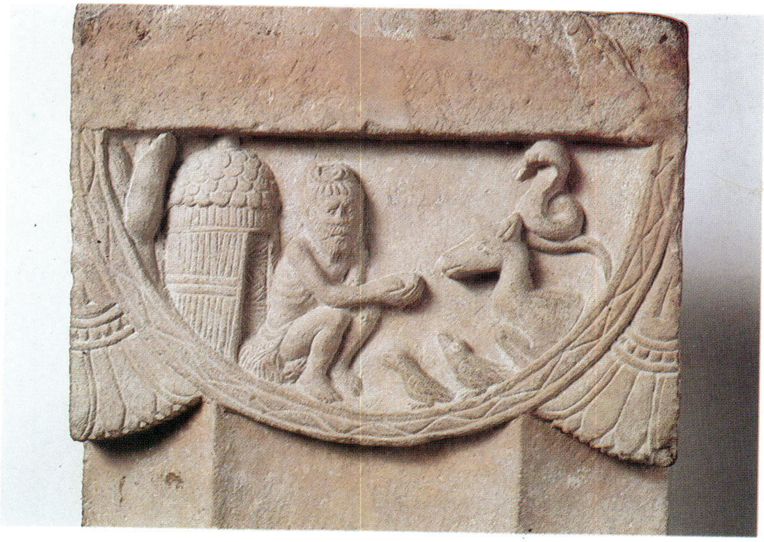

VI. *Jātaka* of the worst Evil, Śuṅga

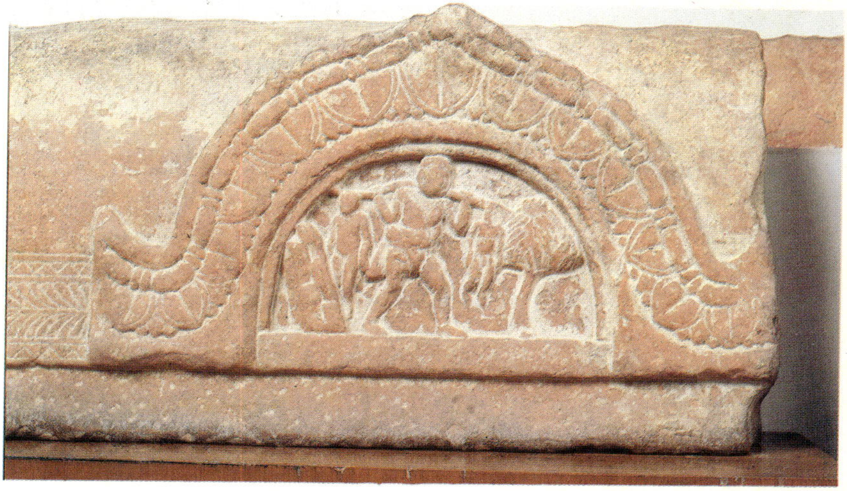

VII. *Sutasoma Jātaka*, Śuṅga

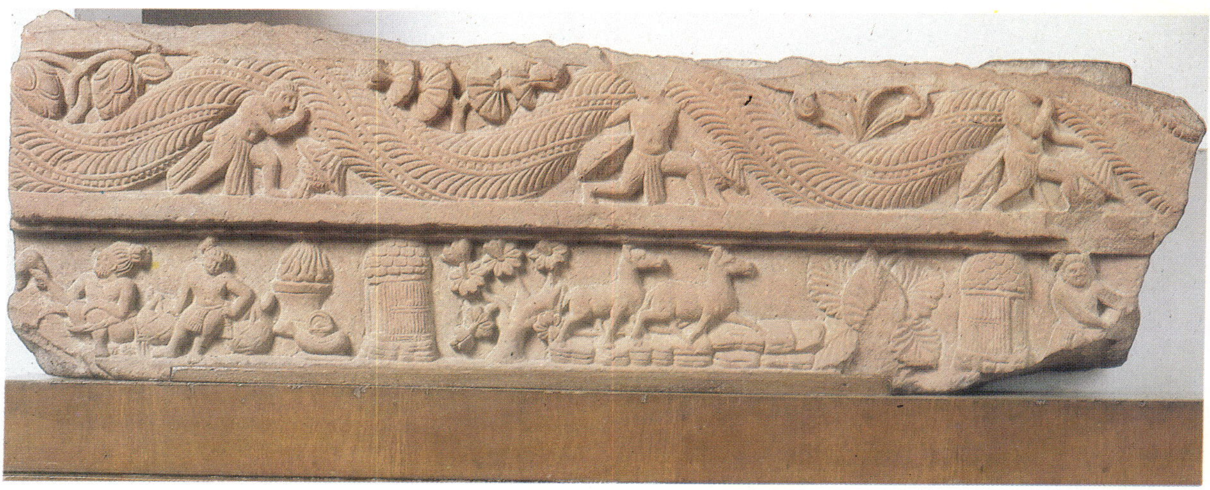

VIII. *Romaka Jātaka*, pre-Kuṣāṇa

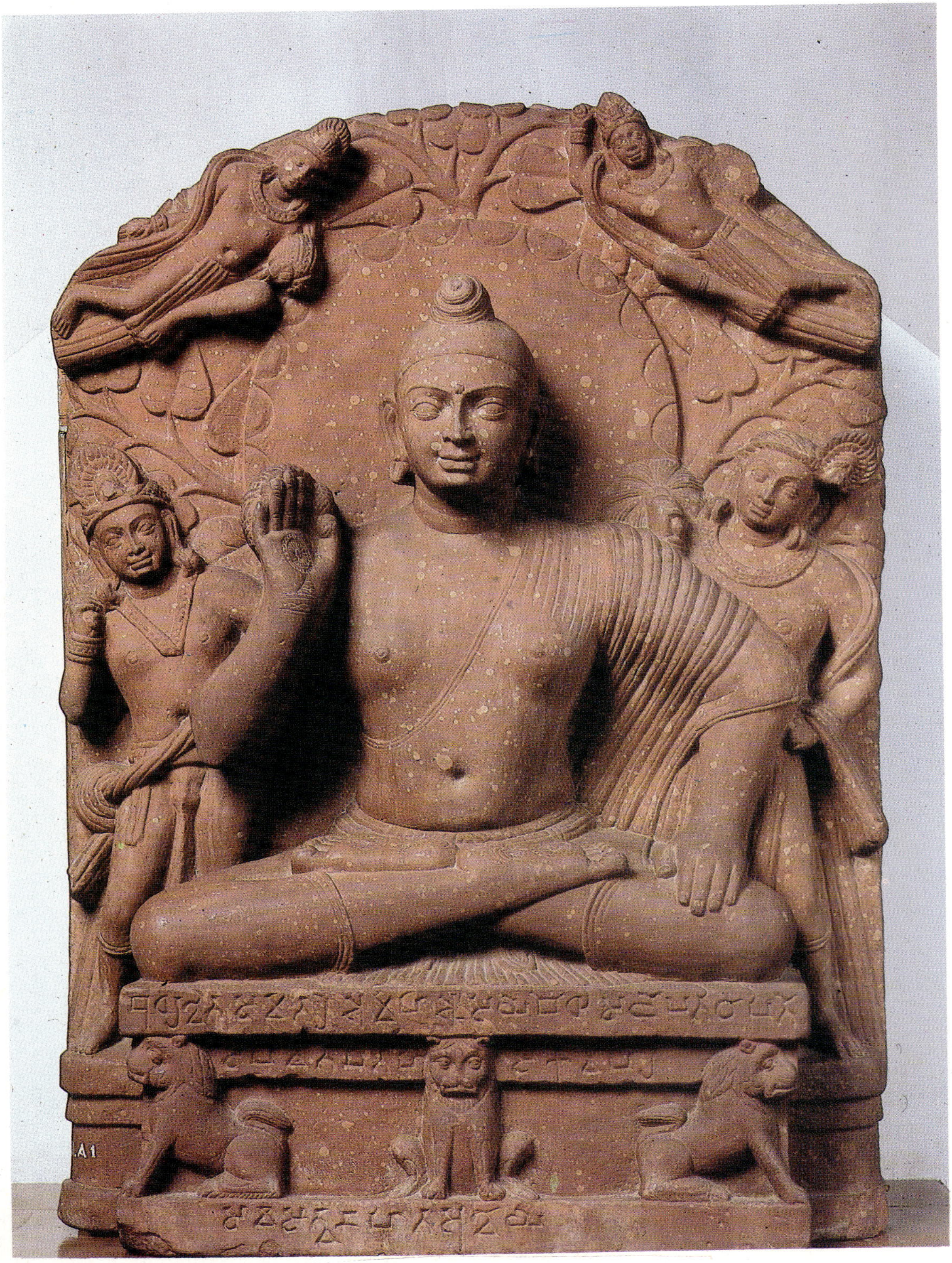

IX. Bodhisattva from Kaṭrā, early Kuṣāṇa

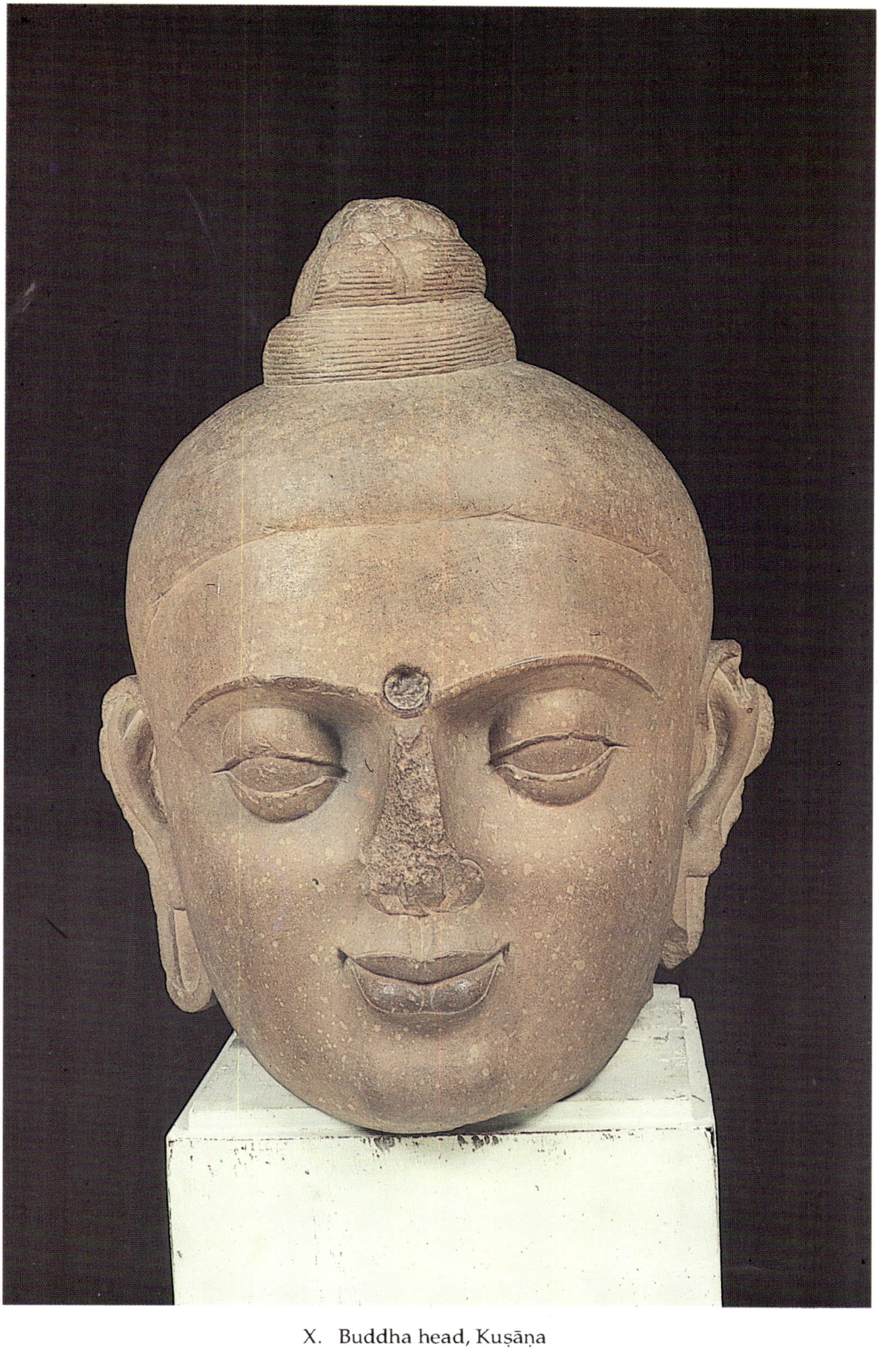

X. Buddha head, Kuṣāṇa

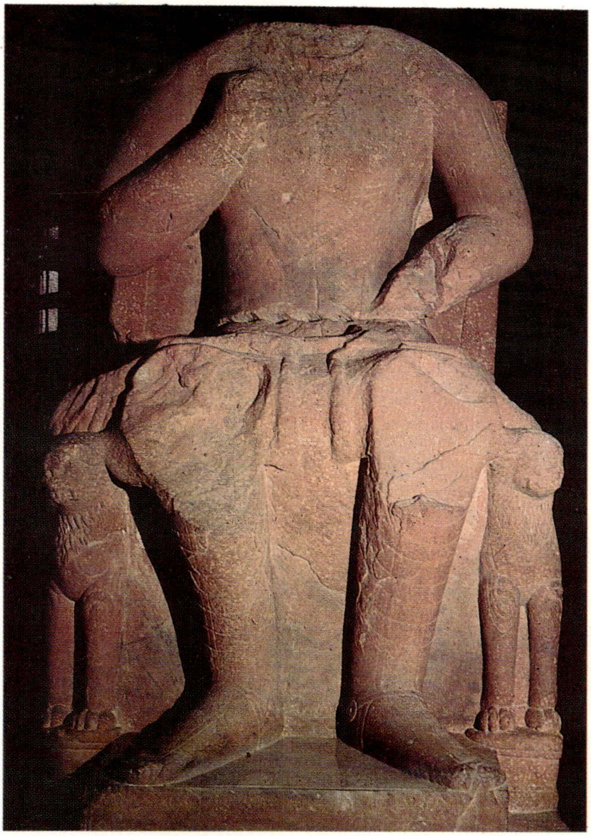

XI. Vema Kadphises, early Kuṣāṇa

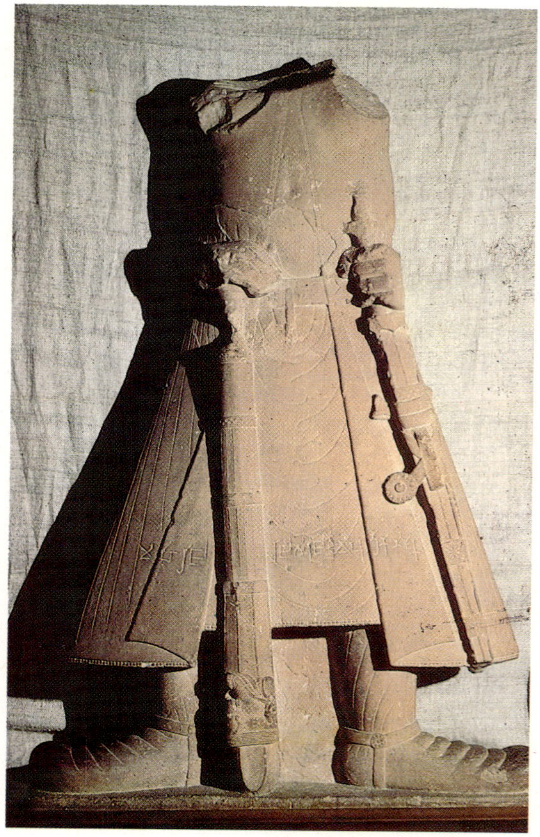

XII. Kaniṣka, early Kuṣāṇa

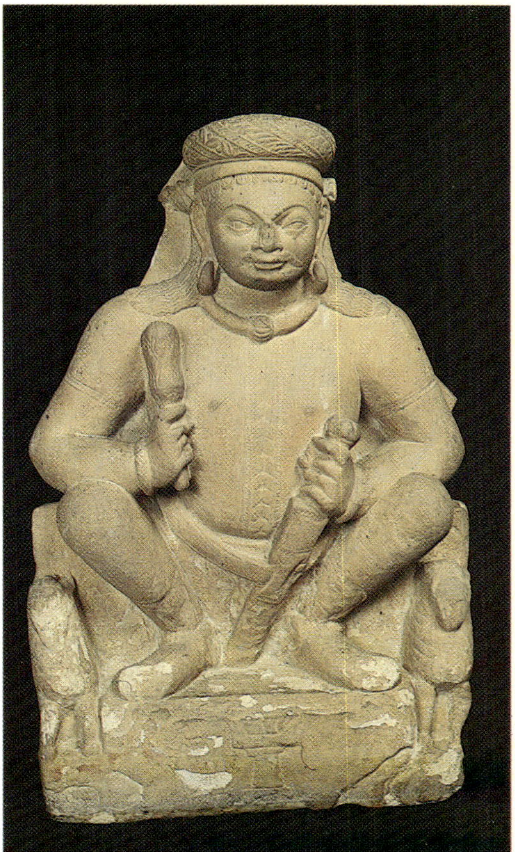

XIII. Sūrya, Kuṣāṇa

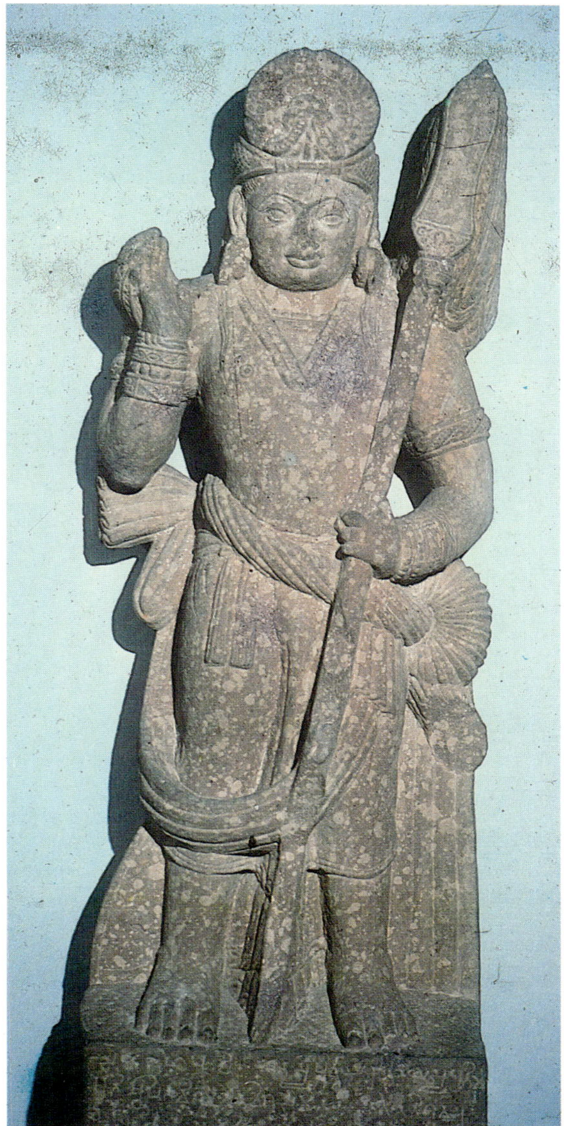

XIV. Kārttikeya, Kuṣāṇa

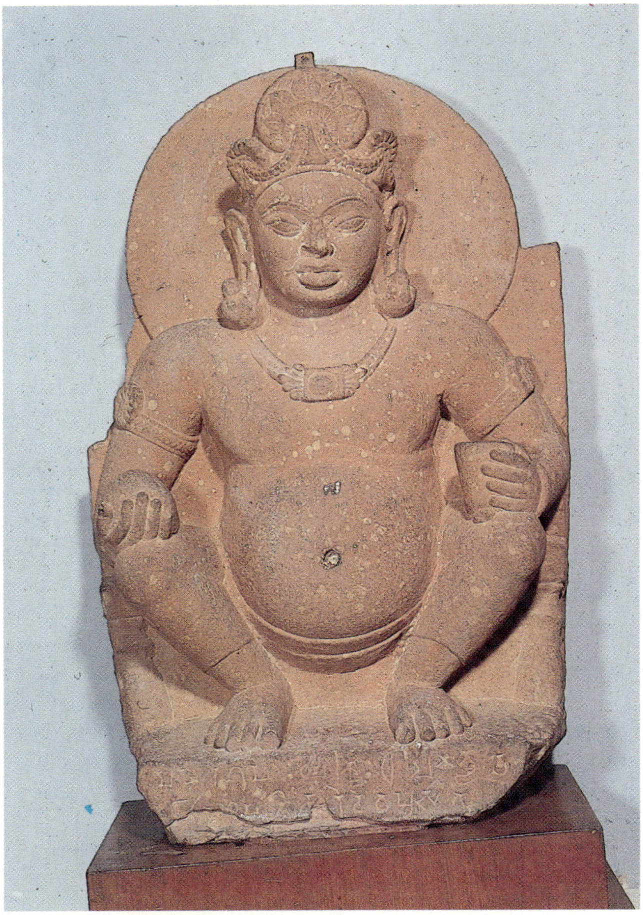

XV. *Yakṣa*,
Kuṣāṇa

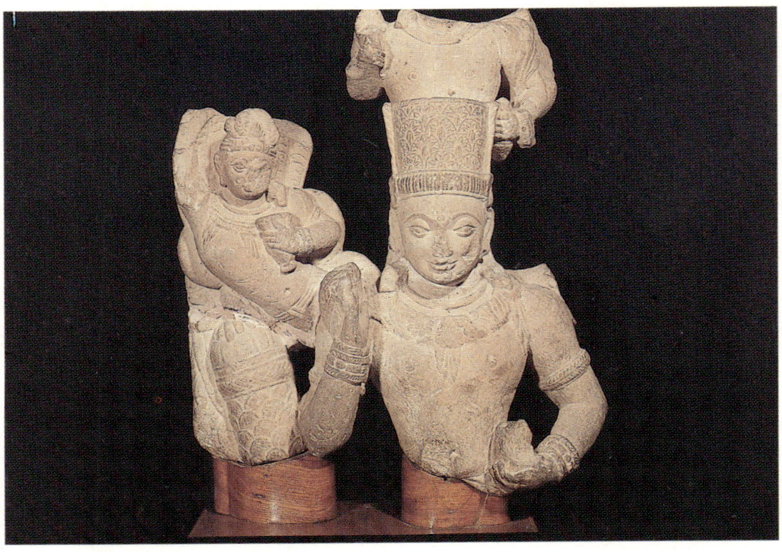

XVI. Multiple form
of Viṣṇu,
Kuṣāṇa

XVII. Balarāma, Kuṣāṇa

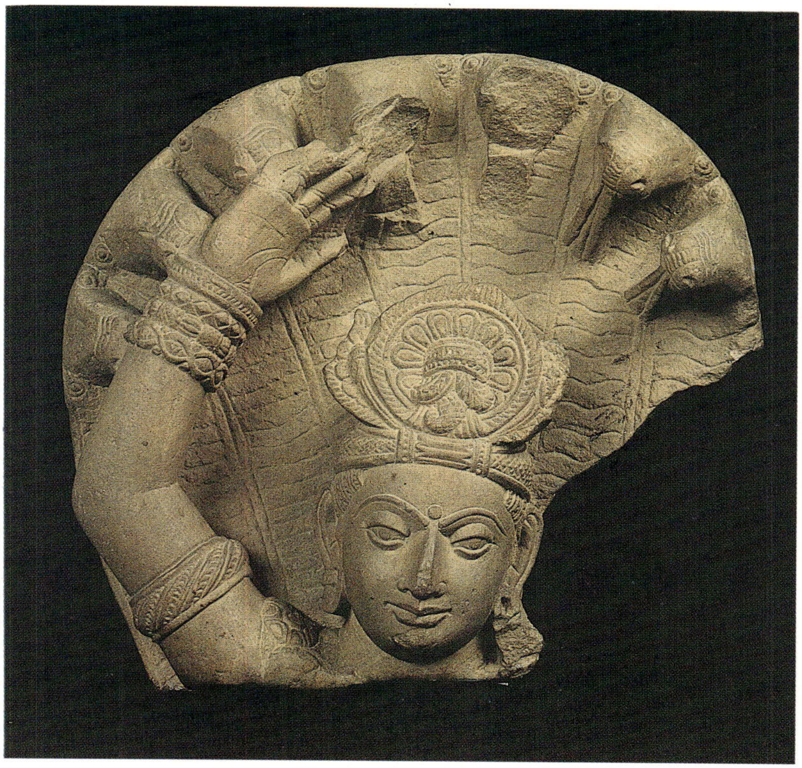

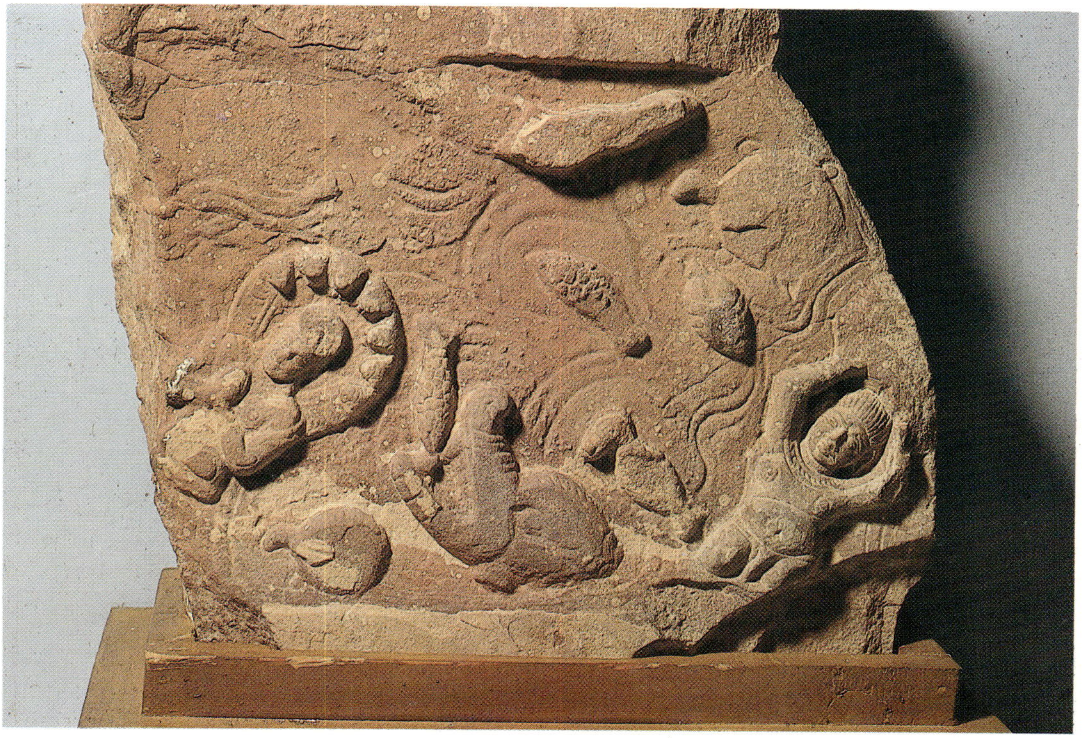

XVIII. Vāsudeva carrying Kṛṣṇa, early Kuṣāṇa

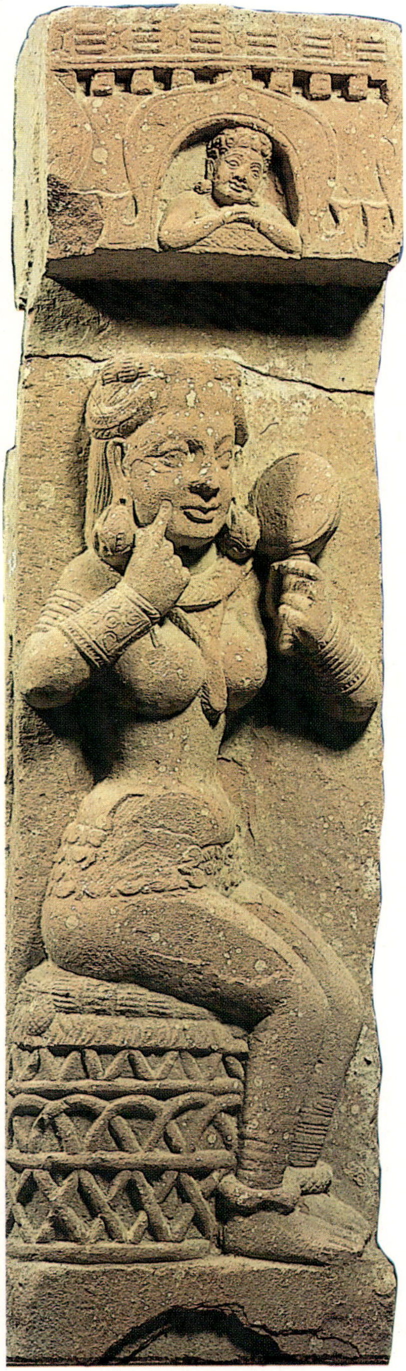

XIX. Lady with mirror, Kuṣāṇa

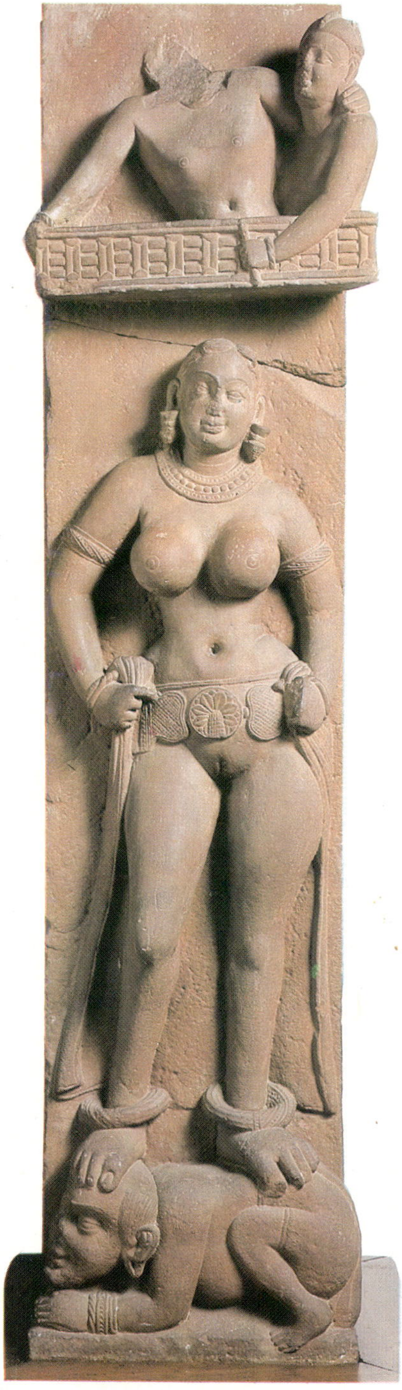

XX. Lady wearing garment, Kuṣāṇa

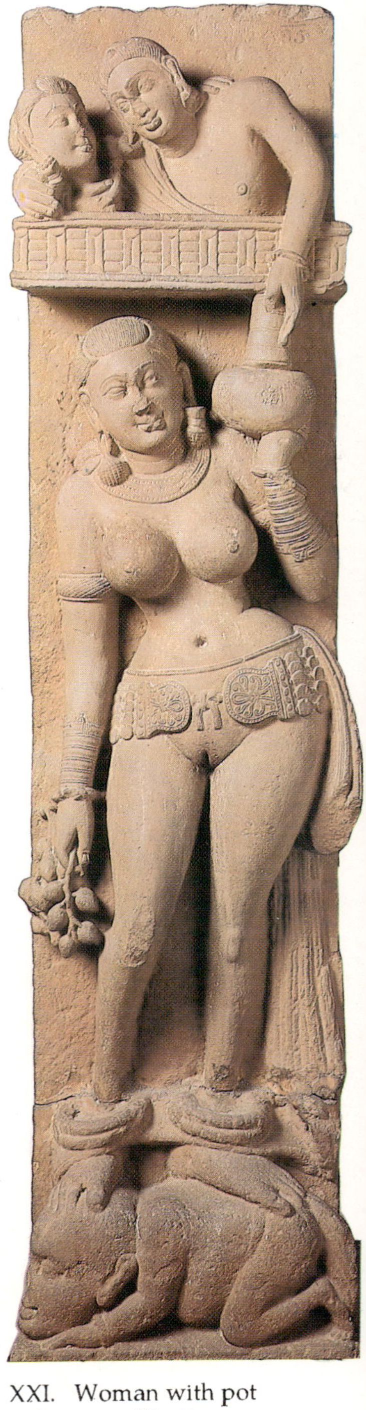

XXI. Woman with pot and grapes, Kuṣāṇa

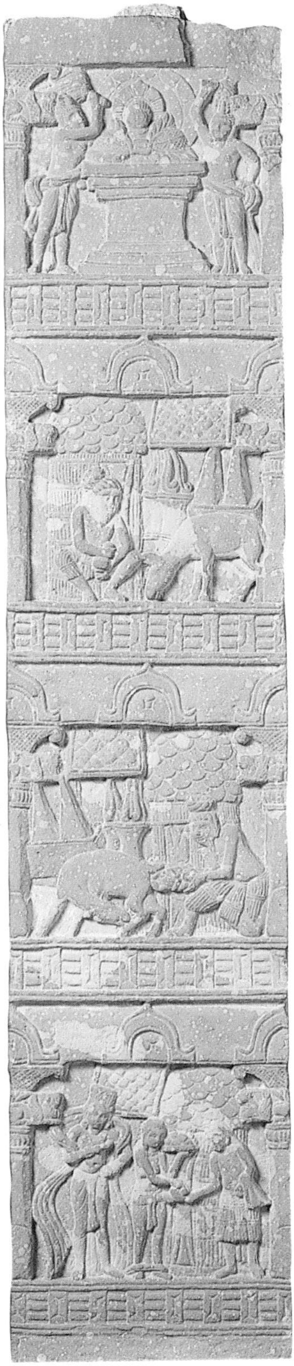

XXII. Birth of sage Śṛṅga, pre-Kuṣāṇa

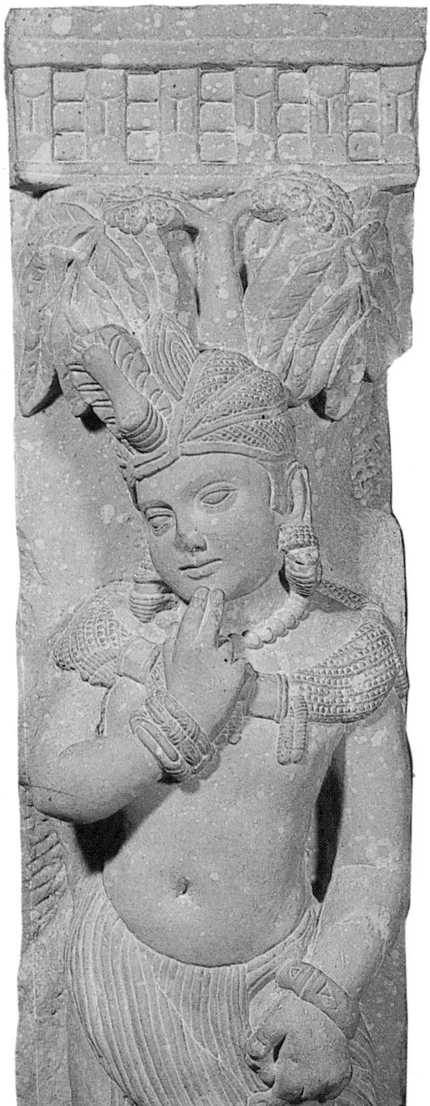

XXIII. Hermit Śṛṅga in ecstacy, Kuṣāṇa

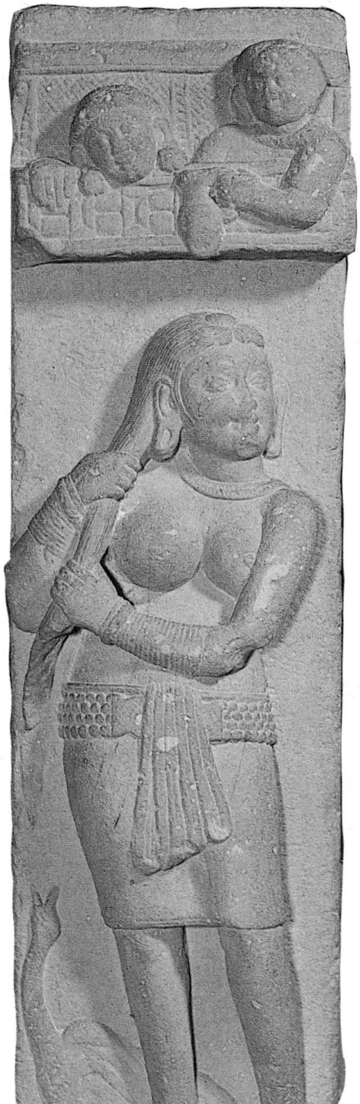

XXIV. Lady squeezing hair, Kuṣāṇa

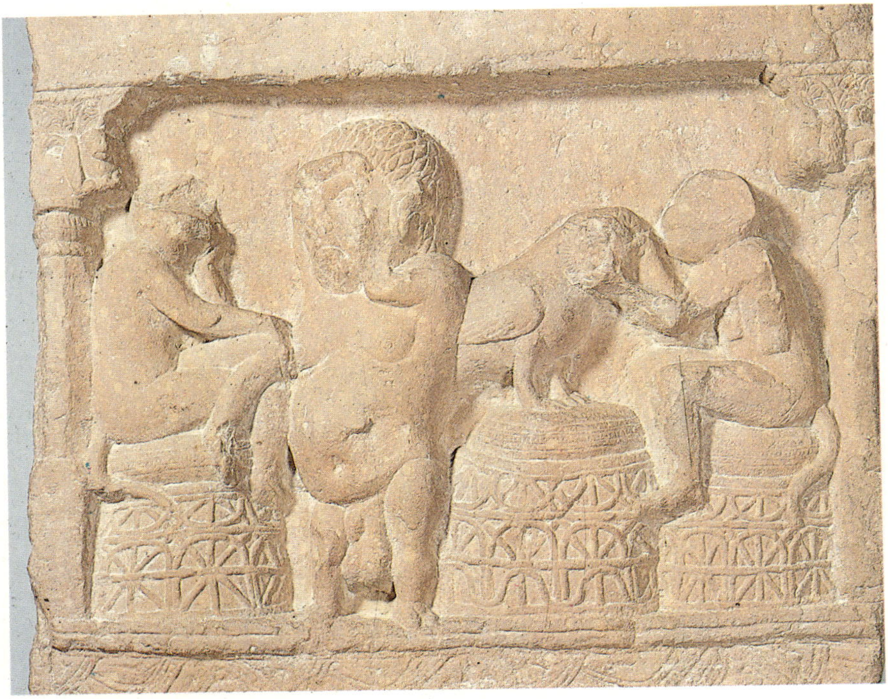

XXV. Veterinary clinic, early Kuṣāṇa

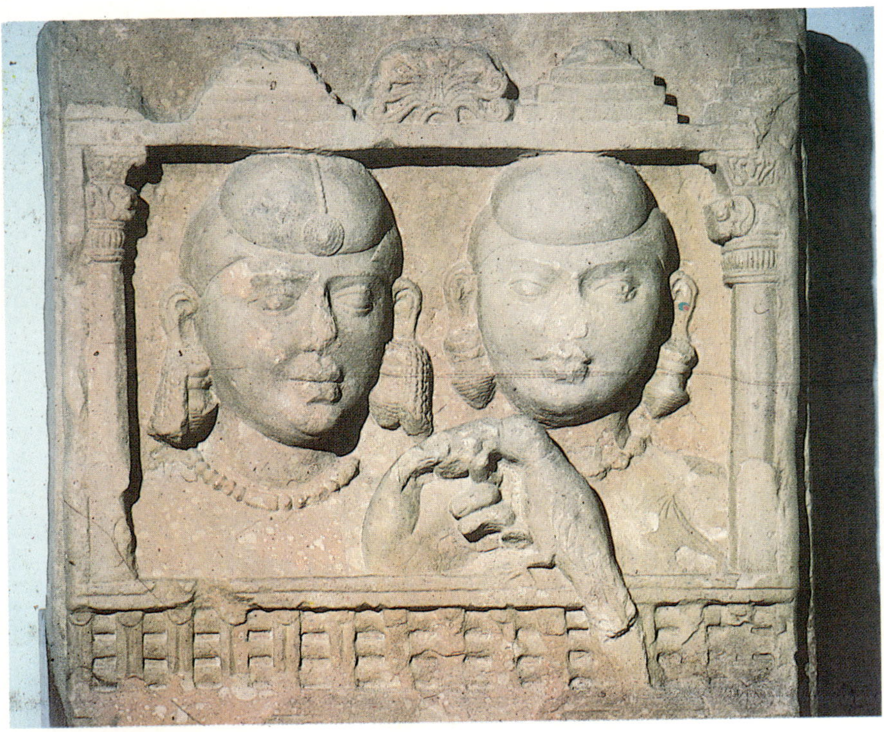

XXVI. Couple feeding parrot, Kuṣāṇa

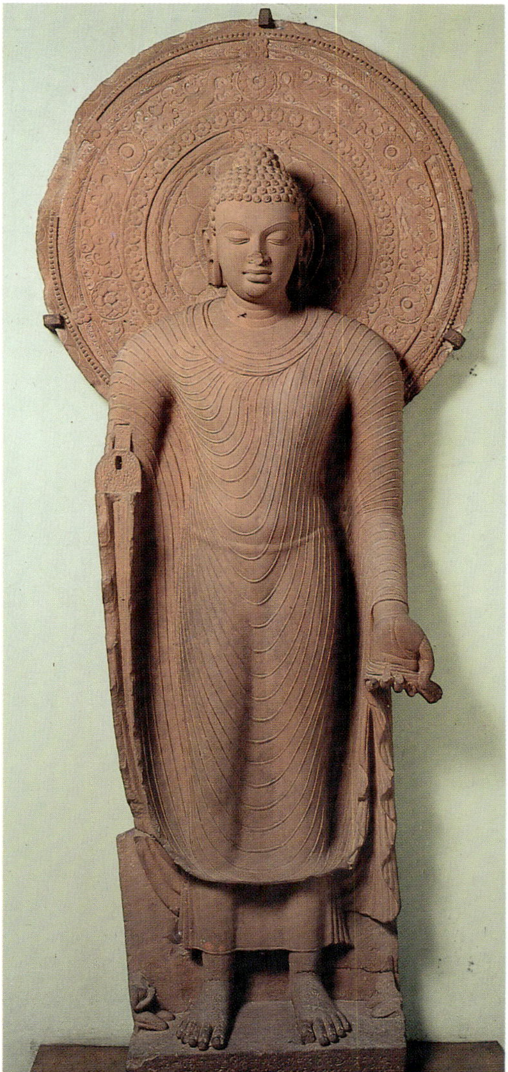

XXVII. Buddha image of Yaśadinna, Gupta

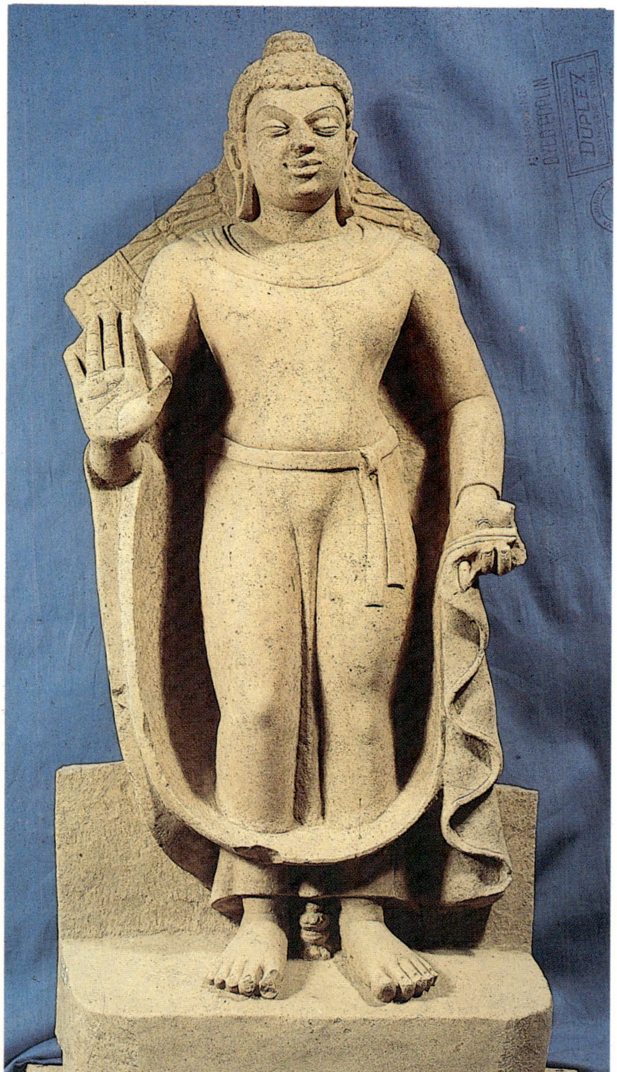

XXVIII. Buddha wearing foldless garment, early Gupta

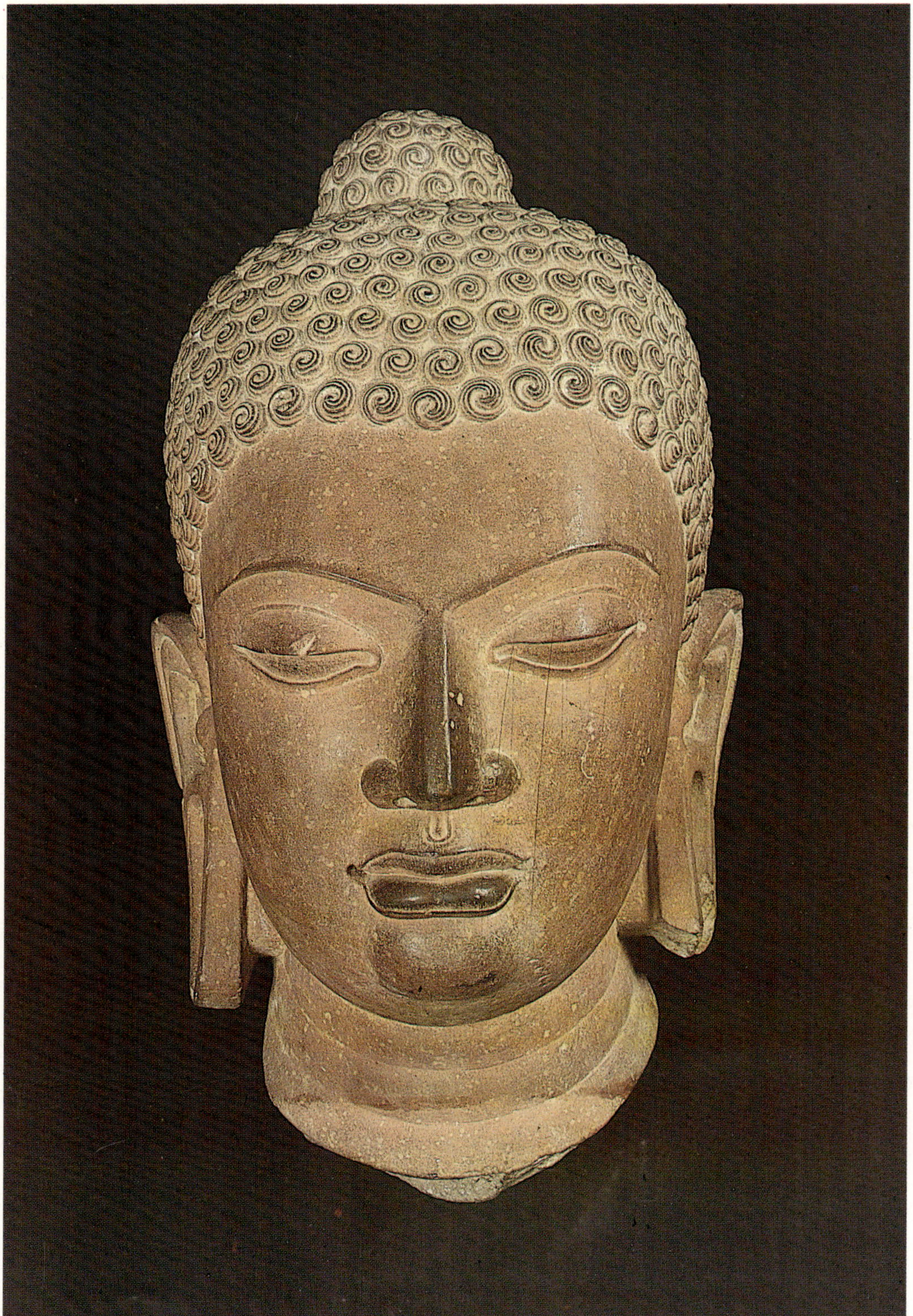

XXIX. Buddha head, Gupta

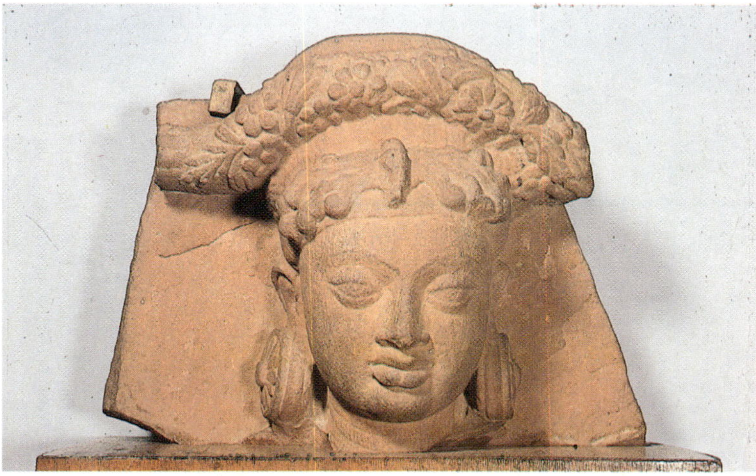

XXX. Durgā head, Gupta

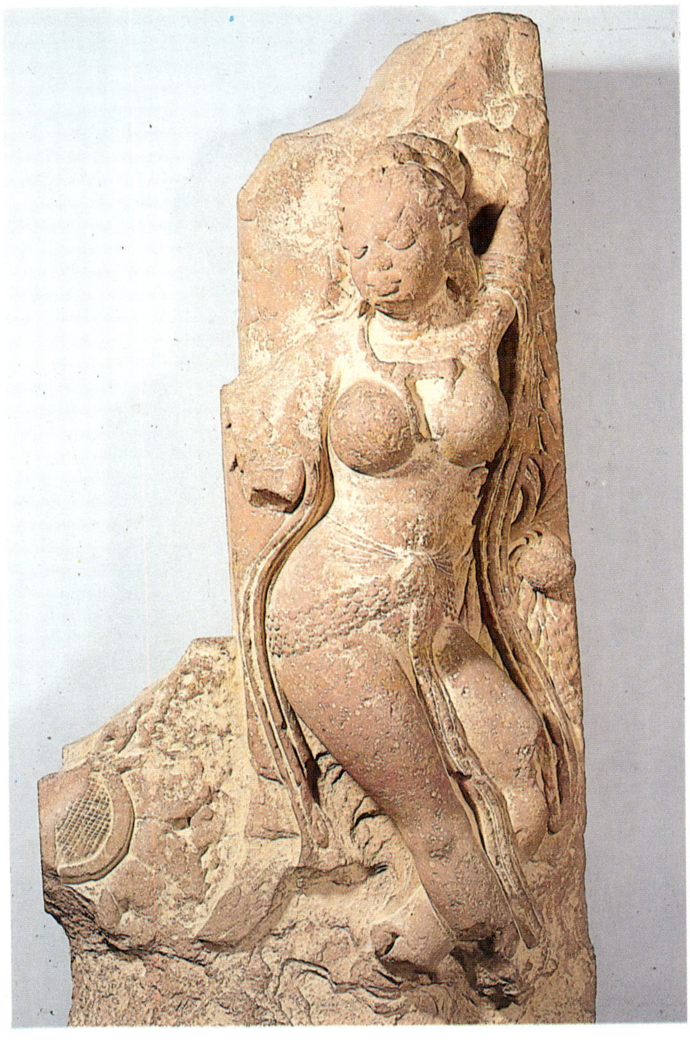

XXXI. River goddess, Gupta

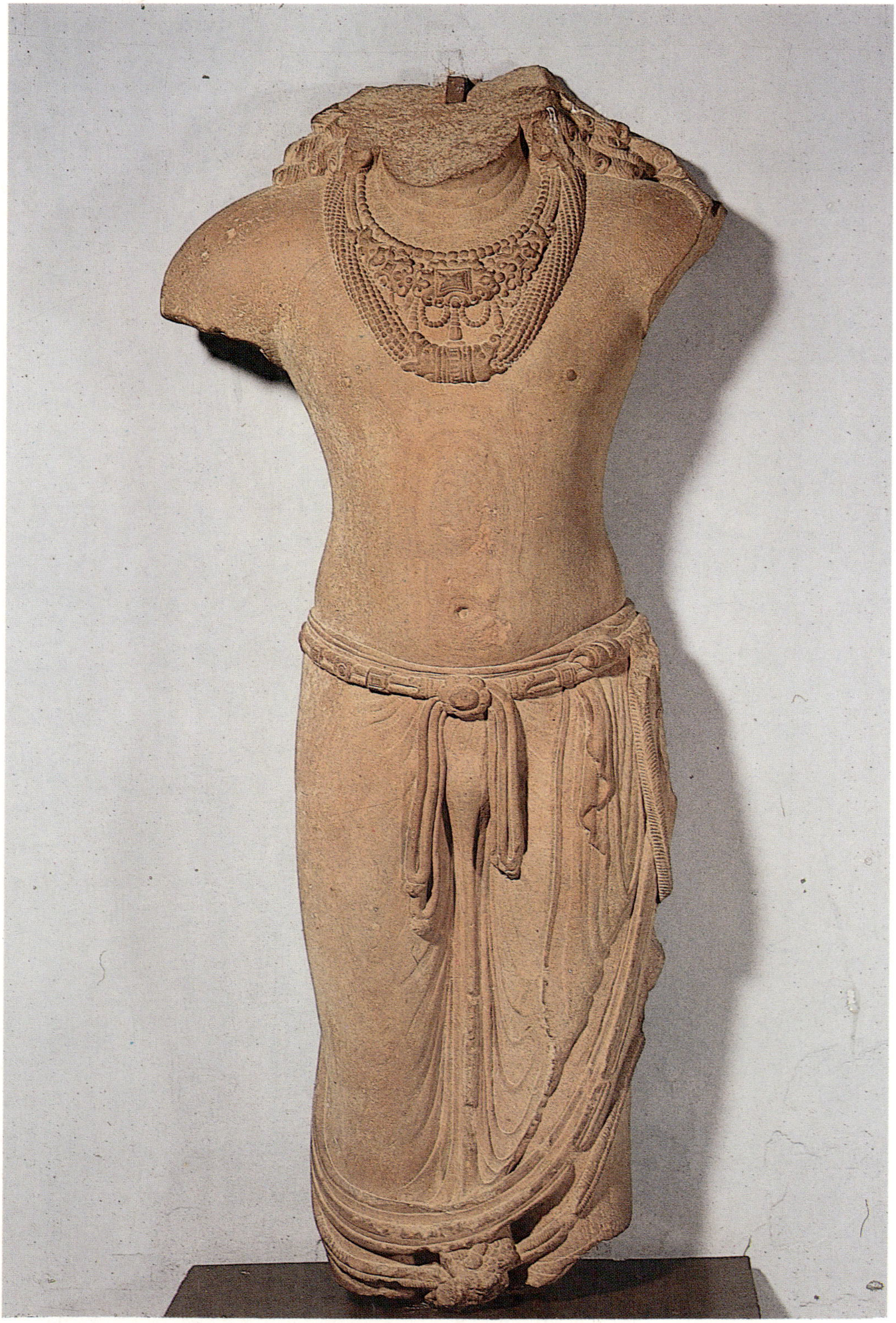

XXXII. Viṣṇu torso with ornament, Gupta

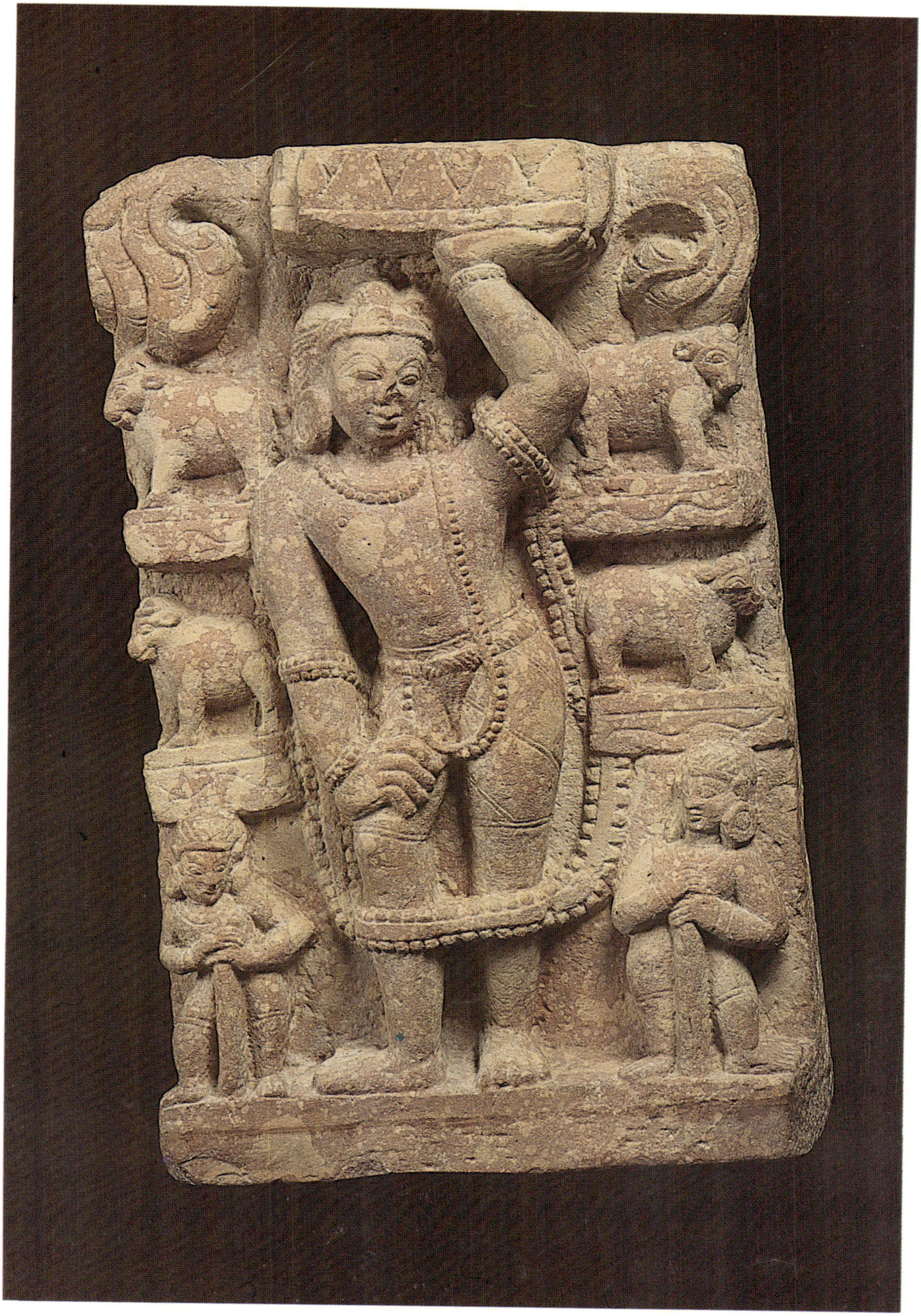

XXXIII. Kṛṣṇa lifting Govardhan, post Gupta

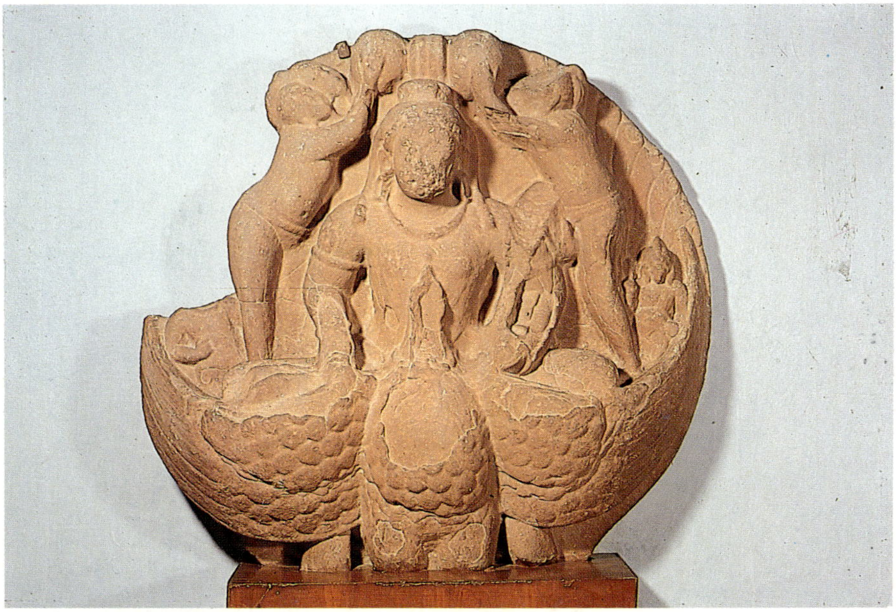

XXXIV. Kārttikeya on peacock, Gupta

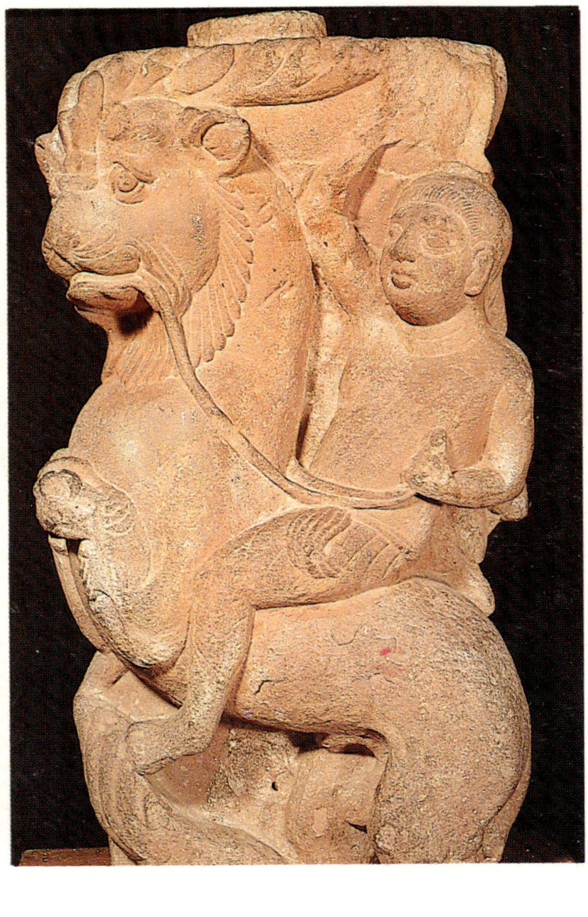

XXXV. Rider on the leogryph, Gupta

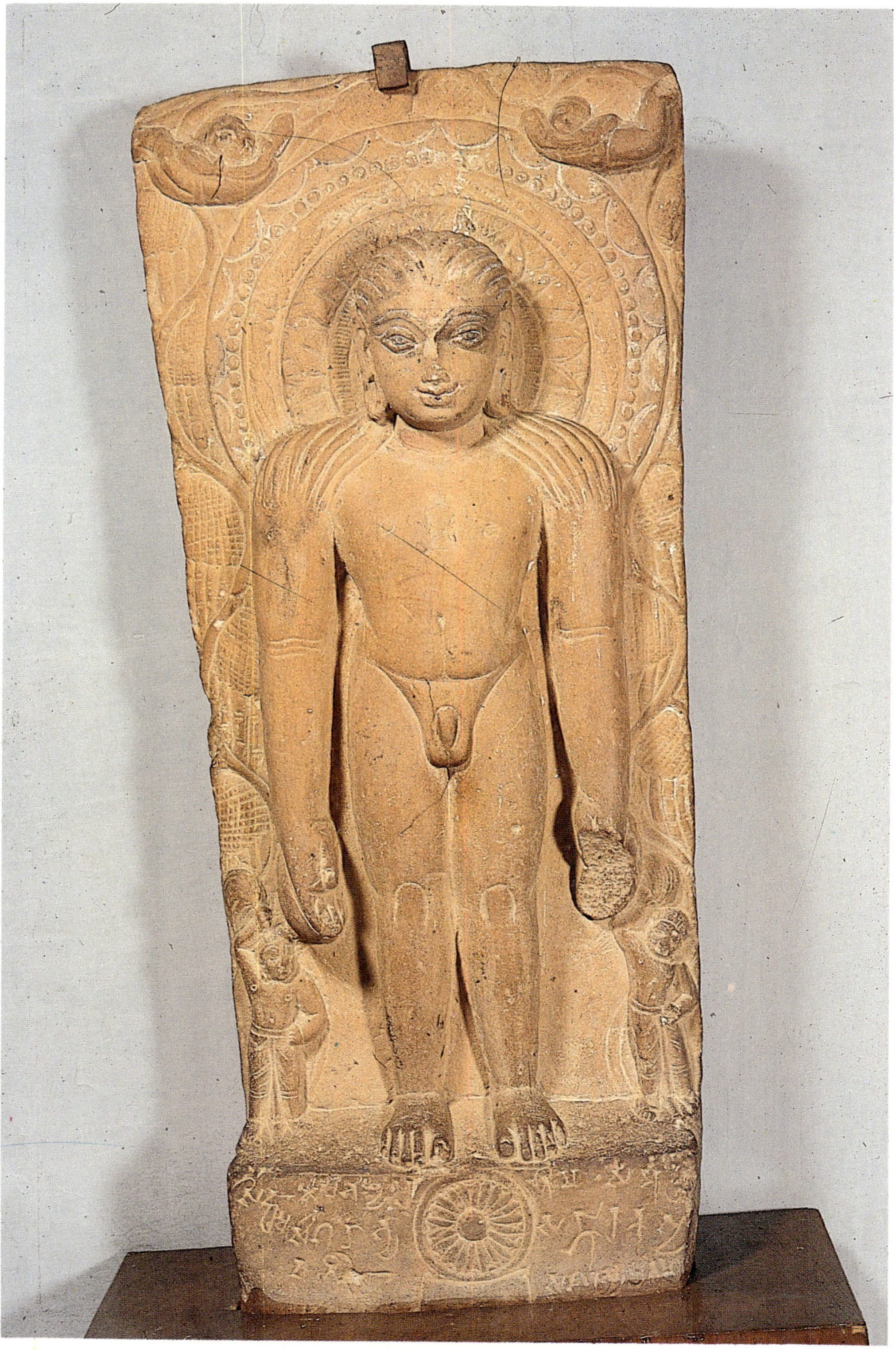

XXXVI. Ṛṣabhanātha, Gupta

XXXVII. Sūrya with family deities, Medieval

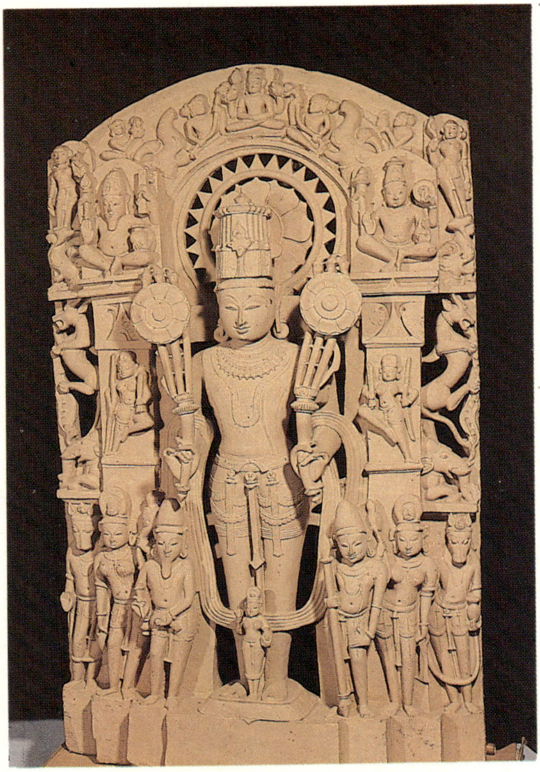

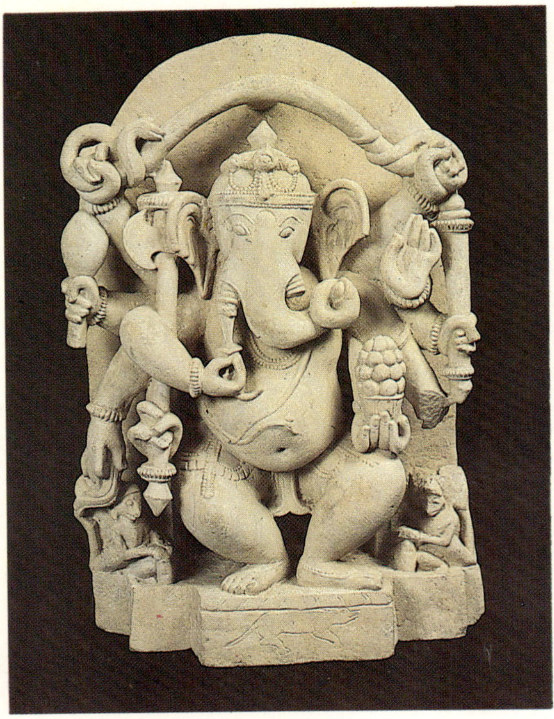

XXXVIII. Dancing Gaṇeśa, Medieval

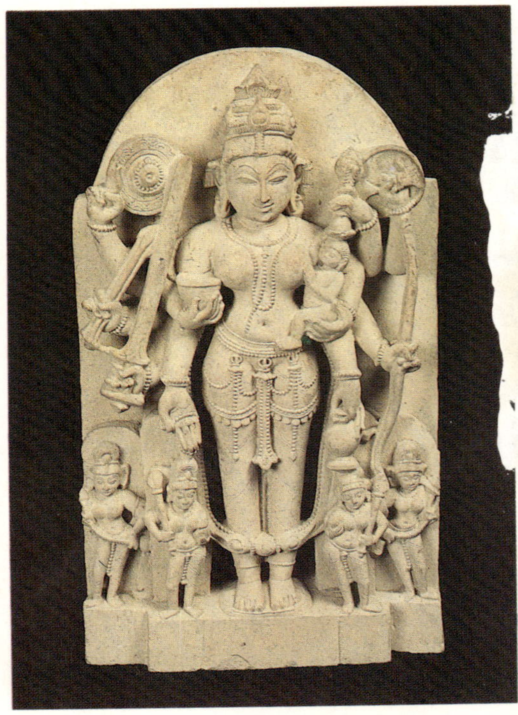

XXXIX. Ambikā, Medieval